The Pantheon Asia Library

New Approaches to the New Asia

The Japan Reader, edited by Jon Livingston, Joe Moore, and Felicia Oldfather
  Volume 1 *Imperial Japan: 1800–1945*
  Volume 2 *Postwar Japan: 1945 to the Present*
A Chinese View of China, by John Gittings
Remaking Asia: Essays on the American Uses of Power, edited by Mark Selden
Without Parallel: The American-Korean Relationship Since 1945, edited by
Frank Baldwin
Chairman Mao Talks to the People: Talks and Letters, 1956–1971, edited by
Stuart Schram
A Political History of Japanese Capitalism, by Jon Halliday
Origins of the Modern Japanese State: Selected Writings of E. H. Norman,
edited by John Dower
China's Uninterrupted Revolution: From 1840 to the Present, edited by Victor
Nee and James Peck
The Wind Will Not Subside: Years in Revolutionary China, 1964–1969, by
David Milton and Nancy Dall Milton
The Waves at Genji's Door: Japan Through Its Cinema, by Joan Mellen
China from the Opium Wars to the 1911 Revolution, by Jean Chesneaux,
Marianne Bastid, and Marie–Claire Bergère
*China's Industrial Revolution: Politics, Planning, and Management, 1949 to the
Present,* by Stephen Andors
China from the 1911 Revolution to Liberation, by Jean Chesneaux, Françoise
Le Barbier, and Marie-Claire Bergère
The Pacific War: World War II and the Japanese, 1931–1945, by Saburō Ienaga
Shinohata: A Portrait of a Japanese Village, by Ronald P. Dore
China: The People's Republic, 1949–1976, by Jean Chesneaux
Ten Mile Inn: Mass Movement in a Chinese Village, by Isabel and David Crook

The Silk Road

Also by Jan Myrdal

Report from a Chinese Village
Confessions of a Disloyal European

Also by Jan Myrdal and Gun Kessle

Chinese Journey
Angkor: An Essay on Art and Imperialism
China: The Revolution Continued
Gates to Asia

The Silk Road

A journey from the High Pamirs and Ili
through Sinkiang and Kansu

Jan Myrdal

*Translated from the Swedish
by Ann Henning*

Photographs by Gun Kessle

Pantheon Books, New York

Library of Congress Cataloging in Publication Data

Myrdal, Jan.
  The silk road.

  Translation of Sidenvägen.
  Includes index.
  1. Sinkiang—Description and travel. 2. Kansu,
China—Description and travel. 3. Myrdal, Jan.
I. Kessle, Gun. II. Title.
DS793.S62M9413   915.1′6′045   78–51796
ISBN 0-394-48231-X

Manufactured in the United States of America

First American Edition

To the memory of my uncles Folke Reimer and Stig Reimer. They made a dark childhood lighter and more bearable. In their home at Kvicksta I began reading about the Silk Road one summer afternoon when I was eleven. As I came home from my journey forty years later they had but a couple of short months more to live.

Contents

List of Maps   ix

Foreword to the American Edition   xi

Preface   xv

1   Tashkurghan, the Old Gateway to China
    on the Roof of the World   5

2   Where Three Empires Meet   22

3   A Border That Does Not Exist   28

4   The Haunted Consulate   37

5   Sinkiang   41

6   It All Began with the Horses   45

7   Roads and Years   48

8   The Uighurs—Are They Chinese?   60

9   The Grave of the Saint   66

10   With Regards from Chairman Mao   74

11   The Despot Had Eighty-two Rooms in His House   80

12   The Empty Grave   83

13   Yipek Yoli   108

14   Let Us Talk of Silk   112

15   A Walk in Khotan   122

16   Party Secretaries Li and Liu Talk of Khotan   130

17   For What Is Khotan Famous? Silk, Jade, and Rugs!   135

18   Keriya, or the Pulse of History   144

19   With Our Own Strength   157

20   The Politics of Sand   166

21   Turfan   172

22 The New Monuments   178

23 Stalin's Cleft Shadow   184

24 The Russian Game   192

25 People's Defense in Dzungaria   202

26 The Production and Construction Corps   221

27 The Revolution Marches On in Nylon Stockings!   227

28 Kansu   233

29 Crescent Lake   235

30 It Rains in the Corridor   243

31 At the Western Gate   250

32 The Kansu Iron Combine   256

33 The Reclining Buddha   259

34 Toward the Divide   263

35 The Yellow River   268

36 Where the Roads Separate   274

Glossary   279

Index   281

Maps

Sinkiang (drawn by Roland Klang)
between pages 41 and 42

The Silk Routes Between the Mediterranean
and the Yellow River   page 111

Kansu (drawn by Roland Klang)
between pages 233 and 234

Foreword to the American Edition

Sinkiang is still the pivot of Asia. The great game continues even though the British left the table decades ago and the Empire is receding into history. But what is so striking as you travel through what formerly was know as East Turkestan is that Russian policy has been consistent since the days of Peter the Great. Now and then a forced halt; once or twice a diplomatic—and even, as in the case of Ili, a military—retreat; but then after some decades a new thrust forward. The Revolution seemed to change the situation. Many of us believed that there had been a change for good and that only some traits were left from czarist days. After all, Lenin had said that czarist policy was ended. But then the game continued as before. Stalin played for Sinkiang and Manchuria. He was outwitted by Mao Tse-tung and forced to relinquish his hold. And maybe he was even prepared for some kind of peaceful and social-ist coexistence with the new China. His successors were not. And now in February 1979, during the border war between China and Vietnam, I was talking to a Chinese friend about the Russian countermeasures.

"They won't make a major strike," he said. "They are not quite strong enough to try for Manchuria. Their communication lines are still bad. But they might try for Ili. After all, they do consider it Russian. They were forced to leave only a century ago."

Russia is still playing the great game for Asia. But the United States now is leaving the table as did the British a generation ago. Twenty-one years ago, when Gun Kessle and I first traveled in Iran and Afghanistan, we saw the United States as not only a great but a dominant power. We believed that it might even have the upper hand in the game. There was an American presence all the way from the Caspian Sea through the Turkoman country of northern Iran and along the Hindu Kush. There was the big base in Peshawar, and com-ing down from Kabul in the autumn of 1958 we met Americans who talked as if there really was going to be an American century. Now all that is gone. The bases are dissolved. The American Century became an American Decade in Asia—if even that. The Russians have moved down to the Khyber and are still playing the game according to the rules of Peter the Great.

Western liberals have as great difficulty today as they did a hundred years ago in seeing that history is real. The Chinese are aware of history. Therefore, when they stood up they were able to force the Russians to a diplomatic retreat in Sinkiang and in the northeast. This record of a journey down the Silk Road from Tashkurghan in the Pamirs along the Kansu corridor toward Lanchow is also a book about the great game, and about the men who played it. Stalin is therefore present. The hand he held is still not played out.

But 1976 was not only a year when we traveled in Sinkiang; it was also a year when we traveled in a China where the "Gang of Four" were trying to gain complete power. Now, three years later, many people— even many intellectuals in China—believe that China is very different. China is not. There are twists and turns along the road, but the nine hundred million or so Chinese continue to shape a new China through their work. The direction this new China is taking cannot be changed by a Lin Piao (who was a very real hero once) or by a "Gang of Four" (who had no historical dimensions).

Those who see China only through documents or who believe that China is a concrete expression of political ideologies will have difficulty in understanding this. To them China seems to be undergoing sudden and violent changes. But if you see the documents and speeches as true ideological expressions of the concrete difficulties, if you see China in historical perspective and look at it from below where the view is clear, then these violent changes become just necessary phases in the development of a new China.

What for instance would have happened if "the Four" had won in 1976? If they had gained power? Some people would have been killed, some people jailed. Some people would have been forced to see the huge economic projects on which they were working ruined. China would have suffered. Education, culture, and technology would have suffered. There would have been minor and medium disturbances in different provinces. The policies of "the Four" would not have been just a necessary phase in the development of the new China. But even so, they would not have changed China greatly. The nine hundred million or so would have gone on forming a new society by their daily work. The struggle against the desert would have gone on. In the end "the Four" would have disappeared without leaving enduring traces in Chinese history. Only if they had started a civil war, which would have given the Soviet Union a chance to intervene, would they have been of real danger to China.

Now that they are gone, China is developing more rapidly. But the direction has not changed.

Some of my Chinese friends agree. Others do not. This winter a Chinese friend stayed with us for two months. We have known each other well for nearly thirty years. She most decidedly did not agree. She had suffered. She was an intellectual. And it is very probable that if I had been Chinese and had been a writer interested in Balzac and romanesque art and things foreign (as I am), then I would have suffered too and would now be saying and writing, like so many Chinese intellectuals, that these last ten years were black years of fascism. It would be understandable, but it would still be wrong. Even these last ten years from 1966 to 1976 were years when tremendous forces were set free in China and when the nine hundred million or so Chinese with their work were building China.

This journey in 1976 was also a journey through the hinterland of China at a time when China watchers in Hong Kong and in Peking were casting political horoscopes. I have always held that you see the historical and political realities better in the hinterland than in the capital. What is decisive is not whether youngsters in Peking drink Coca-Cola or not, or whether they dance this or that new dance, or whether they go dressed this way or that; what is decisive is whether it will be possible to beat back the desert and see to it that the people of China achieve a decent standard of living. If the new China cannot quickly increase production and income for the hundreds of millions in the agricultural hinterland, then it will fail, no matter if the youngsters of Peking go dressed this way or that way. And the only force that can change the destiny of the hundreds of millions in the still poor hinterland of China are these hundreds of millions themselves. Only by their own labor and their own conscious effort can they build a better life. That has been the main direction in China all these years.

When I put it this way, I believe that all my Chinese friends—even those who suffered at the hands of the "Gang of Four"—will agree. After all, China has stood up and is strong enough to hold its own against Moscow. And that is a great hope for us all.

Jan Myrdal

Fagervik
April 2, 1979

Preface

I began planning this book in 1959. Seventeen years later the journey had been made. Gun was in the hospital in Tsingtao for her old TB. There I worked on the manuscript during the autumn of 1976. When she got better, we went home to Sweden. While the book was being printed in Sweden, we were going back to China to make films for the Swedish Broadcasting Corporation.

Much had happened in China since we traveled down from the Pamirs in 1976. We were following the Silk Road through Sinkiang and Kansu down toward Lanchow as the "Gang of Four" were making their desperate bid for power in the summer of 1976. Reading the book in the summer of 1978 in China when the rectification campaign was in full swing, it once again struck me how little the "Gang of Four" really mattered.

Of course there are—and will be—struggles and contradictions among the nine hundred million or so Chinese. But such as the "Gang of Four" were but froth on the surface of that revolution which is carrying China back to its normal position as one of the most highly developed nations. One with a quarter of the world population, though.

Many people helped to make this journey possible. Rewi Alley kept on encouraging me year in and year out. Many Chinese friends—none named and none forgotten—tried to arrange the necessary permits. The Chinese People's Association for Friendship with Foreign Countries helped us arrange everything. The Chinese friends who traveled with us were old friends indeed.

Publishers and editors and people from the Swedish Broadcasting Corporation helped finance our journey. Gunnar Jarring, Anders Lennartsson, Per-Olow Leijon, Jan Stolpe, and Torsten Örn read the manuscript and helped me avoid certain mistakes. For the remaining ones, the responsibility is mine.

For reasons of economy the English version is slightly abridged.

The Silk Road

This book about a journey in northwest China opens in a camp of mountain Tadzhiks in the High Pamirs. Now, six months thereafter, I am writing out these notes in a house built of stone on the edge of the cliffs north of Tsingtao on the Shantung coast. It is autumn and the sea is blue, so blue; the waves roll in, break, and hiss under our windows and Gun is sleeping, wrapped in a woolen blanket, on the balcony. She can breathe easily in the fresh air coming from the Yellow Sea.

It had been a long journey to the East. Had we traveled in the opposite direction, we would be in Athens now. The journey had also been unusual. We traveled both north and south of the Takla Makan Desert. We drove from the Ili valley through the whole of Dzungaria, took the train out of Sinkiang, and continued down the Kansu corridor by car all the way to the Shensi border. There we took the train from Paoki junction down to Chengtu in Szechuan and continued in due course in a river boat on the Yangtze down to Wuhan.

I don't really know of anyone, Chinese or foreign, who has made such a journey in recent years. They fly. And why should anyone drive down the Kansu corridor when there are good trains running all the way to Peking or Shanghai?

The year 1976 was a decisive one in China. When we were about to leave Peking for Sinkiang in May 1976, an old friend of mine said, "You have been to China a couple of times; you can look at it from the outside. Now—What do you think? Will the struggle between the two lines be resolved without an armed conflict? Do you think we will have civil war?"

There was a poster campaign on in Khotan. The young party secretary said, "They accuse me of being a capitalist roader, you know. But their accusations lack substance. It's mainly big words and anger."

Power seizers, self-styled rebels, had taken the hotel in Chengtu. They had occupied it and had been living there for a long time. We had to stay at the back of it.

Different struggling groups attacked each other with posters, speaking at the top of their voices to outshout each other. The opposition group, in a car equipped with loudspeakers, drove up in front of the hotel entrance and let out a volley of denunciations. The rebel headquarters in the hotel replied by turning up the volume of their amplifi-

3

ers. Slogans howled in the air, and the big posters flapped.

The hotel was a liaison office for Szechuan province. From there the attempt to seize power was organized. Cars from all corners of Szechuan were parked in the courtyard, and excited young arrivals hurried to the receiving committee in the entrance hall. But in the street people passed by as if they neither saw nor heard. They didn't even glance in the direction of the uproar. My Chinese friends said, "Who do you think loves those self-styled rebels?"

When we were leaving Chengtu for Chungking, the train was full of evacuees; there was an earthquake warning out for Szechuan province. There had been an earthquake in Yunnan and an even more disastrous one in Tungshan, there was one expected north of Chengtu.

We were in Tsingtao when Chairman Mao died. The grief was profound. We traveled up to Peking to pay our respects at his bier. Before returning to the coast we took a walk in the Fishing Park with one of our old friends, who said, "There are difficult days ahead in China. You and other foreigners may have to leave the country. Let's hope it will work out. But certain people are very dangerous."

Later on, when the news was getting around that the "Gang of Four" had really been taken care of and politically smashed, and demonstrations were spreading all over China, the people of Tsingtao went out to the streets. The relief was enormous. It was the happiest demonstration I have seen in China.

Gun is asleep on the balcony. She has been very ill. We already knew that something was wrong when we arrived in China. Her old TB had flared up. But she kept going and did her work. Even when she was on the verge of collapse in Tunhwang she kept on working. And that was right. If you have the good fortune to be able to work as a writer or an artist or a photographer, you do not work to live but live to work. Gun knew she might have to pay a high price for the happiness of traveling through the Takla Makan, visiting Tunhwang, seeing Mai Chi Shan. It was worth it.

This is a book about a journey. It does not claim to be some kind of reference work on northwestern China. Neither is it a summary of political events during a decisive year in China.

Even if there are only two of us—Gun and I—walking through the dry riverbed outside Tunhwang where the clouds are aflame over the desert in the sunset, we are three. The reader is the third. We walk through Khotan early in the morning, and as we walk and talk we know that we are also talking to the reader. This gives the travelogue its form. This is not just the description of a journey; it is a journey with the reader.

1

Tashkurghan, the Old Gateway to China on the Roof of the World

The camp belongs to Tagarmi People's Commune. The valley below us is wide and open. It is the time of summer migration. Through the green meadows the herds are passing on their way to the summer grazing. The lambs bleat and the ewes answer, and the yaks tread slowly and heavily in front of their calves. The snowy mountains are white as chalk against the deep blue sky. The air is pure and every detail seems emphasized. The cliffs on the other side of the valley are sharp and rough. White clouds form and swirl over the mountaintops. We are sitting on the thick felt rug outside our host's yurt.

The rug has a bold pattern in bright colors. It was made by the women. Making a felt rug takes one winter. It is not only beautiful, it also protects against the damp and cold of the ground. The music is playing. Bone flutes squeak shrilly, and fingers beat the drum skin. Our hosts are dancing to welcome us. The music is of the kind heard in the high mountain lands from the Tsinghai-Kansu border to the Balkans.

The chairman of the revolutionary committee, Mangsurban, comes up to us and starts to dance. He moves his hands in gestic clarity and performs the dance with dignity. One by one our hosts get up and begin to dance in front of us. They are Tadzhiks, mountain Tadzhiks. This is the Tashkurghan Tadzhik Autonomous County in the far west of China.

We came up from Kashgar and drove along the new road just west under Kungur Shan and Muztagh Ata. Kungur Shan reaches 7,719 meters above sea level, and Muztagh Ata 24,757. The last pass was 4,650 meters high. We are now down at 3,700 meters. I feel a little numb. The high altitude begins to affect me.

This is the old road across the Roof of the World. It seems to soar between heaven and earth, as the people here used to say. They passed along this road almost fifteen hundred years ago. But even then it was old and well trodden. Long before it became one of the silk routes, it was a lapis lazuli route to the East and a jade route to the West. This road across these mountains has been described many times. All sorts of travelers have passed here. It is the scene of the wildest adventures of Chinese storytellers. The real Hsüan Tsang himself wandered through this valley thirteen hundred years ago, and the legends around him grew until Wu Ch'eng-en in the sixteenth century wrote *Monkey (The Pilgrimage to the West)* and let Monkey conquer the White Bone Demon in these mountains. The story was one of Mao Tse-tung's favorites, but Chiang Ching tried to put a stop to the performance of the Shaohsing opera version of it. She suspected—and quite rightly—that people identified her with the White Bone Demon disguised as Beauty. So the route is old and legendary.

More and more people are dancing. Men and women get up in front of the musicians and start to dance, dance with strength and pride. The old men—the whitebeards—move with restrained dignity. The last time I saw men dancing like that was farther west, in Albania. The road across the Roof of the World connects us. It is now seven hundred years since young Marco Polo reached these valleys from the West. He noted:

> No birds fly here due to the height and the cold. And I assure you that, because of this great cold, fire is not so bright here nor of the same color as elsewhere, and food does not cook well.*

He was here earlier in the year, and we are farther down in the valley: I see birds. But the pastures are as he described them: "a lean beast grows fat here in ten days."

Verily, this land is good land for the herds, and the grazing is among the best in the world.

"We have 170,000 cattle now," Zaman says. He is vice-chairman of the revolutionary committee of the people's commune. "That is six times the amount we had at the time of the liberation, when there were two animals to each person. Now there are about nine animals to each person. Besides, in the old days a few people owned most of the cattle, and most people had no cattle at all. Now the herds are owned in common."

The dancing is over. We look out over the valley. A cold wind is blowing now, and the herdsmen ride past; they are driving the yaks up the valley. Heavy clouds hide the mountaintops, and we are bidden to enter the yurt. The meal is ready.

It took us a long time to get here. Nineteen years. Even longer, in

*The Travels of Marco Polo, trans. Ronald E. Latham (Baltimore, 1958), p. 49.

fact, because I read Marco Polo for the first time one prewar summer
when I was eleven. I was staying with my uncles on their farm just
south of Lake Mälar in Sweden. It was harvest time but it was raining
that day, and I lay on the floor in the attic reading Marco Polo, listening
to the rain pattering on the roof and the thunder far off. There were
two volumes, almost falling apart. I had found them in the same box
as *Eight Hundred Miles on the Amazon River* by Jules Verne and
Through Asia by Sven Hedin.

Then when Gun Kessle and I started living together, the journey
began to take shape. Each of us brought an edition of Marco Polo along.
She had the Marsden edition and I had the Yule. In the summer of
1957, on the train coming home from Moscow, we began to talk about
a real journey: following Marco Polo's route eastward.

We wanted to travel overland on roads and rivers across all of Europe
and Asia. Six months later we were driving toward Asia in a Citroën
2CV. After another eighteen months we were coming up the valleys to
the High Pamirs from the west. It was in the summer of 1959, and we
had followed Marco Polo up through Badakhshan in Afghanistan:

> We go over the pass and at once the scene changes. It is as though we
> haven't moved at all, but one stage scene had replaced another. The
> ground is still swampy, yet there are white mountains rising, ranged in
> a semicircle in front of us. Pamir and the Hindu Kush. Straight across
> the valley lies the Soviet Union; to the east, Pakistan; and now the
> Ab-i-Pandj goes through the valley below. A great basin of green mead-
> ows, where the upper Amu Darya, coming from Wakhan and Pamir,
> turns northward.
>
> The clouds are flying over the mountains and we drive down into an
> amphitheater. A long green slope redolent with spring flowers, its long
> sweeping lines broken by high black mountains, the white-topped Ish
> Kashim. The key to Pamir.
>
> Here the road goes up to Pamir. The new motor road, which one day
> will go right through Wakhan to Sinkiang in China. The wind is bitingly
> cold, but the fields are green and they tell us we have brought the spring
> with us. The snow has just melted in Ish Kashim. Higher up it is still
> falling. It is July 16. Our odometer shows we have driven 37,480 kilome-
> ters—23,226 miles—since leaving Sweden.*

Six months after that, I was sitting wrapped in blankets and propped
up by a mountain of pillows in a bed in the raw, damp winter cold of
a room on the North Indian plain with my typewriter on my knees,
writing:

*Jan Myrdal, *Gates to Asia* (New York, 1971), pp. 179–80.

I had to give up. I never reached the High Pamirs. I was struck down by illness; only with difficulty could Gun take me down to Faizabad. I didn't make it. I lost all my strength and had to give up. That was the worst defeat I ever had. I saw the mountains and then no more.*

I had still not recovered half a year later when I sat there in my bed writing, while the bleakly cold north Indian winter sneaked through the brick walls and permeated both blankets and woolen sweaters:

I had to return without Pamir. It doesn't help much to know that our little Citroën was the first small car to climb up to Ish Kashim when it could have been—but wasn't—the first on the Silk Road up the Pamir valley. This utter humiliation of sickness. Not to be able to face one's own reflection in the mirror for the sheer shame.†

As soon as I was well again and could make plans ahead, we discussed how we could continue the broken journey. We applied for a permit to visit Tashkurghan in Pamir in the extreme west of China. It took us sixteen years to get that permit.

The women are bringing in the meat. Behind them in the opening of the yurt, the mountains stand out sharply white against the unbelievably dark sky. It's mutton, real mutton: *Ovis poli.* It is not just a great honor. It is true meat.

The people who welcome us here are the same as those we stayed with on the other side of the mountains, seventeen years ago. They too were hospitable and had the same dignity. But this side of the mountains they are no longer poor. They are not ragged. I will discuss economic development later on with the hosts. Not now. We are sitting on the starkly beautiful, thick Tadzhik carpet of felted wool, bowls of meat and sour milk in front of us.

I am happy. Coming here was worth waiting seventeen years. And from here the roads eastward are open. Still, no one will ever say about me that I traveled along Marco Polo's routes. It doesn't help to be the first foreigner to travel in Chinese Pamir since 1949, nor does it help that we have made our way on roads and rivers all the way from the North Cape to the Yellow Sea and that we have been on our way for twenty years, for there are quite a few miles over the high mountain passes between Afghanistan and China that we have not traveled. Next-to does not count.

Perhaps that permit will be granted in another seventeen years? I have an old permit from Pakistan to go up to Tashkurghan from that side, and if only I had a permit to cross the border to Afghanistan and

*Jan Myrdal, *Kulturers korsväg* (Stockholm, 1960), p. 265.
†Ibid.

go down via Wakhan, the journey would be completed, not only that of Marco Polo, but also that of Fa-Hsien and that of Hsüan Tsang. All the things an eleven-year-old boy in an attic dreamed about one rainy day—and even more.

I may be able to get that permit; but if I do I doubt that I will ever make the journey. I can hear the music again. They are dancing out there. I'm beginning to feel the altitude. Heights over 4,000 meters do not suit me. On our way up we were joined by a group from Peking Television. We had met them in Kashgar, and when they heard that we were going toward Tashkurghan, they asked if they could join us. They had a jeep from Kashgar Radio and followed us. But the changes in altitude were too sudden, and when we took a break just beneath Kungur Shan, three of them were sick with mountain sickness. There was too little oxygen in the air they were breathing. Their faces were chalky white, they vomited, and one became unconscious. They were younger than I am. These things happen. I don't get mountain sickness, at least not at this altitude as yet. The pass we crossed was 4,700 meters high. I went to see some graves there, just below the pass. They were like the graves in the Bashgul valley in Nuristan under the Hindu Kush south of these passes. I can still travel there, but I probably won't be able to in ten or twenty years. Even if I were granted a permit it is unlikely that I should ever cross the passes to Afghanistan over there. They are even higher.

It is strange to sit here listening to the music, knowing that we have come so far but no farther.

I am quoting from the notes taken in the camp east of Tashkurghan. I do it in spite of the fact that now in the grey Swedish weather they feel a bit sentimental in my mouth. Traveling has a dimension we don't always like to admit.

The travelers who have passed this way are all very factual and practical as they give an account of their impressions. They have also had quite believable reasons for coming here, either for trading, collecting holy scriptures, investigating the road to China, or drawing a map. All of this is quite true. We too have our practical reasons. I travel in order to report. That's quite right, I suppose. But all this doesn't really explain why I myself have spent more months traveling abroad than in my native country these last twenty years. Nor does it explain the journeys made by the great and admirable travelers. There is a third dimension to traveling: the longing for what is beyond. The dawns when you set off. The good feeling of being dead tired after crossing the mountains. The taste of the sea on your lips long before you reach any shore, the humid smell of crops and wet soil while you're still in the desert. Arriving in a strange city in the middle of the night, standing quite still in the dark listening to the sounds.

Traveling is not just seeing the new; it is also leaving behind. Not just opening doors; also closing them behind you never to return. But the place you have left forever is always there for you to see whenever you shut your eyes. And the cities you see most clearly at night are the cities you have left and will never see again.

Right up here on the Roof of the World, at the moment when I realize that I shall never in my whole life be able to complete the journey I have been working on for twenty years, that I will never cross the high passes—right up here, at this moment, I understand how strong, how overwhelming and all-consuming is my urge to set off, to go on, to go beyond, to leave behind. Reports and articles and accounts are necessary and motivated and rational, but seen from this perspective they become rationalizations of deeper emotional urges.

I don't think a report is made less valid by my accounting for the personal needs that drive me. On the contrary. We are all equal but we are decidedly not all alike. There are people who would say that their eardrums felt pierced and torn by the music of the bone flutes. There are those who simply lack interest in fifteen-hundred-year-old accounts by Chinese monks about the place they are visiting themselves.

There are those who never experience travel itself as exhilaration bubbling through the body. They do not tingle when they approach the mountains. They move from place to place while carrying out their duty to report facts and figures back home despite homesickness, dysentery, blisters, bad plumbing, and hard beds. They may be nice and honest people, good friends, able writers. They may even be revolutionaries with a strong loyalty to the people on whose work they are reporting. But it is obvious that their views and accounts of Tashkurghan would be quite different from mine. This in spite of the fact that Tashkurghan is the same and neither of us is lying.

Tashkurghan is situated 3,600 meters above sea level. It is the city farthest west in China. Tashkurghan means "stone tower," and some people say that this Tashkurghan was the Stone Tower described by Ptolemy in the second century A.D. as being on the road to Sera, the capital of the Seres, then famous for their silk. But that is not very likely. As far as the name itself is concerned, there are two other "stone towers": one Tashkurghan is in north Afghanistan just below the Amu Darya. In 1959 we drove from there toward Kunduz and up to Badakhshan toward Pamir. Tashkent is another "stone tower," from which there are roads leading to Pamir too. We drove there on our way to Pendzhikent in 1960. They are all old cities. They are described in the very first records of these parts. The Afghanistan Tashkurghan was known in Alexander's time, and Tashkent was known during the Sui dynasty.

The Pamir Tashkurghan is an old city by the side of an old road. It is now neat and new. There is a broad main street beneath the heavy mud fort built in the Manchu dynasty, on foundations of an unknown age: *tash kurghan*—stone tower. The fort has not been excavated; there have been no archaeological surveys up here as yet.

The doctor who is head of the hospital in Tashkurghan is a young man. His name is Fan Shi-hung. He is interested in archaeology and folklore. He thinks the finds constantly being made here indicate greater and more important ones waiting to be revealed. He has written a bit about the trade route and its history; one of his papers is to be published in Peking.

"But they take their time. There is a lot of material lying around in the offices of scientific journals. I suppose I'd better write again to remind them."

He has a fine collection himself. Jade and bronze and old coins.

"Of course, we're not making any digs or looking for objects systematically," he says. "That's prohibited; it has to be done properly and scientifically, so that the historic monuments will not be destroyed. History is the property of the people, but every family has a couple of old objects that they have inherited. People keep them because they are beautiful."

He shows me an ivory figurine with an inscription from the Han dynasty. It is very lovely. I can't remember ever having seen anything quite like it.

A patient gave it to me. It was a bad appendicitis case that I had to operate on immediately out there in the camp. The operation was successful, and afterwards the man gave me this as a keepsake. He had had it from his father, who had had it from his. I'm keeping it to show to the archaeologists in Kashgar. I try to tempt people from the Urumchi museum to come here. When they see this, they will realize there are many things worth digging for here, and that's important if our history is to be understood. But Sinkiang is large and the Urumchi archaeologists have so many things to do, they have to work immediately on vast areas where new industries are to be built or new irrigation systems dug. Up here we can wait. But it would be interesting to learn more about the history of Tashkurghan. This was, after all, for very long periods the gateway to China."

Tashkurghan may not have been Ptolemy's stone tower, but it was an important station on the Silk Road. In various epochs it was also an administrative center, sometimes within the Chinese Empire. Mandarins were stationed here then to survey the trade and the frontiers. Occasionally it was the seat of more or less independent local rulers. And even in recent times, caravans passed this way going to or from China.

It is still a market town. The border trade between China and Pakistan is controlled from the border trade office here. The Pakistani traders come here and the trucks from Kashgar with goods for Pakistan go this way. The shops in Tashkurghan, like those everywhere else in western and southern Sinkiang, have piles of almost transparent silks from Pakistan, decorated with gold and silver thread.

Most shops are to be found along the new upper street, where the hospital and the theater and a cinema and the schools are. The shops are well stocked.

"Before the motor road up from Kashgar was finished we had problems with the goods," says Shirinbek, chairman of the county revolutionary committee. "Then it took the caravans a week to come here from Kashgar. Now there's a bus two days a week. The selling price of industrial goods is the same here as farther down in the country. The cost of transport is not added to the price; that is subsidized by the state."

I buy a Sinkiang flora of medicinal herbs in the bookshop. It is a beautiful piece of work, over 600 printed pages and 293 exquisite color plates; names of species in Latin, Chinese, and Uighur and descriptions in Uighur.

"It has just been published," says Ismail, vice-secretary of the county party committee. "We're planning to circulate it in large numbers, to get it out to every production brigade and every work team. People must learn to recognize the medicinal herbs."

"If they take to collecting medicinal herbs seriously," Fan Shi-hung adds, "it will be possible to raise the standard of medical care more quickly. There's plenty of medicinal herbs in the mountains here in Sinkiang. We send quite a lot of them down to the inland."

"The attitude toward medicinal herbs is a political matter," Ismail says. "It is a question of walking on two legs. Comrade Fan here and the other doctors have access to the most modern drugs here in Sinkiang or in other parts of China, and even imported, when necessary."

"By and large our pharmaceutical industry has achieved and surpassed the highest international standard," Fan Shi-hung says. "By exploiting the medicinal herbs and making the gathering of them everybody's business, we can achieve quicker and better results with less money. It is not a question of choice: either the most expensive drugs or the medicinal herbs; we walk on two legs."

The Sinkiang flora is printed in Arabic letters. Now the Uighur language is beginning to be written in a latinized alphabet. That is an advantage, since a Latin-type alphabet is more suited to the language than the Arabic script. It was the same choice that Turkey made, and Uighur is a Turkic language. Besides, the same type of alphabet should be used all over China—it makes educational work and mutual understanding easier. The Latin alphabet was chosen when the decision was made in 1957 to change over gradually to a phonetic script for the Han language.

So for the Uighur language there is now an organized transition to a latinized alphabet with extra letters to suit the needs of that language, in the same way that the Latin alphabet was changed to suit the Swedish or Hungarian or French languages.

"But we still use both the Arabic and the Latin letters," says Ismail. "During the transitional period both are to be used. The main thing is to be understood."

The bookshop is good and well stocked. Most books are in Uighur, the predominant language in south Sinkiang; some are in Han. The only foreign books I found were a few simple schoolbooks in English. There are many editions of the Marxist classics, Marx, Engels, Lenin, and Stalin plus Mao Tse-tung, in different languages and with different scripts.

As is true everywhere else in China, the science and technology section is extensive. It contains simple illustrated popular-science brochures in Uighur and Han and other languages of China booklets about the solar system, the history of the earth, the theory of evolution, the life of animals, and nuclear energy, as well as more specialized works on mathematics, physics, and chemistry. The department for agriculture, irrigation, cattle breeding, and tractor driving is, naturally, also large.

It ought to be pointed out that this bookshop in Tashkurghan in the far west of China is much better stocked than provincial bookshops are in Sweden these days. I bought the Sinkiang flora, a manual for the people's militia edited especially for the local defense men and women of this autonomous Tadzhik county, some children's books, and a roll of posters.

The climate here is harsh—cold winters and cool summers. Above all, the thin air.

"The boiling point of water here is 87 degrees Celsius," Fan Shi-hung says. "And you can see how slowly the trees grow up here. It's the same with people. You adapt to begin with; that's not too difficult, it takes a week or so. Then you realize that you haven't really adapted at all. My wife and I have worked to establish this hospital, and we're quite happy living here. We have asked to remain where we are. But if you look at my hands, you will see that one does not adapt to a permanent life with insufficient oxygen.

"My main work as a doctor is up in the mountains with the shepherds and not down here in Tashkurghan. Just look at my hands! My nails are deformed. And my teeth are getting loose. I want to stay here, where I have my job and I like the people. The comrades tell me I've stayed far too long already, yet I am staying on although they want to send me back to the lowlands. I don't really know what is going to happen. Whenever I go to the lowlands now I become ill: the heavy air down in Kashgar is too much for me."

"Comrade Fan ought to think of his health," Shirinbek says. "Not everyone can live and work up here. And most of his work is done out in the high grasslands. He is not one of those doctors who see patients in an office; he rides from camp to camp visiting the sick, serving the people. But this means he has to work at an altitude of more than 4,000 meters, and a person from the lowlands can't learn to do that; you have to be born to it. But then, he has helped to train other doctors."

Shirinbek is a big man with hands like sledges. His eyebrows are bushy and his chest is like a barrel. We are sitting on the *kang* at their healing spring with the bath-keeper of the third production brigade. He is not actually a bath-keeper; he is a shepherd with a disability pension who looks after the baths, a low building with three large concrete bathtubs. The water is sulphurous. The spring emerges up in the mountains northeast of Tashkurghan. It can be seen from a long way off, and its water colors the stones in the valley green and yellow. The higher up you get in the ravine, the thicker are the sediments, and at last you reach the spring. The water is hot, about 77°C, and we let it cool in the tubs before getting in. The water comes up to our chins.

"Health itself," says Shirinbek. "People here have known of this spring since time immemorial. It cures rheumatism and bad joints and weak lungs. The third production brigade looks after it now. People come here for the baths all the way from Urumchi. If it wasn't so remote it would be one of the most famous springs in all China."

After the bath the bath-keeper of the third production brigade puts out bowls of sour milk and meat. Mutton. Proper mutton.

"This is the only place in the world where you can eat Marco Polo mutton," Shirinbek says. "We hunt quite a lot up here. Our host is a good shot. He got the ram himself. He lives here by the spring and can bathe his rheumatism away."

On the way back to Tashkurghan, Fan Shi-hung says, "Comrade Shirinbek works very hard, but he is no longer a young man. He is a leading cadre with great responsibility and likes to set an example. He has just come back from one month with a work team, being a shepherd among other shepherds. That is a good style of work; it also makes it easier for him as chairman of the revolutionary committee of the whole autonomous county to make correct decisions. He knows the problems firsthand. But he ought to think of his health. He is a veteran, an old cadre who was active in the democratic revolution, leading it against the Kuomintang in the forties. The comrades have suggested that he should accept a leading position that would be physically less strenuous in Kashgar or Urumchi, but he refused. He prefers to live here. In one way that is understandable. It's not easy to acclimatize. People up here are a little different, as you can see for yourself. I don't just mean to say that they are not of the Han people. Most of them are Tadzhik. Tall and big-nosed and with curly hair, and some of them have blue eyes, as you see. It has always been like that here.

"You can read about that in the old dynastic histories. I have just seen a note from the Northern Chou dynasty records of fourteen hundred years ago that people here were known for having deep-set eyes and straight noses! That was written fourteen centuries ago. The people living here now are the same as then. But I don't really mean to talk about the color of their eyes. It is something else that I am trying to talk about. People here are different in a more vital sense. Their nostrils are wider, their rib cages deeper. They can absorb more oxygen. They are physically adapted to the environment. This is not something you acquire just by adapting yourself to the altitude for a week or a year. I reckon it takes the organism about three generations or even more to become really adapted to altitude. I live here and so does my wife, and we have children who were born here, but these children weren't born acclimatized. Still, if they stay here, their children may be better off.

"People can adjust to living at these altitudes and having their organisms adapt to the lack of oxygen at 4,000 meters above sea level. Adaptation and selection too; some leave and some stay on, but it takes a few generations. That's probably why mountain people don't really feel at ease in the heavy lowland air. Still, it is easier to adjust to the lowlands than to the real highlands. At least, that's my opinion. In the beginning I thought differently. Now I believe it takes three generations. Look at my hands and look at my nails: you see! Digital clubbing!"

The new hospital is on the main street in the upper town of Tashkurghan. Doctor Fan himself was instrumental in the building of it.

"It's a county hospital in a border area. It's well equipped. Our equipment here in Tashkurghan is not much inferior to that of Kashgar."

The X-ray equipment in the hospital is new. There are thirty beds. There are also permanent clinics in each one of the county's ten folk communes where simpler operations can be carried out and where there are three to five beds for long-term treatment. There is a medical staff for each production brigade, three people in the larger ones and two in the smaller. There are barefoot doctors in the work teams, and from the county hospital medical groups are sent out with doctors, nurses, and equipment to visit the camps.

"The county hospital also serves as a training hospital. Before liberation there was no medical care at all up here. By the time of the Cultural Revolution there were nineteen doctors with different backgrounds, but now the number exceeds fifty. We have courses here at the hospital. Barefoot doctors from the work teams get their medical education here. I also train surgeons at this hospital. All my junior doctors have been trained here. We do have the most modern equipment available, and so we have organized a system to cover the whole county. We follow the line of Chairman Mao, concentrating on the countryside, on preventive medicine, on treating the most common diseases which cause most suffering to the people. The doctor serves the people. The idea is not to train doctors who dream about becoming world-famous specialists serving some urban overlords. Rheumatism is a bad problem. Shepherding is a hard job. But we've managed to come to grips with syphilis and smallpox, after five years of hard fighting. The general hygienic level has been raised, and we have overcome the high infant mortality rate. The Tadzhik population has increased by 65 percent since liberation."

Tashkurghan is a small town with about 3,000 inhabitants. Its population was once contained within the walls of the old fort. The stronghold is now deserted and just waiting to be declared a monument. From a street in the lower town, which has not yet been rebuilt, we climb toward the fort.

"The age of the fort?" says Shirinbek. "Perhaps five hundred years. We all lived in here. Since liberation we have left the fort and the town is growing. We have mountain strongholds like this at many places. People had to be able to find security behind a castle wall. This fort was the seat of government in those days, for the tax collector, the magistrate, the soldiers. I served there myself. In 1944 the KMT troops left

Tashkurghan, during the democratic revolution. That was part of the general revolutionary movement in China against the Reaction. This was a poor and backward part of the country. But the Tadzhiks were not just poor, they were also exploited by their own masters as well as by the reactionary Han administrators. The KMT was a chauvinist regime. Its administrators despised all non-Han peoples. So the Tadzhiks lived under double oppression.

"Since liberation we have done a lot to overcome the remains of the old Han chauvinism, which bred conflicts between the various nationalities in China and thus assisted the Reaction. We have worked hard training our own cadres. Of all cadres in this county 80 percent are Tadzhiks, 15 percent are Han, and 5 percent Uighurs and others.

"Chairman Mao Tse-tung set it down in his directions for the work in Sinkiang in 1963 that Han cadres working in nationality areas should learn the language and respect the customs of the local population. The Han cadres who work here have behaved well; most of them now speak the language of the people and live like we do up here. The others are learning our language and doing their best.

"We now have 15,000 inhabitants in our county, which is 25,000 square kilometers in area. The Tadzhik population is on the increase. Not that family planning is forbidden or that there are no contraceptives available in Tashkurghan. Whoever wants contraceptives can get them free. But we follow Chairman Mao's line for the family-planning work. China needs family planning. It is necessary for the liberation of the women. Humans have to plan their own rate of increase too, as Chairman Mao said. But if the same policies regarding family planning were applied here and in the Han areas, we would achieve not equality but inequality. It could give rise to conflicts. The Han people are in such a large majority in China that many people would see propaganda for contraception or family planning among us Tadzhiks or among Uighurs or Tibetans or other Chinese nationalities as an attempt to create a China of Han people and conduct a reactionary Han chauvinistic policy like the KMT's. We must be extremely careful in our work to avoid such conflicts.

"The necessity to counter any resurgence of conflicts between nationalities is so important that we are not conducting any family-planning discussions here—or in other nationality areas—even though this in itself makes for certain difficulties."

"The people were oppressed all over China," said Dursland, chairman of the women's organization of Tashkurghan, "but the Tadzhiks were also oppressed by Han chauvinism, and the Tadzhik women were oppressed by the patriarchal male rule. The women were the most oppressed. There are still difficulties; early marriages are not uncommon. There are reactionary forces that still agitate against love marriages. They exploit the religious prejudices that say marrying for love is immoral. We as communists propagate the new idea that a marriage is moral only when it is a freely chosen mutual and lifelong relationship based on individual love between two adults. We have to fight old customs. We are setting our new morals against the old reactionary morals that oppressed the women."

"We have to be very careful, though," Shirinbek said. "We should not give the enemy the slightest opportunity to drive a wedge between the nationalities and thus create national conflicts. You must realize that we've had a great deal of bloodshed in the history of Sinkiang, people slaughtering each other just because they spoke different languages or had different religious beliefs or ethnic backgrounds. This did a lot of damage to us, and we must be on our guard. Especially since the enemies of our country never stop trying to get a foothold by stirring up these conflicts again. We mustn't give the social imperialists the slightest chance to interfere with our business. Here we have the advantage of not having any cadres with dual citizenships, as they have in other places along the border. But the social imperialists have other methods in store. Do you realize that for this visit we have had to double the border guards and give an alert to the People's Liberation Army for stepped-up preparedness? No foreigners have been here since the liberation. You are traveling part of the time within an eye's distance of the border. A border provocation on the part of the social imperialists at this moment would enable them to achieve a great propaganda effect. So we must make sure they can't do it. If you wonder why it was so difficult for you to get a permit to come here to the Tashkurghan Tadzhik Autonomous County, that is the answer. We discussed this at length even after Peking and Urumchi had given their consent. We are directly responsible, you see."

The theater is opposite the hospital. We had been there to see a performance by the county company. The autonomous Tadzhik county not only has amateur groups in the work teams, it also has a permanent company that is developing the local Tadzhik tradition. Afterwards we had a drink and a bite. The night was cold and we were wearing thick sweaters and fur hats at the table.

"We do like dancing," Dursland said. "We always dance and sing at our parties; it's part of our custom. When we have guests we dance to welcome them. From the age of eight the children begin to take part in the adults' dancing. That's how they learn."

"Before the liberation 95 percent of the population were illiterate," said Abuzel, vice-chairman of the county revolutionary committee. "Not many shepherds could read a book. Now 3,800 people go to school—that is 20 percent of the whole population. We have not only established elementary education for all children, we have achieved secondary education for everybody. We have our own teacher's training college even here in Tashkurghan. We also send young people for higher education in Kashgar and Urumchi and Sian and Shanghai and Peking. When their education is completed, they return here to work.

"The Cultural Revolution was very important. Before it occured, schools were practically closed to the children of shepherds. As you know, we are mainly shepherds up here. We follow the herds from summer grazing to winter quarters. Before the Cultural Revolution we all had the right to be educated, but in reality education was only for the children whose parents lived near the school. That meant the working shepherds' children couldn't get any schooling.

"The Cultural Revolution changed this. It was then that we could establish schooling for all. We founded mobile schools for the little children, schools on horseback. Teachers follow the pupils and teach in the yurt. No children lack basic education now. We also established proper elementary schools with two additional classes for the secondary school in each people's commune. These are boarding schools, and the state pays for food and lodging. In that way the shepherds' children have exactly the same chances of an education as those with permanent abodes. It wasn't so easy to do all this. The difficulties were great. But when we had smashed Liu Shao-ch'i's false line regarding education and established the proper course, we managed to make it a practical reality. First of all, though, you have to establish a correct line.

"The young are being educated, but they are not being educated to leave the county and move to the cities, to leave the people's commune. They are going to school in order to be literate, capable, and revolutionary herdsmen. We say that education goes from the people's commune to the people's commune. When they have finished their studies, they help transform and modernize their own native home."

"Not only the men are being educated," Dursland added. "We are educating women from the county too. Technicians, teachers, health officers. Three hundred women already have responsible positions on work-team level. There are 485 cadres in our county on the state payroll; that is from people's-commune level and up. Of these, 97 are now women.

"I was an orphan, and when grown up, being a woman, had only two alternatives to choose from: marry a shepherd and lead a miserable life in poverty, or become a minor wife serving a master at his will, which was even more miserable, and shameful besides. But then, a woman couldn't even choose between these two alternatives. The choice was not hers.

"A woman could be disposed of—sold. The bridal gift was payment. After that she became her husband's property. Men could divorce whenever they wished. A woman could not free herself. Men could beat their wives. They could flog and whip their wives to death if they felt like it. To be a woman was to be a piece of merchandise: something to be bought and sold and handled and used up and thrown away. Women had no human worth. Rich men bought themselves three women or more, but the poor man couldn't get even one.

"A woman could take no part in the political and social life. She couldn't even speak freely with the men. The feudal customs were deeply rooted. It has taken a lot of work to overcome this, and we still have far to go. But it was unthinkable before for a woman to have a leading position in society, to get an education, to freely choose her spouse in a love marriage."

Yes, women are different now!

We are sitting in a yurt in a camp above Tashkurghan. Dzhangul is sixteen, a shy but self-confident girl. They say she's a good shot.

"Dzhangul caught a Soviet agent, a KGB man, last year," says Baygum, the shepherd in whose yurt we are sitting. He pours sour milk for us. "She's a good girl."

"It was on the second of August," Dzhangul says, "in the evening. We were a small camp, just a couple of yurts. I was sitting with my neighbor while the men were out with the herds. We were quite high up in the mountains, and it was getting dark. The other woman said, 'I think there's someone out there.' She told me to have a look. I saw a stranger, some seventy meters off. 'Who are you?' I said. 'My friend has left,' he said, but he didn't sound like one of us. I didn't recognize him and his accent was not like ours, so I called out again. He started to run. I'm in the people's militia, the local defense, so I wouldn't let him go. My brother is one year older than I, and we both started to run after the man. This camp up in the mountains was right on the border. The man tried to escape, but lost his footing and fell when trying to get across the river. He didn't know where to step and that made us sure that he was an intruder, one who shouldn't be there. He turned toward us and fired his gun. I told my brother to go to the border guards of the People's Liberation Army and alert them, while I watched the man, who was shooting at me to keep me at bay. I took cover so that he couldn't hit me. Meanwhile my brother alerted the border guards, who summoned the people all around and blocked all roads and paths around him. In all he fired five shots at me without hitting. At daybreak when the sun rose, he shot himself through the mouth with his last shot, caught as he was, like a rat. When we examined the corpse we found his pistol, some pills, some dried apricots in a bag, some water in a bottle, binoculars, and his documents. He was a KGB agent."

The Tashkurghan Tadzhik Autonomous County is right on the border. The roads run close to the Soviet posts. From the town of Tashkurghan they go on as motor roads over the passes to Pakistan or as caravan routes over the passes to Afghanistan. Tashkurghan is an old town in the extreme west of China.

2
Where Three Empires Meet

The morning wind is cold, the air icy, high, and clear in the sharp light. The clouds gather over the mountaintops, and the tufts of grass on the stony ground cast long, well-defined shadows. But the clay wall of the domed grave already feels warm under my palm when I touch the rough surface. I am in the large necropolis north of Tashkurghan where domed graves rise over saints and holy men.

The mausoleums are of sun-dried brick and clay reinforced with straw.

"The oldest should be about three hundred years old, from the early Ch'ing dynasty," Doctor Fan Shi-hung says. "They should naturally be declared monuments. That will be done as soon as the Urumchi archaeologists have a moment to spare to look around this area."

The same simple domed graves can be seen to the west along the old trade route in Badakhshan and and on toward the large monuments in famous pilgrim resorts like Mazar-i-Sharif. They follow the route east and can be found in groups at the foot of Muztagh Ata and near Little Kara Kul by Kungur Shan on the route to Kashgar, the road between China and Persia.

Most graves are simple mounds, according to Islamic custom. Occasionally you see a stark whitewashed base of packed clay with the horseman symbol rising on it, four legs under a saddle. These graves are for men. Some of the graves are recent. From Tashkurghan the routes lead south across the passes toward old Kafiristan, where horses' heads carved in wood still watch over the graves of dead men.

The old graves of the gentry are surrounded by walls. The flat wooden roofs have been torn down by the winter storms. The walls are weathered and battered, but they still gleam chalky white in the sunlight. The surfaces are full of brightly painted figures and signs,

22

where the sun symbol dominates, its geometric catches and radiating hooks the same as in the well-defined figures on Tadzhik or Kirghiz felt rugs in the yurts. On the walls surrounding the dead also are depicted instruments and embroidered wedding clothes, jewelry, laid-out meals, Marco Polo sheep, the protective hand, horses, and human figures.

These pictographic decorations are related to those which can be seen on teahouse walls near Kunduz in north Afghanistan or on house walls in desert towns in Rajasthan in west India. A folk imagery far older than Islam.

In this valley China's old road to the West forked, one road going directly west at the top of the valley toward Persia and farther to the Mediterranean countries. The other continued south across the watershed down to the Indus valley. This valley, where the roads westward meet and then run east toward Yarkand and Kashgar, is also the fertile part of Pamir where most of the permanent housing is found and where remains of old water mills can be seen.

"Yes," says Zaman, vice-chairman of the Tagarmi People's Commune, "we use tractors now. We have ten tractors and we have twelve harvesters and twelve seeders. We have actually become self-sufficient in cereals here—we even have a slight surplus. Still, cattle breeding is our main line. But don't forget that this is the first time we have ever been self-sufficient in cereals!

"Things are so different these days. I was ten when the democratic movement started; we joined the people in Ili, where the three revolutionary districts had formed their own government. The reactionary KMT regime tried to send troops against us. Then we came to an agreement, but in 1946 the KMT broke their word and came back, burning and plundering. They caught several of our revolutionary comrades here and buried them alive, leaving only their heads above ground. That's a painful death.

"In the month of September 1949, the People's Liberation Army were on their way here. The reactionary troops started to flee then; they were no patriots. Generally speaking, the Sinkiang KMT forces were patriotic and joined the liberation peacefully, whereas the forces here fled toward Pakistan and India, plundering all on the way. The People's Liberation Army came here in October 1949 and liberated the Tadzhik people from their oppressors. In the old society Tadzhiks were despised, looked upon as animals that have no souls. I went through that as a child. At the time of the liberation I was fifteen, so I was able to go to school. I was lucky enough to have four years of schooling after liberation. Now we have managed to establish a secondary school for all children. Learning is important. On leaving the school, I was sent by the party to special courses.

"By studying Marx, Engels, Lenin, Stalin, and Chairman Mao Tsetung, I have been able to change my views on the world and reach a clearer class-consciousness. I am convinced that we will be able to achieve communism, and the more I read about what is happening all over the world, the more convinced I get that Marxism-Leninism will triumph. And out here in our district we see every day how the Soviet revisionists sink deeper; they don't stop at anything. They send in agents against us; they even try to move the border markings. They try to take the stones marking the border and move them into our territory; they are absolutely shameless. They didn't manage to provoke us here the way they did farther up by Ili in the early sixties. But of course, we did not have any cadres who turned out to have double citizenship."

Afternoon is approaching and the air is getting warm. A couple of shepherds are riding toward the camp followed by a trail of dust. The people's militia is practicing over by the stables. Shots are being fired.

"Our girls are not bad at shooting either," Zaman says. "Our people's commune is right on the border of the Soviet revisionists, so we have to be fully prepared."

We enter the yurt where the sour milk and mutton await us, and our host says, "Zaman is a fine man, a good and hard-working communist. That's why we nominated him our delegate at the Tenth Party Congress. He proved worthy of our trust and did good work at the Congress in Peking. He is a responsible party member, and it is as Chairman Mao has pointed out, that the force at the core leading our cause forward is the Chinese Communist Party."

The Tashkurghan Tadzhik Autonomous County is part of the Kashgar district. The road to Kashgar is wide and well maintained, going in huge bends up the moraines. Muztagh Ata rises toward us. It is getting colder and we are enveloped in thick fur coats. The large trucks on their way to Pakistan honk when we meet them. The drivers wave. Just at the pass we leave the Tashkurghan Tadzhik Autonomous County and are no more in the Kashgar district.

The morning in the pass is bitterly cold. The valley ahead of us is in the Kizil Su Kirghiz Autonomous District. Kizil Su means "red water," the Kirghiz name for the Kashgar River. It is a large district that runs along the Soviet border from Pamir to Tien Shan. The road is quite close to the border.

"In the KMT days this valley was closed to us," Sadit Tude says. "It has the best grazing grounds, but the KMT dared not let us in here, as they feared we might establish contacts across the border. It was in

Stalin's days when they were communists over there."

Sadit Tude is the party vice-secretary in the Bulun Kul People's Commune. The camp is a part of the Subashi production brigade, and our host is Akjol, a shepherd.

"We have 130 households in this brigade," he says, "570 people. We have 10,300 animals." Marking with his hand, he gives an account of them: "450 yaks, 45 camels, 63 horses; the rest are sheep. We have private animals, not just collective ones. Each family can have five large and ten small animals. Initially it was different, depending on the size of the family, but that led to such disparity that we don't consider the size of the family any more."

We have had our meal. The men are recumbent, smoking, chatting. The women sit behind the screen, but they take part in the conversation, moving in and out of the yurt. However, they don't smoke. One of the men says, "You must realize that the revisionists are absolutely shameless now, they are absolutely disgraceful. This is plain border country, and we have created a unit between the people's militia and the party organization and the border troops. We have two posts for protecting the border here, which is insufficient. We all have to work at protecting the border to prevent the revisionists' agents getting in. Sometimes they manage to get through, but either we get them or they are caught a bit farther down. One could say that it's probably easier for them to get in than to get out. But the revisionists do things I never would have believed, had I not seen them with my own eyes. They send girls to the frontier. Shameless girls. These girls come all the way up to the borderline when our young men are taking the animals out. They make eyes at them, wriggle their hips, and make a show of themselves, shouting, 'Such handsome young men . . . we have no young men at home . . . we want young men like you . . . come over to us, this is a good place to be in.' "

"It's disgraceful," our hostess says. "But we women are in the militia too, watching our borders."

"Well," her husband says, "the revisionists can't fool us with such simple tricks. They can send as many made-up girls as they like to stand on the border making eyes, wriggling their hips, trying to entice our young men. Our boys still won't go across to them or leave our grazing land for a moment."

Plans for the future are discussed. The production brigade has made its plan for development in the next few years.

"There's a task for us in the plan for China that Premier Chou En-lai put forth. We'll have to build an irrigation system and mechanize the haymaking by 1980. The number of cattle should by then amount to

20,000. In the eighteen years that have passed since the production brigade was created, we have increased the number from 2,500 to 10,000 heads. This should be doubled now.

"We estimate that we should be able to keep 40,000 animals if we use our grazing land rationally. We have a lot of work to do. We have 110 children in the brigade. They all go to school, eleven of them already to the secondary school. The people's commune has a boarding school for them. They study cattle breeding and its problems. It is important to us that they come back here. To enable us to build up our country, the educated young people have to come back to our brigades. Eight of them have already returned after finishing secondary school.

"In our brigade we have three barefoot doctors. There is a hospital in the people's commune. The cooperative medical care is one of the greatest achievements of the Cultural Revolution. The life of a shepherd is not easy. People have to work outdoors in rain and snow and cold at high altitudes. They die of cardiac disease or pneumonia or suffer from rheumatism. The women used to die from puerperal fever, but now we have our own midwives and have managed to overcome this. If you really want to understand the implications of the Cultural Revolution and cooperative medical care, you ought to know that in the year 1965—the year before the Cultural Revolution—nineteen children were born in this brigade. Four of them died, which was quite a normal percentage then; 20 percent of all children born were buried before they were one year old. In 1975, twenty-six children were born in the brigade. One year has gone by, yet all of them except two are still alive. So you see why we think barefoot doctors are a good thing."

The women are now bringing in the food. Huge bowls of meat, carved for me by the host. The women have retired behind the screen.

One morning later on, we are standing by Little Kara Kul. The lake is a breathtaking blue beneath the mountains, and the cliffs have been weathered smooth by the biting wind. A border guard rides past toward Bulun Kul, greeting us. I look toward the lake, to which Sven Hedin came in April 1894 from the "hospitable officers" in Pamirsky Post, "this corner of the great Russia" where he had been "as a compatriot and old friend." Hedin here experienced his first Kirghiz *bajga,* that horsemen's game which in Afghanistan is called *buzkashi:* the snatching of the goat.

He was a typical figure of the period of the great game, this explorer who now is mainly remembered for his discovery of the sources of the Brahmaputra and Indus rivers. A Nietzschean superman mastering his sorrow as his camels fall and his men have to be left to die of thirst and he walks alone out of the desert to salvation. A name-dropper on the grand scale, having General Kuropatkin and Czar Nicholas II, Kaiser Wilhelm II, Lord Curzon, and Chancellor Hitler as listeners. But also one of the great geographers of his age. A man with an absolute carto- graphic eye who made the best maps still available on southern Tibet. A man prepared to serve the czar, the kaiser, Chiang Kai-shek, and Hitler for the greater glory of the imperial idea . . . but still one of the great geographers of the age. Now in 1894, in the great year of the Game, he comes from Russia into the Chinese Pamirs.

And in this lake Sven Hedin almost drowned on October 4, 1894. He was taking soundings from a leather boat he had had made. A strong wind started to blow; the boat drifted and began to fill with water. He managed to get to the shore, "hurried to the camp, and made up a huge fire." I am standing there, trying to imagine the scene, remembering that prewar summer in Sweden when I was a child and lay in the attic, the rain drumming on the roof, wondering whether it was possible to make up a huge fire with yak droppings.

The sky is very blue, the scenery painfully impressive, immense and beautiful here near the little black lake. The border leaves us here, turning off to the west. Our route goes north, toward the next lake, Bulun Kul. It will then move east, precipitate down the ravines, follow- ing the Ghez Darya toward the plain and Kashgar.

It is a strange border. It is no border at all, in fact, but rather a temporary front line for Russian troops, recognized by nobody. A kind of demarcation line, one could say. The Russian troops reached this point at the time when Sven Hedin joined the host of land surveyors, geographers, learned men, and officers on a pleasure trip during a leave of absence. They had begun strolling through the Pamirs from the 1860s until it was—as Thomas Hungerford Holdich, superintendent of the Frontier Surveys for India, put it—"probably the best explored region in High Asia."

The story about this border, which we have followed from Tashkurg- han until it turns off now by Little Kara Kul, is a special story that demands its own chapter. In an attempt to avoid telling this story, the Kremlin leaders have let the world know that China is reclaiming Siberia. This fact, however, is as untrue and incorrect as saying that the three kingdoms—the czar's Russia, the British Empire, and the Chi- nese Empire—ever met at a common border point up here on the Roof of the World.

3

A Border That
Does Not Exist

Some issues become very complicated in spite of the fact that they are actually straightforward. The complications are so arranged and piled up as to cover the simple truth. One such issue concerns the border between the Soviet Union and China in Pamir. The simple truth is, the border does not exist.

I will show this first. Then it will be possible to discuss the historical background as well as the actual implications of this fact.

According to article IX of the treaty made by Russia and China in St. Petersburg on February 24, 1881 (New Style)*, both sides nominated authorized representatives to mark the border. In the Protocol of Novy Margelan of May 22, 1884 (Old Style), the border was established and described as the border between "the Russian territories and the Kashgar province which belongs to China." The third chapter of the Protocol reads:

> The border line goes . . . up to the pass of Uz Bel, also called Kizil Jik (covered in snow most of the year). That is also where the border between the two countries ceases, since the Russian border turns off to the southwest and the Chinese border goes to the south. All the land with the rivers flowing through it which is west of this border line belongs to the Russian Empire, and the land with the rivers flowing through it which is east of this border line belongs to China.

Immediately after this follows chapter four of the Protocol:

> 4. The description of the border in this Protocol together with the attached map with the border line marked between the Russian Empire

---

*Soviet Russia, via Lenin, accepted the Gregorian calendar, effective February 1, 1918 (Old Style), which became February 14, 1918. The Bolshevik uprising is dated November 7, 1917 (New Style) but October 25 (Old Style)—thus, the October Revolution.

and China with rivers, mountain passes, valleys, and border posts, is ratified and recognized by the Russian side and the Chinese as final.

The Uz Bel pass on modern maps is called Kizil Jik and is situated on a northern latitude of 38°40′. Whoever is interested in looking it up for himself ought to get a good, fairly detailed map.

I am using map NJ43 "Su-Fu (Kashgar Kone Shar) Southwest Asia" with a scale of 1:1,000,000, published by the United States Army Map Service, part of their world series. It also contains good information regarding the degree of accuracy.

Let us now, according to this Protocol, draw a border line south from Kizil Jik (Uz Bel) as far as Lake Zorkul (Lake Victoria).

But on this map the line showing the border now held by the Soviet forces makes a wide curve much farther to the east. This border line of more than 300 kilometers, once occupied by the czar's Russia, is not sanctioned by any international treaty.

I want to be perfectly clear: this line is not sanctioned by any treaty between the Russian Empire/the Soviet Union on the one hand and any Chinese government on the other; nor can it be related to any treaty between Russia/the Soviet Union and any third power.

Let me deal with each question separately. The Soviet government holds that its troops are occupying the area east of the border line from Kizil Jik to Zorkul in accordance with the exchange of notes of 1894. (See the statement by the Soviet government of June 13, 1969.) I will come back to the political situation, where these notes were exchanged between China and Russia in April 1894; the important thing at this stage of our discussion is to point out that the Soviet government is making false statements.

The government of the emperor's China did not accept the border line established by the Russian troops. It stated expressly that it followed the Protocol of 1884. There is nothing in this exchange of notes —and nothing in any statement of any later Chinese government—that could be used to define the Russian military demarcation line as a recognized international border.

In the treaty concerning spheres of influence in Pamir formulated on March 11, 1895, between Great Britain and Russia, a Russian southern border to Afghanistan was defined "from the eastern shore of Lake Victoria to the Chinese border." In the description of the border based on the work of the mixed Russian-British commission, the Russian-Afghan border is said to have its eastern limits at "the top of Povalo Schveikovsky . . . which is the border of the Chinese territory." But neither Afghanistan nor China was a signing power. Neither did they participate in the debates or the work of the border commission.

Even if one takes the imperialist stand that a treaty between Russia and Great Britain would be obligatory for China, regardless of the Chinese government's opinion, there is no international treaty whatsoever legitimizing 307 kilometers of Russian military demarcation line in Pamir from Kokrash Kol/Povalo Schveikovsky up to Uz Bel/Kizil Jik.

I am not alone in holding this opinion. On the contrary, it is based on existing treaties and documents. Therefore, Dr. J. R. V. Prescott points out in *Map of Mainland Asia by Treaty** that the present border between China and Soviet in Pamir has no authority in any international treaty.

Basically, the border problem in Pamir is not an impossible one. It is one of many similar problems along the long border between the Soviet and China, where the Soviet troops are now holding areas once occupied by the czar's troops on the Chinese side of borders which—by threat of war and blackmail—the czar's diplomats forced China to accept. Problems inherited from history should be given a solution.

The attitude of the Russian Bolsheviks to this expansionist foreign policy of the Russian czar was clear and indisputable. Lenin and his wife Krupskaya spent the autumn of 1912 in Krakow. He kept in touch with the Bolsheviks in inner Russia from there. On November 13 Krupskaya—who handled the dispatches—wrote a document which she sent on to Russia. It was Lenin's suggestion for the declaration of the Social Democratic Duma fraction. The czar's political police managed to find the document, which was not found again until fifteen years after the revolution, in 1932, in the old archives of the police ministry. This "Declaration of Workers' Deputies" says *inter alia:*

> From the IV National Duma the Social Democratic fraction explains that there exists an indissoluble connection between its activities and those of earlier social democratic fractions in the various National Dumas. . . . The Social Democratic fraction in the IV National Duma objects especially to the foreign policies maintained by the Russian government, rejects the attempts to extend the territory of our state by conquering foreign areas around the Bosphorus, in Turkish Armenia, in Persia and China; it rejects the conquest of Mongolia, by which our good relations to our Chinese brother republic has been disturbed.

After the revolution these clear, indisputable principles guided the foreign policies drawn up by Lenin in a difficult and complicated situa-

*Published in association with the Australian Institute of International Affairs, Melbourne 1975.

tion, with civil wars and foreign intervention. On July 25, 1919, when the war was still going on in Siberia, the deputy people's commissar for foreign affairs, Leo Karakhan, in the name of the Workers' and Peasants' Government, issued a "Declaration to the Chinese Nation and the Governments of Southern and Northern China."

> Now we appeal to the Chinese nation to open its eyes. The Soviet Government has renounced all the acquisitions made by the Czar's Government, which deprived China of Manchuria and other regions.

Because of the wars, this declaration did not reach the Peking government until March 26, 1920. That government was weak and exposed to pressure from Japan and other foreign powers, which then kept China in semicolonial dependence. But in September 1920, a Chinese delegation, led by General Chang Shih-ling, was sent to Moscow. On September 27, 1920, the Soviet government made another statement to the Peking government. Lenin's government then suggested through Leo Karakhan a "friendly agreement" between China and Soviet Russia, based on the declaration of 1919. The draft had eight points. The first reads:

> (1) The Government of the Russian Socialist Federated Soviet Republics declares as void all the treaties concluded by the former Government of Russia with China, renounces all the annexations of Chinese territory, all the concessions in China, and returns to China free of charge, and forever, all that was ravenously taken from her by the Czar's Government and by the Russian bourgeoisie.

On May 31, 1924, the treaty between China and the Soviet Union was signed in Peking, the first treaty on the basis of equality signed by China for more than a hundred years. This treaty says, among other things:

> Article IV. The Government of the Union of Soviet Socialist Republics, in accordance with its policy and Declarations of 1919 and 1920, declares that all the Treaties, Agreements, etc., concluded between the former Tsarist Government and any third party or parties affecting the sovereign rights or interests of China are null and void. . . .

> Article VII. The Governments of the two Contracting Parties agree to redemarcate their national boundaries at the Conference as provided in Article II of the present Agreement, and pending such redemarcation, to maintain the present boundaries.

In China, where the people were beginning to rise against plundering foreign imperialists and corrupt native warlords, and in Asia, where the people had started to fight colonialism and imperialistic oppression, these declarations and this treaty were greeted with wild enthusiasm. The words were like a trumpet call.

It would, in other words, not have been difficult to solve the questions of Pamir and other border areas where the czarist regime had intruded on China's sovereignty and the Soviet regime had inherited the historical situation from the previous rulers. Lenin's policy on that matter was indisputable. In 1924, after Lenin had died, Stalin in his lectures at the Sverdlov University described the foreign policies of the czarist regime:

> The czar's Russia first of all was a seat for all kinds of oppression— capitalistic as well as colonial and military—in its most inhuman and barbaric form. Who does not know the connection between the total power of capital in Russia and the despotism of the czarist regime; between the aggression of the Russian nationalism and the executioner's role in the czarist regime against non-Russian people; the exploitation of whole areas—in Turkey, Persia, China; the czar's conquest of these territories with wars of conquest? Lenin was right when he said that czarism was a "military feudal imperialism." Czarism was a concentration of the most negative sides of imperialism, raised to the second power!

The stand of the present Soviet regime is different. In the statement of the Soviet government on June 13, 1969, it said, among other things:

> The border between Soviet and China is the result of historic events from a long period. . . .
>
> Having been created many generations ago, the border between the Soviet Union and China reflected then, as it does now, the actual settlements of the people in these two states along natural demarcation lines, such as mountains and rivers. In its full extension this border is clearly and exactly defined by treaties, Protocols, and maps. . . .
>
> . . . Neither the declaration of 1919 nor the treaty between Soviet and China of 1924 contained or could contain any suggestions of the treaties establishing the present borders between the Soviet Union and China as being unequal or secret. There was naturally no question of nullifying or revising them.

With this, the Soviet government has gone back to the attitude characterizing Russian foreign politics before Lenin, in the October Revolution, had a chance to formulate—in practice—the principles of a socialist foreign policy. Now the Soviet policy coincides with that of old Russia.

This transition began as early as Stalin's days, although it developed fully only after his death, when the Soviet Union could assume the role of one of the superpowers. Stalin committed serious mistakes in his foreign policy, going against the basic principles he himself, theoretically, had advocated more forcefully than anyone else among Lenin's Bolsheviks before the October Revolution. Later on, though, after China had liberated itself through its own efforts, he was prepared to admit his mistakes to Mao Tse-tung and the Chinese comrades after a full debate. He was able to criticize himself and make policy changes. He did so in 1950. But his successors have developed and systematized what was wrong in his policies. The determining factor in this development is, of course, the social transformation of the Soviet Union during these decades. In order to see the characteristic features of those of Stalin's errors in his foreign policy which his heirs have made the main line in Soviet foreign affairs, we can compare three different quotations.

The first is from one of Stalin's lectures on the basic principles of Leninism, which I have already quoted. It dates from April 1924, when his attitude coincided with that of Lenin.

The second is from "Comrade J. V. Stalin's address to the people on September 2, 1945." Japan had by then capitulated unconditionally. It reads:

> But the defeat of the Russian troops in 1904 in the war between Japan and Russia left bitter memories with our people. It was a dark stain on our country. Our people waited confidently for the day when Japan would suffer defeat and the stain could be washed off. For forty years we, the older generation, have been waiting for this day. Now it is here.

The third quotation gives an opposite judgment of this defeat. It is from Lenin's article "The Fall of Port Arthur" in *Wperjod,* January 14, 1905: "Not the Russian people but the autocrats have had a defeat. The Russian people have won by the defeat of the autocrats."

In step with the change in the Soviet Union from the dictatorship of the proletariat to that of the state monopoly bourgeoisie over the proletariat, these chauvinist tendencies have been developed and systematized along Great-Russia lines toward a new czarism.

The wind is strong on the mountains. The tufts of grass hide together between the stones. The snow on Kungur Shan is glistening white against the dark sky. A Kirghiz shepherd rides past us westward on the road along the south shore of the lake. His pack is carried by another horse, running behind. The telephone poles wander north across stony mountains. The sun burns my neck. My long underwear, which served me so well a while ago in the morning cold, suddenly itches at the back of my knees as noon approaches.

Sven Hedin was staying here by Little Kara Kul at the time the Russian troops marched into Chinese territory and established fortified camps over to the west, on the other side of the mountain ridge. Sven

Hedin had felt at home with the Russian officers; the commandant of the Pamirsky Post had delivered a formal speech in honor of the king of Sweden and Norway, His Majesty King Oscar II. In patriotic rapture, Sven Hedin had drunk the glowing Turkestan wine, while the Russian gentlemen toasted the monarch:

> on the Roof of the World, 3,610 meters above sea level, far from the bustling world, in the middle of Asia, in an area where our closest neighbors were the chamois of the rocks, the wolves of the wilderness and the golden eagles of the sky.*

The Chinese forces had been pushed aside by Russian troops. Their objections had not bothered the Russian staff. No wonder Sven Hedin found the Chinese guards suspicious when he appeared from the Russian lines on the mountain pass, measuring, mapping, and taking soundings in the lakes.

At that time Russia and Great Britain were coming to an agreement concerning Pamir. Not that either had any legal right to the area, which belonged to China and Afghanistan, but they were two great European powers playing the great game over Asia.

In the report of the border commission, printed in Calcutta in 1897, Lieutenant Colonel R. H. Wahab, R.E., reveals the following: "No signs of Chinese occupation were seen in this direction, though the nomad Kirghiz, whose tents were found for some distance up the valley, professed to be Chinese subjects."

If the same argument at the same time had been valid also outside Asia, Russia could have taken the whole of northern Sweden and northern Norway, since the commission wouldn't have found signs of a Swedish or Norwegian in those mountains, although the Lapp nomads whose tents could be found some distance up in the valley claimed to be Swedish or Norwegian subjects.

England and Russia certainly played the game over Asia, and the British representatives in the commission, like the British diplomats, certainly had an interest in keeping the Russian border as far to the north and west as they could possibly force the Russians to accept. But the Russians were after all Europeans and not Asians, and Colonel Holdich writes in his report that the people are

> entirely Kirghiz, and it may, I think, be taken for granted that it will soon be entirely Russian. . . . There is doubtless a tendency on their part toward accepting Chinese domination, which is due to the easy terms on which they are permitted to live within Chinese territory, and the absence of direct taxation; the skins of certain wild animals killed by their

*Sven Hedin, *En fārd genom Asien 1893–1897* [Through Asia] (Stockholm, 1898), p. 143.

huntsmen forming the chief tribute claimed by Chinese authority at Tashkurghan. But the security for life and property will inevitably lead them to the Russian fold eventually, especially as there is no ethnographical distinction whatsoever between the Kirghiz of the Alichur or Alai-Pamir and those of the Taghdumbash. There seems, indeed, to be a certain historical fitness about the return of the Kirghiz to a Christian Government if they are, as they seem to be, a survival of the medieval Nestorian Christian communities of Asia.

The road down through deep ravines where the Ghez Darya breaks through the mountains has been swept away by the spring landslides. It is now provisionally repaired and open to traffic. It hangs like a ledge on the mountainside; the gravel rolls under the wheels and the jeep lurches downward in low gear.

"It's a difficult road," says Rakmov, deputy chairman of the revolutionary committee of Kashgar district. "I saw the slide coming last year with my own eyes; it was as if the whole mountain had moved. It can be dangerous, too. Still, we have to keep the road open. The technical problems have to be solved. This is our link with Pakistan. We're extending it. It used to be impossible to pass during long periods of the year. Now it's open winter, spring, summer, and autumn."

Farther down in the valley, we leave the jeeps and ride up into the mountains. We're going toward the old caravan route. The path meanders up the mountainside; it is narrow. My horse has a saddle with a silver pommel, very smart. But I'm not a good rider, and the path is very narrow. When I look down, the rock drops off vertically more than a hundred meters down into the frothy, foaming water. The rock is black, stones roll over the edge. On the other side the rocky wall sneaks along my knee. I would really have preferred to ride one of the yaks. But Abdullah says, laughing heartily:

"An honored guest couldn't possibly arrive on a yak. Yaks are only for women and children. You are a man and a guest of honor. You just keep on riding. The horse is used to this road, it lives here."

It is late afternoon by the time we reach the Gazi brigade. In the middle of the mountains the meadows open, fresh and green. There is the site of the old caravanserai; we pace out its plan. A little sheep pen is all that remains—the rest disappeared more than two generations ago.

"It was a private caravanserai," says Mahmed Islam, chairman of the revolutionary committee of the production brigade. "The caravans stopped here before getting into the high mountains, or they rested here on their return after descending. The owner was a man called Khulum-bek Hadji; he made a nice profit. Then times changed and there were no more caravans, so he just had the serai pulled down."

It is a valley of fantastic beauty, 2,800 meters above sea level. The air is fresh, the mountains like a protective wall around the green meadows.

"But it's cold in winter," Mahmed Islam says. "About 20 degrees Celsius below freezing. We have 5,557 animals now. Before the liberation there were only 1,500 of them, but they were owned by three families. Nine families—all the rest of us—had to work for them. In 1951, however, we did away with the exploitation, and now life is better. We have three teachers here and all our children go to school. The secondary school is for all, and we have five children in higher schools."

Our host is young, a shepherd called Akjol. We are sitting in his house, about twenty people. On one long wall there are big pictures of Marx, Engels, Lenin, and Stalin. On the other long wall there is Mao Tse-tung plus two diplomas for good work with the animals and for setting a good example with his serve-the-people attitude. In the courtyard the mutton is being grilled on skewers over a charcoal fire. This is a feast. The children sit in a semicircle, pushing each other and whispering. It is getting dark. The sky is still quite light, but darkness is rising through the valley. Two singers have arrived. The song rises, epic, monotonous, and magnificent in the night.

"We Kirghiz people like songs," our host says. "We have so many songs. They have plenty to tell us."

4

The Haunted
Consulate

Gun woke me up in the dead of night.

"Are you awake?" she asked. "I can hear you are. I have been thinking about Macartney. Petrovsky could be so rude to him because he knew Macartney's father had married in China and Macartney's mother came from Suchow. Petrovsky was a brute. I don't think he cared, being one of the czar's diplomats, but he knew what the British were like where race was concerned. You know, it was enough if he said, 'Oh, that Mac- something, Younghusband's* Eurasian secretary! No, I'm not at home to him!' And Macartney had to stop on the steps. The Russian diplomats are good at that sort of thing."

Gun was quiet for a moment. Then she said, "That was probably the reason why it took Macartney so long to get his appointment. He had to work as the British representative here in Kashgar for eighteen years before being allowed to call himself consul. That was due to his mother being Chinese! The British will never forgive a half-caste. You remember how they treated that consular assistant in Kabul who had married an Indonesian woman."

Something is ticking in the wall. The room is completely dark. The heavy velvet curtains are drawn. We are staying in the old Russian consulate, sleeping in the room of the duty officer. The night is still over Kashgar, but it ticks inside the walls, and now something begins to creak in the hall. As shiny black leather boots creak. Somebody standing out there, slowly rising on his toes, bending his knees, his boots creaking. Standing there waiting.

*Captain Francis Younghusband (1863–1942), British officer, explorer, and diplomat, traveled in Sinkiang in 1887 (see p. 174). He is best known for being in political command of the British expedition to and occupation of Lhasa in Tibet.

"Do you think it might be Petrovsky himself standing in the hall, his boots creaking?" I ask Gun.

But she has already gone back to sleep. I hear her breathing in deep slumber. I think of Petrovsky. I met him many times reading Sven Hedin:

> A Russian flag is swaying over the entrance where a couple of Cossacks are on guard. A few minutes later I am in the office of the powerful Russian consul Petrovsky, involved in an animated discussion about my trip and about important Asian issues.*

In 1882 Petrovsky arrived here in Kashgar with a guard of forty-five Cossacks after the St. Petersburg peace when China had to accept a Russian consul in Kashgar who was to help extend mutual trade and assist Russian citizens. He then worked hard according to plan for twenty-one years as the Russian representative in Kashgar, trying to take over Sinkiang for his master, the Russian autocrat.

Sven Hedin later on, when he was over eighty, looked back and portrayed Petrovsky as he had appeared three generations earlier:

> I have to thank my unforgettable friend, the consul and the Geheimrat Nikolai Feodorovich Petrovsky for all these favors. He was a man feared and secretly hated by the Chinese, but admired and esteemed by the natives, the East Turks, who called him "The New Genghis Khan."
>
> Petrovsky was a very learned man, very knowledgeable in the history of Central Asia, in archaeology and in East Turkic languages. He was tall, usually dressed in a local green *khalat* or mantle and a likewise green calotte. His eyes flicked jovially behind his gold-rimmed spectacles.
> In the evening we would sit for hours making great plans.†

I doubt the love of the people for Petrovsk. Other sources give a different picture of their feelings. Still, I find the portrait of him plausible.

I was now lying in the dark, unable to go back to sleep. I felt fidgety, the alcohol was leaving my body. We had celebrated Gun's fiftieth birthday the night before and had had a big birthday party. All our hosts and friends in Kashgar had gathered to eat and drink and dance. Here where Confucius never had great influence, they do dance. After that we went to the theater. We didn't drink all that much but it was enough to keep me awake. I was thinking about Petrovsky. He was a typical Russian diplomat: tough, able, and knowledgeable.

As Engels pointed out, it's easy to underestimate czarist diplomacy because czarism in general was such a misery. But the inner misery was

*Sven Hedin, *Karavan och tarantass* (Stockholm, 1953), p. 137.
†Ibid., p. 138.

balanced by splendid external success. From the time of Catherine the Great on, the czar's diplomatic corps was by far the most skillful in Europe. Petrovsky was a typical representative of this elite corps, far superior to that Indian civil service of a thousand British bureaucrats who ruled over India.

I had brought Engels's book on the foreign policy of Russian czarism. It ought to be interesting, I had thought, for a journey so near the borders of the new czars. Since I was unable to sleep anyway, I got into my slippers and dressing gown and sneaked into the hall to read. It was totally quiet again. When I turned on the light, I could see the magnificent Khotan rugs on the walls. Mirrors and gilding gleamed around me, as I read Engels from 1890:

> You must know, however, the strength of your opponent as well as his weakness. And foreign policy is no doubt the area where czarism is strong, very strong. The Russian diplomacy is somehow a modern Jesuit order, powerful enough to rise above the Czar's whims in an emergency, overruling the corruption among themselves and spreading it even more generously. A Jesuit order, originally and primarily recruited by strangers. . . . The old Russian high aristocracy had too many worldly private interests and family obligations and lacked the absolute reliability which service in this new order demanded. . . . This secret order, recruited originally from foreign adventurers, has lifted the Russian Empire to its present power. With ironlike powers of endurance, eyes firmly fixed on the goal, no scruples regarding treachery, perfidy, assassination, hypocrisy, extending bribes with full hands, never triumphant in victory nor depressed by defeat, walking across the corpses of millions of soldiers and at least one czar, this band, ruthless as it is talented, has contributed more than any Russian armies to move the Russian borders onwards from Dnieper and Dvina across the Vistula to Prut, Danube and the Black Sea, from Don and Volga across Caucasus and to the sources of Oxus (Amu Darya) and Jaxartes (Syr Darya), which has made Russia great, powerful and feared, opening its roads to a world Empire . . . "Progress" and "enlightenment" were in the eighteenth century the czarist passwords in Europe, just as "The Freedom of the People" was in the nineteenth. There was no conquest, no violence, no oppression by the czar unless on the pretext of "enlightenment" and "progress" and "liberalism" and "liberation of the people." And the childish West European Liberals believed in this until Gladstone came—well, they believe it even today.*

I went out onto the veranda, opening the large doors to the night. The air was fresh. Light fell over the courtyard. Kashgar was asleep.

*"Die auswärtige Politik des russischens Zarentums" [The Foreign Policy of Russian Czarism], *Karl Marx—Friedrich Engels Werke,* vol. 22 (Berlin, 1963), pp. 14–15, 23.

The twenty-five-year-old student Sven Hedin came here in 1890 and the Russian diplomat took him on, leading him to his office with books and mercury barometers and aneroids and seismometers. Writes Hedin:

I stop in front of the huge ordnance map of the western part of Asia in order to survey at once the whole 3000-kilometer-long road from Teheran through Khorasan, Transcaspia, Bukhara, Samarkand, Fergana, and East Turkestan to Kashgar, where I have now arrived safely. The map shows that I am not far from the foot of Kunlun and hardly two weeks' ride from the secretive Tibet.*

Much later he was to write: "Marvelous visions and future projects loomed before me."†

And four years after the consul Petrovsky had taken on this Swedish student, Hedin was up in Pamir. The Russian troops in the meantime, following consul Petrovsky's direct orders, had marched in and started to occupy the country. The Chinese border guards had become suspicious of traveling strangers. Sven Hedin was mapping out valleys and passes and waterways on the side where the Russian troops had not yet arrived; he sailed in a leather boat on Little Kara Kul and nearly drowned when taking soundings. He had a lot of other strange experiences before he made his way down to Kashgar, where he stayed with his fatherly friend, the consul Petrovsky, and they sat up late at night talking about Asia and its problems, about scientific progress, geographical discoveries and interesting new maps.

I closed the large consulate doors and turned out the light in the hall. Mirrors and gilding no longer gleamed. I groped along the rugs on the walls, going toward our room. As I entered, Gun said through the dark, "Do you remember what Hedin said? That he came to Kashgar the first time in 1890 and even that same evening Petrovsky took him to see Younghusband, where he met Younghusband's interpreter called Macartney whose mother was Chinese and who looked Mongol and lived with the servants? Who do you think told Hedin all that? Younghusband? Macartney? Petrovsky was really a cunning devil who knew how to put his words!"

She fell asleep again before I had time to reply. I lay in the dark listening to the large house around us. I could hear again, quite clearly, the creaking of boots in the hall.

The consulate was haunted.

*Sven Hedin, *Genom Khorastan och Turkestan* (Stockholm, 1893), p. 448.
†Hedin, *Karavan,* p. 139.

5
Sinkiang

In older literature: East Turkestan with Dzungaria; East Jagatai, Little Bucharia; High Tatary, Kashgaria, Chinese Tatary. The extreme northwesterly province of China. Official name since 1955: Sinkiang Uighur Autonomous Region.

Provincial capital: Urumchi (previously Tihua). Another three towns form separate administrative units directly under the province: Karamai (the oil city), Kashgar, and Ining (previously Kuldja). There are eleven districts, five of which are autonomous districts of different nationalities (Hui, Kazakh, Kirghiz; two Mongol). There are eighty counties, six of which are autonomous counties (Hui, two Kazakh, Mongol, Sibo, and Tadzhik). Within the autonomous region—the province, which is Uighur—there is an autonomous district—which is Mongol—in which there is an autonomous county, which is Kazakh. That is one example. The principle is: Nationalities living in a concentrated settlement should have autonomous administrations.

Area: about 1,600,000 square kilometers, one-sixth of the total area of China, more than England, France, Italy, and Germany combined.

Three large mountain ranges cut through Sinkiang: Altai in the north, Tien Shan in the middle, and Kunlun in the south. Between these there are two huge basins without outlets: the Dzungarian basin north of Tien Shan and the Tarim basin south of Tien Shan. East of Tien Shan there are high plateaus, where the Turfan depression is also found. Its lowest point, 154 meters below sea level, is the lowest point in China. To the west, adjoining the Soviet border, is the Ili valley below Tien Shan. Along the Altai range the Irtysh River flows west. That is the only river in Sinkiang connected to a sea, the only Chinese river flowing toward the Arctic Ocean. To the extreme west of Sinkiang, the mountain ranges rise to the Roof of the World: Pamir, where China borders

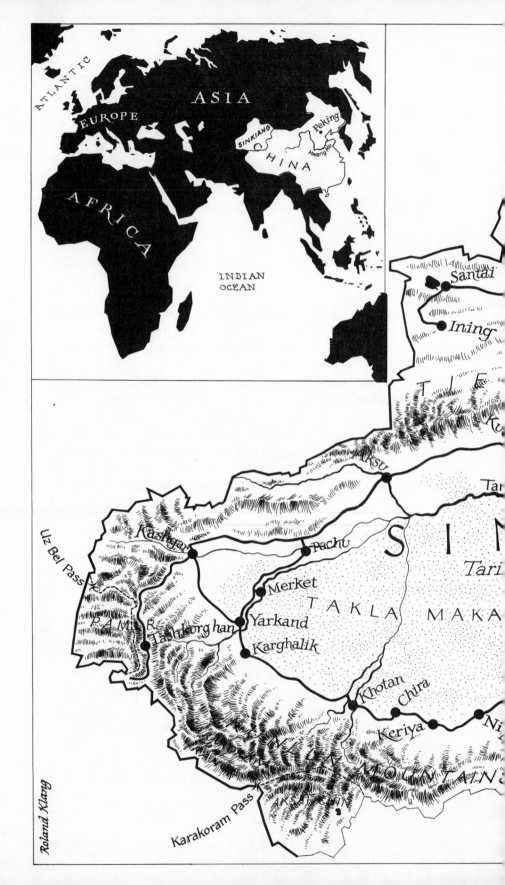

ATLANTIC

EUROPE

ASIA

SINKIANG

Peking

CHINA

Hwang Ho

AFRICA

INDIAN
OCEAN

Santai

Ining

T I E

Ku

RSU

Tar

Kashgar

Pachu

S I N

Uz Bel Pass

Merket

Tari

TAKLA

MAKA

PAMIR

Tashkurghan

Yarkand

Karghalik

Khotan

Chira

Keriya

Ni

MOUNTAINS

Karakoram Pass

Roland Klang

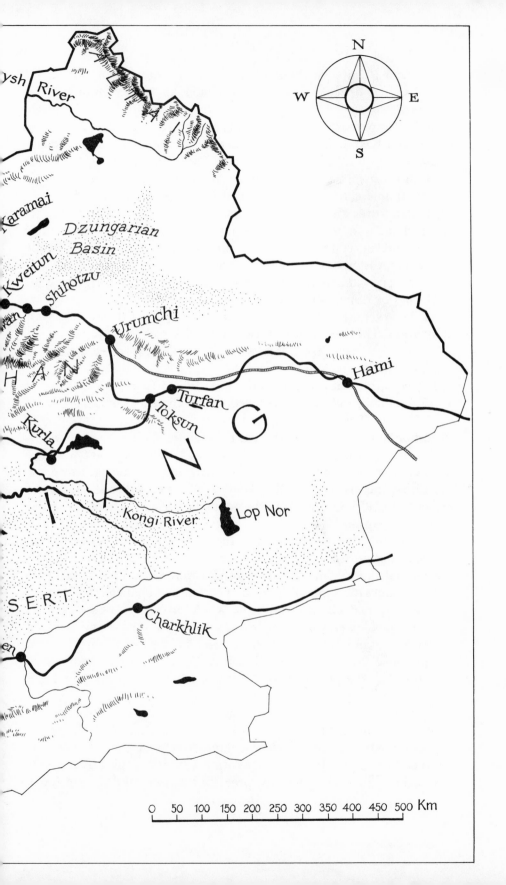

on the Soviet Union (without a fixed border), Afghanistan, and Kashmir (disputed between Pakistan and India; that part being held by Pakistan).

In the Tarim basin is the huge Takla Makan Desert of 370,000 square kilometers. East of Lop Nor the sand desert becomes a stone desert.

Climate. This is the innermost part of Eurasia at the farthest distance from all oceans. North of Tien Shan the average annual precipitation is 250 millimeters and the number of frost-free days is 150. South of Tien Shan the average annual precipitation goes down to 100 millimeters and the number of frost-free days goes up to 210. The average temperature in winter is c. $-20°C$ and in summer c. $+35°C$. In the Turfan depression the July temperatures exceed $+46°C$. The day variations are very wide; each day and night can be said to have four seasons.

The *agriculture* is 90 percent dependent on irrigation. North of Tien Shan, however, there are grazing lands and potential new areas for cultivation. The area south of Tien Shan is a pure oasis area.

The *natural assets* are great. Oil, coal, uranium, iron ore, gold, salt, sulphur, and so on. Sinkiang is rich.

The *population* at the time of the First World War was estimated at 1 to 2.4 million, and in 1953 reached 4.87 million, 74 percent of which were Uighur. The increase since then has been great, mainly due to migration to newly cultivated areas in Dzungaria, oil fields, and industrial areas. The census in 1957 showed 9.3 million inhabitants. The number now amounts to 11 million, distributed among thirteen nationalities, the main ones being Uighur (45.7 percent) and Han (41.4 percent). In 1953 75 percent of the population lived south of Tien Shan in the oases around Takla Makan. Migration and economic expansion have now given northern Sinkiang the main part of the population.

Roads and railroads. The ancient trade routes to China from India, Persia, and the Mediterranean countries were here. Present roads in general follow the same directions. The railroad connecting Urumchi with Peking and Shanghai and the whole growing Chinese railroad system is now extended from Urumchi toward Kashgar and Khotan. Urumchi has an international airport and has developed into a center for air traffic. In southeastern Sinkiang, beyond Lop Nor and toward the border of the provinces of Kansu and Tsinghai, China conducts nuclear experiments.

Borders. China borders in Sinkiang on the Mongolian People's Republic, Afghanistan, Pakistan, and India. The borders with the Soviet Union and Afghanistan are clear, delimited by treaty, mutually recognized and demarcated. The border with Kashmir occupied by Pakistan is awaiting a final solution of the problem between Pakistan and India, delimited, recognized, and demarcated by Pakistan and China. The border with Kashmir occupied by Pakistan is—awaiting a final solution of the Kashmir problem between Pakistan and India—delimited, recognized, and demarcated between Pakistan and China.

There India claims about 30,000 square kilometers northeast of the Karakoram Mountains, the high plateau of Aksai Chin. This is held by China and is administratively part of the Khotan district and cut by the old—now extended—road between Sinkiang and Tibet. There were fights here in the 1962 border war between India and China.

There are now many indications that this conflict between India and China is gradually approaching its solution. The realistic compromise will probably be the one recommended by the Afro-Asian states, which Premier Chou En-lai was prepared to accept. Each side will keep more or less what it has and the border will be measured accordingly. China on the whole will accept India's claim in the east on the border stretch between Bhutan and Burma, and India on the whole will accept China's claim on the west. The actual present border line would, in general, then be the one recognized, delimited, and demarcated.

Regarding the Soviet border, China maintains partly that it is a result of unequal treaties made under threat and that the Soviet Union, in previous declarations and treaties, has declared that it is prepared to take up the border question again to achieve a new demarcation; and partly that Soviet forces are now present even on the Chinese side of this border in several places.

By a skillful misinformation campaign, Soviet propaganda has managed to give the impression that China has reclaimed all areas annexed by czarist Russia during China's weak period in the nineteenth century. China wants all of Siberia, they say. This is simply untrue.

China demands that the Soviet Union, according to promises made in declarations and treaties, agree to redemarcate the borders and in the meantime keep the present border lines.

The Chinese Foreign Office expressly declared on October 8, 1969:

> The Chinese government's stand for an overall settlement of the Sino-Soviet boundary question is, in summary, as follows: . . . 2. In consideration of the actual conditions, take these treaties as the basis for an overall settlement of the Sino-Soviet boundary question through peaceful negotiations and for determining the entire alignment of the Boundary line. China does not demand the return of the Chinese territory which czarist Russia annexed by means of these treaties.

Since the Soviet propaganda so loudly proclaims that China wants Siberia, it should be emphasized that the stand of the Chinese government is indisputable. The border line established by these—unequal—treaties should be taken as the basis for the redemarcation of the border.

China is not—repeat: not—demanding Siberia back!

There is, however, one important border issue, which is completely open: Pamir. The only treaty and the only written agreement in existence between any Chinese and any Russian or Soviet regime regarding this area is the note in the third chapter of the border Protocol of May 22, 1884, according to which China's border runs south from the Uz Bel pass (Kizil Jik). In the Russo–British race for Central Asia, Russia at that time occupied Pamir up to the line now seen on the maps. This means that this border has no basis in any internationally recognized treaty. No country other than Russia (the Soviet Union) has ever agreed to it.

The people's militia at the Soviet border in Pamir

Tashkurghan, the old fort: the "stone tower" in Pamir

Tadzhik welcoming music at the Tagarmi People's Commune

Equestrian games on the Roof of the World

Shepherds riding into the camp

Apak Hodja's mausoleum in Kashgar

Women being trained to tie rugs in Ining

Tursun Mehmed serves tea to guests in his home at the Pakhtaklik People's Commune, Kashgar district.

A local power station in Yukuri Urlez People's Commune, Khotan district

Ruzi Khalla and others responsible discuss the "Eighteenth of August project."

The goldminer Kasem Suchi and party secretary Li Shu-san

The canyon at the entrance of the "Eighteenth of August project," Niya county, south of Takla Makan

Harvesters at Chapchal, Sibo People's Autonomous County, Ili district

6
It All Began
with the Horses

The population is agricultural and resident. They grow rice and wheat, make wine from grapes, and have many good horses. The horses sweat blood and originate from the heavenly horses. The cities are surrounded by walls. . . .

That was General Chang Ch'ien reporting, more than two thousand years ago, to Emperor Wu Ti from his mission to the westerly countries. He was talking about what is now Fergana, west of the mountains shared by Uzbekistan, Tadzhikistan, and Kirghizistan in the Soviet Union. The year was 126 B.C.

Twelve years before, he had been sent as ambassador to the Iranian peoples in Central Asia to establish an alliance in their joint fight against the Huns. At this time Rome had just defeated Carthage in the third Punic War.

The Huns had taken advantage of China's temporary weakness in order to extend their power. They now held the oases along the old cultural road west. The great Emperor Wu Ti of the Han dynasty reinforced the unity of the Chinese Empire, carried out reforms, and fought the Huns.

After many adventures, a long capture by the Huns and extensive journeys, General Chang Ch'ien came back. He gave a precise account of his journeys. China was arming against the Huns. In 221 B.C. Ch'in Shih Huang Ti had united China. The new state was strongly central- ized with a uniform bureaucratic rule. Coins, weights, measurements, and written language were standardized as well as the calendar. The old kingdoms and duchies were defeated. All barriers for trade within the empire were removed. The track width between carriage wheels was standardized, and broad highways radiated out over the empire from the emperor's capital. Land could now be bought and sold and the landowning class created a state according to its needs.

The administrators were to be nominated for their ability. They had to carry out the will of the emperor in a united manner, and they exercised control over each other. The centralized feudal autocracy was established. This kind of state was to last for two thousand years. When formed, it was a great victory for progress. Two thousand years later, when it was demolished, it had become a reactionary, oppressive state in decay.

This new state, however, was not just a liberating development. It also allowed the possibility of exploiting the farmers, the working people, with unequaled efficiency. Three-quarters of the harvest could now be claimed for the new needs of the state. This state also triumphed thanks to its new military technique. The cavalry had broken the old kingdoms. But the exploitation was increased to the brink of the unbearable and the first dynasty was crushed by huge peasant revolts as early as 207 B.C.

China seemed to be falling apart again. The Huns assumed even greater power and influence, but the new state organization, too progressive to be effaced, was a historic necessity for the landowning class. They might have rejected parts of Ch'in Shih Huang Ti's official ideology, but they accepted the actual results. Out of the confusion a new rule arose, which developed fantastic possibilities offered by this instrument: the centralized bureaucratic state. The Han dynasty re-established the unity of the empire and took up the fight against the Huns. The cavalry was reinforced.

The blood-sweating horses from the West, on which Chang Ch'ien had reported, turned out much superior to the Mongol horses. Emperor Wu Ti sent one ambassador after another to procure some. On General Chang-Ch'ien's advice seeds for blue lucerne were imported. Wu Ti had large areas next to his palace sown with this new plant, which fed the "heavenly horses" now used by his cavalry.

The Huns were to be driven back across the deserts, and the road west was to be secured. Trade and cultural contacts were to be increased. The Huns' power over trade was to be broken. This was the time when the Chinese adopted, among other things, grapes, grape wine, and garlic.

The Huns were beaten in one campaign after another. In 121 B.C. the Chinese troops had driven the Huns away from the whole Kansu corridor and stood directly in front of the huge desert in the Tarim basin. In 114 B.C., just after General Chang Ch'ien had died, the first trade caravans wandered west. Up to twelve caravans went west across the deserts every year with some hundred people each and a great number of loading animals. Each camel could carry a load of about 140 kilograms. They walked about 30 kilometers a day. But the trade was still hesitant, and China would not admit any merchants from the West. The Chinese merchants were badly received in the West. They complained to the emperor.

In 105 B.C. Emperor Wu Ti changed the trade policy of the empire. Foreigners were admitted into China. Trade increased. Silk was made for export. The oases in the Tarim basin were in alliance with China, but the trade on the roads was disturbed by attacks. In a masterly, well-organized campaign, General Li Kuang-li then took 60,000 men through the desert. The whole of the Tarim basin submitted to the emperor's supremacy. That was in 102 B.C. The roads to Iran and India and the Mediterranean countries were now open. Trade flourished.

Ever since, the people around Tarim have had their fate linked with the people around the Yellow River. China has periodically been united and strong; then the oases have been part of the Chinese Empire. That has been the case in about five hundred out of the two thousand years here in Kashgar, the Far West of China, and in about a thousand of the two thousand years farther east. China has sometimes been divided into several kingdoms by internal fights. The oases were then attached to one of these or established their own local dynasties. Conquering armies have occasionally broken in to occupy the oases and at times, the condition has been as in the twenties, thirties, and forties of our century, when Sinkiang was a Chinese province. It was not independent, but the central government had no power or only shadow power. The troops were managed locally. Foreign powers made intrigues. There were bitter, confusing civil wars with many victims. Sinkiang remained, however, part of China.

Still, it all started with the horses two thousand years ago, when the emperor of China wanted allies to combat the Huns and so armed his cavalry.

7
Roads and Years

Kashgar can hardly be called a beautiful city. It is grey under the yellow sky. The desert smokes over the city in the strong wind and the sand grits between the teeth. They say the airport has been closed for several days now.

Our hosts show us schools and craft cooperatives and hospitals. They would like Kashgar to be newer and more modern, more of a show-place. They would like to present a Kashgar of glass and concrete and steel. But the city extends, grey like clay under the yellow sky.

Kashgar is not a city of misery. The worst jumble was cleared up long ago. The bazaars have been tidied up. Kashgar is not the city seen on photographs in travel books from the twenties or thirties.

"We go from nothing to something, from small to big now that we industrialize," says Rakmof, deputy chairman of the revolutionary committee. "We have about 350 industries in the whole of this district. We have built power plants and concrete factories and we make fertilizers. We have factories for agricultural equipment and repair shops in each county to take care of tractors and agricultural machinery and cars. These are also starting to manufacture spare parts here and there. We have a textile industry and a silk mill, and we make carpets. We have started to manufacture our own diesel engines in Kashgar."

Still, Kashgar is not an industrial city. It is the dusty capital of a rich agricultural district. They show us the new department stores. People gather to stare at us. The hosts are apologetic: "They are not used to strangers here."

As we leave the store and cross the square in front of the mosque, a crowd has gathered. Turning around, I find that Gun has disappeared among the people. She is small and dark with short hair, so she can join the Kashgar crowd. Uighurs are 90 percent of the population here—

but she could have been a Kazakh. She does not attract any attention. I, however, seem to lead a small demonstration. Strangers are unusual.

We visit the mosque. It has been restored. It is cool under the trees. Old men are praying.

"Let's not disturb the believers," the hosts say.

We pass through the bazaar streets by the mosque. They have been cleaned up. The interest in us is decreasing. People are friendly. The men sit in the teahouse around the teapots, smoking and chatting. Only a few children follow us now. They hang over the parapet of the teahouse platform, glaring at me. The men chase them away: "Don't embarrass the guests!"

The streets on the outskirts where the old Russian consulate is are wide and shady. Large poplars grow along the covered ditch. Irrigation water flows there through the city and is brought into the gardens at fixed hours. Kashgar is an oasis: a desert town. The midday heat is thick and yellow over the city.

In the shadow of a large billboard we see the old consulate in front of us. Large, brightly painted letters tell us to be vigilant and watch out for the new czars. The consulate is now a guest house.

"But I suppose it was built after Petrovsky's great time," Gun said. "Swedish missionaries were there giving technical assistance to the Russian craftsmen."

The city was still in the midday heat. We walked up the path toward the main building of the old consulate, opened the heavy door, and went into the cool hall. It was the hour of the midday rest.

Gun had been looking for the old British consulate. She wanted to take a picture of it. It took her some time to find it. It had become an overnight hotel for truck drivers, where they can take a break coming down from Urumchi before continuing around the desert toward Khotan. It was clean and tidy, although little remained of its former imperial splendor. The only tokens of the British Empire were some British watertaps and a lavatory called "Victory." It was dripping quietly.

"How are the mighty fallen!" Gun said, as she told me about it.

"Second Book of Samuel," I said.

We went to school in the days when one was expected to know the Bible from Genesis to Revelation. This overnight hotel for truck drivers seemed to be the only remaining trace of the Swedish missionaries' activities in Kashgar.

The British consulate was Swedish built, and here in Kashgar was the Swedish mission for East Turkestan. Gun had read about that in the school library of her childhood. We asked about it now. Did anyone remember the Swedish missionaries?

No. They thought there had been missionaries there once. They might have been Swedish, but it was long ago, they disappeared long before the liberation. Rakmov, deputy chairman of the revolutionary committee, thought he remembered Swedish missionaries, but he didn't know for sure. If we were so very interested, they could look into it. There should be some documents in the city archives. And perhaps they could find some old people who remembered the Swedes. If there had been a missionary school, with hospital and everything, there ought to be someone who remembered them. But that might take a day or so.

Two days later, however, we were to be in Pakhtaklik People's Commune and then on our way to Khotan. We were to visit the Institute of Uighur Medicine. Gun, who had been to see the mausoleum Hazrat-i-Afak, wanted to go back there. The mosaics were lovely.

"Being in Kashgar, I prefer Islam for religion," Gun said. "If I have to choose."

"Yes," Rakmov said, "that is our monument. The missionaries did not belong here. I am not saying anything against Swedish missionaries," he hastily added. "I know nothing about them."

The missionary activities in Kashgar went on for many decades. It cost a lot of money and even poor people in Sweden donated money to spread light in one of the three cities which, according to the missionaries, were the darkest in Asia. The other two were Kabul and Lhasa. They believed in what they did. But it is as though they had never even existed. The work of the missionaries wasn't even written on the water. They moved in Kashgar's yellow air for a while and then disappeared. Where is the shadow of these people who passed by here two generations ago? In Kashgar they are forgotten.

That is actually a good thing. If they weren't forgotten and if their writings were to be translated and spread among people here, it wouldn't be too pleasant to be a Swedish visitor. I wouldn't then have been able to appear as a friendly foreigner in front of a crowd of curious but kind Kashgarians. I would have had to run. Or would any people like to hear this about their poor grandparents:

All believers in Islam have a deep-seated distrust of each other. This mistrust is justified, since almost all of them, especially in East Turkestan, are extremely dishonest and prone to lying.*

As I said, if this had been translated into Uighur, it wouldn't have been easy to be a Swedish visitor.

The missionaries were not bad people. We know who they are. Their parents were small farmers and poorly paid teachers. They had worked hard to get an education and were sincere and ambitious. They did not belong to the upper classes and they had good intentions. Neither did they behave badly. But they shared one conviction with their British and Russian brethren, the deepest conviction of all, that of European superiority. The Christian faith was less important than the over-all colonial ideology.

> The bulwarks of Islam are firm and closely connected with its followers' innate desire for a life devoted to evil and unnatural lusts. . . . How lost and forgotten the missionary feels every so often in this remote land, where he is separated from the rest of the world by mountains constantly covered with snow rising far above the clouds, and by hostile deserts, where whole caravans have perished! To be surrounded on all sides by all these insurmountable barriers and severed from any civilization and any decent company, to live through one year after another in the difficult task of awakening the interest in the Christian faith, in virtue and morality among lethargic, indifferent, hostile, and in every way depraved people certainly demands more than human strength.*

Another quotation. This time from Lars Erik Högberg, who worked as a missionary here in Sinkiang, 1894–1900, 1903–1909, and 1911– 1916:

> You rarely see in individuals or in the whole people a real grief, rarely a shiver in the face of most tragic events, seldom a true expression of joy in the face of happiness. You rarely hear heartfelt laughter. It is strange that this quality is found in the children as well. You have to force them to say thank you for a gift. . . . The people are cowards, lack courage and force and the ability to organize. . . . If a servant is treated well and given affection by a European master, it is only in exceptional cases that he will attach himself with devotion to the master or mistress.. . . . No notion of a mechanical invention or an improvement to any tool or anything similar seems ever to have entered the minds of these natives. . . .†

The missionary Gottfrid Palmgren, however, had some nice things to say about these miserable people:

> We must give our workers their due. They may be lazy and ignorant but they are kind and amenable. They only know of the working hours indicated by the sun. Thus, in summer, they work for fifteen hours. Strikes and trade unions are to them unknown phenomena. Their wages only cover necessities, but they are still happy with their lot.‡

---

*J. P. Norberg, Preface to *På obanade stigar, tjugofem år i Ost-Turkestan* [On Untrodden Paths: Twenty-five Years in the Service of the Mission Association in East Turkestan] (Stockholm, 1917).
†Lars Erik Högberg, "Folkkaraktären i Ost-Turkestan," in *På obanade stigar*, pp. 91–95.
‡Gottfrid Palmgren, "Några erfarenheter från ett stationsbygge," in *På obanade stigar*, p. 346.

When old Grandfather tells the little children in the Kashgar nursery school about these evil old times, they listen in open-mouthed astonishment.

We had been to an outdoor cinema to see an air force picture on the subject of the Korean War. The night was rough, dark, and hot. We had tea in what was once the duty officer's room in the Russian consulate. On the wall were the splendid Khotan rugs the last Cossacks could not take along. Our tea glasses rested in old Russian silver holders. We were discussing the annihilation of Christianity in Central Asia and its transient existence in China.

There had been many Christian communities here. Up to the nineteenth century there had been native Christians in some places. Then European imperialism came, preceded by the missionaries; where the missionaries trod the tax collectors and merchants stepped in; the flag followed the cross.

"The missionaries came and religion went," Gun said. "Whoever wants to check the facts can read their own documents and reports. He that hath ears to hear, let him hear."

"Matthew 11:15," I said.

Many religions took root in China—Islam and Buddhism. But Christianity—in its different versions—remained a foreign religion. It was annihilated or transient, however you want to see it. Around 1949, after a century of intensive attempts to reform the people, hardly 1 percent of China's population were even called Christian. Today the Christian group in China is insignificant. There are Moslems and Buddhists still.

Religions can disappear. Here in Sinkiang Manicheism once was an established religion, seemingly on its way to becoming a world religion. In 762 it was declared the state religion by the khan of the Uighurs. It had great influence and started to spread down through the Kansu corridor and south in the Yangtze valley. When the Uighur conflict with the Chinese state intensified, Emperor Wu Tsung of the T'ang dynasty, issued, for political reasons, a decree in the third year of his reign—in A.D. 843—prohibiting this religion. A century later Islam had become the dominant religion in the west of Kashgar. In Europe Manicheism lived on as a secret lore among sectarians and heretics. Later, when the Holy Inquisition had wiped it out, it lingered on in isolated covens as a belief in witchcraft; today only scattered popular superstitions remain. Religions certainly can disappear. But the Christians had a firm base in countries where their religion was ordained by the state, and they devoted a lot of energy to making converts. Still, they disappeared. Today it's more difficult to find a Christian in Kashgar than a Jew in Kaifeng.

On three occasions Christianity seemed to be on the verge of playing a role in China. Each time it withered away without ever rooting and becoming an established Chinese religion like Buddhism or Islam. But the reasons for this are found in the countries where Christianity was the ruling state ideology. The reasons were political.

In the sixth century A.D. the countries around the Mediterranean were Christian. It was a time of bitter political struggles in the eastern Mediterranean countries. Christianity was the state religion in the Eastern Roman Empire. The Persian Sassanid Empire was fighting successfully with the Eastern Roman Empire, having proclaimed Zoroastrianism their state religion. There were, however, increasingly large groups of Christians in the Sassanid Empire, and the areas that the Sassanids tried to conquer from Eastern Rome were Christian.

This was the situation when the Christians began to discuss the second person in the Trinity. Orthodoxy in church matters had been decreed since 380. The Church, and not the religious concepts, was the pillar of the state. Heresy thus became a state crime. With the Council of Nicaea in 325, the nature of Godhead became a matter of state. On June 19, 325, it was established by a majority vote that Jesus Christ was God incarnate and at one with the Father, the first person of the Trinity. The state was empowered by the council to install the decided-on faith among the inhabitants of the empire. As a consequence of that Nicaean decision, the Unity of God and True Nature of Jesus Christ became of immediate state political interest, to the Sassanid rulers as well.

The fight about the True Nature of Jesus Christ became a political struggle which interested the Sassanids in the way that, for obvious reasons, they saw the view decreed in Constantinople as subversive. The view that the emperor in Constantinople held to be dangerous to the state, the Sassanid rulers on the contrary helped to propagate.

As long as Monophysites—of which the only surviving church is that of the Jacobites who still cross themselves with one finger to show that they consider Christ to have had but one nature—kept their influence in Constantinople, their followers were persecuted by the Sassanids in the area under their power. The emperor of Constantinople's concern about them had the political purpose of protecting the territorial integrity of the empire and increasing its influence.

The Jacobites had strong support in Armenia and Syria. The Sassanid politics were the same as Constantinople's, only directed by the opposite interests. At that time the Sassanids supported the Nestorians, who maintained that Virgin Mary had borne a son who was merely human but with whom the Divine Word was united, and then left its temporary dwelling when the mere human died on the cross. The Sassanids supported the Nestorian missionary work among Christians within the Sassanid Empire as well as without.

On principle both Nestorians and Jacobites were then heretics according to the decisions of the various church meetings. In order to achieve total power over a monolithic church and reinstate the Roman Empire to its full extent, Emperor Justin I (518–527) let the decisions of the Council of Chalcedon be carried out. Christ had two natures, each perfect in itself and each distinct from the other, yet perfectly united in one person, who was at once both God and man. No discussions could help any more in this matter. All one could do was to believe because it was without meaning.

Jacobites now were just as damned as Nestorians, and the Sassanids no longer had to persecute the Jacobites but could treat all the different sects in one and the same way. These sects then carried out missionary work eastward along the trade route. The Nestorians had a congregation in the imperial capital in China, one among the wealth of groups in the swarm of foreigners who had gathered around the emperor's court at the east end of the trade route. The Nestorians were known as astronomers and doctors. But their religion lacked the characteristics that could make it a useful ideology for the millions of peasants who were being driven to revolt by increasing oppression. These were better served by Taoist and Buddhist ideas. Neither could the sophistic Christological interpretations of the Nestorians appeal to the rationalistic administrators who had risen to power through the system of examinations based on careful study of Confucian classics. The warlords had need to legitimize their attempts to seize power and create independent realms, but they found nothing of use in these Western sects. Had the Nestorians not had time to carve their names in stone, they would have disappeared from China's history as if they had never existed.

Here in Kashgar and all over Central Asia, Nestorian and Jacobite congregations survived a relatively long time. As a popular belief, Nestorianism was soon pushed aside by Manicheism, which had the armed power of the Uighur state behind it. Still, congregations lived on. It was Islam, an ideology useful in quite another manner, which eventually wiped out these congregations. Only scattered sects of no significance survived. Nestorians and Jacobites could be used by various rulers, but their ideology could not, due to its nature, be an efficient tool for an armed prophet. And—as Machiavelli pointed out—all armed prophets have been successful and all unarmed prophets have been unsuccessful. When people do not believe any more, they have to be forced to believe. Moses, Cyrus, Theseus, and Romulus were successful, but Savonarola was not, since he lacked the material power to retain those who had believed and to force the nonbelievers into believing.

In the fights around the countries between the Eastern Roman and the Sassanid empires, Nestorians and Jacobites were ground down to sects and heresies. Only Islam, a few centuries later, proved a usable faith to the people of these countries. In other words, the first Christian attempt to convert China never had any chance at all.

The next attempt is better known and, for that reason, does not need any long discussion. The Catholic Church tried to gain admission into China for five hundred years, first through the Mongols. Opposing Nestorians and other sects, the missionaries tried to gain the loyalty of different groups of rulers. In the fourteenth century there was a Catholic church in Peking, the land for which had been donated by an Italian merchant. But that mission disintegrated with the group of rulers whose support it had sought.

The Jesuits then worked during the Ming and the Ch'ing dynasties to gain influence among the high bureaucracy. They adjusted as far as possible to the ideas and customs of this bureaucracy, and used their own scientific and technical knowledge to try to convince the bureaucrats that a fusion of Confucian tradition and the new science and technology taught by the Jesuits would be possible within the framework of a Chinese Christianity of a Confucian-Jesuit type. In China—as in Europe—they tried to win the ruling class to their new state theory and their political aims.

Regardless of how the Jesuit mission is judged from the aspect of the Chinese people—they not only brought science and technology, they also attempted to provide the ruling class with even more efficient tools for political oppression—this Jesuit mission came into conflict with European interests. In China the Jesuit politics became much too independent in relation to the European powers, which had now started the race for world rule.

The battle over the rites—whether the ancestors and Confucius were the objects of respect or adoration, the former allowed and the latter forbidden according to the first of the Ten Commandments—could, for general political reasons, only be decided by the pope to the disadvantage of the Jesuits. The mission had to make a clean break with what Catholics thereafter had to regard as worship of the ancestors and Confucius. That decision could not be avoided by the Church.

The Catholic faith was a state ideology in several European powers now expanding over the world. That ideology had to serve the interests

of the state. Jesuit politics began to threaten state interests. In China
—as later in metropolitan Europe itself—the state interest demanded
the destruction of Jesuit power and influence.

With this decision, however, Christianity became a religion in opposition to the Chinese state and was treated accordingly. The high-
ranking bureaucracy considered it an extra disadvantage that this religion was ruled from abroad. Christianity was not only in opposition to
the state, it was a threat to state security.

Almost five hundred years of Catholic mission in China thus ended
in total defeat. When the Vatican decision of 1704 to combat the
Confucian rites was known in China, Christianity was transformed
from a religion into a conspiracy, inimical to the state. These rites were
at the very core of the Chinese state ideology. And thus the second
attempt to convert China to Christianity failed for political reasons.
The Papal Bull of 1742, forcefully renewing the decision of 1704, put
the final seal on that defeat.

The third attempt was made by the missionaries. Great Britain won
the Opium War of 1840–1842 over the weak late Ch'ing-dynasty China.
The empire was falling apart. China had to accept import of drugs, and
had to pay 21 million silver dollars to cover the war expenses of Great
Britain. China had to agree to open five ports for trade. So the missionaries could get down to work.

Certain Christian ideas had been spread over the years. In the Taiping Revolution it looked for a moment as if China would be able to
recover from the humiliation and as if the peasant wars would give rise
to a democratic China of the people. The rebels—or at least some of
them—believed that they were Christians. Christianity was about to
start playing the same ideological role as it had done in Europe in the
sixteenth century. It was not, however, in the interest of the European
powers that China rise from the decay of the Ch'ing dynasty. They
therefore helped to combat and wipe out the only movement of the
Chinese people that ever had any contact with the Christian doctrine.

The missionaries remained learned representatives paving the way
for the foreign powers that tried to conquer China. That is how the
Chinese generally regarded them too. Missionaries were protected by
international treaties and foreign troops, but they were hated. Those
Chinese who were converted to Christianity were an insignificant marginal group.

It did not help that the Vatican in 1942—when Mussolini had formed
an alliance with Japan—announced that it had had second thoughts
regarding respect for Confucius and the ancestors. The Chinese people
were then liberating themselves from the Japanese and other imperial-

ists (also from their missionaries and ideologists of various kinds), as well as from the awe of Confucius and the ancestors which had kept the people down and oppressed.

"Here in Kashgar there aren't so many who remember the missionaries now," Gun said. "Nobody cares for what they did. It's remarkable to imagine all these Anderssons and Högbergs and Bohlins and Engvalls and whatever they were called, fighting and striving here, suffering in the heat and the dust from the desert, kept by poor Swedish sharecroppers and craftsmen who got together for prayer meetings and missionary coffee parties all over the country, sending money to the missionaries in Sinkiang which would have been better used for their own children. It's incredible that all these Svenssons and Törnqvists and Martenssons and Nyströms have been totally forgotten as if they had never existed, while the 'natives,' the wise men who were so despised then, are now respected and held in awe and paid homage, as pioneers of progress and medical care. I wonder what they would have felt if they had known what the outcome of their mission in life was to be. What a waste!"

We had been to the hospital of traditional Uighur medicine and were on our way back to the old consulate. The afternoon was hot but a little less windy. The air was grey, no longer yellow, and no more desert dust gritted between our teeth.

"Whatever is without roots disappears," Gun said.

We had spent some time at the hospital talking to the old Uighur doctor Zunun Kari. He mentioned the Swedes, but not by name:

"The traditional Uighur medicine is based on seventeen hundred years of experience," he said. "We guard our knowledge and systematize it. We are respected now. But it wasn't always so, we've had some hard times. As far as I know there were only Uighur doctors here seventy—eighty years ago. Then one or two Westerners arrived with their own medicine. There were more and more of them arriving, pushing us traditional Uighur and Han doctors aside. We weren't good enough. The magistrates and the rich went to the Westerners. We could only tend the poor who couldn't pay for it, and it became increasingly difficult to earn one's living as a doctor. The greatest Uighur doctor of all, Yusup Hadji, was driven away too; we were all discriminated against and called witch doctors. The authorities persecuted us until no more patients came to see us. We had to go along the streets selling our herb remedies, and try different professions in order to survive. Our traditional medicine was dying out. We didn't have any printed books to carry our knowledge forward. And then, when we had lost all our patients, Yusup Hadji in his lonely old age sat down to write a book about our traditional medicine. He wrote a summary of our knowledge in this, the most difficult time.

"Since the liberation, we have gained respect again. Chairman Mao Tse-tung and the party gave us new life. Yusup Hadji's book has now seen several editions, the third having been published last year. Chairman Mao Tse-tung said that our experience is valuable. Young doctors come to us now to learn, even those who have studied Western medicine. We're not enemies any more. We all want to serve the people."

Zunun Kari gave us Yusup Hadji's book and wrote a dedication in it himself. An honored old man with a white beard. The hospital was large; it had 150 beds and saw 300 outpatients every day.

"We have to record and systematize the valuable experience of the Uighur people," said the senior doctor, Mur Imat. "This is an important part of medical care as well as the policy regarding the national culture. We have complete modern equipment now with X-ray and EKG, combining Western methods with traditional Uighur herb remedies.

"The traditional Uighur medicine has four methods of diagnosis. First, it's the general impression given by the patient. How does he move? What's his posture like? How does he look? Then we ask the patient. How does he feel? How has he been? What treatment has the patient had before, and how did he respond to it? After that, we examine the different pulses. As in Han medicine, we think that there are several pulses, which have to be examined very carefully. We then smell the patient's breath, look closely at the urine and smell it. These are our traditional methods of diagnosis. We achieve quite good results when we combine them with Western methods.

"We also use the medicinal herbs that grow here in Sinkiang. In some cases we use gold and silver, too. But the herbs are very cheap. And all the remedies used by us have been examined with great care to make sure they can't be harmful.

"We have been especially successful in the case of two illnesses. One is gallstones. The other one is vitiligo. People are coming here now from all over China to have their vitiligo cured. We've had 578 patients from other provinces treated for vitiligo. We are now busy systematizing our results scientifically. The effect of our treatment is quick and obvious. Uighur medicine still has a lot to offer to the world."

Barefoot doctors from other counties who have come into Kashgar to get further training were taught Western as well as Uighur medicine.

"First they have to be given a proper basic knowledge of the uses of certain safe selected medicinal herbs," the old pharmacologist Abdulrahman Kirim said. "After that they can learn more step by step."

"That's why they failed."

It was not only the Swedish missionaries in Kashgar who were so opposed to learning from the natives—it was a typical attitude. Typical, however, for one definite historic situation. One could say that people from Europe and North America, from the early nineteenth century up to about 1950, generally lacked ability to learn from China and India and other parts of the present Third World.

There are many ways to watch the change of attitude to Asia. One method is by using encyclopedias. Look under the word "Chine" in the seventh volume of the *Encyclopédie* by Diderot-d'Alembert. The article is brief and factual. Not one mention of the word "strange." China is large. It has its own technology (the great canal, above all), its own laws and administration, but it is not strange.

One century later Pierre Larousse tries to continue the Diderot-d'Alembert's tradition with his *Grand Dictionnaire universel du XIX siècle*. There is a long learned article about *Chine* . . . but as early as in the fourteenth line, China has become "mysterious" and "peculiar." The unfamiliar has become exotic.

Learning and acquiring knowledge is not the same thing. Learning means learning *from* as well as learning *about*. There was knowledge enough—Larousse is more knowledgeable than Diderot. But colonialism made learning impossible. It was as unthinkable for a "Western" doctor to learn cures for vitiligo from Yusup Hadji as it was for a European diplomat to follow Chinese ceremonies when received by the emperor in Peking.

Colonialism is an ideological system too, a huge structure of laws and notions and tricks and various so-called truths created by the colonial exploitation. A structure, however, not only consisting of legitimizations and cover, but also a systematized all-embracing view of the world, guiding even the religious faith and the results of positive sciences.

The Swedish missionaries in Kashgar never managed to liberate themselves from its blinkers. When China liberated itself, however, Yusup Hadji's views on the treatment of vitiligo could also be changed from superstition and bigotry to experience and science.

Not until now has it become possible for European scientists to learn and not just gain knowledge in Asia.

"Yes," Gun said, "thanks to the liberation they shall know the truth!"

"John 8:32," I said.

"But in the right context," she replied.

8
The Uighurs
—Are They Chinese?

I'm on the second floor of the bookshop in Kashgar buying posters. I find twenty-three of them that I haven't seen before; some are from Shanghai but most are from Sinkiang. Each province has its own publishers. The province can be identified by the number in the bottom right-hand corner. Posters from Sinkiang have the number M 8098. Usually, however, they can be identified by their style. The Sinkiang artists work in a harder, rougher style. They are closer to the early socialist-realist posters of the thirties. Besides, one can see immediately that the poster is from Sinkiang by looking at the text. Most posters from Sinkiang have Uighur text written with the Latin alphabet.

The twenty-third poster shouts: HARVEST! HARVEST! HARVEST! The sky in the poster is blue and the clouds white as the summer sky over Ili. The field is golden and the wheat is ripening; the spikes are heavy. In this mighty river of wheat stand two young men. The grain reaches above their waists. They are Uighurs. They are young, sunburned, have broad shoulders and bulls' necks. They have their arms around each other; brotherly. In their free hands they carry large sickles. The sickles are newly ground; the steel of the edge shimmers blue. With clear eyes they look you frankly in the face; their teeth glisten and they tell you:

ARMIYE BILEN HELK KELBDAX BOLUP ITTIPAKLIXIP MOL HOSUL ALAYALI—"When the army and the people unite as of one heart we will take a bumper harvest."

A farmer and a soldier from the People's Liberation Army. Young brothers in the sun. That is a poster such as Deineka, Malennov, Pimenov made during the heroic years of the first Five-Year Plan in the Soviet Union.

We have rolled up the posters. I am on my way out and I pass the window from which Gun is looking down into the street.

"Can you see the camel carriage?" she says.

A carriage with two camels in front is making its way through the swarm of bicycles. A red bus passes. It has just started after picking up some passengers. It honks at the cyclists filling the street, and they pull aside to leave room for the bus. It is a hot and hazy afternoon.

People are going home.

The greater number are men; a few are women, most of whom are wearing skirts. They wear boots, skirts, and head scarves. We haven't seen any women in veils. In the cities women used to wear veils.

The streets are wide, the pavements are separated from the roadway by a green streak between two large gutters, glittering with water. The trees haven't had time to mature yet. This is a new area. On the opposite side of the street is the cultural palace which we visited yesterday. There is a library and a reading room there, exhibition halls and conference rooms. Farther down the street is the large ironmonger's shop. It serves agriculture. Representatives come in from the production brigades to get special machinery and tools. Next door is a shop selling local goods made cooperatively. There are rough handwoven fabrics, hardware, and beautiful articles of wrought iron.

We look at the camels, which are now way down the street. The afternoon air is thick and dusty and it's hot. People hurry past. Kashgar is a Central Asian town in the far west of China. Most inhabitants are Uighurs. The others are different nationalities—Han, Hui, Kazakh, Tadzhik, and others. Fourteen nationalities live in this city, according to Pashakhan. She is from the Youth League and accompanies Gun, shows her around.

"In the city of Kashgar the percentage of Han is slightly more," she says. "In this city we have now about 200,000 inhabitants and most of the Han people in the district live here."

"As a matter of fact," Rakmov says, "the situation is now such that 85 percent of the party members are Uighurs, 75 percent of the cadre of the party are Uighurs, and 65 percent of the party secretaries are Uighurs. The party committee of this district has the same proportion."

"Concerning the state cadres," says Liu Kai-shan, expedition chief for this district, "we have about 33,000. A little more than 22,000 of these are Uighurs and other nationalities—that is, not Han. The working class in this district is almost 35,000, and 65 percent of these are Uighurs. That's the situation, from a statistical point of view."

"You must remember," Pashakhan says, "that the feudal and patriarchal traditions are still there, although we are trying to overcome them. It won't happen overnight. Between 1970 and 1975 we have sent 1,120 students from this district to university. But of these, 745 were men and 375 women. Out of the 33,000 state cadres only 9,394 are women. And merely 125 have leading positions above people's-commune level, and only 14 women have leading positions in county and district. Overcoming the past isn't done overnight."

"But remember that 95 percent of the school-age children go to school now," Rakmov says. "We won't say 100 percent, that would be inaccurate. There are nomads in the mountains who haven't had the school question solved satisfactorily, and there is the occasional case even here of children who don't finish their schooling. Still, 95 percent of the children go to school now, up to the intermediate, boys and girls alike. We will overcome the remnants of sex discrimination just as we are overcoming the remnants of national discrimination."

We go down the broad stairs of the bookshop. Downstairs the shop is jammed with people coming to look at us.

"Give room to our foreign visitors," Rakmov says.

People move away, leaving a passage free. They laugh. Some grab my hand, press it hard, and shake it. They are all Uighurs. Some have caps but most wear skullcaps.

But are the Uighurs Chinese?

Well, are the inhabitants of Nykarleby, in Österbotten province in Finland, Finns?

The inhabitants of Nykarleby in Österbotten are Finlanders but they are not Finns. The Uighurs in Sinkiang are Chinese but not Han.

The problem is that the word "Han" is not normally used in our languages. By Chinese we really mean two things: we partly mean Chinese nationals, in the same way as we say "Finlanders" about Finnish nationals. But we also say "Chinese" generally about Han people, using it in the same way as "Finns."

The situation is complicated by the fact that we can't talk about Han people as we talk about Finns. In both cases the words are used as an ethnic definition, but it is really a question of two different types of *ethnos*. The Han people contains groups as different in looks and physical build, customs, culture, eating habits, and spoken language as Norwegians and Spaniards in Europe. They can't understand each other's speech, find it difficult to eat each other's food, behave in different ways. They still maintain that they belong to one people with one culture and one language.

It is true that the characters of the written language are the same. But they are also the same as those of the Japanese. Even those who can't write and thus can't overcome the linguistic barriers are convinced that the different groups belong to the same one Han people.

It's even more complicated. One of the nationalities in China is the Hui. They think of themselves as a different people from the Han and are recognized as a separate nationality. But they speak the same language as their Han neighbors and have the same culture, with two exceptions: they don't eat pork and they wear white skullcaps. They used to be Moslems, and some of them are still practicing. In China they are a separate nationality with their own administrative units.

We don't speak of Huguenots and Catholics in France as different "nationalities." The difference between them is religious, not ethnic. In China both Hui and Han see the difference between themselves as ethnic. I write this to show that the definitions we find natural in Europe are not necessarily so in countries with a different historical background. The questions of nationality are different in Europe and China—or India.

China is a multinational unified state. It has a long history as such. During this long period different national and ethnic groups have had the dominant role. Often it has been the Han people. So it was during the Han dynasty (206 B.C. to A.D. 220, the dynasty that gave Han its name); the T'ang dynasty (618–907); the Sung dynasty (960–1279); and the Ming dynasty (1368–1644).

The Chineseness of China, its culture and traditions, was also formed during other dynasties. They could be Turkic like the northern Wei dynasty (386–556), when the specifically Chinese tradition of sculpture was developed. The Mongols ruled during the Yuan dynasty (1271–1368), a period of technical development and administrative changes. Manchus ruled and were the dominating group during the Ch'ing dynasty (1644–1911). Tibetans established their dominion in the west, and made their contribution to the Chinese philosophical tradition. What we know as China and Chinese culture are a creation by many ethnic groups and nationalities.

The Han culture predominated and Han people had the leading position during most dynasties and also assimilated other people and their cultural traditions. But during its whole long history, China was a multinational entity. Even during periods when the unity of the realm was broken and other more or less independent states were established, often within "natural" boundaries, "China" did not break up. The bonds were strong. When the necessary time had passed, the parts once more coalesced into China.

Sun Yat-sen admitted this specific and multinational character of China. To him Hui was one of the nationalities of China. But Chiang Kai-shek did not accept this. After the counterrevolution he led in 1927 "the nationality of Hui" became "the believers in Islam." Chiang Kai-shek and his followers in this respect also broke with the democratic tradition of Sun Yat-sen.

During the KMT time Han chauvinism became an official ideology. All nationalities were to be assimilated into the Han people. This was a policy of harsh national oppression against the national minorities. These national minorities might—according to European standards— be large populations, though they are an insignificant minority compared to the huge majority of Han.

After the liberation the different nationalities within the united but multinational China became officially equal. Han, Hui, Uighur, Tadzhik, Kazakh are all Chinese with equal rights. But the struggle against "Great Han chauvinism" is still necessary. The Uighurs in Sinkiang are Chinese. But certainly not Han!

However, this question is not quite so simple either.

"This school was founded in 1953," says Maram Khirip, leader of the workers' propaganda team at the first secondary school in Kashgar, "but only in 1970 was it developed into a complete secondary school for teaching in both Uighur and Han. There are students of eight nationalities at the school, but apart from Uighur and Han, they are just single individuals, seven Hui and one Tadzhik, you know. We have 1,497 students now, 706 boys and 791 girls. Twenty forms with alltogether 866 students are taught in Uighur. They are also taught Han three hours a week. Fourteen forms with altogether 631 students are taught in Han. They study Uighur three hours a week all through their time at school. The number of Han-nationality students among the 631 students in the Han-language forms is, however, only 544. The remaining 87 are mainly Uighur. This is for different reasons. They cannot go to the Han forms without knowing Han. Thus they must have been to a primary school where Han was the first language, perhaps because that school was nearer to them."

"Of the teachers," says Musa, vice-chairman of the revolutionary committee of the school, "61 are Uighur and 42 Han."

"The students are admitted after examinations," Maram Khirip says. "They must be given the right kind of teaching. Of course we have regular examinations. For the sort of knowledge they have to learn by heart we don't allow any aids. Still, it's not like the days before the Cultural Revolution when the teachers treated the students as enemies who were to be outwitted and exposed. Now students and teachers cooperate to achieve the best possible results, and the students help each other to learn."

"Besides, our students are quite mature," Musa says. "They are twelve when they come here and seventeen when they leave."

"It is a great achievement that all children go through the secondary school," Maram Khirip says. "That's why it's so important that we, from the workers' propaganda team here at the school, help them keep to the right direction. They must not forget how it used to be."

9
The Grave of the Saint

Just outside Kashgar is the mausoleum of Apak Hodja. We went to see it several times, not because this was the holiest of pilgrim resorts in southwestern Sinkiang—old Kashgaria—but because this mausoleum is a remarkable and beautiful building.

The wind played in the poplars. The roses were glowing. It was afternoon and the gardener was drawing water out of the irrigation ditch for the rose bed. We were sitting in the shade drinking green tea and eating mulberries out of large saucers. It was still, almost cool. Down by the gateway of the palace a bus had stopped. Visitors swarmed out and wandered up toward the mausoleum. We could see its green tiled dome between the trees. Beyond that, beyond the greenery, a town of the dead next to the holy mausoleum, shimmering with its tiles. The graves are made of mud and lie like low huts, row upon row. The ground is dry and burnt. Ground and tombstones and a wall of the same intensely reddish-brown earth. Not a green leaf—a town of dead people in *terra di Siena.* The dark green tiled dome, also in an earth color with a dim luster; the sky, clear of its yellow haze here outside the city, deepening to a dark blue above the poplars; and all the time, the sound of the irrigation water in the ditches, the glowing roses, and the black mulberries in my hand, squashed to a dark, sour sweetness.

This is now a cultural monument and a picnic place, one of the great and famous protected monuments of this province. The curator's name is Hassan. He is a historian. He offered us some bright red, transparent little cherries, tasting fresh and dry.

"Gun prefers the sour to the sweet," he said, "I know that. Some of us do. Sweetness easily becomes insipid."

"Five generations of this Hodja family are buried in this mausoleum," he said later. "Seventy-two people in all."

Those who lie in the siena-colored graves outside the wall are not part of the family. They had to pay a high price for their graves. Apak Hodja was a saint. He could protect the dead even after he was dead. This mausoleum used to be a religious foundation, a *wakf.* It was very rich. The Swedish missionary Gustaf Ahlbert wrote sixty years ago that this mausoleum owned "large areas of land to support itself and its head and administrators—not only in Kashgar but also in Yarkand and in other places."

To this mausoleum belonged: "about 43,470 hectares of land, forty-eight pairs of millstones, fifteen large farms, a high school with large areas of land, etc."

Feudalism and its economic structure are gone now. The mausoleum is a historical monument, maintained by the state, which also pays the administrators' salaries. Anyone can now bury his dead here by the mausoleum of Apak Hodja. The cemetery is free of charge.

"The dome was damaged in the twenties," Hassan said. "It was rebuilt during the over-all restoration work in 1956. In 1972 a complete archaeological and architectural-historical investigation was made, when specialists from both Urumchi and Peking worked here. We are waiting for the first results to be published."

The Hodja family mausoleum was built in the seventeenth century of our era: a great period in Moslem architecture. It was the time when Jahangir ruled over the India of the Mughals, when Akbar's mausoleum was built at Sikandra outside Agra; when Abbas I ruled in Persia and his architect Muhammad Riza Ibn Ustad erected Masjid-i-Shaykh Lutfullah in Isfahan in memory of the father-in-law of the shah. Apak Hodja's mausoleum, though, is not an exclusive and refined building. It is harsher, more compact. It is reminiscent of the buildings of the great and stringent nineteenth century in Khiva. The same severity; the same decorative sparseness and strength, possibly determined by poverty. But Apak Hodja's mausoleum is two centuries older.

The dark green tiles of the dome are not of a kind with the Timurid blue tiles of Herat; they are related to the Peking tiles. But I've not seen even in Khiva the grand effect created by these large tiles. Rows of green tiles broken by irregularly inserted solitary white, deep blue, or siena-colored tiles and stripes of tiles. The surface lives, a decorative plane without dead symmetry. As the equilateral geometric forms are broken up, an austere rhythm develops, and as you come quite close to the wall, the white and seemingly uncolored tiles open up, disclosing soft patterns of blue lines. Different shapes of flower ornaments and suddenly, here and there, obvious symbols, swastikas. The tile decoration on Apak Hodja's mausoleum is independent and original, but still turned both toward great China and the khanate of Khiva.

Up in the gallery just below the dome, the windows open out in all directions. The lattice work is done in decorative geometrical designs, in one window originating from Herat, in the other from inner China. Here a meandering pattern, there a swastika pattern, here cloud bands and to the right ice lines.

We return several times to Apak Hodja's mausoleum while we are in Kashgar. We walk in the garden; circle and take in the massive building, walk up to the walls and stand close to them, looking into the mosaic. Then turn and ascend through the dark stairway inside the wall and come out onto the gallery and view the siena-colored graves down below in the city of the dead, through lattice work in thunder-scroll or Timurid patterns. Down below us the seventy members of the Hodja family rest in their graves.

When the Mongol Empire fell in China and the Yuan dynasty was succeeded by the Ming in 1368, the oases around Tarim were dominated by Jagatai's heirs. The land north of Tien Shan was totally devastated by the constant wars and became grazing land, but the southern oases were protected by the desert. Here rulers came and went during confused battles, without leaving any traces and without contributing to any economic development.

Babur—who later made himself ruler of India—met in 1502 with his uncle Ahmed, who was then involved in bitter fights over Tashkent. He describes the uncle in his memoirs:

All the younger khan's [Ahmed's] men had dressed themselves up after the Mughal fashion. They had Mughal caps, frocks of China satin, embroidered with flowers after the same fashion, quivers and saddles of green shagreen, and Mughal horses dressed up and adorned in a singular style.

The younger khan came with but few followers; they might be more than one thousand, and less than two. He was a man of singular manners. He was a stout, courageous man, and powerful with the saber, and of all his weapons he relied most on it. He used to say that the mace, the javelin, the battle-ax, or broad ax, if they hit, could only be relied on for a single blow. His trusty keen sword he never allowed to be away from him; it was always either at his waist, or in his hand.

As he had been educated and had grown up in a remote and out-of-the-way country, he had something of rudeness in his manner, and of harshness in his speech.

Such were the lords and princes fighting each other for the rule of Kashgar and the other oases of the Tarim basin. Kashgaria was then one of the feudal states rendering more or less sincere homage to the emperor of China. But as the lords came and went, though, there was one significant change for the people during this time. The victory of Islam. Several rulers were Moslems and fought the infidels, the remaining Buddhists, as well as the Christian sects that still had churches in Yarkand when Marco Polo traveled there.

Some years into the sixteenth century, the learned descendant of the holy prophet, Hodja Makhdumi Azam came from Samarkand. He became the *khalifa,* the spiritual director of the ruling khan. He was granted land in fee and died in 1540 in Kashgar, surrounded by great holiness. From him descended that Hodja family that during ever more tangled struggles seized power in Kashgar from the Jagatais and founded a theocratic state.

The Hodja family split into two groups, each supported by different Kirghiz families: Ak Tagh—White Mountains, and Kara Tagh—Black Mountains. Its economic power was based on land ownership and dominance over the sanctuaries that owned *wakf* property. These foundations possessed more than land; they also owned serfs. The power of the Hodja family was based on religious feudalism, creating its theocratic state. This meant that the politics of the Hodja power necessarily encouraged expansion of religion at any cost. New religious institutions were founded with land and serfs in accordance with the *wakf* rules. The power of the Hodja family increased and its members might have been holy, but they were no more loved than the rapacious khans and warlords of the Jagatai lineage.

Late in the autumn of 1603 the Jesuit Father Benedict Goes came here to Kashgaria. He was traveling east, having left Agra about a year before. Maybe he was a scout for the Mughal emperor Akbar disguised as a priest; maybe he let the end justify the means and took Akbar's four hundred gold coins and passport to make easier the holy task of finding the route from India to China. He had come up from India over the high mountains, and now stopped in Kashgaria until mid-November 1604, when he followed a caravan east across the desert. He never reached Peking, however. He had no passport to present at the Great Wall down in Kansu. In the city now called Kiuchüan he waited seventeen months for permission to continue. Then he died on November 11, 1607. The permit never arrived.

But in the year Father Goes was in Kashgaria, he was a diligent writer of letters and sent extensive and detailed accounts of conditions in the country back to the Jesuit order. In 1615 Father Peter du Jarric published parts of Benedict Goes's letters from Yarkand.

This was then the center where merchandise traded between East and West was reloaded. The caravans from Kabul came here, and new caravans were formed to go to Peking. The ruler of Kashgaria was lord of the trade, selling the caravan rights to the highest bidder. The caravan leader whom Benedict Goes later was to follow bought the rights of his caravan for one hundred bags of musk. He then ruled the entire caravan alone with full power during the whole journey. Four partners had bought shares as envoys, and 172 merchants had to pay him a high price to be allowed to participate in the caravan. A caravan privilege was worth a lot.

Religion was organized properly in this land so recently converted to Islam. Each Friday an official went into the bazaar to remind the people of religious commandments. After that twelve men went out from the large mosque carrying leather whips, scourging anyone found in streets and squares during prayer time.

During a period marked by devastating wars and social disintegration, religion gave the Hodja family not only an efficient ideology but also an economic basis: the religious feudalism of the *wakf* property as well as the physical means of power to mold a theocratic state.

That Apak Hodja who rests under this green dome and who has given his name to the mausoleum was Hidajetulla Hodja. He was a saint of such great holiness that people swooned and fell to the ground in front of him, the deaf heard, the blind recovered their sight and the lame danced for joy. No such holiness had existed since the Prophet himself. But in addition to that, he also became a worldly ruler who negotiated on equal terms with the Dalai Lama in Lhasa and with all sorts of khans and chiefs. No intrigues or diplomatic tricks were alien to him. He secured the Kashgarian theocracy.

Then the Ming dynasty (1368–1644) fell. It had had Kashgaria as a tribute-paying feudal state. The Manchus grasped, re-established, and reinforced the Chinese state. The different Hodja parties divided Kashgaria between them after bitter fights. To gain his rule Hidajetulla had once called on the lord of the Oirats for assistance. The Oirats are West Mongols and at that time ruled by their own might over Dzungaria. The struggling Hodja parties had them as overlords. They were kinsmen of the Manchus and for some time it was not clear how they stood in relation to those tribes that had become masters of the Chinese Empire.

On their own they had established relations with the Russians in Siberia and obtained firearms from them. They seemed to begin the creation of a new empire of the steppes, based on the might of their cavalry as once Genghis Khan had done, and as they rode against Peking in 1690, the Chinese army intercepted and defeated them badly. As they then did not heed the command of Emperor K'ang Hsi (1662–

1722) to appear at the court in Peking the year after and formally ask the emperor's pardon, they were labeled as rebels. In 1696 a Chinese army of 80,000 men led by Emperor K'ang Hsi himself defeated the Oirats at Urga in Mongolia. A prince, faithful to the emperor, became the new Oirat ruler. But he turned against Tibet, interfering in Tibetan politics, and in 1717 sent an Oirat army from Kashgaria toward Lhasa. Thus the Oirats once more were rebels, and Emperor K'ang Hsi ordered his troops to drive them out of Lhasa and to their own grounds.

In 1718 the Chinese army was beaten back by the Oirats at Lhasa, but in 1720 the Oirats were defeated and driven out of Tibet.

At the same time Emperor K'ang Hsi had sent his ambassador Tu Li-shen to Ayuka, the khan of the Torguts—the Kalmucks of the Volga —to invite them to return home. These Torguts had left Dsungaria in 1618 with 40,000 tents and now lived along the Volga. (During the journey of Tu Li-shen through Siberia the Russian authorities showed the Chinese ambassador and his escort some Swedish prisoners. Tu Li-shen later reported to the emperor that these Swedes "behaved properly and seemed well fed.")

The Torguts remained at the Volga where the grazing land was good, although they considered K'ang Hsi's invitation to return. When the Russians pressed on toward the Volga, colonizing the country in the middle of the eighteenth century, the situation became worse and the Torguts decided to return home. They left on January 5, 1771, then numbering 400,000. The migration took eight months. More than 100,-000 Torguts died on the way, but the survivors eventually reached China. The Emperor Ch'ien Lung received them with honors and granted them land in Ili and Dzungaria, 185,000 animals, tents, materials, cereals, tea, and silver. The Oirats were then defeated. That had been the precondition for the Torguts' return.

The little Oirat wars had not ceased, neither after the defeat at Lhasa nor after the promise of peace in 1739. Chinese troops had placed under Chinese administration the oases of Hami and Turfan, but the little wars continued. In 1754 the Oirats were defeated. Two years later the new Oirat prince revolted. The Chinese defeated them again, but as soon as the Chinese troops had gone away, the Oirats revolted once more. This time the Emperor Ch'ien Lung decided to give Dzungaria an organized bureaucratic administration. General Chao Hui became the governor. His residence was in Ining in the Ili valley. The emperor had large steles erected, inscribed in Han, Manchu, Oirat, and Tibetan:

Hear ye people of Dzungaria. . . . For generations you have behaved like thieves. The mighty have oppressed the weak, the many have oppressed those who are but few. . . . Now Heaven has established the great Ch'ing dynasty. It was not done by human power.

In 1757 and 1758 General Chao Hui established law and order in Dzungaria. It has been said that one million Oirats were executed as rebels. Others say it was half a million, and yet others maintain that it was less than half a million. Still, everybody knows that they were many and that this country, devastated and depopulated by so many generations of wars, was even more depopulated, and even more arable land became grazing land. But the wars were over, even if the confused internal strife continued in Kashgaria.

Governor Chao Hui had an order sent to the rival Hodja groups to stop their unruly behavior at once, keep the peace, maintain good relations, and ensure trade and civilized order. They ignored this command and even killed a Chinese envoy in Yarkand. Chao Hui then marched into Kashgaria with 3,000 men in October 1758. In February 1759 he was reinforced, and Kashgar fell in July of that year. On the east shore of Yeshil Kul in the High Pamirs the remaining forces of the last Hodja ruler of Kashgar were defeated, in 1759. The Hodja ruler fled toward Badakhshan. The Chinese had a memorial stone raised over the place of victory, which was also a border stone. On June 22, 1892, Colonel Yonnov arrived there with his Cossacks, in the service of the Czar. They wiped out the Afghan border guards and took the Chinese border stone to the Tashkent museum. Yeshil Kul is now well inside the Soviet Union.

There was now peace in Kashgaria. The Chinese administration did not interfere in local religious or popular customs. The *wakf* institution remained, and feudalism did not change its character. But trade was open all the way to Peking, and for the first time in many generations the pressure of taxation was eased at the same time as the irrigation system was put in order and the roads became safe.

"Her name was Mamrisim," Hassan said. "She was of the fifth generation buried here in the mausoleum. She rests beside her maternal grandfather, Apak Hodja. At the Peking court they called her Hsiang Fei—'the Fragrant Concubine'—because she was one of Emperor Ch'ien Lung's lesser wives."

Mamrisim's grave is the smallest under the dome. Her sedan chair is there too. She was sent by the Hodja family as a concubine to the Emperor Ch'ien Lung as a token that they were no longer rebels. She was accepted by the emperor as a symbol of the reinstated peace. For three and a half years she was carried in a sedan chair from Kashgar all the way to Peking, where she was painted by the Italian Jesuit Giuseppe Castiglione (1688–1766).

This remarkable artist worked in Peking for fifty-one years and became court artist to the Emperor Ch'ien Lung. He is known in Chinese art history under the name Lang Shih-ning, mainly for his battle pictures of the emperor's victories over the Oirats. In Europe he was renowned for deep religious feeling, although there exists no painting of his with a Christian subject. As the emperor's court artist, he portrayed this Moslem concubine as a Chinese divinity wearing Portuguese armor.

One year after arriving at the court the Fragrant Concubine died under mysterious circumstances. I have read that she hanged herself. Three months later her brother, who had accompanied her, died. The funeral procession with the dead twenty-nine-year-old princess and her dead brother took three years. When they were buried under the green dome next to their holy ancestor, the Kashgar bazaar was full of goods from the inland. Kashgar's short period of independence was over.

The road into Kashgar was dusty. It was late in the afternoon and the sun was low. On the road people were coming from the market, men on donkeys, young people on bicycles, tractor-trailers with whole families, and young girls walking along, the dust whirling about their feet.

"This road will be asphalted," Rakmov said. "That has already been put down in the plan."

10
With Regards from Chairman Mao

On March 23, 1952, people from the marshlands at Kizil Darya just outside Kashgar gathered in Pakhtaklik village. They were celebrating the victory of the land-reform movement.

Then 636 families lived here, 226 of them with no land at all. Poor-peasant families owning just some hundred square yards of land each numbered 140. There were 31 landlord families with 330 hectares among them. They were all poor.

In 1949 rents and wages had been brought under control and it had become possible to check the worst exploitation. Now, on March 23, 1952, the landless and the poor peasants and the lower-middle peasants had been able to unite and carry out the land distribution reform. The thirty-one landlord families lost their land and their power.

The party representatives delivered speeches. The poor peasants gave speeches. There was great joy, since here were gathered those who had gained by the land-reform movement. Everything would be different from now on. A letter was sent from the meeting to Chairman Mao in Peking with a report of the victory in the struggle for the land.

On August 30 of the same year, Chairman Mao replied.

"He did not dictate it, he wrote it himself," said Mehmed Abdullah, chairman of the revolutionary committee of what is now Pakhtaklik People's Commune." We were having tea in the reception room of the people's commune. Around the table were representatives of Konishahr county and Pakhtaklik People's Commune. They offered us raisins and melons from their own harvest. The responsible cadres gave an account of the history of the people's commune, its economy, and its problems, as the custom is in China when visitors arrive.

On the wall was a copy of the letter from Chairman Mao written twenty-five years ago.

74

"He thanked the peasant comrades of Pakhtaklik village for the letter they had sent in March when they had won victory in the land reform movement. He pointed out that they had now become emancipated from landlordism. They should strengthen their unity and increase their production. On that basis they would increase their material living standard. Thus they would also be able to raise their cultural standard.

"Now, twenty-five years later," Mehmed Abdullah said, "we have drained the marshes, we have dug ditches and planted shelter belts against the desert wind. We have leveled the fields and grow ten varieties of cereal plus cotton. In the old days they could only grow rice. We are not fully mechanized yet but we have by our own means got nine tractors, a number of little walking tractors, and two trucks and threshers and many other things. The standard of living has certainly improved. Out of the 2,258 families living here now 608 have bicycles. The bicycle ownership rate is 36 percent. And 147 families—that is, 16 percent—have sewing machines.

"The arable land has now reached 1,600 hectares.

"In 1949 there were in this area three elementary schools with thirteen forms, 17 teachers, and 360 students. The literacy rate was 10 percent. We had no hospital and no doctor. Today we have seven elementary schools and one secondary. Of the school-age children 98 percent go to school up to and including the secondary stage. We have 85 teachers and 1,800 students. Only this year we sent 20 young people from the poor and lower peasant families to study at the universities and high schools in Urumchi and Sian. We have our own people's commune hospital. Each one of the seven production brigades has a clinic, and we have barefoot doctors in all of the forty-three work teams.

"We are altogether 47 cadres at the people's commune level. That is 47 state employees. Of these, 43 are Uighur and 4 Han. The Han are: one vice-chairman, one tractorist, one clerk, and one technician. All the cadres of the production brigades and work teams are Uighur.

"I would like to point out that our development has been very rapid since the Cultural Revolution, which liberated great potentials. Between 1965 and 1975, for example, the number of teachers rose by 65 percent, and the number of students by 78 percent. We are now aiming to be a people's commune of the Tachai type. We are resolved to achieve this in two to three years' time."

"Yes," Harnisahan said, "we have followed the advice of Chairman Mao and have certainly raised our material standard of living as well as our cultural level."

On the way from the reception room out to the fields, Mehmed Abdullah said:

"It's not always easy and seldom painless. The thirty-one landowning families are still here, not a single member of them was executed. Of course, some of them have died by now, but their mental attitude hasn't changed. We just had a big meeting to criticize Sidik Barat. He was a landlord before the land reform. He has been working in the first production brigade. He seemed to behave well, and to have changed. But he had not. When the great debates and discussions were taking place, it turned out that he was trying to get his land back. He spread rumors. We found out that he was trying to bribe the cadres to keep quiet. He was a fawning, cajoling person. But worst of all, he inveigled a young boy from an honest family into becoming a profiteer and a thief. The masses have now criticized Sidik Barat. We keep our eyes on him. The boy has had a strict warning. You have to fight the illness to save the patient. This was a month ago. We'll see what happens."

The leader of the seventh work team of the first production brigade is Nur Ashim. He is thirty-six and has three children, two at school and one who is still preschool age. The family includes four adults: himself, his wife, his father and mother. They all work. They took home 1,160 yuan in cash among them last year, plus 360 to 380 jin per person of cereal, vegetable oil, vegetables, and melons. No member of the family has needed medical attention the last few years.

"I was selected leader of the work team in 1971. The question was discussed by the masses and the cadres. My name was suggested after the cadres' discussion, and the masses accepted it. There are three demands on the leader of a work team:

"1. Political consciousness.
"2. The will and the strength to work hard in productive labor.
"3. A certain level of scientific agricultural knowledge and the ability to plan and lead the work.

"The leader of the work team is responsible for the political studies as well as for directing the agricultural work and checking the quality of the products. It's not a salaried post. You get nothing extra in pay or kind for being elected. It is an honor and a political responsibility. The leader of a work team has to work two hours more than the others each day; he has to get up an hour earlier to plan the work and leave one hour later to check that everything is in order. I was very proud when I was nominated. To lead a work team is to serve the people.

"There are six cadres in each work team: the leader, a vice-leader, one leader for the women of the team, one accountant, one storekeeper, and one representative of the poor and lower-middle peasants. There are 209 working in our team. The men take home an average of 450 yuan a year and the women 250 to 300 yuan. The difference is due not so much to different daily income as to different numbers of working days per year. Women and men have the same points for the same work. The highest cash income per day is 1.50 yuan and the lowest 1.20.

"On top of that they get cereals, vegetables, oil, and so on. Plus, of course, schools and medical care and so on. This is where our main problem lies. It is necessary to propagate Mao Tse-tung Thought in such a way that we can achieve an increase in productivity in a planned manner. We must develop the collective economy. But it can still pay to go to the market and sell products there from the private lots. There are instances of people speculating and profiting by selling dear during temporary shortages. That can make the difference quite large between what one can earn by selling products from the private plot on the market and what one can earn by taking part in collective labor. So far we haven't had any really serious cases. There was a boy who got involved in this kind of trade last year, but we talked sense into him. We have to make everybody aware that we can develop only by collective work and in the long run only thus raise the material standard and cultural level of everyone. What the harvest will be like is a matter of politics. Our harvests are directly dependent on the planned work we can carry out. This year has given a bumper harvest. The masses have reached unity through political discussions and have taken great initiatives in production.

"I myself went to school for six years. Now we're already sending young people to university!"

The leader of the first production brigade, Tursun Hodja, said:

"We are now preparing the fields for mechanization. By 1978 all the arable land of this production brigade is to be ready. It will have taken us three winters. We take about 120 hectares each winter. That makes about 3,000 days' work each time.

Abdurchut Kur is the leader of the sixth production brigade. He said:

"The problems of agricultural development have been very thoroughly discussed, particularly after the Fourth National People's Congress in January 1975 when Premier Chou En-lai, according to Chairman Mao Tse-tung's great plan for the development of China, stated the goals for an all-out modernization of agriculture, industry, and defense as well as science and technology in order that China at the turn of the century should have attained the front ranks among the technically and scientifically developed countries.

"After having carefully studied the reports from the People's Congress and conducted general and open discussions on the grassroots level, we tackled the questions in an organized fashion. We had a meeting for the whole of southern Sinkiang in Kashgar in August 1975, where we exchanged experiences in agricultural development. We then sent a delegate from the party committee of our county, Konishahr, to the National Conference on Learning from Tachai in Agriculture, which was held in September-October 1975. Have you read comrade Hua Kuo-feng's summing-up report of October 15, 1975? He there represented the Party Central Committee, and he summed up the criteria for a Tachai-type county in six points:

"1. The county party committee should be a leading core which firmly adheres to the party's line and policies and is united in struggle.

"2. It should establish the dominance of the poor and lower-middle peasants as a class so as to be able to wage resolute struggles against capitalist activities and exercise effective supervision over the class enemies and remold them.

"3. Cadres at the county, commune, and brigade levels should, like those in Hsinyang, regularly participate in collective productive labor.

"4. Rapid progress and substantial results should be achieved in farm-land capital construction, mechanization of agriculture, and scientific farming.

"5. The collective economy should be steadily expanded, and production and income of the poor communes and brigades should reach or surpass the present level of the average communes in the locality.

"6. All-round development should be made in farming, forestry, animal husbandry, side occupations, and fishery with considerable increases in output, big contributions to the state, and steady improvement in the living standards of the commune members.

"These were the six conditions posed by comrade Hua Kuo-feng. This is how we have worked in past months. Directly after the large national conference the party committee of the county arranged meetings where our delegate reported back to the masses what had been discussed and decided. Thus the masses were mobilized and raised the demands, which we then could shape into a firm economic plan for the county through repeated meetings and discussions.

"Our fields were too small for mechanized agriculture. To make it possible, it was necessary to join them into large fields suitable for tractors. Immediately after we had begun to discuss the plan in the autumn of 1975, we decided to carry out this project within three years. Last winter 400 people worked for 15 days on this in our brigade, so we devoted 6,000 days' work to the task.

"We have set up a plan and are firm about getting it realized, which means that our whole brigade is to be prepared to convert to mechanization in three years and the mechanization is to be completed within five years. All heavy work in the fields, such as plowing, should then be mechanized.

"At the same time irrigation and drainage systems should be improved and pump stations built."

We were approaching the newly built village for the first production brigade of Pakhtaklik People's Commune. The houses were embedded in greenery, and the vines shaded the courts. Mehmed Abdullah said:

"Three hundred educated young people have returned to live here after having completed their studies. It's quite usual since the Cultural Revolution, when their views on life changed. The intellectuals now return to their families. Before, if a boy could go to school and learn to read and gain knowledge, he became an intellectual who left his family and his village and didn't want to know his father any more but went into town to have a career there. He became a learned man and considered himself too refined to dig in the earth. Now that the students' world outlook has changed, they return to the country and take part in the work teams, contributing to the development of the countryside. We need people who have studied. We have to change the countryside. Look here at Azad Tiliwaldi!"

Mehmed Abdullah pointed to the representative from the county party committee.

"He came back to us after the Cultural Revolution. He has behaved well. The poor and lower-middle peasants, after a few years, elected him to a responsible position on the work brigade. Now he is vice-secretary of the party organization of the whole county. He behaves well, takes part regularly in the work in the fields. We try to stick to the three-in-one combination for the leading groups. Young people should be given responsibility and thus be able to test themselves. Azad Tiliwaldi is a good comrade and a good worker. Thus we bring up successors according to the directions of Chairman Mao Tse-tung."

11
The Despot Had Eighty-Two Rooms in His House

Our host was fifty-six years old. His name was Tursun Mehmed and he worked in the first production brigade. We were sitting in the room of his house, on the beautiful Khotan rug. The tablecloth had been spread. On it were dishes with delicious koftas of minced, well-seasoned mutton on skewers, kebabs with grilled mutton, good bread with a nice salty crust; sheep's cheese; sour milk; pilau where the rice formed a white mountain over the meat and the lard dripped from the fingers when we ate it. There was plenty of food. Good food. The women had been cooking for days before we arrived. The host served liquor in little cups, and we toasted one another.

"We Uighurs have always liked our drink," Mehmed Abdullah from the folk commune said. "Even in the Hodja period," he added.

The Han cadres of the party followed the country custom, eating the mutton and taking the rice with the fingers of the right hand. Comrade Chen, however, whispered to Gun that she would give Gun her mutton when our host was not looking. She came from Shanghai and had never learned to eat mutton.

"I'm a minority here," she whispered, "so I have a right to have my local customs respected." Then she laughed.

It was a big party. We ate and drank and ate again, sweating from heat and food, our faces red, sweat dripping down our backs as we took more meat, the good taste of mutton in our mouths, and Harnisahan said:

"So far nobody has ever left an Uighur home hungry, as long as there was food in the house."

The host poured more liquor, saying: "Have some more! Have some more!"

The women brought new dishes and we ate.

"The poor used to suffer a lot," he said. "People weren't worth much in those days. We were a family of five, my parents, myself, and my two sisters. We worked for the landlord, we had no land of our own. We slept in a shed behind the animals. In summer the sun burned us, and in winter we froze. Sometimes we wondered whether we would have to carry this heavy yoke forever. Were we never to be free?

"The landlord took one of my sisters to be a servant in his house. He sent her out pregnant to work in the fields. She was nine months pregnant and bled to death out there.

"My other sister had two children. One day she was making up a fire in the large oven. She must have become dizzy, for she fell into the fire and was burned to death. My mother had to bring up her children. She treated them like her own, but she had little to give them in spite of the fact that she and my father and I struggled all day long.

"The landlord was called Ahmed. He was a hard man. He had thirty hectares of land, and a house with eighty-two rooms. He owned five water mills and twelve working animals. He was a rich man, and very hard. I worked seventeen years for him. He flogged me. Look at my hands! He hung me on the wall to flog me, he hung me with loops around my wrists, and since then I cannot straighten my fingers. In the daytime we had to work in his fields and at night in his house. How we hated him! When the liberation came he changed his behavior completely.

'Don't believe those soldiers,' he said. 'Wait and see! One day they will be gone again but we shall have to keep living together. Don't listen to them!' But I did listen to the People's Liberation Army. Now that Ahmed could not punish me, I left his service. Ahmed tried to be friendly, but we hated him.

"I remember when we began the land-reform movement. We confiscated his property. I got the rug you're sitting on and a sheep and a cow and two sacks of rice. We struggled with him in a mass meeting; we all brought out our accusations against him. He was then sentenced to five years in prison. This was all done in good order. It should be done properly. He is dead now, but he died from sickness and old age; we did not execute him. He had committed many crimes and been guilty of great cruelties, and my sister's blood asked for revenge, but he was just another despotic landlord. They used to be like that. Those who were executed had committed crimes that were much worse.

"He's dead now. But the memory of the old times must not die. I'm illiterate; when I grew up the doors of the school were closed to people like me. But my daughter has gone to school. She's a barefoot doctor now and goes to special courses to continue her education. My son drives a tractor. One of my nephews who had such a bitter childhood has the honor of serving in the People's Liberation Army now. We must not forget how it used to be. These evil times may return unless we keep the revolution in firm memory.

"In the old society, only the landlord could afford a sewing machine. Now our family has a sewing machine and a bicycle and a radio. Do you think people like us could have offered our foreign visitors a meal like this in the old days? Oh no, the guests would have had to be content with the best thing we had to give then: a handful of corn.

"Chairman Mao Tse-tung showed us the way, showed us how to be masters of our own homes. I tell the young people over and over: Never forget what it was like before. Remember it always!

"This house was built in 1966, when we made up the plan of a new village here in the first production brigade. We then decided to build a new village, and the architects and technicians from Kashgar came here to discuss the project. There were certain basic principles. We were building a new socialistic countryside. The houses should be adapted to the size of the family, the style uniform to make the village neat and beautiful to look at. The technicians came here to help us, but we made the decisions. We let them help plan and design, but all decisions were taken by our own cadres after the masses had discussed the questions thoroughly and had their say. We then built the whole area with mutual aid, and with contributions from the collective. Everything now is the way we want it. Our homes are better than that of the landowner, in spite of his eighty-two rooms. Chairman Mao's guidance helps us do what we want to do."

12

The Empty Grave

The night is stifling, the air heavy. Gun is reading Sven Hedin in bed, I am listening to the radio. I have heard Tashkent and New Delhi, I have tried Voice of America, and I am now listening to the BBC. The commentary after the news is not very interesting. I turn it off and pour some tea. Gun says:

"A hundred thousand people were killed fighting in Sinkiang in the early thirties, maybe even more. No wonder people became bitter. They were the same kind of warlords as in Jagatai's day. Babur's uncles were not in the least more romantic than Ma Chung-yin. What Hedin writes about General Ma might as well have been written about one of the Jagatais:

"Ma is said to have sent out a proclamation, which reads: 'I am the king of Altishahr' [the six cities, or East Turkestan]. But the people say: 'He made Sinkiang a desert. We used to have everything in abundance, now there is nothing, we are all hungry and poor.' "*

After a little while she continues:

"It's even stranger, really. The army that secured Sheng Shih-ts'ai's power as governor-general of Sinkiang and liberated or captured Hedin in Korla on the north route in the spring of 1934 was a mixed army of White Russian emigrants and Soviet soldiers commanded by a White Russian emigrant. Listen to this:

"Another man answered my question:
'We're coming here troop upon troop all day long from Karashahr. Today about one thousand Russians, half White, half Red, arrived. . . . When we asked how White and Red ones could possibly work together, a sturdy blond man replied, "It's easy when you have the same

*Sven Hedin, *Stora hästens flykt* [The Flight of the Great Horse] (Stockholm, 1935), p. 208.

83

goal." He added, "Last January and February the Urumchi situation was awful, and we expected any minute the city to be taken by Ma. Then the Governor-General sent a radio telegram to Moscow asking for help. It came. . . ." '

"I wonder what the people thought about all that," Gun said. "Ma Chung-yin was a crook and a bloody bandit just like his relations who were warlords in Kansu and Tsinghai and Ningsia. But did people like to have the Russians here? They were not just any Russians. The Red ones mentioned by Hedin were GPU troops without any badges. How come the GPU troops and the czarist Cossacks could unite under a czarist general from the White side in the Russian civil war and consider their goal the same? I wonder after all if those GPU troops were not part of Stalin's 30 percent. Mao Tse-tung says that Stalin's policy was mainly good but up to 30 percent bad. That common goal which the Red and White Russians had in Sinkiang seems to belong to those 30 percent!"

"As a boy I always had problems with Hedin," I say. "One of my very first memories is of going with a relation to the large exhibition at the Liljevalch Hall in Stockholm, where the Hedin expedition showed their collection. That was the first time I saw pictures of lion dancers. Later, when I worked with the Chinese People's artist troupe I understood the dance and the movement. Then I learned that it originated in Sinkiang. Lion dancers from Kucha brought the dance to Changan, the emperor's capital, the present Sian, in the T'ang dynasty. It was in 1952, twenty years after I had seen the pictures of lion dancers as a child in Liljevalch's in Djurgarden. It was Wang Di-tse, the leader of the artist troupe, who told me about it. But when I took him and the artists to the Ethnographic Museum in the old barracks behind the Technological Museum—I used to spend my winter holidays there— he was annoyed, and the artists turned away, demanding to be shown back to their hotel. They regarded that kind of exhibition as an insult to China.

" 'The Chinese people have stood up,' Wang Di-tse said. 'Our country cannot be shown in this manner. It does us wrong. The comrades from the artist troupe are deeply hurt. Comrade Fan Li-chen, who does the number with the flying trident and knows well the old society and the opium smoking and other things shown in your museum, wanted me to tell you that the artists realize that you did not mean to hurt them and had no evil intentions, but you must remember that the Chinese people have stood up, and we are fighting the bad old customs. As far as I am concerned,' Wang Di-tse added, 'I find that it is this way of

looking at us that we find insulting. It is an imperialist way of looking at other people. As if we were strange animals in a zoo.'

"I returned to see these collections some time after this. I tried to see them with Chinese eyes, and realized then that they were right. We show our own history in the local museums as part of our hard-working Swedish people's past, but their past is shown as if it only concerned exotic strange customs and habits in strange countries. Hedin wrote the speech the king gave during his attempted *coup d'état* in 1914. Hedin was a reactionary politician and admired Hitler, and you can sense all this in his work in Asia."

"But Hedin did not only attempt a *coup d'état* in Sweden and admire the Czar and the Kaiser and Hitler," Gun said. "He did other things as well. Listen to the speech he says he delivered to the czarist Russian general whose GPU groups had taken Korla and were holding him prisoner. It sounds like a grand speech, but the contents are quite all right:

"I assure you that our aims are far beyond this miserable competition about the transient power over the province of Sinkiang. From our point of view, the war between Sheng Tupan and Ma Chung-yin is but a second on the clock of history. But, finding ourselves in the middle of this war, we have to watch its course carefully, for the sake of our own security. Still, we are disgusted by the sight of devastated cities, burning villages and gardens transformed into deserts, and a people whose shattered survivors are doomed to die from starvation and disease. This miserable war has made a whole people into beggars and destroyed what had been created in centuries and generations. It has moved the borders of the Gobi Desert hundreds of miles to the west. I assure you, general, that neither I nor any of my staff want any connection with this unfortunate war.*

"At that time Hedin was in Sinkiang on behalf of the Chinese government and not for the sake of Russia or Germany. I think his sentiments about China, the people and the country, were relatively decent in these books from the thirties."

The night is stuffy, but a wind is blowing up and can now be heard in the poplars outside in the dark. I am thinking of Gun's words about Hedin. People are difficult to judge, life is long, and we all have time to change many times. I had not seen Wang Di-tse in twenty-five years; I did not know what his views and behavior had been during this time. I did not even know if he was still alive. I had not given him a thought for many years until the lion dance reminded me of him. But we had

*Hedin, *Stora hästens flykt,* p. 260.

had this serious conversation—"exchange-of-hearts conversation" as the Chinese call it—on our way from the Ethnographic Museum in Stockholm in the autumn of 1952, and he had tried to make me understand how Europo-centric and culturally imperialistic our views on Asia and its people were. This helped me then to write about Afghanistan. And Hedin, in his books of the thirties, not only talks like an admirer of Hitler and a reactionary member of the Royal Academy, he also takes a certain stand for the Chinese people.

But when I turn around to tell Gun about this, I see that she is already asleep. She has *The Flight of the Great Horse* over her face and slumbers peacefully. I take the book, put it on the table next to the teacup, and turn out the light. I then lie in the dark, listening to the wind in the trees. The sound of the wind increases, drowning the sound of Gun's breathing. I fall asleep.

Gun says something to me in the dark, waking me up:

"Are you awake? I can hear you are. Are you?"

It is a quarter past three and by now I am awake.

"I was thinking about something," Gun says. "There is also an empty tomb by Apak Hodja's mausoleum. Anuven once was buried there. We should have asked to see it. They know which one it is."

"You mean Yakub Beg's tomb?" I say.

"In pictures it looks just like the other tombs in the large field outside the mausoleum. I could take a picture of any of those tombs and say it was that of Yakub Beg. It has been empty these hundred years. But that wouldn't be honest." She adds after a while: "He died in May. May 1877. Maybe he was poisoned by his relatives or battered to death by them or perhaps he died on his own in the midst of defeat. But hated he was—nobody stood up for him at the end. His soldiers rose against him and joined the Chinese government soldiers who were coming back toward Kashgar. Yakub Beg's own followers wrote to the Chinese officials, begging to be freed from Yakub Beg.

"They didn't even fight when the government troops returned here. Yakub Beg's son Beg Kuli Beg fled across the mountains toward Russia. He lacked power. The only man who was really punished for the revolt was Yakub Beg himself, and he was dead. They took him from his grave, burned his body at the stake, and sent his head to the emperor in Peking. That's why his tomb is empty. I would have liked to have a picture of his tomb. The emptiness is exemplary.

"Ma Chung-yin made me think of him. They were the same kind of warlords and murderers. Of course the people preferred to have the Chinese government back; they did not have their cities and villages plundered; their friends and relatives killed, and to be flogged themselves and survive only by luck. People want peace and order and good irrigation canals and low taxes. They don't want glorious cavalry rulers, and they certainly don't want warlords who are as worthless as they are cruel.

"Hedin describes how Ma Chung-yin and his war extended the desert hundreds of miles over the oases. Aurel Stein tells how Yakub Beg ruled so harshly that the population of certain oases was diminished by half.

"Aurel Stein was a Hungarian Jew who knew what oppression was like. But he was a faithful British civil servant as well. An imperialist British patriot, knighted for his difficult intelligence work in Sinkiang. What he wrote and said about Yakub Beg's oppression coincides with what others have written about Yakub Beg and his rule.

"Yakub Beg tried to create an independent realm and contacted the sultan in Turkey and Queen Victoria in England, and he said that he fought for the True Faith. But the people did not want him. He was not of the country even but from the other side of the mountains. Besides, he had started as a dancing-boy serving old gentlemen, then his slyness and cunning advanced him further. He was a plunderer. He sucked the blood of the people."

"I've read in other books that he came from a most respected family, where both father and grandfather were religious judges—*kazi,*" I said, but Gun interrupted me:

"That doesn't matter. We have met drug-pushing male prostitutes from good families in Stockholm. Their morals did not improve as they later rose in society and politics. Same thing with Yakub Beg. People refuse to be ruled by such a man. They don't want to be plundered and risk being killed. Even if they can't live in the best of societies, they prefer a law-abiding, proper administration where the civil servants are punished if they oppress the people, and where taxes are low and somewhat just and are used for the maintenance of irrigation canals and roads. Never in their history did the Uighurs show any inclination to accept warlords like Yakub Beg or Ma Chung-yin. They want to live and work in peace. That is why they did not support Yakub Beg and that is why Beg Kuli Beg had to flee west across the mountains, and why this province became an ordinary Chinese province, Sinkiang. I would say that this explains a lot," Gun says, "because I have been wondering how come Sinkiang stuck to China even in those long periods when there was hardly any central Chinese power and hardly any Chinese troops and Sinkiang could not be forced to remain in China. I have thought a lot about that."

In this abandoned Russian outpost in Kashgar, the question of Sinkiang's Chinese character becomes an important issue. The wind is rising outside but the air in the bedroom is still heavy and stifling hot. Yakub Beg could let himself be named an *atalik ghazi,* father and hero, but he was certainly not the *badaulet,* "prince of luck," that he called himself, because he never became a hero of the people; he was betrayed by his followers and murdered by his family, and his body was taken from its grave and burned at the stake, while his head was sent to the emperor's court and his name was forgotten. He was a man of ill-luck and ill-fame.

"If I understand you rightly," I say to Gun, "you mean that neither Ma Chung-yin nor Yakub Beg nor even Hidajetulla—Apak Hodja resting out there in his mausoleum—could become what Ahmad Khan became for Kabul? The founder of the realm; the father of the state."

But Gun does not reply. She is asleep again, and I can hear her breathing. It is hot and I am wide awake, unable to sleep. I get up, put on my dressing gown, and enter the large reception room. As I turn on the light, the mirrors gleam and the gilt shines, but the chairs stand there with white covers, and the Khotan rugs on the walls have a deep luster. I ask myself whether the Cossacks in the end did not have time to take the rugs or whether they were brought here later on, to be hung in this Russian reception room of the officer of the watch. I pour some tea and sit down at the desk.

I've put the books I'm reading in a pile to my left. White pieces of paper show how far I've read, and at the back I've noted pages and references.

I think about the things we've been discussing as I look for something I marked the other day.

Yakub Beg and Ma Chung-yin rode like devastating desert storms over Sinkiang, leaving death and annihilation in their tracks. As war-lords they could not build up a nation. Neither did Hidajetulla Hodja leave a durable state behind, although he died in great holiness in 1693–94 and lies buried in his beautiful mausoleum. But his power was based on holiness and feudal ownership. It was not organized and not constructive, and his successors fought one confused war after another in the oases. Ahmad Khan was of another kind: his power was different.

In 1747, when Nadir Shah of Persia had been murdered, his Afghan bodyguards broke camp and were freed of their fealty and started to march homeward to their own mountains. The leader of the body-guards was Ahmad Khan of the Saddozai lineage of the Abdali tribe. Him the elders of the tribe then crowned Shah Durr-i-Durran—"the Pearl of the Ages." And his tribe took on the name they still bear: Durrani. This was the origin of the Afghan state, which, after long wars of independence, was transformed from tribal federation to state. When the elders crowned Ahmad Khan as shah with wheat ears, this became a symbolic act in a historic leap forward: the kingdom of Kabul served the Afghan people in their development. But who were the ones who benefitted from Hidajetulla Hodja and Yakub Beg and Ma Chung-yin? It is not just a question of cruelty; Ahmad Khan could well be more cruel than Hidajetulla Hodja, and I doubt that Yakub Beg's hardness of character even approached that of his contemporary Abd-er-Rahman, of Kabul. Ma Chung-yin can be put aside. The point is what needs the cruelty fulfills. Abd-er-Rahman's cruelty was founded on a reason. His policy could be defended—he defended it himself with great eloquence—by the need to secure the lives and safety of his subjects, to make the trade routes secure, to safeguard the kingdom's independence against threatening great powers. The grim wars of independence against the British were costly for the country and delayed its development, but Abd-er-Rahman's policy secured independence and contributed to overcoming British aggression. His policy—like that of Ahmad Khan—was historically progressive.

But who benefitted from Yakub Beg? Not the merchants. Not those who tilled the soil nor the landlords, since the oases became depopulated and agriculture impoverished; not the miners who were forced to dig for gold in appalling conditions to pay for Yakub Beg's regiment. He remained just a warlord, unable to accomplish any historically progressive task in Sinkiang; thus he could not create a state.

Now to the books. To Tashkurghan I had brought with me, among other things, John Wood's *A Journey to the Source of the River Oxus,* the edition that his son Alexander Wood published in 1872. On New Year's Day in 1838 John Wood—then a young British lieutenant spying out the land of Badakhshan—was in Jurm in northern Badakhshan. He was talking to Ahmed Shah, the leading *mullah* in Jurm. He had left India in 1809 and spent a long time in East Turkestan before going to Jurm. He told much about the Chinese and their customs:

> Of the jealousy which characterizes the Chinese, their fear and distrust of foreigners; the wakeful vigilance with which their frontiers are guarded; and the efficacy of their restrictive measures, he had many anecdotes to tell: while, like every other native of these countries with whom I conversed on the subject, he praised their probity and good faith.
> . . . A foreign merchant informed the magistrates of Eela that he had lost his *koorgeen,* or saddlebags. The man was required minutely to describe them, and to make oath to their contents. He swore to the value of one hundred silver yambos, and was dismissed after being told to come back on a given day, when if the saddlebags were not recovered the State would make good his loss. On the appointed day the merchant presented

himself, when, to his great chagrin, the *koorgeen* was produced. It had
not been opened, and much to the crafty man's annoyance, this was now
done by the authorities. Instead of the sum he had sworn to, the articles
it contained were found not to exceed a few yambos in value. A circum-
stantial report of the whole affair was transmitted to Peking, and the
emperor decided it to be for the benefit of his exchequer and the moral
good of his subjects that the admission into the country of barbarous and
unprincipled foreigners should forthwith be prohibited. This may or may
not have been the case; but from the story we learn the high estimation
in which the Chinese character is held among those most intimate with
them.*

This story, heard by Lieutenant John Wood from the *mullah* Ahmed
Shah in Jurm on New Year's Eve in 1838, explains why the people of
Kashgaria preferred to be subjects of a multinational Chinese empire
—then ruled by the Manchus—rather than be under the rule of this or
that warlord.

But just as interesting in this context is the footnote added by Wood's
son Alexander regarding Yakub Beg in 1872: ". . . and though his career
has presented all the characteristics of intrigue and murder which are
inseparable from the foundation of an Eastern dynasty, still . . . he
appears to be a ruler under whom trade is likely to flourish, and who,
to a certain extent, encourages intercourse with foreigners. . . ."†

That which made Yakub Beg acceptable to the British, and which
caused his policies to be followed with more than just interest by the
Russians, made him less acceptable to the people who were subjected
to intrigues and murder and such trade as foreigners hoped to gain
from. But if the re-establishment of Chinese administration in Kashgar
was a liberation from insufferable lawlessness and barred the expansionist policies of both the British and the Russians, it was still carried out
by those very troops that had recently drowned a large popular revolt
in an ocean of blood. The troops were led by one of China's most
ruthlessly reactionary and efficient administrators, Tso Tsung-t'ang.
That liberation was not a liberation; it was establishing rational feudal
oppression in due form. However, for the merchant class and the feudal
landowning class for which the *mullah* Ahmed Shah spoke in Jurm in
Badakshan in 1838, the Ch'ing dynasty mandarins were honest and
sincere. In comparison with Yakub Beg, they appeared to the laboring
people who carried the whole feudal system as sufferable.

They would have been insufferable, however, without this comparison. The Ch'ing dynasty was decaying. It had taken over the centralized

*Captain John Wood, *A Journey to the Source of the River Oxus* (London, 1872), p. 181.
† *Ibid.*

state power from the Ming dynasty and centralized it even more; its power rested on an alliance between Manchu tribal chiefs who had become ruling aristocrats and on a mandarinate based on landlordism. But as early as the turn of the century, when Chia Ch'ing succeeded Ch'ien Lung in 1796, the dynasty proved an obstacle to China's development, hampering all progress. Corruption, administrative high-handedness, oppression, and incompetence contributed to worsening the social and financial crisis that shook the empire. The tax reform of 1725, bringing together all different taxes into one to be paid in silver, was implemented differently in the various provinces, and local administrators added their own taxes. The economic assets that should have been released by the reform were absorbed by the increasing tax pressure and the augmenting corruption. China's industry did develop, but haltingly.

The Ch'ing dynasty did not even manage to maintain the prohibition against drugs. The British were pumping opium into China and taking out silver. In the 1830s they got out every year between 20 million and 30 million taels in silver, that is, between 850 and 1,275 tons of silver annually. China's coinage system was based on the silver standard. The taxes were taken out in silver. But the silver price doubled in a hundred years in relation to the copper coins normally used for trade and simpler payments. Agricultural products were paid for with copper, but taxes were to be paid in silver. Up to the Opium War the basic tax was thus doubled at the same time as the people were impoverished, and the administration was paralyzed due to lack of cash.

The government made a desperate attempt to protect the laws, the finances, and the health of the people by an attempt to maintain the prohibition against the importation of drugs. The British struck back with armed forces and forced China open. The Ch'ing dynasty could not even fulfill its first task: to protect the country against foreign aggression.

The defeat in the war brought immediate increased exploitation in China. The masses of peasants were pushed further into poverty; small tradesmen and craftsmen had to go begging. The war damages China was forced to pay were drawn from the people by higher taxes; foreign capitalism pumped silver out of China, while drugs destroyed more and more people. All over China peasants, craftsmen, small dealers, patriotic intellectuals, and honest officials started to revolt. On January 11, 1851, "the Taiping Heavenly Kingdom" was proclaimed in Chintien village in Kweiping county in Kwangsi. The official ideology was Christian. This was the greatest uprising in China since the fall of the Ming dynasty. The Taiping economic program meant land reform giving land to the tillers, support to the craftsmen, freer trade, low taxes with simplified collection. Its social reforms included prohibition against drugs, rights for women, prohibition against binding girls' feet, against selling girls and keeping them as concubines. The foreign policy was aimed at friendly contacts with all foreign states based on equal rights and trade to mutual advantage.

The Taiping Revolution in China was one of the great democratic wars for freedom of the nineteenth century. In Europe it was hailed by socialists like Marx as well as by radical democrats like Strindberg. But after fourteen years of hard fighting, the Taiping movement was defeated. The foreign great powers had united and given their support to the corrupt decaying Ch'ing dynasty against the people in revolution. Only foreign help could keep the Ch'ing dynasty in power.

But while China in this way was made safe for foreign capital, the Ch'ing dynasty had simultaneously lost what is called in classical Chinese tradition "the mandate of heaven." From the mid-nineteenth century, the Ch'ing dynasty thus ruled as a corrupt clique without historical legitimacy. China sank to a semicolonial country.

The increasing oppression made the different nationalities of China rise against the Ch'ing dynasty. The foreign powers that had helped to defeat the Taiping Revolution also helped the dynasty fight back these other revolts. This proved profitable for them. The Ch'ing dynasty safeguarded not only the foreign powers' interests in China, it also sank deeper into debt to the foreigners, pawning its sovereignty bit by bit in order to keep the various nationalities from rising against its rule.

In Shensi and Kansu the Hui people rose. In European literature they are called Tungans after the name given to them by the Turkic-speaking people. The revolt went on from 1861 to 1873 and cost a vast numbers of victims. After the Taipings had been defeated, Tso Tsung-t'ang financed by British merchants, was sent to fight the Hui. Step by step his troops advanced up through Kansu.

In present Sinkiang the Ch'ing dynasty had a special administration. The viceroy had his seat in Kuldja in the Ili valley, with two deputies, one for the area north of Tien Shan and one for the area south. These deputies—*ambans*—took care of all internal affairs. However, any matters pertaining to borders or external issues had to be referred to the viceroy, who had direct contact with Peking. There was an executive administrator under the *amban* with four advisers, one military, one civil, one financial, and one judicial. These in turn had one deputy each who managed the administration as such.

There was at the same time a specific Uighur administration, managed by a *hakim beg,* responsible for tax collection and the judicial system. He was answerable only to the *amban* himself. The Ch'ing dynasty gave him land and also a salary.

The administration was very slow, but—as the *mullah* Ahmed Shah says—it was a functioning administration well into the nineteenth century. The taxes were kept within reasonable limits, trade flourished, the judicial system worked, and the administrators were not too corrupt.

But the decay that marked the whole Ch'ing dynasty administration toward the middle of the nineteenth century was twice as bad in so-called Chinese Turkestan. Here—as in certain other areas—the administrative positions could be held only by Manchu aristocrats. This meant that the quality of the administrators was lower than in the rest of China and the population was exposed to double national oppression. From the 1820s on one revolt after another flared up against the Ch'ing dynasty in Chinese Turkestan.

To safeguard its rule, the Ch'ing dynasty began to give the merchants from the khanate of Khokand west of the mountains certain privileges. From 1832 on the khan of Khokand had a right to exact tax from those of his subjects who lived in Chinese Turkestan. These were organized by his own *aksakals* (agents) who were ruled by a Khokand representative who had his seat in Kashgar.

In this way the Khokand merchants became a caste organized like a state within the state having their own administration, obeying a foreign prince, and forming part of a foreign power's state system.

Later czarist Russia, after conquering the khanate of Khokand, would take over its feudal privileges in Sinkiang and keep the whole system of local *aksakals* directly obeying the Russian consul-general in Kashgar. During the years before the First World War, Russia seemed to be taking over Sinkiang with this organization's assistance. In the early 1960s the new rulers, in a similar way, organized the "league of Soviet citizens living abroad" and made it directly dependent on their consuls. With their help they tried to seize power in Sinkiang. The conflicts in 1962 and the Chinese confusion over the sudden appearance of tens of thousands of "Soviet citizens" can be explained historically by the treaty between the Ch'ing dynasty and the khanate of Khokand regarding the Khokand merchants' privileges of 1832. I shall come back to 1962. We are still in the mid-nineteenth century and the representatives of the Ch'ing dynasty in what was then Chinese Turkestan are becoming less and less fit to fulfill their job.

The Khokand merchants took advantage of their position of power to gain the trade in the bazaars around Tarim. They pushed aside the local traders in oasis after oasis—the local Uighur as well as the Han. In the fight over the market they also took advantage of their religion.

At the same time Russia was pressing on. In the Peking treaty of 1860, Russia had forced the Ch'ing dynasty to open Kashgar to Russian trade. After the defeat in the Crimean War, Russia had turned its eyes east. The Czarist diplomats took skillful advantage of China's difficulties, and Russia turned out to be the power victorious in the French-British war against China 1856–60.

In June 1860 French-British troops occupied and plundered Peking. The Russian diplomat Count Ignatiev had been told by the French minister, Baron Gros, that the French-British troops were not going to stay in Peking. They were to be withdrawn after the conquest and the pillage. With this knowledge Count Ignatiev would now carry out one of the great diplomatic coups of Russia.

During the war Russia had already forced the Ch'ing dynasty to give up vast areas of China's territory which were Chinese according to the then valid border treaty of 1689 between China and Russia. The methods were unscrupulous. Muraviev, governor-general of East Siberia, had negotiated the Treaty of Aigun and skillfully worked with various versions in different languages. In this way he had managed to rob the Ch'ing dynasty of more than it realized. For this Muraviev was raised to the rank of count and given the name "Amurski," after the river Amur.

This is when Count Ignatiev performed his masterpiece. The twenty-eight-year-old Prince Kung was to look after the Chinese foreign contacts on behalf of the Ch'ing dynasty during this crisis when the French-British forces were occupying Peking. Count Ignatiev turned to him, pointing out that Russia had always been the true friend of China. Russia felt love and affection for China and wanted to help. Russia would use all its influence and all possibile ways of pressuring the French-British occupation troops to leave the emperor's capital, Peking. As a modest compensation, Russia just wanted the land between the river Ussuri and the sea plus various additional little concessions, including the right to trade in Kashgar.

Prince Kung accepted on China's behalf the Russian conditions for assistance. On November 5, 1860, the French-British troops left Peking. On November 14 the treaty between Russia and China was signed. A couple of days later Prince Kung became aware of the fact that he had been cheated. The Russian diplomacy used confidence tricks. The smart of this deal still hurts, which is one of the reasons why the Chinese foreign ministry demands that the Kremlin agree to declare this disgraceful treaty null and void. If the Kremlin were to agree to that, China would accept as a valid boundary the border line that Count Ignatiev craftily made Prince Kung accept. This request does not ap-

pear unreasonable. The sixth article of the Peking treaty of 1860 reads
as follows:

> Kashgar will be opened for trade on trial on the same conditions as in
> Ili and Tarbagatai. The Chinese government shall in Kashgar surrender
> enough land for a factory with all necessary buildings such as domiciles,
> store houses, church, and so on, plus a cemetery and grazing land as in
> Ili and Tarbagatai. The Kashgar *amban* is, without delay, to surrender
> this land. . . .

Thus, Russia had a foothold in Kashgar. But the borders of the
Russian Empire were still far from Kashgar. North of Kashgar was
China's border at Lake Balkhash. Beyond the mountains northwest of
Kashgar was the khanate of Khokand, and to the west China extended
across Pamir toward the khanate of Bukhara and the kingdom of
Kabul. Russia was far away.

But the Chinese border in Central Asia could now be broken, just as
the Chinese coastal cities had been opened to foreign powers. The
Ch'ing dynasty was falling apart. It could neither defend itself against
foreign powers nor play the diplomatic game. The generals of the
Ch'ing dynasty deserted their troops, and its diplomats let themselves
be taken in by the simplest confidence games.

It was only against their own people that the dynasty managed to
wage war, but then only with either open or indirect support from the
foreign powers already established in China, who were dividing the
empire between them. The Ch'ing dynasty was corrupt and was op-
pressing the people. The peasants' armies and agitators of the Taiping
spread revolt wherever they went. The Chinese peasants were on the
march, as they had been over and over when a dynasty had turned
corrupt and decayed and no longer could rule. But now in the mid-
nineteenth century the peasants' revolt was different: the Taiping revolt
was growing into a revolution.

The Taiping agitators made contact with the Hui people, the Moslems, in Shensi in 1862. These were badly oppressed by the Ch'ing
dynasty, not only exploited by landlords, oppressed by taxes, and exposed to arbitrary officials; they were, moreover, trampled on and
insulted as a people. In the 268 years of the Ch'ing dynasty rule in
China, only forty-five of the great Hui people were allowed to reach
higher administrative positions in the empire. In May 1862 the Hui
people rose spontaneously in Shensi, and before long, the revolt had
spread all over northwest China.

It was a peasant war, a war of liberation against the Ch'ing dynasty.
Like the European peasant wars, this one, too, was in religious disguise.

It is important to keep in mind that this does not mean it was "in reality" a social war, in religious "disguise" for tactical reasons. Look at Thomas Münzer in the German peasant war of 1524. The social contents cannot be separated from the religious preaching. Münzer himself would have interpreted his own behavior in religious terms. But it is just as impossible to transform him into a "purely religious" apostle. Religion is the ideology of the peasant war. Taiping, a peasant war growing from revolt to revolution, was an ideology about to take the leap out of religion. The war of the Hui people was conducted within the framework of religion. Late in the autumn of 1761, a man called Ma Ming-hsin, a native of Anting in Kansu, had arrived in the Salar area in the upper reaches of the Yellow River in Tsinghai province. He had studied in Kashgar, and now preached "the new teaching," *hsin-chiao.* He was a visionary and a mystic. His teaching was akin to Sufism: it was strict and ascetic and at the same time opened up the doors to ecstasy. The true believers stamped, sang, and danced as did the followers of contemporary Christian sects in the European cottages. The devotees of the new teaching fought the old one. They struggled even with arms. After two large revolts, "the new teaching" was forbidden in 1783 by authorities as antisocial. It continued as an underground movement, a visionary sect in constant revolt against the state. In 1862 its leader, Ma Hua-lung, the direct successor of the founder and saint Ma Ming-hsin, would lead what became one of the largest peasant wars in China's modern history.

Here in what was then Chinese Turkestan, all command posts were held by men from the "eight banners," descendants of those who had taken arms in the Manchu struggle against the Ming dynasty in the seventeenth century. They were organized in eight sections within the army, each with its own color: yellow, white, red, blue, with and without borders. Within each banner, Manchus, Mongols, and Han were organized separately. These "eight banners" formed the spine and the armed might of the Ch'ing dynasty.

There are statistics about the officials who held the thirteen highest positions in Chinese Turkestan up to 1874. They were in all 234 men, 229 of whom were definitely recruited from the "eight banners" and 5 —two *ambans* in Urumchi, one representative in Hami, one adviser in Kashgar—possibly from outside the "eight banners."

This system, which initially seemed to secure the border areas and keep them in faithful hands, had toward the mid-nineteenth century begun to threaten the security of the state. Positions were filled by nepotism. All over the empire, relations and connections overruled skill and ability—but here they meant everything. The quality of the administration went down, and oppression increased. Here in the far west there was no real supervision, and incompetent officials who had obtained their office through pull or graft seized the opportunity to enrich themselves. When the Hui people rose in revolt, the links of communication with the rest of the country were cut off. On July 13, 1864, Urumchi rose. The revolt triumphed in one city after another. On July 16 Yarkand fell; on July 30, Kashgar.

There was no leadership of the revolt. A time of great confusion followed when various local feudal lords resumed power in different cities. Aksu, Urumchi, Kashgar, Khotan, and Yarkand each had its ruler. These soon fought each other in war and cunning intrigues.

At the same time Russian troops had started to move and now marched into the khanate of Khokand from two directions, through Chinese territory from the Ili area and from the bases established by Russia on the river Syr Darya. On September 22, 1864, the two detachments united after having conquered Dzhambul, Turkestan, and Chimkent. While the Russian troops were on the move, Russian diplomats acted swiftly and efficiently. On October 7 (September 25 Old Style), 1864, the Chinese authorities signed the border protocol in Chuguchak. They were cut off from the rest of the country, the rebels holding the roads behind them. All they had was a little streak of land up in Ili. Under Russian pressure they now surrendered all the land between Lake Balkhash and Tien Shan, hoping for Russia's aid.

When the Russian advance in Central Asia began to arouse attention, the chancellor of state, Prince Gorchakov, had circulated a document to the foreign powers through the Russian envoys abroad, announcing the guiding lines for Russian policy in Central Asia according to the Russian government. The circular was characterized by sympathetic comprehension of international fear. Russia now wanted to calm public opinion, and the envoys were to explain the high principles to the various governments.

Gorchakov held forth that Russia, with a heavy heart, had had to extend its territory—which was already more extended than necessary—because a civilized nation bordering on semiwild tribes, in the name of its own security as well as of general trade, had to safeguard "a certain superiority over neighbors whose unsettled nomad instincts make them difficult to live with." Gorchakov writes as an experienced statesman, chastened by political realities, pointing out the following:

> All powers in the same situation have had to do the same thing, the United States of America, France in Algeria, Holland in its colonies, England in India—they have all been forced to follow a course where

ambition is less important than the pressure of necessity and where the main difficulty is knowing where to stop.

Russia eventually achieved a natural, safe border. The steppes were under control and the border right on the "agricultural and trading people tied to their land with a more elevated social organization, thus giving us a basis for friendly relations."

Russia now had no more need for any expansion whatsoever in Central Asia. Russia merely hoped that the bordering states, "in spite of their low culture and their dim political development . . . may one day achieve those real connections which can remove, in our mutual interest, the obstacles at present barring their progress."

At the same time the minister of foreign affairs, Gorchakov, could not keep himself from noting the following:

> People in recent years have been kind enough to give us the task of civilizing our neighboring countries of the inland of Asia. The progress of civilization has no safer ally than trade relations. These in all countries need order and stability for the sake of expansion. Asia also needs a transformation of popular customs.

Such a transformation of the customs of the Asian people can, however, be carried out only by a firm political organization, a government. A strong society is necessary. Therefore, Russia's task, according to Gorchakov, was first to secure its borders to discourage any disorder, insecurity, and war. Russia's task would then be to assure the neighboring states their true independence by a just, reasonable policy that taught them to live without violence. Russia was not their enemy and did not want any more conquests; Russia was their friendly helpmate.

> As the Russian Empire devotes itself to this matter, it is only in the interests of the empire; but we consider the completion of this task also to serve mankind and civilization in general. We have the right to expect fair and loyal appreciation of the policy we follow and the principles which have fixed it.

GORCHAKOV

Thus Russia achieved its extreme, safe, natural, and final border. In the following year Russian troops occupied Tashkent.

The British government was again worried. On July 31, 1865, Lord John Russell suggested an exchange of notes between Russia and England with the aim of guaranteeing a status quo in Central Asia plus the independence and integrity of Persia. In reply, Prince Gorchakov expressed his joy over England's friendly suggestion, but Russia, not desiring any expansion of land in Central Asia, did not consider an exchange of notes necessary. All Russia wanted was peace and security for all parties in Central Asia. Russia wished peaceful trade to flourish. In spite of this, Gorchakov said, it would have been easy to make the required statement, if only the emir of Bukhara was not behaving threateningly toward the khan of Khokand. In September of the same year Czar Alexander II, the Russian autocrat, emphasized to the British ambassador, Sir Andrew Buchanan, that Russia had no territorial ambitions at all in Central Asia. Russia worked for peace and appeasement even in these barbaric areas. In October Prince Gorchakov sent a note, pointing out that Russia had only peaceful intentions in Central Asia, wanted to respect Afghanistan's independence, and, in agreement with Great Britain, wished to support the Persian monarchy.

Concurrently with these diplomatic maneuvers, conquest was in progress. The army of the emir of Bukhara was defeated, and Russia occupied Khojend between Khokand and Bukhara in May 1866. In July 1867 the government-general of Turkestan was established, comprising the recently conquered territories. In May 1868 Russia took Samarkand. The emir of Bukhara had to pay war damages, and Bukhara became a Russian protectorate. Russia had reached the Amu Darya, the Oxus of ancient times. The khanate of Khokand was shrinking, owing to the continued Russian advance, but was still wedged between the government-general of Turkestan and the Russian protectorate of Bukhara in the west and the southern part of Chinese Turkestan in the east.

Chinese influence in Chinese Turkestan was apparently being eliminated. Only east toward Hami and Barkul was there still Chinese administration. In Ili government troops and high officials had held out for eighteen months. The viceroy had asked for 40,000 men from Peking but had instead been dismissed and replaced on November 1, 1864, by Ming-hsu, military commander in Chuguchak. The situation of the besieged deteriorated. There was famine. People even ate their cats. Typhoid fever claimed between fifty and one hundred lives a day. Russian authorities offered no assistance. The Chinese officials, who had recently given up such large territories of the Heavenly Empire to gain Russia's support, were given only excuses as they begged for assistance from the Russian governor of West Siberia. The Russian authorities watched the destruction of the Chinese without doing more than waiting. In the winter of 1865–1866, when the siege had been going on for more than a year and the situation was desperate, the foreign officer in Peking—Tsungli Yamen—tried repeatedly to get the Russian minister to intervene, but was given only noncommittal replies. On March 6, 1866, Ili fell, and the new viceroy, Ming-hsu, as well as his predecessor and both their families were killed.

On April 11, 1866, Chuguchak fell. The Russians considered that the ripe fruit had fallen and all they had to do was pick it up.

That is what they did in the summer of 1871 when it seemed likely that the Ili territory would form part of Yakub Beg's realm. General Kolpakovsky, governor of Semiryechie—"Land of the Seven Rivers" —then marched across the border with 1,785 men and 65 officers to occupy a territory of almost 3,200 square kilometers, the most fertile land in this part of Asia. The rest of the world knew nothing about this until September.

In old Kashgaria fighting between the different feudal rulers in the winter of 1864–65 had resumed as formerly in the Hodja time. Sadik Beg of Kashgar, with the intention of fighting back Rasheddin Hodja and his dominion in Aksu, had turned to the khan of Khokand asking for someone from the "White Mountain" branch of the Hodja family. The khan of Khokand then sent Busurg Hodja, who brought with him a Khokand general, Tadzhik-born, who had lost many battles against Russian troops. His origin was slightly disputed, but he was renowned for his courage and ambition, and along with him were sixty-three men, sent by the khan of Khokand. This man was Yakub Beg.

With the aid of Khokand merchants subject to the khan of Khokand's *aksakals,* and with the previous Manchu troops—now officially Moslems—Yakub Beg dethroned Sadik Beg who had summoned him. He also had the local ruler of Yarkand deposed and placed Busurg Hodja on the throne. Once his power was stabilized and his forces organized, he deposed Busurg Hodja, calling him a notorious debau-chée who had forfeited all right to his inheritance. Yakub Beg now approached the emir of Bukhara and inveigled him into bestowing the honorary title of Atalik Ghazi, "Father and Hero." The emir was defeated by the Russians and made a Russian tributary, but Yakub Beg continued his conquests, deposing one local ruler after another. He now took the name of Badaulet, "the Prince of Luck." In 1870 Yakub Beg ruled over most of southern Sinkiang, his capital being Aksu, and had 1,015,000 people as subjects.

The British made contact with him, giving him diplomatic support. While Russia continued her conquests, taking Khiva in 1874 and finally occupying Khokand in 1876, Great Britain tried to strengthen Yakub Beg's position as an independent monarch. The Turkish sultan recognized him as khan of Kashgaria and Amir-ul-Muminin, "Commander of the Faithful," in 1875.

Within the Imperial Government in Peking intensive disputes were going on regarding the choice of policy. General Tso Tsung-t'ang, who had crushed the struggle of the Hui people for freedom in Kansu in

1873 (a campaign financed by foreign merchants in exchange for security in Chinese customs and Chinese taxes and 10 percent annual interest), demanded to be allowed to continue and thus defeat Yakub Beg. After various debates he was granted permission. His troops took Urumchi on August 18, 1876. In April of the following year the Chinese government troops defeated Yakub Beg, first at Turfan and then at Toksun. In May 1877 Yakub Beg died. Chinese sources claim that he committed suicide, others that he was killed.

The state that Yakub Beg had tried to build collapsed. His army had consisted of mercenaries, but these came from Khokand and Badakhshan and the Afghan tribes. He had trusted them, and they had been faithful to him for as long as he could pay. The Chinese troops he took over when intriguing to seize power over Kashgar from Sadik Beg for his then lord and master had been left in their quarters. Yakub Beg had never dared take them out of Kashgar and Yarkand. The Uighur infantry had proved unwilling to battle for him. It was unreliable.

The Khokand merchants had stopped supporting Yakub Beg when the bazaar trade was driven to ruin as the economy of the oases was devastated. Yakub Beg's secret police—so well organized that it had gained fame as far way as Persia—was certainly able to trace those who were actively dissatisfied, but it was unable to create supporters for his rule.

Great Britain on and off had lent its support to Yakub Beg. This support was part of the great game played by its diplomats and statesmen with their Russian counterparts over Asian power. But the British support had not been too strong, and not forceful enough to secure Yakub Beg's dominion. This very British-Russian game over Asia had been the decisive factor when the highest officials of the Chinese Empire discussed whether their limited resources were to be spent building a modern coastal defense against Japan in the east or securing the western parts of inner Asia which were under the rule of Yakub Beg.

In spite of the fact that Japanese forces—led by an American chief of staff and transported on American ships—had already once attacked Taiwan and been forced back, and that the powers had compelled China not to pursue its victory but instead pay a war indemnity and recognize the special interest of Japan in the Ryukyu Islands, the Turkestan situation was deemed to be more serious. The governor of Hunan emphasized the following:

If our troops retire one step, the Russians will advance one step. If our troops lose one day, the Russians will gain one. Nothing is more urgent than this. Different states like England, France, and the United States can also take advantage of the situation. Another deterioration of the Russian issues will lead, inevitably, to difficulties on the coast, and our defense can hardly meet a double threat. The consequence could then be an unthinkable situation for China's foreign relations in the future.

When General Tso Tsung-t'ang's troops advanced through the desert and it was obvious that Yakub Beg did not have the power to resist, the British government made a last effort to save him. On July 7, 1877, the British government suggested that Yakub Beg should recognize China's suzerainty but continue as a local ruler. Tso Tsung-t'ang remarked to Peking that the whole thing was part of the British-Russian game. Yakub Beg did not come from Kashgar. The power there had been taken by a little group of Andijanis from Khokand. Now the Russians had advanced and occupied Khokand. The British diplomatic action was a trap:

> The men from Andijan belong to a tribe living outside the Kashgar district. Great Britain and Russia are both friendly states. If Great Britain wishes to protect Andijan from a Russian attack, this is no business of ours. . . . If Great Britain wishes to establish an independent state somewhere for the men from Andijan, Great Britain can give them some British territory or some part of India. What reason have we to seek the gratitude of these men by giving them our fertile land?

The British suggestion was turned down by the Chinese government. The matter was, they told the British, completely an internal one. If Yakub Beg had anything to say he should not send a representative to London to ask the British government to speak on his behalf but turn directly to General Tso Tsung-t'an, who was the official responsible for this matter.

This British support accelerated the ruin of Yakub Beg. It became twice as necessary for the Chinese government to finish his dominion immediately. The Russians had played against the British by delivering grain to the Chinese troops. After conquering Khokand, Russia gave aid to China to eliminate Yakub Beg. Russia assumed that the armed resistance against the advancing Chinese government troops would be so strong that even when Yakub Beg fell—which was inevitable— Kashgar would be without a ruler for some time and in that way automatically could slide into the Russian fold by itself. To prevent this development, the Chinese troops were given the order to advance quickly toward Kashgar. The resistance that Russia had hoped would detain the Chinese government troops did not exist. Yakub Beg had no support. His dominion collapsed. Kashgar became neither Russian nor British.

The past is not gone. All those who acted in the great game of a hundred years ago are long since dead, and Yakub Beg does not even have a grave, although he believed for a while that he would be able to found an empire. But Kashgar is not a city without history. It has been formed by these long-dead men. How would it be possible to understand the politics of Sinkiang today without taking history into account?

Outside the window the night is still deep. I've been drinking much tea in these hours; two thermos flasks are empty already. The third is by the door; I can see that it was made in Urumchi. It is beautifully painted, a Kazakh girl laughing outside a yurt, a lamb in her arms. Behind her wooded slopes rise toward mountaintops with snow against a blue sky. The grass is fresh and green.

A hot desert wind is blowing through the night outside. My skin is dry, and when I walk across the rug toward the table, I am charged with static electricity until the hairs rise and my fingertips spark against the door handle even though I am wearing rubber soles. I'm sitting here in this deserted hall of mirrors in Russian provincial empire style, arranging my notes on Kashgar. The Cossacks are gone, and as I look up from my papers I can see myself in the large mirror. The amalgam is getting yellow and flaky by the golden frame, and behind me where the room loses itself in darkness at the entrance hall I can see the folds of the heavy red curtain. The wind whistles under the heavy door, and in the fatigue of the late hour I ask myself who is standing out there in the darkness. There have been uninvited guests there before. My eyes are burning, and I stick the notes together and insert them into my file.

Kashgar was one of the cities that seemed to be at stake in the big game. Other such cities were Teheran and Kabul, Khiva and Merv, though Peshawar and Lahore seemed to be won first by one side, then by the other. In the whole of the nineteenth century Russia and Great Britain maneuvered against each other for dominion of inner Asia. Khiva and Merv and much else was taken by the Russians, Punjab and Sind and much else by the British. The agents, the diplomats and adventurers of the two great powers, made surveys and plots. Persia, Afghanistan, and Sinkiang were eventually not taken by either side. This big Asian game brought immense suffering to the people. The British troops in Afghanistan behaved like the Germans in Yugoslavia in the Second World War. And they met the same fate.

The past is not dead, and the bids in this great game still affect the future of the people there. This makes it necessary to go back to the Protocols over and over again and try to clarify what actually happened. Of course it is possible to find out what is true and what is false.

What is important to us is determined by our own time. We know that Bismarck distorted the contents of the Ems dispatch. But this in itself does not once and for all determine the character of the initial stage of the Franco-Prussian War. It is for the sake of this great game that I get no sleep this night in Kashgar. When I here watch this game between Russia and Great Britain in the nineteenth century, the pattern changes, although the minutes are the same. I wonder how come I did not see this before.

Once I spent three years reading accounts from the time of the great game. Diaries and memoirs and travel descriptions and recent accounts. That was not so strange. I had arrived in this part of Asia, and I had to get my historical bearings. In the spring of 1958 I sat by a hired desk in a little basement apartment by the old Shemiran road north of Teheran. That was then on the outskirts of the city, quiet and peaceful. The area is now long since surrounded by the growing city. Gun was painting but I could not even start writing, because I had come to realize that my European chronological map did not apply. In 1959 we lived in Kabul. I used to go to the library of the French Archaeological Delegation to borrow books. They were helpful. In 1960 we rented the ground floor of a house in Defence Colony on the outskirts of New Delhi. I had begun writing in Kabul. Here I finished my book.

The way from Teheran through Kabul to Delhi naturally gave a very special perspective on the great game. Each city and each village offered fresh evidence of British brutality and British outrages against humanity. Each book I opened testified again to British deceit and British cynicism. The difference between the British officer and gentleman and the Prussian *Junker* and SS man was reduced to the fact that the British gentleman did not do it at home. (Except in Ireland, of course.) This attitude was quite natural to my friends. United States imperialism had succeeded to British imperialism in this area. That was the great danger. And the fight against United States imperialism, just like the fight against British imperialism, was the same fight for liberation. In the evenings we met friends in Delhi. The older ones told us about years of imprisonment under the British and about assault and torture.

This was all correct. I had read the minutes properly. The mistakes I made and the mistakes in my Afghanistan book have nothing to do with this particular discussion. They refer to questions such as how to judge the Pashtukistan dispute between Afghanistan and Pakistan or the estimated number of inhabitants in Afghan cities.

Looking at the great game from the Kashgar horizon the picture changed. It was understandable that the Russian actions had seemed less prominent when I had looked at history from cities where the ruins left by the barbarity of British troops and the monuments remaining after the departed imperial British lords dominated the view. But that which could be seen so clearly and prominently here in Kashgar I ought to have been able to discern also from Kabul or Delhi.

In the nineteenth century Russia was economically backward, it was corrupt and inefficient, an empire of mud and lice and poverty, whereas England was the richest country in the world. From London was governed a dominion mightier than all previous ones. But how did the great game go?

Was it three thousand men the Russians lost when they conquered the countries between the Caspian Sea and Pamir? In the same period the British lost whole armies in countries they were never even able to conquer. How did they get involved in these strange wars?

Look at China! The British waged war there. But Russia won.

What about the game over Kashgar in Yakub Beg's time? The British attempt to exert influence gave Russia a chance to march into the Ili area. When the British intervened to help Yakub Beg survive and suggested that the Chinese government accept him as a vassal, the British government signed Yakub Beg's death sentence, since the officials who quietly had been prepared to let Yakub Beg exist were now forced to decide to get rid of him, the sooner the better.

From the Napoleonic wars onward, Great Britain and Russia certainly took part in a great game—a cold war, we would say—for dominion over the countries between the Caucasus and the Pamirs. Certainly British diplomats and British officers, decorated, brave, and wellborn, and British agents, spies, and politicians, all brave even if not all gentlemen, played the game . . . but the Russians won. The British got involved in wars they had not expected; they were exposed to the whole world as the crooks they evidently were (it was evident); they lost their diplomatic cards before they had had time to play them; whatever they did and said was turned against them, and at the end of the century, a safe boundary was to be drawn to secure the northern border of India, it was said. The British then signed a treaty regarding the border between Afghanistan and Russia in the middle of Chinese territory without even managing to consult China. The British diplomats were proud of the security they had now gained, since the Russians accepted in silence that the British had grabbed a bit of Chinese territory. Naturally, the minister and consul-general Petrovsky smiled in Kashgar.

I was not wrong in seeing the British as crooks in the great game from the horizons of Teheran, Kabul, and New Delhi. They certainly *were* crooks. But my mistake was not to take a closer look at the Russian maneuvers. They were the winners right through this century. With absolutely superior skill, the shrewd diplomats of this corrupt and decayed autocracy outwitted the representatives of the rich and mighty British Empire.

The Russians were crooks just like the British. The people tried to stay away from them for as long as possible. What had been gained by Russian diplomats with skill and refinement was then ruled with a knout by corrupt Russian police and officials. British colonialism needed for its existence native teachers and officials; the British founded industries and opened roads to increase their profit. British colonialism was all exploitation, which at the same time, of necessity, created a national bourgeoisie with its own schools and colleges and a free press (which actually did exist). This was necessary; this was how the empire was made profitable. But British imperialism also had to bring up its successors. It is now thirty years since the British had to leave their Asian empire.

This became visible to me in Kashgar. But it ought not have been necessary for me to go to Sinkiang to get this view of the nineteenth century. That was after all what Marx and Engels saw. They wrote a great deal about the great game.

Now the morning is hot and misty and yellow. The night is over. I must wake Gun. We have to pack. We're off to Khotan today. My eyes burn from lack of sleep, I pack up my notes and books.

Of course, I know why I didn't want to see the part old Russia really played in the great game but was content to state that Russia was as bad as Great Britain, two of a kind, and then to describe British brutality. Here in this old czarist hall of mirrors in the extreme west of China, I know very well. I put Engels' work on Czarist foreign policy into the larger of the two bags of books. It was certainly not unknown to me in 1960, but I did not then let it explain to me Russia's nineteenth-century foreign policy but stopped at the point where I said that Russia and Great Britain had both acted like crooks. It was true, but it did not explain anything.

The czarist policy in Asia became clearer to me and I found it easier to understand Engels when I traveled in Turkmenistan in 1965 and saw the increasing national oppression of the Turkmen people. The occupation of Czechoslovakia in 1968 was pure czarist policy. This made it necessary once more to evaluate the nineteenth century. And here in Kashgar I could now see the great game from another angle.

The past regains life. If I were now to write about the Danish-Swedish wars of the seventeenth century, I would very likely deal with the battles in a general way, and stress the suffering of the people. It is less likely that I would discuss the politics of Sweden and Denmark. Possibly this is wrong. I know for sure, though, that my 1960 description of the great game has become insufficient.

In a position where Moscow more and more openly follows the tracks of the czar, the czarist policy assumes great importance. Today's events won't change the reality of the past, but they may change our view of the past.

These questions are far from abstract. Take the border issue. Whoever wants to understand why the Kremlin today has opened such a barrage against China, pretending that China is demanding Siberia and wants to cut large pieces out of Soviet territory, ought to study the basic documents. They were infamous. China also sees them as such today. The Kremlin ought to be able to afford to agree with Marx and Engels about czarist policy and agree with Lenin that they ought to be revised. China is after all prepared to accept as boundary the border line drawn up by these unequal treaties. That would not only be a decent policy, it would also serve the interests of the population on both sides of the border and fulfill the tradition of Marx and Lenin. But the Soviet propaganda campaign against China becomes quite comprehensible if the Kremlin's present foreign policy is seen as a continuation of that of the czar.

The documents prove that the troops now holding Pamir do this without support from any valid international treaty. The question could of course be solved; that would not in itself be difficult. But to admit that the question can be solved implies admitting that there is a question to solve, and this would mean great risks to the Kremlin leaders. If China can have an unequal treaty rendered null and void, what about Japan? And Rumania? And what about Poland? By continuing the czarist policy, the Kremlin has ended up in an impasse.

I go in to wake Gun, but she is awake already, and reading in bed. "Have you been up all night?" she asks. And then: "It will be hot today."

After we have packed and are having our breakfast tea, she continues: "Of course the Russians wanted Kashgar. Kashgar and Ili are the granaries of inner Asia. What did Rakmov say yesterday? The resources available hold a potential of multiplying the arable land thirty times and multiplying the yield. All they have to do in Kashgar is to use water rationally and scientifically and build proper dams and canals. Kashgar is a rich agricultural area already and it could become even more so. But that technique existed a hundred years ago as well. No wonder Petrovsky sat in this consulate spinning his intrigues!"

13
Yipek Yoli

The red wind blows, hot and dusty over Kashgar. I've eaten a large bowl of sour milk and poured a bucket of cold water over my head, but I still feel the same thirst in my throat, and my hair is cracklingly dry again. We pack our luggage, lash the typewriter cover which keeps coming off, and spread white cotton cloths over Gun's camera cases.

It is morning. The asphalt glitters with water. The water trucks have passed and flushed the dust of yesterday away. We drive toward the center of town. Gun wants to get four knives of Kashgar steel. She made up a list at breakfast: "This for uncle, that for aunt . . ."

On our way to town we see three trucks coming down from Pakistan, now driving the last stretch over the plain toward Kashgar. The trucks are dusty. The drivers wave.

"We all know each other here," one driver says. "I've driven that route. You need a health certificate to be allowed up there. Heart and lungs and all that. If the weather is bad in the mountains you may have trouble sometimes."

Of course Kashgar is still a market town. The bazaars are waking up in the streets behind the mosque. Shutters open, and behind them bicycle repairers and shoemakers, goldsmiths, tailors, and copper-smiths are at work.

"But the forms of ownership change," Abdullah says. "We won't let capitalism take root and grow again. The craftsmen have set up a cooperative."

The large department store has opened and is already full of people. They have come in from the villages of the district to do their shopping.

A young woman in a head scarf and a flower-printed skirt is unlocking the large double doors of the handcraft emporium.

"She's a Kazakh," Gun says. "Look at her boots!"

Abdur Rahman, party secretary, with the sixth production brigade, Chira

Nur Ashim, leader of the seventh work team of the first production brigade, Pakhtaklik People's Commune, Kashgar district

Rotsemi Salan, vice-chairman of the revolutionary committee at the rug factory in Khotan

Ruzi Khalla

Ruzi Turdi, chairman of the revolutionary committee, Turfan

Ushur Nijaz, kareze builder, Turfan

Mehmeduli, Ili

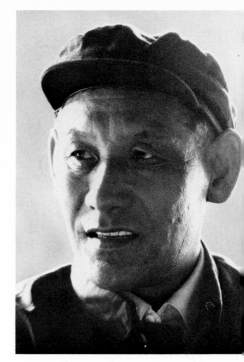

Elyashar, Ili

Chepisem, Ili

Kaderbeg, Ili

Yang Yung-chen, work-team vice-leader of the ninth company of Regiment 145, Shihezi

Chang Yu-lan, party secretary of the Chauyang Production Brigade, Santakuo People's Commune, Ansi county, Kansu

Chou Wen-chi, a young oil technician, and Chu Yu-chen, the oil technician in charge, Yümen

In the wide shop windows on the square there are beautiful embroideries, skillfully forged Kashgar daggers, instruments, jewelry, and silver articles displayed on rugs in lustrous colors with shades of blue and pink. The patterns are bold and free.

"But the rugs come from Khotan," Abdullah says.

"In the long run the department stores and their cooperative selling centers will take over the functions of the old bazaar," Rakmov says. "The old customs will change in due course. In other oases, the smaller and more remote ones, bazaars are still what they used to be in Kashgar, minus the haggling and cheating, of course. Things are changing here. Kashgar is becoming a modern town, a big city. The young people generally prefer to shop in the department stores when they come to town. There are not just one or two or ten different models of transistor radios in this big department store; there may be up to twenty of them, you know. And they are not only from Sinkiang but also from Shanghai and Peking and other places. There are goods from Pakistan and from all over Sinkiang and all over China. Supply is a matter of importance, since it serves the people. When people come to town from the remote production brigades, they like to go to the department store. It's like an exhibition, too, where we show what we can produce.

"People in the Kashgar district can now buy 78 times more than they could in 1948. They buy expensive consumer goods such as sewing machines and bicycles and watches and high-quality transistor radios with world-wide ranges. We aim at every family getting these 'four bigs.' And families save money to get them. The income is secure and we encourage saving. The people now have 350 times more money in their bank accounts than they had in 1950. But we also have to make sure that there are goods to buy and that they are of high quality. The retail trade is a political question.

"Of course there are difficulties. The marriage age, for example. We have managed to raise it to twenty years in general. But that is still too low. This is an important question for the revolution. The women are 'half of heaven.' The old custom of early marriages, of girls becoming wives before they get to be independent, still survives. But we have to fight it in a proper way, for it is in just such questions that the reactionary forces are at their strongest. The class enemy won't tell the old poor peasants that it is too bad that they can buy 78 times more than they could before liberating themselves from landlords and usury. That wouldn't work. But he can send a reactionary religious preacher to whisper about the indecency of girls going to school and becoming independent instead of being married off while they are still children.

"We must be very careful there. Any mistake on our part, gives the class enemy a chance to succeed in destroying the unity of the people. So we go about it slowly and gently. But the women have to be given all our support in their fight for equality and liberty. That means we must never give up the claim of free choice and mutual love as the only basis for marriage as we strive to raise the age of marrying."

As we drive out of the city center, the wide new esplanades open; young poplars are growing and converting the new road into a shaded avenue. They are planted in double rows along the open gutter where water runs toward the city gardens. The gutters here in inner Asia are not for sewage but for irrigation.

"That's the new railroad station," Rakmov says. "It's almost ready. Once the railroad is opened to regular traffic, everything will be easier, and we shall also be able to increase industrialization. Great efforts have to be made if we are to succeed in developing the agriculture as we hope to. We have the sun and the land; water too. All we need to add is work and plants, machines, phosphate, and ammonium sulphate.

"The old trade route from China to the West went from Kashgar. This rich agricultural land between the great desert and the high mountains was one of the important stations for reloading, and merchants from all over Asia would meet in the Kashgar bazaar. The caravans came there by two large roads from the East. These roads went on either side of the great desert, the one north of it connecting the oases below Tien Shan. A railroad is now being built there, which already reaches from Urumchi down to Korla via Baghrash Kul. It then continues down under the mountains over Kucha and Aksu to Kashgar.

"The tunnels take much work," Rakmov says. "In some places it was as difficult to build a railroad here in Sinkiang between Urumchi and Kashgar as it was to build one from Chengtu in Szechuan to Kunming in Yunnan. There were many technical problems in constructing the tunnels. We set up the basic plans immediately after the liberation, and worked out the details in 1958. But only in recent times has the work of construction really begun. The railroad should be open for general and regular traffic in 1985, and it must be ready for it before then."

But the rail connection is not only for Kashgar. One line is planned all around the Tarim basin. It is now extended toward Khotan and is then to go on to Keriya and Niya and farther east. This road south of Takla Makan where the railroad is now to be built is the oldest of the two large trade routes eastward from Kashgar. It is one of the roads of humanity, older than all history.

On this road across the mountains and deserts, the people of the Tigris and the Euphrates, of the Mediterranean countries and the Nile, were in contact with the people living around the Yellow River, long before our written history had begun reporting on journeys or diplomats and armies. From these mountains down toward Pamir, lapis lazuli was taken in Badakhshan and brought west to Sumer and Egypt five thousand years ago. Jade from Khotan was taken to the Yellow River. When the road was first described in chronicles, it was already an ancient one.

It is now one hundred years since the route was given the name we know it by: "The Silk Road." In 1877 a professor of geography at Bonn University, Count Ferdinand von Richthofen, gave a lecture entitled "Über die zentralasiatischen Seidenstrassen bis zum 2. Jahrhundert n. Chr." He was one of the founders of modern physical geography. The name he gave to the route was useful. I buy books and posters at the Khotan bookshop. Among them is a book on the newest textile finds from excavations along the Silk Road. The title is *Yipek Yoli*—"The Silk Road."

Among the footnotes I see a reference to the great French Sinologist Edouard Chavannes, and one to Berthold Laufer's basic work *Sino-Iranica* of 1919. I know that a Chinese edition is being published of Joseph Needham's monumental work *Science and Civilization in China*. China respects those scientists who have contributed to the development of knowledge. That Sinology, however, which is a part of the intelligence services of the superpowers, or that which is used as an ideological disguise for imperialism, colonialism, and various types of racism, is looked upon in China as hostile and fundamentally unscientific activity.

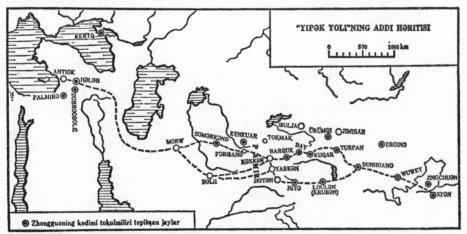

The Silk Routes Between the Mediterranean and the Yellow River

It is not too difficult to identify the various names of the places, since the Uighur alphabet is based on the Latin. Xi'an = Sian (old Changan). Hoten = Khotan. Kaxgar = Kashgar. Turpan = Turfan. (Map from *Yipek Yoli—Han, Tang Tokulmiri* [Xinjiang halk naxriyati, 1973].)

14
Let Us Talk of Silk

We don't have to start with the Roman emperors. Look at King Henry VIII of England! When he was dressing up, he pulled on his silken hose. Elizabeth, his daughter, became such a mighty queen that she could wear her black knitted silk stockings every day. This created envy and fame in European courts.

Nothing is like silk. In the northern Germanic tongue there are two words for it—one for the cloth and one for the yarn. But the meanings of the words intermingle. The word for the yarn traveled up the large rivers and along the trade routes through Eastern Europe, and remains of silk have been found in tombs from the Viking era. The word for the cloth came from the continent. Both words originate from China, the country of the Seres. They were called *seres* because silk in their language was *se*.

Silk is the noblest of all textile materials. It is light and strong, cool and warm. Undyed, it has a living, pure hue; dyed, it assumes a deep luster. It is comfortable to wear, beautiful to look at. It protects without clinging, allows the skin to breathe without chilling it. The thickest knotted rugs are most beautiful in silk, and the thinnest veil is durable in silk. There's nothing like silk, pure silk. Creamy yellow and soft. Spun by the larva of the true mulberry spinner *Bombyx mori*. An animal tamed five thousand years ago.

There are plenty of different types of silk as such. Spiders' webs are of silk. There are numerous moths who spin cocoons to enclose themselves when they are pupae. Many of them are wild, and in Bengal and other places people make raw silk from cocoons where the thread is too thin to be wound. It is carded and spun. But the real mulberry spinner feeds on mulberry leaves and can be cultivated. *Bombyx mori* is a

112

domesticated spinning moth that has lived with man for thousands of years and is dependent upon him.

The eggs laid by the spinning female are minute, weighing about 0.9 milligrams. They can be kept for some time at a low temperature. At the right moment—when mulberry leaves are available—the temperature is increased to about 28°C. After ten days to three weeks the larvae hatch. They are then given fresh mulberry leaves, and develop incredibly fast. After one month and four changes of skin, the fully grown larvae are about 6 centimeters long. That is when they spin their cocoons. If the cocoons are left alone, the moths will break out of them after a few weeks. Grey, insignificant moths who copulate, multiply, and die.

The cocoons used for silk production are taken away, killed by heat, and dried. They are sorted: cocoons showing any sign of disease are put aside. Cocoons of similar quality are gathered in series and immersed in hot water, which must, however, not boil. If the water is too cold, the cocoon will not dissolve, and if it is too hot, the cocoon will fall apart and cannot be used. Then the cocoons are brushed, and the external threads come off. What is left is a little ball on a hard core, and this ball is now unwound. The thread that is used is very fine, between 300 and 900 meters long. While it is being wound, five to seven threads are wound together to make it strong enough to be used.

Silk production, in other words, demands a highly developed agriculture with specialized techniques, and a well-defined scientific tradition. The leap from gathering the cocoons in the woods, dissolving them in hot water, and carding and spinning and producing raw silk, to cultivating mulberry spinners and producing silk, is vast. Not only are the careful cultivation of mulberry trees and the proper regulation of temperatures and standardized routines necessary, but also the unwinding procedure that distinguishes silk from various forms of carded and spun raw silk demands machines and high technology.

It was the highly developed Chinese science and technology that made the step to silk production possible. This science and technology in itself was the result of the Chinese working people's fight for increased production. The silk production then posed new demands, which spurred technology forward. The basic inventions and the great scientific breakthroughs are not achieved in isolated ivory towers but by the working people involved in active production. Diderot realized this when he and the other encyclopedists represented the rising European bourgeoisie. He therefore focused his interest on the reality of production. In his day the intelligentsia of Chinese feudalism had become a rigid mandarinate, which hampered China's development.

Today one can spend an afternoon in Khotan discussing with Chinese intellectuals of various nationalities the history of cranks and driving belts and eccentric motion. Theirs is now the same fascination that once was Diderot's. The European intellectuals, however, discuss beauty and tradition and art, just as the feudal mandarins once did in China.

The problem was to take a sticky little ball of silk, about 3 centimeters long and 2 centimeters in diameter, and unwind a thread of almost 1,000 meters. Two thousand years ago, the Chinese farmers had learned the principle of the crank and designed a winnowing fan driven by a crank. The crank was one of the fundamental inventions. From the eleventh century we have the first printed description of a silk-winding machine using a foot pedal and a driving belt to unwind silk thread from cocoons. The silk waste was spun with a spinning wheel, an invention of the Indian cotton growers.

"You see," Jin Ching said, "The people are the driving force in world history: Chairman Mao is right. That goes for the silk technology as well."

It was afternoon in Khotan, and we were sitting in the meeting room of the revolutionary committee discussing the history of silk in Khotan. Jin Ching was a lecturer at the teachers college. He said, "There are some of us who used to get together to discuss problems regarding Khotan's history, things like the interpretation of old documents or new archaeological finds. We can also discuss such things as the social situation and the class struggle at the turn of the century. I have studied history at the university and also lecture in history at the teachers college, but these discussions of ours have nothing to do with the school. We take a personal interest and have different individual experiences, and we get together to discuss these issues. It certainly has a political aim; we are taking part in the fight for the superstructure."

The other two delegates were Abdur Rahman, an older technician from the experimental plant for silkworm breeding, and Jo Li-chun, who worked in the Department of Traffic and Industry of the Khotan district.

"You need good cocoons for good silk," Abdur Rahman said. "Two things are required for good cocoons: experience and a suitable climate. Of these two, the experience of the people is the most important.

"We have now in China mulberry trees from Hainan in the south to Heilungkiang in the north, from Shantung in the east to Khotan here in the west. The genuine silkworm comes from China and has spread all over the world.

"In ancient times it was wild. People gathered cocoons. They then started to breed it intentionally, which was a great step forward. The cocoon as we know it now is not a natural product, it is cultivated. We have found cocoons in tombs from the Late Stone Age. Five thousand years ago they were using the silkworm. There are other indications of this, like the traditional decorative patterns based on the shape and behavior of the silkworm. And in the Chinese language the signs for silkworm and mulberry tree appear very early.

"The center was the valley of the Yellow River, and then the Yangtze valley and Szechuan. There is a chronicle about a Chinese princess who smuggled silk eggs here in the fifth century during the Northern Wei dynasty, and so silk culture started here. But we have had silk longer than that. The cultivation of silk spread west from here. The Silk Road was a cultural road too. Silk spread from Khotan toward India and Iran and then farther west all over the world."

"In 1959 we opened a tomb north of Niya," Jo Li-chun said. "It was the tomb of a Niya ruler, a local lord. We found two coffins with mummified bodies in them. We have a dry climate. It was a man and a woman; the woman was dressed in silk, with a pattern of written characters. The find dated from the Eastern Han dynasty, that is the first two centuries of the Christian era."

"Khotan has long been an important focal point in China," Jin Ching said. "This was China's function with Central Asia and Europe. The silk caravans were of great importance; with the caravans silk was exported as cloth.

"On his way home, General Chang Ch'ien passed by here, and ever since then we have had organized relations. The envoys from the emperor's court brought silk as gifts to the local rulers. They sent their sons to study at the court in Changan, the present Sian, and the ruler of Khotan was the first local ruler of the Tarim basin to be nominated an official of the empire, after he had spent some time in the capital. The road was properly organized at the time of the Western Han dynasty, and Khotan was an important station on this route.

"The southern route went from Tunhwang here to Khotan and then via Yarkand to Persia and farther on. The fact that this trade route was secure meant that international contacts grew. Trade increased, as did cultural exchange and mutual visits. China exported various goods west, but mainly silk. The caravans were large, comprising several hundred people. The journey took a long time; they had to reckon eight or nine years to go from Changan to Persia or northern India and back. At that time many merchants came to China from the West to buy silk. They settled along the trade route and in Changan.

"This was a luxury trade. Before the silk reached Rome, its price rose so that it had to be paid for by its weight in gold. We have made a number of finds of silk cloth along this route. Especially since liberation, our archaeologists have been able to do some research on the trade with the help of these fragments of cloth. The Niya finds are part of a whole series of similar discoveries. Thus we know now that silk was sent to Khotan at the time of the Western Han dynasty before the Christian era. The documents confirm this. We also know that silk cloth was used by the ruling class here in Khotan during the Eastern Han dynasty at the beginning of the Christian era. We know that the tradition of breeding silkworms and producing silk spread west through Khotan.

"It is more difficult to tell when the people here started to breed silkworms and produce silk locally and how long they were just receiving gifts of silk and transporting and using it. It is not a question of invention alone, but of a complex cultural unit as a whole, of various different kinds of knowledge connected together: from the growing of mulberry trees and the treatment of larvae to the art of unwinding the silk thread from the cocoon. We cannot tell yet when Khotan began to produce its own silk.

"Khotan recognized the suzerainty of the emperor quite early. Its ruler spent long periods in the capital, and contacts were frequent. Local coins were minted according to the Han dynasty pattern, and the administration and the titles of the officials were basically those of the empire. Its cultural influence was strong too. Even in the time following the fall of the Han dynasty the Silk Road was kept open, and the Northern Wei dynasty tried to strengthen the connections with Persia and kept the route via Khotan open. It is in this period that Khotan became a center for silk production.

"Khotan flourished in the T'ang dynasty. Large routes led west from Changan: one route north of Tien Shan past what is now Ining in Ili; another just south of Tien Shan to Kashgar and farther west; still another through Khotan, later splitting into two. Afterwards, one branch joined the route from Kashgar and continued toward Persia and farther west. The other branch turned off across the mountain passes down toward the Indus valley, and down by the sea the goods were loaded onto vessels sailing to the Western countries.

"The best description we have of Khotan from this time comes from Hsüan Tsang. He had been to India to study religion and collect Buddhist scriptures. He spent a little more than six months here in the winter of 644–45 and then continued east with a caravan. Khotan was then under the emperor's sovereignty, and Hsüan Tsang, who had defied the emperor's prohibition to leave China, was waiting here for a pardon for his defiance and for permission to return with the scriptures. The emperor was glad to greet him, and he arrived in Changan sometime in the spring of 645. While working on the translation of the scriptures he had brought home with him, he at the same time dictated the notes on his travels to a monk, who compiled them into a coherent story. Hsüan Tsang was not the first Buddhist monk to pass through Khotan with holy Indian scriptures—far from it. Many monks and pilgrims wandered along this route. Neither was he the first one to describe his journey. Fa-Hsien passed through this place in A.D. 400 on his way to India, and he described Khotan as 'a rich and happy country with a thriving people. All inhabitants are Buddhists and relish in their Faith.' But that is all he says about Khotan. The rest are religious descriptions of rich monasteries and ceremonies and the difficulties of traveling through the desert. They are valuable in their own way but tell nothing about silk. Hsüan Tsang, however, or the one who wrote down and compiled his stories, tried to be as careful and detailed as the historians when they wrote accounts of foreign countries.

"He describes Khotan as mainly a stone and sand desert. But the fertile land, which is limited, is very fertile and gives rich harvests and much fruit. In Khotan they make rugs, felt, and fine silks. They also mine white and black jade. The climate is agreeable but there are sand storms. Customs are refined and the local crafts highly developed. The people are thriving and well settled. They appreciate music and like song and dance. A few of them wear hides and wool, but most of them wear silk and cloth.

"He also says that they are Buddhists and have five thousand monks and that they write like the Indians. Hsüan Tsang also tells how the silk reached Khotan. His account has become well known. In olden days, Hsüan Tsang says, they knew nothing about mulberry trees or silkworms. But they heard that these things existed in the East. Therefore they sent a delegation to ask for the secret of producing silk. The emperor, who preferred to keep it a secret, would not let others find out how silk was made. He had all border stations watched and allowed neither mulberry seeds nor silkworm eggs to be taken out of the empire. The king of Khotan then asked to marry a princess of the emperor's house as a token of his fidelity and his veneration. The emperor kindly agreed to this wish. The king of Khotan then sent an envoy to the princess and asked this envoy to tell her that Khotan had neither mulberry trees nor silkworms. If she wanted to wear silk, she would have to bring some seeds and eggs, with which they could make her beautiful dresses.

"The princess heard this and considered it, and then obtained secretly some mulberry seeds and silkworm eggs, which she hid in her voluminous hairdress. When she reached the gate the guards searched her thoroughly, but they dared not touch her hair. The princess was taken with great pomp to the royal palace and brought her mulberry seeds and silkworm eggs there. In the spring she had the seeds sown, and when it was time for the larvae to hatch, leaves were gathered for them. At first they had to eat any kind of leaves, before there were any real mulberry leaves obtainable. The queen then had an inscription made on a stone, which said: 'It is prohibited to kill the silkworm. Only when the moth has left the cocoon may the silk be used.'

"This story indicates that they first used raw silk, spun silk, before changing over to real silk. But it should be remembered that this was written by Buddhist monks who, due to their religious ideology, were against the killing of the silkworm in its cocoon. It is hard to tell to what extent Hsüan Tsang's story reflects the real silk production in seventh-century Khotan. But we do know that the story of the princess bringing seeds and eggs was widespread. In Dandan-Oilik out in the desert, a painting was found during the excavations of 1914, showing the princess arriving in Khotan with a basket full of cocoons. One of the girls in attendance points at the princess's hair and another girl is weaving. This is one of the pictures essential to China's history. But it was found by Aurel Stein at a time when imperialists could still rob China of whatever they found and when our historic relics were stolen from us to be sold by antique dealers in Europe or America or to museums in various Western cities. We respect and admire foreign researchers like Joseph Needham, whose work has increased our knowledge of our own past. Our researchers too contribute to the exploration of our people's history. But we consider those who stole or robbed or removed cultural monuments as thieves, regardless of whether they stole in China or Greece or Egypt. That is our principal stand."

We were now eating melons and ice cream. The ice-cream factory in Khotan worked intensely during this hot summer. Ice cream was being sold on every street corner. Jin Ching said:

"You can buy ice cream in the streets without fear, it's completely hygienic. It is important to make sure that people have access to good harmless ice cream in summer." After we finished eating he continued: "Shall I continue? Good! There are other variations on this theme. In one version the princess brings the silkworm eggs without the king knowing it. When the larvae hatch, the king's ministers accuse her in front of the king of breeding poisonous little snakes. The king commands her to burn all the little snakes, but the queen, not daring to tell the king the truth, since he does not know what silk is, saves some of them and breeds them secretly. Later on, when she shows the king the silk, he repents and confesses his sin to a monk. To expiate his sin, to have burned so many silkworms, he has a large stupa built. This would have happened in the Eastern Han dynasty, and this story comes from Tibet. It also gives an account of other Khotan kings who married princesses from the Changan emperor's court in the Han dynasty.

"When you go to Tunhwang you must be sure to go and see a cave from the time of the Five Kingdoms in the tenth century. There are large paintings there of the king of Khotan, Li Sheng-tian, marrying the daughter of the ruler of Tunhwang, the powerful viceroy. Such things have happened many times in history. The princess who figures in the stories probably had her prototype in many aristocratic girls from the inland who really existed. And there is very likely some core of truth in the account itself. At least the story reflects the true fact that the knowledge spread to Khotan at the time when Khotan was connected with China. The economic relations were strong then as well.

"According to written documents we know that silk production began in the Wei dynasty in the fifth century. This is pointed out specifically in the official chronicles. But there should have been some local silk production even before. Later in the T'ang dynasty it was extensive enough to be remarked upon, and Khotan became one of China's silk districts.

"The question how this happened won't find its answer for some time. The history of silk in Europe is not clear either. Possibly two Christian monks wandered this way in the mid-sixth century with silkworm eggs hidden in their staffs. If they had been in China for as long as it is said, they must have heard about the princess with the silkworm eggs in her hair. It sets one wondering. That story is not really confirmed either, although we do know that Greece at the time of the T'ang dynasty became a center for its own silk production.

"Extensive archaeological research will be necessary, and it will be long before we can clarify these facts. But the Urumchi museum sent some people here in 1959 to excavate around Niya, and they found quite a lot, not just seals from the Han dynasty and silks and coins but various tools and equipment, pieces of rugs, and waxed cotton. It will take time to ascertain the value of all this. Only after liberation were we able to study the old iron mines of the Han dynasty in the mountains twenty-five kilometers away from here."

"Khotan now has 60 percent of Sinkiang's silk-cocoon production," said Abdur Rahman. "The silkworm is bred in each of our seven counties. Our climate is suitable, and we have the best eggs now. Some brigades achieve a profit of 10,000 yuan annually selling cocoons to the state. So it is an important secondary activity.

"The reactionaries and the KMT kept production down. The years 1940–1941 were all right, but then production went down, owing to various factors. For one thing, the social oppression of the breeders was very bad. Besides, different kinds of artificial silk were taking over the market. Silk production did not pay off, the prices were squeezed, and the breeders suffered. The eggs degenerate after some time; high quality cannot be maintained for any long period of time if the breed is isolated. Also, the cocoons were afflicted by several diseases. All this contributed. But the social and political oppression made it impossible to stop production from diminishing. In 1949 the total production of cocoons in Khotan was only 17 tons.

"Chairman Mao Tse-tung emphasized the importance of silk production, and after liberation the party led the work with great attention and arranged several study courses. We now produce 450 tons of silk cocoons, and by deliberate cross-breeding we have overcome the degeneration and raised the quality and fought the diseases.

"The party has paid great attention to the planting of mulberry trees. Since the liberation, we have planted 5,750,000 of them. We now have 5,900 nurseries with different varieties of our own and those from other parts of the country, 136 in all. One has to select and cross them and find the tree that gives the best result in each place. The quality of the silk also depends on the leaves. One has to select the right leaves for the larvae at the right moment. The dark varieties usually are best for the larvae that are to give silk for dyeing. The right luster demands the right larvae on the right leaves at the right moment. Books cannot teach you that; it takes experience and guidance. That is why the party makes sure the young learn from us and carry our experience further. The party does not accept any negligence."

"The feudal exploitation led to bad quality and reduced production," Jo Li-chun said. "One could say that the Khotan silk production was on the decline during the whole of the Ch'ing dynasty and in the time of the warlords and under Sheng Shih-ts'ai and the KMT. Khotan was declining as a center for silk production. Yes! All of China went down and was pushed out of the world silk market.

"The silk weavers could not afford to wear silk; it was for the nobles, and thus was called *khanum etles*. If the silk was of high quality and woven at home, the master might keep one-twelfth, but ordinary silk gave only one twenty-fourth to the producer. In 1949 there were only sixty looms left in use here. Khotan produced four tons of silk, and the home-woven product was only 14,000 meters. That was all that remained of the Khotan which had once been a center of world trade.

"Now we produce 144 tons of raw silk annually. In 1953 we started to build the new silk mill, but we are also increasing the production of home-woven silk. We walk on two legs! Seventy work teams in eleven folk communes work with homespun silk. We have four hundred such looms going, producing 126,700 meters annually. In that way we also develop the artistic traditions of the people. If we add up all the different varieties, including velvet and brocade, more than two hundred different types of silk are now manufactured in Khotan. This is not only sold in China and abroad. No, the people here use silk. It is not called *khanum etles* ["lady's cloth"] any more; it's only called *etles* ["cloth"].

"The quality is steadily improving too. In 1955 77 percent of the production was first class. Now it is 86 percent. Khotan is again becoming a great silk center. Most of our export goes to Pakistan, where they appreciate our patterns."

15
A Walk in Khotan

Khotan is a dusty town. Light grey clouds whirl up around our feet as we walk the narrow streets. The desert wind is heavy with dust, and already at daybreak it has spread a thin red veil over the city. But the morning is fresh.

We have almost an hour and a half before the day's program is to begin. We have taken morning tea made with our thermos water, poured cold water on our heads, and are now up and dressed. It is in the morning that we can walk and talk things over. We work during the day, and in the evening I arrange my notes. I also have to check our equipment, blow the dust off the cameras, and take out film for the next day's work for Gun. She writes the journal.

"Do you remember," she says, "how we laughed when Börje Sandelin was given the king's personal scholarship and went to the royal palace to have tea and King Gustavus Adolphus VI told him: 'Young man, always remember to write your journal every night. Louise and I have always done that when we travel. When we are back home Louise reads me the journal in the evening. That way you see so much more. We have kept a travel diary for almost twenty years now. It's practical.' "

Khotan is not a big town; it is low and grey. Houses of clay with flat roofs. It has only 40,000 inhabitants. There are few monuments. The streets are wide and asphalt-paved in the center where the large roads intersect. The houses are three stories high, and there are the department stores and offices. Following the asphalted street west one passes the new industries. Later it becomes a highway toward Yarkand. To the east it goes toward Keriya. To the north are the market square and the cinema. That street is a shopping area with a bookshop, a hardware store, a shop for local cooperative products, a textile store, and many

122

others. Farther away is the new road. Khotan is to develop and be transformed, and the large new asphalt road from Yarkand to Keriya and on toward the inland runs in a bow north of the town. The traffic is to be eliminated in the town center. There are also new three-story blocks being built and new detached houses of burnt brick. Following the street south from the center, one reaches the remains of the old town wall, preserved as a cultural monument. To the west of this wall is where we live, in the district guest house. It is adjacent to the theater and some assembly rooms in a little park.

It is now a long time since the last mandarin left his *yamen* in China, but even if the name *yamen,* like the mandarins, has disappeared, tradition still retains a certain significance. The *yamen*—the flag gate —in the days of the empire was the residence and offices of the magistrate with an official seal. His retainers lived and worked there as well. It could be compared to a provincial governor's residence. The district offices with guest houses and assembly rooms still form a detached group in smaller towns all over China. It is practical: cadres traveling on business need a place to spend the night. There is tradition in practicalities.

It is early morning, and the air is still fresh. We leave the guest house and wander past the dining room and the theater. At the gate a truck is parked, hood open. Three men of about twenty are standing next to it, all in green military trousers, although they are not soldiers. Two of them are wearing the Uighur cap, whereas the third does not wear a hat at all, being Han. One of the Uighurs takes out the carburetor and blows, while the others watch. They discuss it. When we pass, they wave. Yesterday we met them in the dining room. They are drivers from Yarkand. They have been educated and taught to drive in the People's Liberation Army and have just been demobilized and given work in the Yarkand Traffic Office.

We walk along the old town wall toward the main street. Yesterday we walked straight to the south when we went out of the gate, and then we were behind the wall, beyond the old city. We had seen housing there, little streets meandering beside the irrigation canals. Water ran under the walls into hidden gardens, whose green branches hung over the wall onto the street. Women were standing in the doorways looking at us, and little children playing in the road stopped in the middle of their rope-skipping and stared at us. We continued through the village walking along the irrigation canals. People on bicycles on their way into Khotan got off their bikes and stared after us.

"It's not surprising that people stare at strangers in Khotan," Gun said. "I remember when I was a child, in northernmost Sweden we had never seen a real foreigner close up, and then one day we saw a German in a green coat and a funny little green hat with a feather and he had yellow gloves and gold-rimmed spectacles and a cigar. All the children stared at him till their eyes popped out. If we had seen him walking along our ditches, I don't know what we would have done. People are no different in Khotan than in northern Sweden. There are so few foreigners here."

By then we had already crossed the road and followed the little footpaths and canals to reach the wide road coming from Yarkand.

"I wonder about all these foreign journalists who say they were not allowed to walk the towns of China on their own," Gun said. "They seem to think that China is hiding her secrets in the outlying districts. But it is only a matter of normal courtesy. We join our foreign guests for a walk if we see them walking into the moors in the early morning. China is not like Chicago where we were warned at the university against going out, especially walking, at dusk. China is a civilized country."

All these years we have walked around the towns and villages that we've visited in China. Sometimes our hosts have accompanied us; that depends on the local authorities. Here in Khotan they were convinced that we could look after ourselves. Khotan still was one of the poor Chinese towns, but also Khotan was one of the politically most turbulent towns. Posters cried out slogans for and against the local party leadership. People stared at us, but nobody worried about where we went.

We now continued along the remains of the old town wall toward the main street running north–south. We turned off to the left, walking toward the center. On the walls posters were hanging like sheets to dry, fixed with pegs on lines extended from one window to another.

It was not quite morning yet, and all we saw in the street ahead of us were three women. One, dressed up in an Uighur silk dress with silk stockings and black pumps and carrying a flowered plastic bag, was hurrying toward us. An older Uighur woman in a flowered dress and trousers was sweeping the pavement in front of the door of the three-story building said to be the militia office and the department of public security in Khotan. Her dress, too, was of Khotan-patterned silk. The third woman was a young Han girl in a tidy blue cadre dress, standing at the bus stop.

"I bet she wears a beautiful flowered silk blouse under her blue jacket," Gun said. "The girls do. I can't understand where male journalists look if they don't see that. The girl students from Peking and especially Shanghai, who wear tattered and torn blue trousers that look as if they had just come from the canal works, let a little strip of patterned silk peep out from below their top. They find it chic. And the journalists don't see it! That girl was from Shanghai; one can recognize a Shanghai girl anywhere. It's like the Parisian girls in France—you see immediately where they come from. It has nothing to do with beauty or expensive clothes, it's just a fact. But the girls from Peking and Chungking are easily recognizable too. The Peking girls like to look serious and prim; they don't show as much silk, but prefer to hide it. The Chungking girls are the opposite; they have short skirts and bare legs. Young couples walk hand in hand in Chungking at dusk. They would never do that in Peking. You ought to write about that some time."

The women walk more proudly here than in the inland. They are used to being more free. No Confucius killed all laughter and forbade all dancing and made people false and boring. The mandarins complained about song and music and dance out here, finding it indecent. It was from here that many large dance troupes and orchestras used to come. All over China song and dance troupes from Sinkiang and Tibet are employed to inspire people to get rid of Confucian rigidity. It's possible, but it takes time. Still, a lot has changed in these fifteen years. There's a considerable difference.

We passed the town center, and continued over to the vegetable-market square. The first vendors had arrived. We walked in the alleys north of the square. They were old and meandering. Mud houses, one story high with flat roofs, clung to each other. The dust lay in drifts, tickling the throat, soft under our soles. A black sewage stream had dug through the sediments of street dust. We took a step over it. It didn't smell in this dry heat. The next time we go to Khotan, all this will be gone, the party secretary had told us. But large parts of Khotan are still like the towns in northern Afghanistan, mud and dust.

"What about its bygone beauty?" Gun said.

"Marco Polo said it was a noble city. Rich. What could he have meant by that? There are those who believe that in the eighteenth century Stockholm was a nice city with gay parties and lovely palaces, but in reality Stockholm in those days was the most miserable city in Europe with the highest mortality rate. Stockholm then was like a little Calcutta. I wonder what Khotan was actually like in Marco Polo's days."

We turned east again, going back to the main street. The alley in front of us was filled with a solid cloud of dust. There was noise and bustle;

the morning had already begun. A whole block of mud houses was being demolished. The workers had arrived. They were to build four-story residential blocks of burnt brick.

We discussed the politics of silk. It assumed its significance very early. Ezekiel talked about the silk raiment of Jerusalem upon which she had played the harlot in her exceeding sin. That was almost six hundred years before our era. If it was silk—you can never trust Bible translations. Aristotle seemed to be talking about silkworms and silk, but his zoology is not all that reliable. Cows don't wave their horns, and lions' legs don't spark, in spite of Aristotle's evidence. Still, it may be silk he is speaking about when he describes "a large worm with antlers and thus different from others. When this worm has spun himself a cocoon, women unwind the thread and spin it. They say this was first spun in the island of Kos by Pamphilia, the daughter of Plates."

This means either that, in the fourth century before Christ—that is, eight hundred years before, according to legend, monks came wandering from China to Emperor Justinian's court around 550—some form of thin and transparent silk or mixed silk was manufactured of un-wound silk or spun silk from some native moth's cocoon; or that the Kos women unwound Chinese silk and made their famous thin Kos cloth, or something else again. No finds of Kos cloth have been made. As far as I know, no tools have been found that could answer the question. That was why Jin Ching said that the European part of the silk history was not clear.

"At least it has been confirmed that the large silk consumption in Europe at the beginning of the Christian era was of silk transported through Khotan," Gun said. "Since this trade was so important, the silk production in any Mediterranean country must have been insignificant."

We had come back to the main street and were walking toward the market square again. The bicycles were now a ringing stream passing us on their way to the center.

The silk trade paid off. It paid the merchants a hundred times what they gave. That was the problem in Rome. Silk was the epitome of luxury, so luxurious that it was really indecent.

When the founder of Christian theology, the apostolic father Tertullian, was tormented by his young wife, he wrote the following: "You are the door of the devil, you fell for the tree of knowledge . . . you persuaded the man." He even considered it the fault of the woman that "God's son had to die."

Tertullian then listed some of the disgraces of the female sex. They wear "silken raiments, purple clothes, golden jewelry, and pearls."

He looked at the young flesh to whom he was wedded and wrote: Necks usually covered by pearls and emeralds are not prepared to bow down to the executor's sword. Away then with all jewelry! This is the time of the martyrs. Bend your necks for the yoke of Christ, your heads for your husbands!

After seventeen years in the Church, the marital suffering became intolerable, and he broke out in schismatic enthusiasm and fell out with the Church. But his condemnation of silk remained orthodox and accepted by the Church.

Silk had a bad reputation. Even in the eighteenth century Gibbon disdainfully wrote about the poor Heliogabalus—who in 222, at eighteen, was killed by his mother—that he stained male honor by dressing in silk.

This moral reaction had a material basis. The soldier Emperor Aurelian, born at about the time when Tertullian broke with the Church, refused to wear silk himself and forbade his wife to have even a single silk garment. Silk was paid for by its weight in gold.

For more than two hundred years the Roman authorities had fought silk. It came from China, was carried past Khotan along the Silk Road toward the Mediterranean. When the land route was blocked, it was transported across the passes to India and then sent by sea to Rome. But Rome's trade balance with Asia was negative; it imported more and more luxurious goods from India and China but had nothing to export. Rome imported silk and spices and itself had only glass, baubles, and trash to offer. There was nothing from Rome that China and the Indian states could not do without. Rome had to pay with silver and gold for its imports of luxury goods. Its ruling class demanded luxury; the imports had become a need for them.

Emperor Tiberius pointed out to the Senate that the coins went east as payment for luxury goods. Pliny the Elder explained the implications of this. Rome lost annually—and that's giving a low estimate—100 million sestertia to India, China, and Arabia.

It is easy to underestimate the role of Khotan in world history. The silk caravans passing through here two thousand years ago carried luxury goods for a small upper class only. And there were few caravans. One could say that this was a marginal matter after all, that the Roman moralists exaggerated; that neither the flow east of currency nor the trade as such had any great significance to general history.

But in 1938 Professor Frederick J. Teggart, of the University of California at Berkeley, had one of these wonderfully beautiful books published which in one stroke wipes out complex speculations and clarifies the issues. The title is *Rome and China: A Study of Correlations in Historical Events.* It deals with the period from 58 B.C. to A.D. 107. Frederick J. Teggart asked the question whether there existed any historical pattern. He just asked it simply and naïvely, and answered with an investigation any schoolchild could have done in the past centuries. Many historians still have not recovered.

Frederick J. Teggart noted country by country those events, wars and turbulence, that have been recorded historically. He then placed these lists next to each other. The result spoke for itself; there existed a correlation.

Every revolt in Europe took place following directly a war either at the eastern Roman border or in western China—Sinkiang. The connection was so exact that wars at Rome's eastern borders were followed by revolts on the Rhine and lower Danube, and wars at Tien Shan were followed by revolts at the Danube from Vienna to Budapest.

Of the forty revolts or invasions that took place in this period at Rome's European borders, nine in the Upper Danube area had followed wars at Tien Shan, and the remaining thirty-one, on the Rhine and lower Danube area, had followed wars on Rome's eastern borders. Of these wars in the east, eighteen have followed wars in what is now Sinkiang. Teggart could thus prove that in the case of twenty-seven revolts and fights at Roman European borders, the events had been preceded by political acts in what is now Sinkiang, carried out by the Han emperor's Chinese government.

The connection is obvious. It was not visible to the Roman and Changan statesmen, nor to those acting and battling in Turfan or around the upper Danube. A reasonable conclusion would be that the trade giving a hundredfold profit, according to Roman as well as Chinese sources, did not have just a marginal interest to the people between China and the European Rome. The Silk Road was the civilized main vein in a barbarian trade network. The caravans stopping in Khotan were interesting not merely to a limited group of the emperor's administrators, wandering merchants, and Roman luxury consumers.

Rome, however, did not have enough goods to pay for its trade, and had to pay for its imports with the gold and silver that the Roman legions were stealing from the conquered and colonized people. This negative trade balance was not decisive for the worsening economic crisis in the Roman Empire, but it contributed to that worsening and the increased exploitation which was corroding the slave society.

The pattern of Europe's trade with China still remained after Rome had fallen. Europe had no really valuable products to offer India or China. The Portuguese, Spanish, and British brought their cloths and hats and honey and oil and glass pearls, wanting silk, spices, lacquer work, and china. They bought it all from China with silver stolen from Africa and South America.

Some years into the nineteenth century the outflow of precious metals to China was about twelve times greater than in the time of Pliny. The British then broke with armed forces the resistance of the Chinese authorities against Bibles and drugs. It was only the opium trade and the missionaries that made trading with China really profitable for Europeans.

At the bus stop outside the cinema opposite the vegetable market, there was already a queue. The street was now full of people on bicycles on their way toward the center. People going to work.

"Whoever doubts that the age of imperialism is gone lacks any feeling for history," Gun said. "The days are over when it was possible to plunder one country in order to buy luxury goods from another, and when missionaries and soldiers could force people to become drug addicts, to enable the businesses in Europe and America to flourish. The people of the Third World are conscious of the connection."

The pavements filled up with more and more people. They did not look at the big character posters shouting their accusations in bold strokes of a brush against party secretary Li Shu-shan, blaming him for being a capitalist roader.

In the center a policeman dressed in white was now directing the traffic. The new industries are to the west. Khotan was awake, the freshness of the morning gone. The sun was burning and the dust made our skin itch and felt gritty between our teeth.

"You have only ten minutes before the discussion about Khotan with party secretary Li," Abdullah said. "Hurry up!"

16
Party Secretaries Li and Liu Talk of Khotan

"I haven't been here more than a year," party secretary Li Shu-shan said. "Khotan was one of the places where there were violent confrontations during the Cultural Revolution. There was all-out civil war, as Chairman Mao said. Just now there are big criticism campaigns but also bad factional activities. You can see for yourselves on the walls of all houses."

We are having tea in the reception room of the guest house. Party secretary Li Shu-shan is about forty. He wears a uniform; he is on leave from the People's Liberation Army. During the Cultural Revolution he was responsible for guarding the frontier and the security in the Huo-cheng area up in the Ili valley. He was selected party secretary because he was considered calm and reasonable. Khotan, then shattered by factional activities, needed a young and capable party secretary prepared to work hard under difficult conditions.

There were those who considered him too young for such a responsible position. Besides, Khotan is a border district. On the walls of houses in Khotan there were now posters flapping with attacks on him. He mentioned them:

"They accuse me of being a capitalist roader." But he did not indulge in any polemics against them. Li Shu-shan is rather typical of the younger cadres in the People's Liberation Army. He is also said to have been a good troops officer. When the film about the Long March was to be shot, his regiment was given the task of honor to re-create the march across the mountains. To make sure the shots were good, he did this march with his men five times in all. He was tanned and sinewy and spoke in a calm, relaxed way:

"The district is about 220,000 square kilometers, 920 kilometers from east to west, and 420 kilometers from north to south. It is divided into

130

seven counties: Khotan, Moyu-Karakash, Pishan-Guma, Chira, Yüti-en-Keriya, Minfeng-Niya, and Lop. Certain counties have double names like Yütien-Keriya. Both names are very old; one is Han and the other Uighur. They have equal value.

"We have fifty-eight people's communes, eight state farms, and a forest by division. We have 1,198 production brigades, 5,900 work teams, and at present a population of 1,020,000 people. That is twice what it was in 1949. Ninety percent are Uighur.

"There are 24,000 party members in the Khotan district. Of these 22,000—that is, 90 percent—are Uighur; 9,600 of the 14,000 cadres are Uighur—that is, 60 percent. These national cadres form the real backbone. We attach great importance to having women cadres. Atik Kurban here, vice-chairman of the revolutionary committee of the Khotan district, grew to political consciousness during the hard class struggle against the local feudal masters, to decrease the rents."

Atik Kurban, sitting at the end of the table, now joined the conversation: "Formerly we women were veiled. Now 32 percent of the women are cadres. The vice-chairman of the silk mill is a woman, as is the vice-chairman of the rug factory. She was also a delegate to the Fourth National People's Congress.

"Khotan is a district with high mountains and huge deserts. But it is in fact very rich. There is coal, copper, gold, tin, and asbestos here. Now we are drilling for oil. Before liberation there was no industry here. Now it is being developed. We are extending water power, we have two coal mines, a rich coal field 120 kilometers from here. The road there has not yet been built, but that will be done next year to open the mine. We need the coal, because the water power is insufficient for our energy requirements in winter. We have opened repair shops in all counties to care for agricultural equipment and tractors. These repair shops are now being developed further into small-scale manufacturing industries. We have been able to open regular bus routes serving all counties and all people's communes. Our light industry works well— silk mills and rug factories. We are organizing a large new textile industry and expect to have 15,000 spindles in operation in five months' time.

"We have established telephone communication with every work team in the whole district. The airfield was opened in 1957, and we have three flights a week to Urumchi and also a direct connection with Lanchow. We are extending the main road and planning a railroad.

"We consider cattle breeding very important. In 1949 we had about 1 million animals. Now we have 2.3 million. Wool from our sheep is especially well suited for the manufacture of rugs and goes directly to our rug factory. Khotan has always been famous for its fruit. We have a large selection and sell both fresh and dried fruit. We have grapes, apricots, peaches, pears, apples, figs, walnuts, melons, watermelons, dates, and many others.

"Water is vital for agriculture here. We are fighting the sand, planting shelter belts, digging canals. In the past eighteen years we have built 8,500 kilometers of canals. The Khotan district is now completely self-sufficient as far as agricultural products are concerned.

"Before the liberation we had a teaching college and 145 elementary schools but no secondary schools. In the last decade, especially after the Cultural Revolution, we have taken a large step forward in education. Now 90 percent of the school-age children go to school. We have 1,231 elementary schools, 66 secondary schools, 7 high schools, and 121 workers' universities.

"There were three hospitals here before the liberation. Now we have nine large hospitals, one for each county plus two here in the main town of the district. We have clinics in all production brigades, and the cooperative medical care now reaches every work team. We are extending the network of barefoot doctors.

"We have striven to establish amateur art troupes and work hard with the literacy campaign, popularizing the Latin-type alphabet which suits the Uighur language, and aim at overcoming the remains of illiteracy. That is, very briefly, a survey of our work here in Khotan."

"I like party secretary Li," Gun said. "He is clear, logical, and straightforward. He doesn't fancy himself. If people like him are capitalist roaders, I am the Virgin Mary!"

Party vice-secretary Liu Hou-shan was about sixty. An older party worker, a bit thoughtful. On our way to the silk mill he discussed Khotan's problems.

"Looking back at the thirties . . . you know what it was like here. And at the time of liberation, Khotan was a nest of reactionaries. We had some armed struggles here in 1951 and 1952, when the reactionaries organized themselves as raiders. But we mobilized the masses and destroyed the whole underground reactionary movement. Some of the reactionaries even came over to our side. They exposed the others. You know that we work politically and are lenient to those who admit their crime or mistrust. Violence is only for extreme cases. The important victory over the reactionary forces was political. When the masses were mobilized, the reactionaries were defeated. But if the proletarian dictatorship is lenient it is not indulgent. When necessary we use armed force. Still, politics decide.

"In 1974 the reactionary elements again tried spreading rumors.

That is not so strange. Look at the class composition. Khotan was a district characterized by the worst class oppression before liberation. In the oases four or five landowners ruled over 80 percent of the land. In general, it could be said that 90 percent of the population owned 20 percent of the land. The standard of living was lower than anywhere else in Sinkiang; Khotan was poorer than any other place. This made political work here easy, and the masses could be mobilized quickly to form agricultural cooperatives and people's communes. But at the same time this background often makes the class struggle very acute here. During the Cultural Revolution, this led to some heavy fighting. Those who in reality served the class enemy managed to split the masses and cause actual fighting here in Khotan. Even later on factional activities remained a problem.

"Khotan is now agriculturally self-reliant, which is fine. But we have to go further. The private plots are a problem. If we want to continue, we shall have to carry through great collective labor with the planting of trees and irrigation systems. But if the work of the people's commune members is centered on the private plots, this will be impossible. At the same time the question can be put in a different way: If the collective is not able to guarantee its members more than 320 jin of grain annually, they are forced to use private plots. Only when the collective can guarantee each member 360 to 370 jin of grain annually will the private lots be superfluous. The most successful production brigades we have can now guarantee their members 400 jin of cereal annually. But that is not general; such is the problem.

"Transport here is expensive. The cars are ruined by the long bad roads. It is difficult to keep the desert roads open; the surface suffers each July because of floods, when water gushes through the desert. We have so little good stone to build proper roads. That is a difficulty we must overcome. We shall asphalt the surface of the road in 1977, but our transport problems will really begin to be solved where there's a railroad.

"We do not have enough irrigation canals. Not enough to lead the water into the fields; not enough to save the fields from the floods. In April and May when we need water, there is too little of it, there is a drought. Cotton, wheat, and vegetables suffer. The snow on the mountains does not really start to melt until May, so the floodwaters reach here in July. Then our canals cannot get rid of all the water, and we lack dams which could store it. It just runs away, losing itself in the desert after causing damage. The problem can be solved but that requires massive efforts.

"Communications are another problem. It is a large district, almost as large as the whole of Rumania. Think about the medical care, the difficulties of transporting acute cases to hospitals for treatment. Now it's better than it used to be, but people are still dying unnecessarily. They get treatment too late. That is a great problem.

"The population is on the increase. There are several reasons for it. Prenatal care and confinement hygiene are greatly improved. The fight against infant mortality has been successful, especially where diphtheria and pneumonia are concerned. The fight to combat venereal diseases has also been successful. Before the liberation a large proportion of the population suffered, and many became sterile. In addition, there is a certain planned migration here from the inland, for example, skilled workers for the textile industry and such. Concerning birth control, we are, as you know, very careful. Whoever asks for contraception will have it, of course. It is free here as in the rest of China for anyone who wants it. But we are not conducting a campaign, for political reasons. Still, even for the future it is likely that the planned population increase in an underpopulated district like Khotan will exceed that of a highly populated inland area. The optimal size of a family is not given once and for all, and can't possibly be the same everywhere.

"We are very successful where education is concerned. We have generally been able to establish elementary education for everyone, and are now achieving a situation where most youngsters go on to secondary school. We are raising an educated generation, which is a decisive change for the better.

"We are now forming 'Seventh of May universities' out in the brigades. Anyone can take part, young and old, literates and illiterates. Five hours a week in spare time. Reading and writing, basic medical knowledge along with hygiene and agricultural techniques. The young people especially, those who settle down in the countryside after school, are the driving force of this educational program. The movement is becoming general, which means that the cultural level in the countryside rises, and we can build a socialist countryside, one of a new type.

"But of course, we have serious problems to face. Our progress may appear great compared to the past, but in comparison with what is necessary, it is quite modest."

17

For What Is Khotan Famous?
Silk, Jade, and Rugs!

The party vice-secretary of the silk mill was an Uighur woman. But I do not have her name; that note was obliterated by a heavy downpour when we reached Tunhuang much later. But she was a woman, Uighur and alert.

"The silk industry was in bad shape at the time of the liberation. The quality was bad, for good tradition deteriorated in the reactionary era. We started to build the factory in 1953 and began to produce in 1954. But at that time we only unwound the cocoons and then sent the silk to the coast.

"We have developed according to Chairman Mao Tse-tung's principles, going from a small to a large industry. We have relied upon our own resources and developed our own initiatives. Only in 1962 were we able to produce silk georgette. Now we manufacture all kinds of silk products, from silk cloth and velvet to silk rugs and filling for quilts and winter jackets, even to soap made from cocoon oil. We have mechanized and given a free hand to the creative initiative of the masses, where technical development is concerned. That means, we have let politics lead.

"At the very beginning we sent out eighty silk weavers to learn the new techniques. At the same time twenty veterans from the inland brought us their technique. This group still forms the backbone of our work. The eighty came from families who have worked with silk for centuries. They also brought over all of the modern techniques from Shanghai.

"When we built up our industry, 500 workers came from the inland. Now 1,500 people work here at the factory, 60 percent being Uighur, and 70 percent of them are women.

"The party organization at this factory has 202 members, 113

Uighur; that is 56 percent. Of the members of the Youth Organization, 45 percent are Uighur. The leading cadres of the party as well as of the administration and technique are all Uighur. Several cadres have also been selected from here for responsible posts in the area and the district, and have contributed greatly to developing the production and the political movements. We elected Guli Khan our delegate to the Tenth Party Congress. She is a woman and a silk worker descended from generations of silk workers.

"Seven of our national cadres have studied in Peking. I myself studied at the National Institute in Peking in 1951. During the past decade we have sent about a hundred cadres and workers to Shanghai and other coastal cities to study and exchange experiences. We have many nationalities represented here in the factory, and they get on very well together. We are, after all, like a family.

"The question of the cadres' participation in production is a matter of principle. All cadres here must take part in the physical work for at least a hundred days a year. Also, if there are any sudden difficulties in production, the cadres responsible ought to take part regularly in the work procedure to find out what the difficulties are at that particular place. At the end of each period after the cadres have worked in production, we have a meeting to summarize the experiences. The masses then give friendly criticism to help the cadres.

"This also brings about a quicker technical development of the production. This method makes it easier to establish technical initiative groups by the three-in-one principle, where skilled workers, technically educated cadres, and politically responsible cadres belong to the same united innovation group. That way we solved, for example, the problem of removing the wax from the silk mechanically. It used to be done by hand. Also, we have mechanized the procedure of withdrawing the cocoons from the simmering water after they have been softened and before we unwind the thread.

"Salaries are paid according to the proper degree scale, the highest being 152 yuan a month and the average 58 yuan a month. Added to that are medical care, pensions, and guarantees against accidents and disability. All medical costs are covered for the employees 100 percent, and 50 percent for their dependents. Medical costs, for instance for appendicitis, are 12 yuan. The employee pays nothing for his operation, but 6 yuan for a dependent. Ninety-five percent of the employees have their own savings accounts in the bank. If someone gets into difficulties, the factory will, naturally, assist him.

"Women workers retire at fifty, women cadres at fifty-five. Men at sixty regardless of their position. The pension may vary slightly owing to different circumstances, but it is about 60 to 70 percent of the income.

"Costs for funerals, for accidents, and for schooling are paid by the factory. We have both an elementary and a secondary school. The number of pupils is now about eight hundred. We have clinics, day nurseries, and a workers' club, and also a 'Twenty-first of July university' at the factory, with political as well as general and technical classes."

We go through the resident area of the factory. Dormitories have been built for the unmarried and small family apartments for the married. Chen Jung-ju is twenty-five and unmarried. She was a Red Guard and went to the countryside to be re-educated. She has now been at this factory for six years. She works in the dye house. She shares a room with three other girls in the dormitory. The rooms are on both sides of a corridor in the middle of a low, long clay building. On the table by the window is an alarm clock, but there are also a transistor radio, tea mugs, a mirror, and books. The floor is of wood.

"We're shift workers," Chen Jung-ju says. "I work on the second shift. We share a kitchen and a bathroom. We each pay 2 yuan and 47 fen a month for rent, electricity, and water."

The children are playing outside the dormitories. Laundry hangs on lines between the trees. The sun is hot and the dust swirls.

"We have done a great deal but we still have a long way to go," the woman party vice-secretary says. "Did you see the hands of the workers? They used to be ruined by fungus; their hands used to be corroded. The heat and the damp and the work with the silk ruined them. Now we have combatted the fungus with crystalline acetic acid and penicillin. That occupational hazard has been overcome."

In the light—but hot and damp—halls where the silk thread is being untangled from its cocoon and unwound, and where the silk is reeled up, the workers were sitting on chairs moving on rails. They kicked themselves back and forth while grabbing the thin silk threads from the cocoons and bringing them together in such a way that the reeled silk kept an evenly high quality. Their hands were red and slightly swollen and the skin was spongy as if they had spent a long time washing dishes —but it was unbroken.

"We still have a long way to go," the party vice-secretary said when we said goodbye.

Khotan is famous in the world for three things: silk, jade, and rugs. The fame for jade is the oldest. Jade has gone from here to the inland of China for four thousand years. It is a strange material. Jade in your hand is cold like ice. It is hard but not sharp. Steel can't scratch fresh uneroded jade. When jade has been lying in a grave it will, however, become eroded and loose on the surface. Jade has depth, and light will penetrate thin jade. It feels smooth and slippery and oily to the fingertips when polished. Jade sings when struck. Jade is white, and jade is dark with a greenish tinge.

Jade is the name of a stone that looks like jade and feels like jade. The word has a Spanish origin—*piedra de la ijada,* "kidney stone." The Chinese called it *yu.* But it became a title of honor for a stone fine as jade. What we now call jade is mainly two minerals: jadeite and nephrite. Up to the eighteenth century, when the Burma jadeite started to spread in China, the Chinese jade was nephrite. And almost all of this nephrite came from Khotan.

Chinese documents tell how the Khotan people looked for jade in the riverbeds. High up from the Kunlun Mountains two rivers flowed down through the Khotan district, joining in the desert to make their way, occasionally, as far as the Tarim River: Karakash (Black Jade) and Yurun-kash (White Jade). Khotan was the country of jade. The surest places to find it were where the moonlight filled the riverbed. Khotan jade could be said to be moonlight crystallized into stone.

Ornamental and cult objects of jade are known from many cultures. They belong especially to the Late Stone Age. Jade also played an important role in the cultures around the Pacific Ocean. The Indians on the northwest coast of America, the Aztecs and Mayas in Central America, and the Maoris in New Zealand, besides the Chinese, all gave jade a central part in their culture. In China its significance extended far beyond that of an ornamental stone. The stories of jade and of jade objects became one of the main branches of Chinese cultural history and art history. And Khotan supplied the jade.

In the winter when the riverbed was dry, people looked for jade that might have been brought down by the melting snow. But the great jade mining in Khotan was not the jade that people could find in the riverbed but blocks that were dug out of the mountains. That work was hard and painful and unhealthy; those who dug for jade had to work at an altitude of 5,400 meters. They burned away the snow and ice and broke off pieces of jade from the ground. One year of hard work could yield 300 kilograms of jade, provided the digger lived and worked high up in the mountains all the time. The profits went to the merchants down in Khotan and farther on along the trade route.

Nowadays the work is mechanized. There are five jade mines with three hundred employees, and the annual production of the district has increased to 200 tons. The laborers get a bonus for high-altitude work, they live in tents insulated against the winter, and goods are now taken there by truck and tractor. Nobody has to carry his own equipment any more. They use pneumatic drills and explosives. Jade of different qualities and types is then shipped from the Khotan jade center to all provinces, and is sold to other countries at the Canton fair. The digging of jade in Khotan is an export industry. But jade, no longer a cult material nor just a material for beautiful pieces of art, is now used for boring heads and in electrical industry.

Jade is a material which, like gold, has changed from being an ornament and a value standard into a precious industrial raw material.

The Khotan rug factory, Hotan Rayonluk Gilam Karahanisi, is situated outside the town of Khotan, in Lop county four kilometers east on the bank of the Yurunkash River. It is not a mill, it is a factory; rugs are manufactured. Old masters and their younger apprentices here manufacture rugs, and all the rugs made out in the production brigades are collected here. Most of the rugs are exported, which involves certain problems.

The vice-chairman of the revolutionary committee is a woman called Rotsemi Salan. Her father was a rug weaver before her. We have tea with him, an old master. She herself was the Khotan delegate at the Fourth National Folk Congress.

"Take the Khotan rugs," she says. "This is a state enterprise with three workshops and 405 employees, 48 percent of them are women. Our weavers are 61 percent women. This industry is important for China; we earn the money here which can be used to provide our country with modern industries bought from abroad. We have an important task on the production front. We must remember that. China has bought petrochemical industry from abroad, for example. How could China do that unless there were things China could sell? Our rugs are in demand all over the world. We fight in our way for the revolution and for the modernization of our country.

"It is now two thousand years since Khotan rugs were sent to the emperor. They were real knotted rugs of pure wool. The tomb finds show the same thing; the rugs are traditional products, based on our good wool, our old patterns and simple tools. Khotan was a center of rug making in Sinkiang. Rugs were sent from here to Russia and England. We traditionally used natural dyes and still do: leaves, walnut shells, pomegranate peels, and so on. We made various experiments before the Cultural Revolution with synthetic dyes, but we did not achieve satisfactory results; the rugs were uneven and too bright. Now after the Cultural Revolution we have solved the technical problems with synthetic dyes and activators. We need to increase the capacity of the production. Our rugs are wanted by the export market. But the natural dyes give more lively, shimmering shades.

"On principle we try to develop the tradition. We have experimented with new patterns, and knotting landscape pictures. We can now make larger rugs. We have also refined the wool and achieved higher qualities. One could say that we can now make rugs that are more durable, more pliable, more shiny, and more even.

"The rug maker's life was miserable before the liberation. He could make 4 square meters in forty-five days. That gave him 50 jin of corn. When the rugs were not in demand in Europe, the rug makers here in Khotan were thrown into starvation and misery. The great profits were taken by the merchants in the bazaars. There were rug bazaars in Kashgar and Turfan and also here in Khotan. The one in Kashgar was the largest and dominated the market.

"The liberation came in 1949. In 1950 we formed a production cooperative. To begin with it was small, seventy households with about one hundred workers in all. Then we assumed collective ownership and developed the factory step by step.

"Our production up to 1962 went mainly to the Soviet Union, which meant that we made rugs according to the patterns wanted by the Soviet importers. The Soviet Union refused to import rugs made by our own traditional pattern units. Our production since 1962 is exported mainly to England, France, and West Germany. We now export 10,000 square meters of rugs every year.

"Our production is increasing, due to the fact that we spread the rug making to more and more production brigades. We now have one hundred sub-suppliers among the production brigades. Our budget is about 1 million yuan for the sub-suppliers' work. Our technicians from this factory travel around helping them set up looms, and also discuss qualities and patterns and colors with them.

"Naturally, there are long-term problems in our production. We are now mainly satisfying the need of the international market. This implies that the foreign buyers give orders for a certain number of rugs of certain sizes and certain qualities with certain patterns to our export organization for rugs. We then fill these orders. The rugs we sell are made according to our traditional patterns. But they are selected and to a certain extent modified by the foreign buyers.

"Looking at the handmade rugs, one can see that the Persian ones aim mainly at being attractive. They are of a very high quality. Tekke Turkmen are strict and straight, often with extremely close knots. The Afghan rugs often have very bold patterns and the knots are not so close. We have our own tradition. For one thing our dyes are different; we often have stronger colors. Also we have, apart from the strictly geometrical figures, a tradition of a series of patterns that connect us with the inland of China. It can be seen, for example, in the cloud ornaments. I don't suggest that Khotan has a mixture of styles. We have our own tradition, which is related to several others.

"Our problem is that we do not make more than very few rugs for our own needs. At the moment it's not possible. We have to adapt to the demand, which means that European buyers decide the nature of our work. That is why we also devote much work to maintaining and developing our own tradition; rugs to us are not an industry, but a form of art. We distinguish between these. On the walls here we have rugs made by our old masters, which their apprentices study. We are keeping their rugs, carrying on the tradition. We use only natural dyes for these traditional patterns developed by the masters. They are more expensive and often difficult to produce, and in the first instance reserved for this type of rug. The old masters will discuss what patterns to use. We are aware of the dangers in producing for the international market; we saw what almost happened when our production was determined by the Soviet rug importers. They gave us patterns to use which had nothing in common with our traditions. Such development is not unlikely to recur here. It is a contradiction we have to study carefully. It is, for one thing, necessary that we increase our production and serve the economy of our country and keep an evenly high quality. We must also be aware that the taste of the buyers directs our work, and we have an obligation to keep and develop our traditions and let them serve the people.

"The party tries to help us pass on all our knowledge to the young generation," Mahmud Tailaki said. He was one of the old masters present. They followed the conversation intently, their teacups in front of them. He then continued:

"I myself am sixty-one. I was thirteen when I started to make rugs. In those days we told and sang the patterns. We learned them while working with the elders. The merchants we worked for in those days were very cruel. I was flogged with a rope when they thought I didn't work hard enough. They had complete power over us. They even cut the fingers off an apprentice who was no good at rug making. Then they kicked him out. These things happened when I was young. I worked for them eighteen years. Then I went to the meeting where they had to answer to the charges for what they had done to others. I told what they were like. They were inhuman.

"Among us old masters, the party has now arranged two special courses. We discuss politics and go through all the things we have seen. We also try to pass on all our knowledge to the young. There are so many things that can't be written down in books. There are several youngsters here who have a serious attitude and real feeling for rugs.

Not all of them have got the feeling, but you really can't expect all of them to have it. Still, our youngsters are all good, because they respect our traditions and their elders. But some of the young also have the feeling that helps them understand the rugs and enables them to create new patterns."

The following day we had another discussion on traditional patterns. These years the Khotan rug production is exported almost 100 percent. What is not exported is used to adorn public premises. The silk, however, is mainly sold locally; only a small part of it is exported. Exactly the same patterns are sent abroad as are sold in Khotan and farther out in the oases along the road south of Takla Makan. It is exported across the mountains to Pakistan, from where very thin Pakistan silk saris are imported. The patterns differ, but they complement each other.

Jo Li-chun from the district office for industry and traffic clarifies the situation:

"The old silk cloths you can see reproduced in books or the originals in the museums of Urumchi and Peking came from the inland. We have copied these old patterns, which have become very popular in big cities like Peking and Shanghai. But these are not part of the Khotan tradition. They were fabrics transported through Khotan and were used here by the ruling class.

"We have different aesthetic traditions. You have seen the silk we use, the ordinary silk manufacture. The warp is stretched and dyed in wide crosswise bands. Then the weft is woven, so that a specific effect is achieved, which people around here appreciate. However, you must remember that these patterns not only differ in various countries; they also differ considerably from one district to another. In Kashgar, for example, they like to work with the seven-hue pattern. We do not use it here so much.

"Silk used to be a luxury material, reserved for the small ruling class. Now one could say that every woman has a silk dress. Silk is still used for festive clothes, but everybody now has a silk dress. We strive to satisfy the people's need for silk. Most of the silk we use is not made as handcraft but woven in the mill. The question of what patterns to weave demands serious consideration. The pattern department first makes a sample and attaches it to a wall of the silk mill. The workers there can discuss it and give their points of view. You must remember that Han and Uighur have differing artistic tastes and therefore different demands. It is important that the girls discuss the pattern fully if it is to be used for material for dresses for Uighur girls or jackets for Han girls. When the pattern is being woven, the salespeople for the retail trade gather views and criticism from the masses. Our commercial employees have been charged to gather and systematize this criticism and pass it on to the mill.

"In order to be convinced before a totally new product goes into manufacture, we establish work teams with representatives from the mill and from the salespeople, and then they travel from one people's commune to another listening to the opinions of the masses, showing different samples and discussing them.

"That is how we develop and further the traditional patterns in a way that serves the people."

18

Keriya, or the Pulse
of History

Keriya is an old town on the trade route south of Takla Makan. It is also known as Yütien. We had driven in from the desert on our way west from Khotan. It is hot, and we are sitting in the garden talking to the party secretary, who is quite young.

"Well," he said, "we have some antiquities here. But they are disappearing. We construct huge irrigation projects, then these remains disappear. Nothing is very old in this town itself. But in one of the communes thirty kilometers off there are considerable remains, even though they are disappearing now that we are building irrigation canals and leveling the ground."

That had a nasty sound to it, seemingly confirming all our worst fears. And he said it himself as he poured more tea and offered us apricots and raisins. The modern development was annihilating its own past.

"It's an old oasis," he said. "The name is mentioned in the historical chronicles from the Han dynasty onward. The oasis has probably moved over the centuries, but it has always been on this road where the Keriya River comes down from the mountains and continues into the desert. Way out there it disappears; it never reaches Tarim. We are now increasing the arable land. In 1950 it was 230,000 mu; now it is 430,000, which is almost double. We have built twelve large reservoirs for water, and we have 325 kilometers of paved and cemented canals. One hundred and three dams have been constructed to protect against floods and to help irrigation.

"Generally, it could be said that we have combatted the floods. But we now protect ourselves against them—we are still not able to make use of all the water brought down by the flood after the snow of the

144

mountains melts. Drought is still our worst enemy; we have an evaporation of more than 2,000 millimeters here.

"Irrigation is a highly specialized business demanding plenty of
knowledge and experience. To put conditions right, the experience of
the old poor peasants must be employed. They know their land. The
ground-water level in places is quite near the surface, especially near
the river. This can have serious consequences. If the ground water is
drawn up to the surface and evaporates, the minerals won't evaporate
but stay on the surface. It becomes critical when the ground-water level
reaches between one and three meters down from the surface, depending on the minerals carried by the water. But if the ground water
reaches one meter from the surface, the situation here is always critical.
The consequences of improper irrigation may be the transformation of
a desert into a salty marsh after a brief interlude as an arable field.

"We have increased the arable land and we are on guard against
salinas. We have had a certain success. We grow rice now, on our own
rice fields. We have never been able to do that before; rice used to be a
luxury. Now people can eat both bread and rice. But our production is
not very high, and the standard of living is low. We have taken the
question of learning from Tachai seriously. Within the next four years
we shall have to carry out our part of the plan. We have three main tasks:

"One: By learning from Tachai, double the grain production to 150
million jin per year.

"Two: Overcome the conflict between drought and water running
away to no use, by building three reservoirs.

"Three: Build three large water-power stations. Our ten communes
now have twelve water-power stations. With the additional three,
which we are building at present, we shall have enough energy to
continue mechanizing the agriculture."

It was a bazaar day. People had come into the Keriya center from
the whole of the oasis. All roads were full of people, coming to do their
shopping, and also to meet and talk.

"You have to distinguish between general shopping and the bazaar,"
the party secretary had said when we had tea. "We are fighting private
trade, which keeps creating capitalism and delays development. But the
bazaar is a national custom. We Uighurs do not just want to shop in
the bazaar; we go there to meet friends and relations and to discuss
politics and hear the news. It cannot be replaced by department stores.
But we are building both a department store and a restaurant. The trade
here in the bazaar is to a large extent state or cooperative retail trade.
You have to remember that the bazaar is not quite the same thing as
the inland private market. Our tradition is different. The bazaar re-

mains, but it keeps losing significance for the trade. The turnover of the trade as such here in Keriya has increased along with economic progress: from 110,000 yuan annually in 1950 to 7,600,000 yuan this year. In a few years, the bazaar will be of no more significance for buying and selling. But people will, very likely, still come here to meet and talk and eat, according to our tradition. That is why we built this large restaurant next to the bazaar."

The midday heat lay like a thick blanket over Keriya. We were eating pilau. The mutton lard was dripping from the rice. The party secretary said:

"It's all local produce. Keriya is really quite rich. The agriculture here goes back to the oldest times long before history, for on the frontier here between the high mountains and the large desert, the river runs forth and the land yields richly to the one who knows how to use it. We have wheat, we have rice and barley and corn, we have peaches and melon and grapes, and we have 400,000 animals."

The sour milk was cool and refreshing. The party secretary poured us some liquor.

"We distill it ourselves. A pity you are here for such a short visit. But a glass does no harm although it's summer. When I heard you were expected I first thought you might stay for some time. There's a lot to see here in Keriya. At the moment we're busy modernizing. It is still a poor oasis. You can see how the people live? That's no good. But we have just completed the brick works, and in the next ten years every family will live in a proper house. They should be built solidly, and the walls should protect against both winter cold and summer heat. No external wall shall be thinner than one and a half stone, thirty centimeters. Each house shall have a garden with an orchard and a vineyard. You see, we live out of doors in summer, and then we need the vines for protection. The vineyard is a patio. So, in ten years, every family shall have a proper new house with brick walls and plaster. By then Keriya will look different!

"The roads won't be dusty any more; we shall asphalt them. And the main road south of the desert will pass through here. You have seen, haven't you, all the bridges built over the desert gullies? These run dry now but fill up with water when the melting snow runs off. Unless we build bridges, we can't keep the road open all year round. We shall plant another million trees, to give shade and wood. We do all this by our own efforts. There have been great discussions about this. We carry out our plans now, to make life better here."

Afterwards Gun and I go to the bazaar. The state retail trade organizations had their stands there, but others also sold handcraft and home produce. Still, it was mainly industrial goods from the department store, about the same selection and prices as in the department store a little farther down in the town. But the bazaar was swarming with people. There were seldom any foreigners there, and they talked about us.

"The man must come from Pakistan, that's obvious, but the woman must be a Han, since she is wearing blue trousers."

Abdullah stood outside the department store, laughing:

"One doesn't have to worry about you two getting lost, that would be impossible. I could see you a long way off, like a huge black bee-swarm of people."

We had been given rooms in the county guest house. It was nice and clean with a stamped clay floor and wooden beds and curtains at the windows. They had brought us hot water, and we poured it in the basin and washed off the dust of travel.

"How strange," Gun said, "when I was a child and read about people washing off the traveling dust, I never knew what they were talking about. But since I came to Asia I understand."

When I went out to the courtyard to pour the washing water over the vegetables, the neighbor from the room next door was smoking a cigarette in the hot night. His name was Muhammed Beg, and he came from Urumchi but worked now as a doctor here in Keriya. He had just come back to the county from a production brigade out in the desert.

"There are certainly problems," he said. "Many mothers are still too young, for example. Older men still try to marry young girls. I'm not only concerned about it medically, although there *is* a medical aspect to it. The main issue, however, is political. It is a matter of consciousness. Women have to fight for their liberation.

"The venereal diseases are more or less overcome. Syphilis used to be very common here. It wasn't transmitted only through intercourse; people were born with syphilis. But now, both syphilis and tuberculosis have been eradicated.

"I am here to learn and teach. It is not enough to work only in the Urumchi hospital and become a better and better specialist. It is of extra importance to us doctors not to lose touch with the real problems of the people.

"I have three main tasks here in Keriya: work with the patriotic health movement; treat patients; educate and further the education of barefoot doctors.

"Concerning the patriotic health movement, that means we organize the people in a campaign for hygiene and sanitation. If we can solve the basic hygienic problems of sewage, drinking water, housing, and infant care, the questions of health will be very much easier. This is the line of Chairman Mao Tse-tung. The most important thing, as regards the health of the people, is not to transplant hearts but to make sure that the flies do not go from the sewage to the children's food.

"What do the people in Keriya suffer from? Dysentery in summer, pneumonia in winter. Why is that? Bad water, bad clothing, bad housing. What is that? That is political! Health is a political issue. As far as clothing and housing are concerned, we are now carrying out a plan to double the agricultural production in four years, and in ten years we will provide each family with a new modern house, fulfilling all the health authorities' demands for insulation and freedom from drafts with fresh air and protection against both summer heat and winter cold. The patriotic hygiene movement fights against dysentery, which is caused by sewage and the condition of the drinking water.

"Old ideas are hard to eradicate in our culture. People think that water purifies itself. Look, they say, spit in the water and it will run clean in a little while. So they take their water straight from the irrigation ditches, in the old, traditional way. We fight it with information; we make sure that the cesspools are constructed in such a way that they can't infect the water. We make sure that refuse is properly handled and composted.

"This is not something I can just command people to do. It is an extensive hygienic campaign for the people. The masses have to realize themselves why this campaign is so necessary; only then can results be achieved. This is a national campaign, even if conditions vary in the different parts of the country. Our people like to drink cold water; they find it refreshing. They do not like boiled water. In the inland they say the opposite: they do not like raw water. It is an old custom here to use unboiled water, just the way the inland custom is to use boiled water. The question, then, is not just whether the custom is old but whether it serves the people. In the inland the custom serves them, and here the custom doesn't. We must, in other words, explain to people here that unboiled water is dangerous. We must show them all the germs that may appear in unboiled water. It is not easy to break with an old tradition. It is easier to convince young girls that they shouldn't marry old men because their parents wish it than to convince people that cold and refreshing water is more dangerous than tepid overboiled water. This old, erroneous idea of the water not being dangerous is a serious complication. You can even see responsible cadres drinking water directly from the irrigation canals. We must present the matter to them in a political way and criticize them for it. If they catch dysentery they won't be able to work. It is not serving the people to drink unboiled water and then have to squat in the latrine all day long. That is a political question, a question of what line to follow, and a question of consciousness. We must be able to expect political consciousness from the cadres, as far as the hygienic campaign is concerned.

"Regarding the education of barefoot doctors, we now have hospitals and clinics in the people's communes and fairly well trained medical staff in each production brigade. We also have six barefoot doctors in each work team. Here in the center we have one hospital with 280 beds. We have 120 fully trained doctors and nurses. The barefoot doctors keep attending special courses; we have to improve on their education all the time. They have to start with simple lessons on hygiene and first aid. Then, step by step, they develop their knowledge while at the same time working in production. This has been rather successful. We could say now that we have introduced the big hygienic scheme extensively. It should reach every house and every latrine. Injuries or illness are treated within the work team. If it is more serious, it is treated within the production brigade or even in the county. If somebody is critically ill, there is a chance of sending the patient to the district hospital in Khotan or to a specialist in Urumchi or elsewhere.

"That is how we have organized the medical care. It's still just beginning; there are gaps. Our resources are limited, too; transport is a problem. Sometimes we may not have time to treat the patient successfully. We haven't enough fully trained doctors. We must go on developing preventive care as well as direct medical care. But the principle of concentrating on sanitation and trying to treat illness prophylactically, like the principle of catering to the majority of complaints and not just those of a handful of high administrators, that is to serve the people and concentrate on provincial medical care and the diseases afflicting many people. Those are principles advocated by Chairman Mao, which are right and correspond to the needs of our people and to the experience of the doctors who take their profession seriously.

"We are not against transplanting organs or against specialist attendance to rare diseases. But we are against the publicity that has developed around heart transplants and such in other countries. That does not serve the health of the people but the fame and income of the specialists."

The summer night was dark and dense. The heat trembled over Keriya and the air was stuffy. We went into our room. Gun was peeling apricots; they were refreshing but sticky. We had tea and then lay down in the dark talking about Keriya.

"He said the antiquities are disappearing," Gun said. "One could have replied that some remains from an old settlement now being sacrificed is a low price to pay for the citizens of Keriya to have a tolerable life. As far as I could see, not many people in the bazaar had inflamed eyes, and the kids did not have green snot hanging from their noses. The men did not have open wounds on their legs, and no beggars were lying along the wall. People were gay and kind and not starving. The party secretary told me that Keriya now has 270 tractors and 520 different types of machines and a repair garage of its own already. One could ask which is more important.

"If that *is* the question," she continued. "All over the world the old is eradicated by the new, that's the law of evolution. China as a whole is being transformed.

"There wasn't much left of Khotan's ancient wall. During our recent visits to China I haven't seen one single town of the old Chinese type, with a town wall and gates and all that. Perhaps Paoshan down in Yunnan on the Burma frontier was the last town we shall ever see of the old type. That was in 1962 and by now its walls may be gone. It is necessary, or people could not survive. Skansen in Stockholm and other local history museums are good and they fulfill Chairman Mao's wish to 'keep a sample.' People, though, should not be condemned to live in eternal misery just to show how the old places looked. And if something is really bad, I see no reason to keep even a sample of it. A picture and description will do. There is not one girl left now in China with bound feet. That's fine."

"You're rushing through the arguments," I said. "You want to prove too much. Be careful you don't end up with the ultra-left which attacked stone statutes and cultural monuments, believing they were serving the future. The leaders of those groups were crooks, but those who were drawn into the movement had the same opinions as you just expressed."

"But I think local history museums are a good thing," Gun said.

"You want to prove too much. Mind that you don't harm the museums in that way. The antiquities are no real problem. All large monuments and excavations are protected. There are placards proclaiming it at every important mosque and at every burial place. They are as protected in Sinkiang as in the rest of China. Nobody digs irrigation ditches through national monuments."

"That was not what I meant," Gun retorted. "Of course I know that if a production brigade suddenly comes across remains of walls they have to call for archaeologists, and if there are paintings they have to protect the whole area."

We had some more tea. It was hot, and we lay talking in the dark about the problems of Keriya. There are problems. And we reached them via the antiquities we began discussing.

The new building projects in Sinkiang are visited by archaeologists from the Urumchi museum. They secure and protect what is considered necessary. In Sinkiang—as in the rest of China—the great campaign to protect antiquities has been carried out parallel with the new landscape transformation such as terracing and breaking new ground. Archaeology is like the medical care: it is real only if it concerns the whole of the working people and not just a few specialists.

Keriya is extending into the desert with the new irrigation system, reclaiming areas once conquered by the desert. Now that Keriya is again using the land cultivated more than a thousand years ago, the remains of the deserted cultivation which once existed inevitably go.

"That is what Aurel Stein wrote from his second journey in this area," Gun said. "When he returned the desert had been transformed into arable land. He describes exactly the same procedure as the one described by the party secretary. The remains of old walls disappear with irrigation. Only if the desert was allowed to rule all Sinkiang could all antiquities be protected. We could save the whole world like that, but it would not do us any good. One can't build without demolishing. Chairman Mao is quite right. That's why the Chinese conduct the archaeological mass campaign at the same time as they build."

But Stein's description from his journey seventy years ago also coincides with the accounts of other contemporary travelers. After the fall of Yakub Beg and the establishment of the Chinese administration over South Kashgaria, new cultivation had been introduced so successfully that the country had flourished as it had not done since the T'ang dynasty.

This is remarkable and explains some of the later history of Sinkiang. The Chinese administrators toward the end of the empire were in many ways bad and corrupt. But their administration worked better and with less violence than that of Yakub Beg (or of the Russians west of the mountains or of the British south of them). This peaceful administration meant that the irrigation system was again extended and large areas were cultivated. In Sinkiang the time from the end of the nineteenth century onward was a period of increasing welfare, totally different from inland China.

The troops at the Chinese administration's disposal were few. Sinkiang was not held by military force; it was connected to the rest of China by other ties. Even when the Chinese administration collapsed at the center, and China went through decades of fighting, Sinkiang stayed within China. Only when General Ma Chung-yin roamed Sinkiang was the province seriously hit by the devastation created by the Chinese warlords. For fifty years—from the fall of Yakub Beg to the invasion of Ma Chung-yin—Sinkiang was a Chinese province of slowly increasing welfare. Outside its borders kingdoms collapsed, and in inland China the civil wars grew into a huge national people's revolt against foreign oppression and domestic reaction; but here in Sinkiang the administration continued as before. Taxes were comparatively low, the administrators comparatively honest. The arable land was extended.

Certainly it was poor, people were oppressed, of course there was exploitation and class struggle, but still that poverty was the greatest development to have taken place in Sinkiang in a thousand years. It explains why Sinkiang was not severed from China, in spite of all the attempts made in those fifty years with foreign aid, and in spite of the numerically almost nonexistent military force in Sinkiang.

"But if all this is so," Gun interrupted me, "whatever happened to the Oriental despotism? I, too, believe that those first fifty years, when Sinkiang was an ordinary administrative unit within the Chinese Empire, were a time of progress. That is confirmed by all contemporary sources, even if they describe poverty. Conditions were miserable, but not miserable like Bengal, held by the British. They were progressing slowly, and the irrigated area increased in a way it hadn't for a thousand years. The administration was reasonably honest, but at that time it was not a powerful Oriental despotism. The moment the administrators lost local support, they disappeared. The state was not despotic. Still, the theories claim that a despotic power is necessary to establish, extend, and maintain an irrigated agriculture. Learned writers even try to go the other way and prove that China is now a despotism because it can be proved that the irrigated agriculture in China is increasing more than ever, and they then refer to the 'well-known fact' that irrigated agriculture can only be extended by Oriental despotism. Ergo, China is an Oriental despotism. How do these theories then apply to Sinkiang?"

"As badly as they do to India."

"But then we can say the opposite! The Chinese administration was both weak and slightly corrupt, but still honest and running smoothly and organized enough to enable the landlords of these oases and the various village communities to extend the irrigated agriculture. That sounds reasonable. But then the theory of Oriental despotism and the 'hydraulic society' is unnecessary."

"It has always been unnecessary, as far as reality is concerned. It has been fabricated to legitimize oppression."

But if the theory of Oriental despotism and the hydraulic society does not apply, when you scrutinize past events in Keriya, what about the theory of the progressive desiccation of the Tarim basin? Sir Aurel Stein described seventy years ago how they had achieved the cultivation of land deserted a thousand years ago. Now the cultivated area is being extended; Sinkiang is being cultivated as never before. How does this apply to the desiccation? Has the pulse of history beaten again? Is there more water now?

The answer is that events in Keriya do not comply at all with the theory of desiccation. The extensive new cultivation now taking place in Sinkiang shows that the theory of Sinkiang as desiccating, fatally growing poorer every day, is basically a false theory.

The remarkable thing, though, is that this theory could have survived for so long.

Geologically, there has certainly been a change of climate here. But from the same viewpoint, mountains have been oceans and continents have risen and sunk and been cleft and joined again. Geological time measures tell very little about history.

The theory of desiccation, and the theory of that pulse of history which forced the people of inner Asia to wander toward India, Europe, and China, driven by the lash of climatic change, just like the theory that only countries with a climate like the English manage to produce intellectual achievements, all have one thing in common: they give a nonhuman explanation for historic development. At the same time they fly in the face of all obvious facts and are embraced with passionate conviction by various types of historians and writers.

"It's amazing," Gun said, "how appealing some theories are. Most people who have dealt with Sinkiang seriously agree that the desiccation is an illusion, but those historians still keep talking about it as an obvious fact."

The landscape here has not changed much in the past two thousand years. There are Chinese chronicles describing the roads, and they apply today as well. Settlements have varied and places have moved: that is all. The chronicles of the Han dynasty fix the number of households at 103,000 in the oases from Khotan to Turfan, which is about 600,000 people. This means that it can be established that the population has increased in the past two thousand years, tripled since the Han dynasty to the liberation in 1949.

The climate is the same now as it was then, the drought the same. Stein described it like this. The houses deserted a thousand years ago still stand as they were. What has not weathered away mechanically— the sand scraping through the rooms and the wind lifting the roofs—

is kept just as it was when the last person left without closing the door behind him. Later on we visit the dead in the burial ground of Astana in Turfan. Down in the tomb the dead man lies dried up but not decomposed. His closed eyelids have not been open since Charles Martel won the battle of Poitiers in 732, and yet the old man lies there. If one stands quite still in front of him, one feels that the gnarled remains could get up from death at any moment.

It is dry. It has been dry for a long time. Put a piece of paper under a stone and come back in fifty years. The paper will still be there. Even after fifty generations, the same piece of paper will lie there undestroyed. A theory like the one about inner Asia's desiccation in historic time, which contradicts both written sources and observed facts, is so incredible that it can only be explained by the fact that it fulfills a social need.

The best known representative of the climatological historical theory was Ellsworth Huntington, a Yale professor, and the president of the Association of American Geographers as well as of the American Eugenics Society. He died at the age of seventy in 1947 and was long considered a scientific pioneer. But his theories of the pulse of history were based on weak facts. As far as Palestine's history is concerned, he had got his facts wrong, and as far as Sinkiang is concerned, even contemporary researchers claimed that his facts did not apply.

The interesting thing about Huntington, however—as about his racist contemporaries—is the fact that his scientific arguments keep losing themselves in the fantastic. In the volume presented to Sven Hedin on his seventieth birthday in 1935, Huntington writes with deep scientific earnestness:

> It happens that such winters, with a mean temperature a little above the freezing point, are the best for mental activity. Thus the climatic conditions that now prevail in the main centers of civilization appear to be the best that can be found with the present distribution of climate.
> ... Thus the distribution of civilization then, as now, was in harmony with the climate—the highest civilization being located where the climate approached most closely to the optimum for the stage of culture then attained by man.*

This was in 1935. Huntington's theory of climate was an Anglo-Saxon variety of racist ideologies. Not a science, that is, but merely rationalization and bad ideology. But the theory of climate, like the

*Ellsworth Huntington, "Climatic Pulsations," in *Hyllningsskrift tillägnad Sven Hedin på hans 70-årsdag den 19 februari 1935* (Stockholm, 1935), p. 601.

theory of race, served. These theories were needed to give imperialism a certain historical justification.

"But even in 1973 the German researcher Annemarie von Gabain writes about the deterioration of the climate," Gun said. "Strange how these ideas survive. These historians don't seem to dare face the thought that human history is human and that neither God nor fate nor race shapes destiny but man makes himself."

But is it not possible, after all, to imagine that the natural conditions have changed and that this has influenced settlement and agriculture? It is quite obvious that arable land was deserted and large settlements became sterile desert. Is it all so unthinkable to imagine that there are other explanations for this than just a sort of historic pulse controlled by the climate?

Of course it is possible. Settlements in western Sweden, for example, in the eighteenth and nineteenth centuries were determined by the herring-fishing periods. They in turn were decided by the supply of plankton. Of course natural conditions can change and influence settlement, but that does not motivate an ideology like that of Huntington. And have natural conditions in Sinkiang changed in historic times?

That's what Aurel Stein felt. He thought Huntington was wrong about the climate, but he believed the water supply to the rivers had sunk in historic times, which, according to him, had led to changes in the arable area and to countryside becoming desert.

He considered the explanation to be a long-term change of climate. Agriculture had to be irrigated. The water comes when the snow on the Kunlun Mountains melts. Suppose that the annual melting of snow exceeds the annual precipitation in the mountains. Then it is fossilized ice that melts, and the supply of water becomes gradually reduced.

When the snow on the Kunlun Mountains melts, the ice from the latest glacier stage melts. Thus a much earlier change of climate—a change on a geological scale where such changes are really noticeable —would manifest itself by diminished water supply and consequently decreased arable land, changing settlements, and eventually increased poverty. At the same time the piece of paper could be left under the stone for fifty generations, bearing evidence that there has not been a change of climate.

Unlike Huntington's theory, this one is feasible. The only thing is, it is unnecessary. In Kashgar, in Khotan, in Keriya, we have discussed the water supply. Everybody expressed the same views. They have so far no ways of retaining and utilizing the water running down from the mountains; it still runs into the desert, useless. The danger of flooding continues to be a real threat with the approach of high waters from the melting snow of the mountains. This water will suffice for a huge increase in arable land, a multiplying of the areas far beyond the wildest imagination of previous generations. In addition, there are large natural reservoirs of sweet water under the desert. Stein, of course, may be right in the long run about the melting of glaciers on the mountains, even if this has so far not diminished the water supply in a way that yet affects the agriculture. I don't know. I asked in Khotan and Urumchi and Peking for data regarding the glaciers and the mountain precipitation. But they replied that the question was being studied.

Settlements, however, have moved. One could also talk about a periodic change of the arable land in the oases. Whenever the Tarim basin has enjoyed peaceful and organized conditions, the arable land has increased. Irrigated agriculture needs care (not despotism). In the decades around the fall of the empire, conditions were calm and the administration reasonably organized here in Sinkiang. Oppression was moderate and irrigated land could be extended. And, as Stein described it, what was a monument one year became a cultivated field the following year.

Still, this evolution has always brought about its own destruction. Owen Lattimore wrote about it. You can see the same thing everywhere: the irrigation canals of a desert agriculture will constantly silt up, and the settlement has to move after a few generations. Not only Lop Nor sweeps back and forth across the desert; this wandering is typical. Within a couple of centuries a large area will be covered by ruins and remains of settlements, in spite of the fact that the arable land has been kept fairly constant over the eras.

This pattern is now being broken. People in the oases south of the desert, with the aid of modern techniques and research, have gone beyond the limitations up to now prescribed by nature. The arable land is on the increase to an extent far beyond what has ever been achieved. And the character of change is itself changing. In Keriya people not only take back areas lost; they have gained new ground.

History is not ruled by fate.

19

With Our Own Strength

Beyond Keriya, the road plows into the desert. Here in southern Sinkiang, the oases are like islands with the bare red mountains to the south and the arid spaces to the north. The oases, like islands facing an ocean, can be enlarged by construction or reduced if the protective work ceases and maintenance is not kept up. But they will remain islands. The oases stop suddenly; greenery plunges to sterile stony desert.

The gravel shoots away from the wheels as we drive the long Gobi stretches. High above is a steely grey, shining sky. Far away on the horizon a possible glimmer—a green streak of fertile ground. As we approach, it dissolves and fades, and we drive on, gravel spraying round the wheels, the car rocking forth, following the lurching road.

On these wastes under the steely grey sky, we seem to be anchored by the heat.

We pass some caravans, walking their routes from one well to another. In the mountains to the south there is grazing land, but here around the oases there are no steppes or grazing land; here is desert. The oases are both exposed to and protected by the desert. The southern Sinkiang oases belong to the early agricultural settlements. They are fertile, the soil is rich, the water comes from the mountains regularly at the same time every year. The lack of rain is a freedom from the vagaries of weather. The peasants of Keriya and the oases here, like those on the Nile or in southern Turkmenistan, never had to worry about the weather, never had to long or hope or pray for rain. The water came when it was due, and as long as they irrigated the land, it yielded profusely.

It was here at the edge of the desert that agriculture could be developed. The isolation of the oases on this desolate waste is also partly positive. The desert routes, from one well to another or from one resting place to another, lead via these oases across the arid desert. North of Tien Shan up in Dzungaria, the oases are connected by steppes. There is grazing land. Thus the oases have no protection. There rode the mounted warriors or the nomad tribes. But here south of Tien Shan and south of the desert, there is grazing land only in the mountains. The oases are protected by the deserts. Nomad raiders could not exist here, and thus trade caravans could go this southern way in relative safety.

The land now changes character. From the north the sand blows in over us, the road is dry and dusty. Thirty meters high, the sand dunes come up from the inner parts of the desert and roll southward. The road twists and turns to avoid them. The sand swirls on the dunes, veils of sand pass over the road, it's like a snowstorm. Then an arm of yellow sand stretches across the road, and we are stuck. The driver says, "It was free here only ten days ago. It's difficult to keep the road open; the sand keeps wandering." The road has now left the sand-blocked roadway and meanders like deep ruts between the dunes. It is marked by large white-painted lumps of concrete. "We'll see what the new highway will be like," the driver says. "They might be able to get around the sand dunes."

Then the air changes taste in our mouths, though we are still among the dunes, and we drive away from them across the marsh leading to the oasis. It was the same when Hsüan Tsang passed this way 1,300 years ago. We are on our way to Niya, and Niya is an old oasis, even if Marco Polo did not bother to mention it.

Niya is also called Minfeng and is the largest county in China, 74,000 square kilometers in area. But it has only 20,500 inhabitants and 5,496 households. Up to 1949 this was a remote, poor oasis, reached by the melting water only in the middle of June, lacking any rich grazing land. At that time 10,000 people lived here in 2,830 households, 29 of which were landlords. They owned 30,000 mu. The other 2,801 households shared 2,000 mu. Of the 119,000 animals, 9,000 were owned by the 2,801 households. There was plenty of wind and sand and poverty here. The caravans to Khotan took seven days.

But they did have a police station, two herb doctors, and a school with 154 pupils and ten teachers.

"The feudal exploitation was bad," party secretary Mattusun Chirip said. "There were two real despots among the twenty-nine landlord families. They had people flogged to get them to work harder. But the people starved. Corn was the only possible harvest, because the water was so late. The harvest did not suffice for the whole year. All we had in plenty was beggars, sand, and wind.

"We shot Yakub Hadji after the liberation. The masses demanded it, they met and claimed his life. He was a thoroughly wicked man, an oppressor. The masses would not have understood if we had not shot him; they absolutely demanded his life. The other landlord was a despot too, but he was spared by the masses. He was allowed to die of old age. The other twenty-seven landowning families had less land. Now they all work in the people's communes. The path of socialism was the only way to lead us out of misery. We now have enough grain for our requirements, and can even sell some to the state. Last year we sold 800,000 jin of grain and 12,000 sheep to the state."

It is a small town. We walk along the main street. The literacy campaign is taking place and all walls are covered with writing. There is a bookshop and a department store. Even here in the desert the selection is impressive, and the prices are the same as in Kashgar or Urumchi. I buy some posters in the bookshop.

"We now have twenty-two cars and fifty-five tractors in the county," Mattusun Chirip says. "Eighty percent of the families have radios. We have telephone communication with most of the production brigades in our four communes, we have hospitals and secondary schools, and the retail trade last year turned over 419,000 yuan. We learn from Tachai and create it all by relying on our own strength."

There is a performance in the evening. Young people have come in from the nearby production brigades to sing and dance.

"They are a little nervous," Mattusun Chirip says. "They are amateurs, after all; they've never performed even in Khotan. And now they are to give a show to foreigners. You are the first foreign visitors we have had in Niya."

An Uighur girl steps forward and sings in a high, clear voice "I am a militia girl." We all applaud her. She blushes slightly and sings another song: "Our party secretary visits the work team."

"It's the young people who have amateur groups," Mattusun Chirip says. "They have learned to sing and dance at school, and when they leave and join the work teams, they stay together as a group and sing and dance together. The party encourages that, we find it quite important. We have always enjoyed a lot of song and music and dance. Uighurs have always loved singing. Confucius never had a strong influence here; he preached that it was immoral to dance and sing and express one's joy."

Two Han girls are now singing "Tachai shows the way."

"We have defeated Confucius, and now even Han girls can sing. They never experienced the oppression to which previous generations of women were subjected. They have all learned to sing and dance and work at school, and they have learned to overcome the old national prejudice employed to sunder the nationalities of China."

An Uighur boy steps forward, carrying an instrument, a *rahab*. He sings a ballad: "We follow Chairman Mao."

"There are 616 party members in the Niya county; 532 are Uighur. The Youth League here has 1,175 members; 1,035 are Uighur. I am the secretary of the party committee; four of the seven members are Uighur. There are 647 cadres on state level, that is, on commune level and higher, and 413 of those are also Uighur. This distribution shows what we have achieved in these years. But many things remain to be done—for example, the issue of women's rights. Still, 124 of the 647 cadres are women, that's a step in the right direction."

Four girls are singing "On the shore of Niya River," a song of their native home in construction.

"They wrote that song themselves in their production brigade. It's good that they are proud of what we have done. They have listened to the old people talking about what it used to be like. It's quite a good song. It is already popular here. People like to sing about their own life and their own area. But there is still so much to be done; we haven't even a proper asphalted road to Khotan. And the road to Tunhwang can't be used by ordinary cars; it has to be widened. And we must have a railroad. Also, we have to develop our county. It will be a long time before this area is on the same level as the rest of the country, and it will take a lot of hard work before China is a strong and developed socialist country."

The whole company are now performing, singing the final song together: "We greet the Eighteenth of August project." We go around thanking them. When I shake their hands, I feel that they have rough working hands. They are amateurs and meet only at night to sing and dance.

"It is the Youth League that is responsible for the amateur activities," says the girl who sang about the party secretary visiting the work team. "We who have returned to agricultural work after going to secondary school live and eat together, and at night we learn songs and dances. The older people appreciate our singing and dancing."

"Everyone dances here in Sinkiang," Mattusun Chirip says.

When we go back to the guest house, the night is black and velvety around us. Standing in the courtyard is Li Shu-shan, the party secretary from Khotan. He has driven here in his jeep. He throws down his cigarette butt and puts it out with his heel:

"The Eighteenth of August project is really something. The Niya people have good reason to be proud of it, as I told you even in Khotan.

Tomorrow you'll have an early morning, we must be off to the mountains at daybreak. One has to take advantage of the cool morning air."

We have come to Niya to see the Eighteenth of August project. Li Shu-shan had talked about it in Khotan. When we asked to go there, he said:

"It's more than three hundred kilometers of bad road across the desert. The new road isn't finished yet. That trip will take some time. But if you want to go, we'll change the program."

"Yes," Gun said. "We do want to go to Niya. I have always wanted to go there."

"I'll telephone Urumchi to arrange for a permit," Li Shu-shan said.

And here he was now, in the courtyard at Niya.

"I had to come here anyway," he said. "This was a second reason."

When we enter to go to bed, Abdullah says:

"He is a good cadre, he does not stay behind his desk. He is known to sleep little and work hard and spend plenty of time in the various production brigades. He lives with the masses and listens to them. I consider him a good party secretary, even if some people think otherwise."

As we drive south through the desert in the morning, the mountains emerge from the dust. We follow a paved irrigation canal cutting through the sterile ground, and then continue across some low hills, reaching a deep canyon just below the mountains. They now burn arid and red ahead of us.

"What was the situation?" says Wang Wen-ho, the man responsible for water construction within the revolutionary committee of Niya county. "What was it? Three months a year Niya had water. From the end of August there was a drought again. The annual rainfall is only a few millimeters. In February and March they didn't even have drinking water. The herds were thirsting. It was impossible to develop the agriculture."

"In 1964 Chairman Mao advised: Learn from Tachai!" says Imin Tursun, who works in the water construction department of the revolutionary committee. "When we were studying this directive we asked ourselves: What would that mean in Niya? The party raised the question with the masses, who pointed out that we were short of water in Niya, but there were waterways and springs in the mountains, which had water all year round. But the stony ground there was completely sterile, and it was tens of kilometers away. The water then seeped away in the stony ground, disappearing before it ever reached any arable land. The masses said that this water ought to be brought to the fields. Then Niya would never have to suffer from droughts again. But it was tens of kilometers away airline distance, and the ground conditions were difficult.

"After discussing the matter with the masses, the party and state cadres together with the People's Liberation Army formed a hydrogeological investigation team. It brought food and water and made a detailed measuring of this area according to the directions and instruction of the masses. They worked at it for two months. The investigation team had sixteen members and found four good spring flows that could be used. All four of them are now being worked; this one and another two are already in use, while we're extending number four.

"But then, in 1964, the investigation team brought back all the information and we had long discussions. We even commenced the work but it was stopped by Liu Shao-ch'i's line. So we could only map it out before the Cultural Revolution."

"The water here has dug a canyon," said Ma Chi-min. "This valley meanders like a deep cut through the mountain and the stony mass. But the ground is such that the water will trickle away and evaporate, and the whole water supply disappear within a short distance. When we say that Liu Shao-ch'i's line stopped the exploitation of this water, it's quite right. The party committee discussed the issue, and certain leading comrades of the county stopped the project, influenced as they were by Liu Shao-ch'i's line. They saw only the difficulties, not the possibilities. But we must realize what their actual mistake was. The project put forward by the group assumed the digging of a canal, several tens of kilometers long. It was to be dug through mountains and huge strata of gravel. We had neither machines nor concrete. Postpone it! was their reaction. Many good comrades wavered. But then they joined the view that it was an impossible task. If the state would not help us technically with iron and concrete and machines, the project was impossible to carry out."

"That was how Liu's line showed itself here," Mattusun Chirip said. "But it really was an impossible project. The mistake was in the whole issue's not being referred to the masses but becoming a technical discussion, where the actual possibilities were not realized. They only discussed a project suggested by engineers and found that it was too technically demanding and too expensive to carry out.

"Now, however, the Eighteenth of August project has been realized as a tunnel, 6,400 meters long, leading the water to the irrigated areas. And this project was carried out by two people's communes through their own efforts. They had no engineers. Until the summer of 1966, there were heated debates in Niya, and the decisions were scrapped twice. At last the work commenced on August 18, 1966. That was when

Mao Tse-tung received the Red Guard at T'ien An Men Square. That is why the tunnel is called the 'Eighteenth of August project.' "

"In the spring of 1966, when the discussion was again intensified, we had given up the thought of a canal for the suggestion of building a tunnel," says Ma Chi-min, vice-chairman of the revolutionary committee, one of the educated who have gone to settle in the countryside. He was in the Red Guard during the Cultural Revolution. The masses raised the issue and raised it in a new way. In the summer of 1966 the decision could thus be taken.

"Those who had eventually been able to agitate to such an extent that the masses agreed with them and could convince the party committee were two old poor peasants: Kasem Suchi and Ruzi Khalla. The management had stated in the summer that it was not possible to build a tunnel because there were no resources. There were neither machines nor engineers nor material for the work, not even instruments. Kasem Suchi then said:

" 'Should we not be able to drive a tunnel six kilometers through the mountain with the incline we need by relying on our own strength? You say that we would not be able to keep it straight! All we need are three lamps and a level. Trust the masses, comrades!'

"Kasem Suchi and Ruzi Khalla were not merely poor peasants; they had worked as goldminers up in the Kunlun Mountains before the liberation."

"All the time we had considered an open canal an impractical idea, absolutely out of contact with reality," Kasem Suchi said. "We said so too. A tunnel is the only sensible thing for such big constructions.

"The cadres then said that a straight line could certainly be drawn on the ground, but it was a different matter to carry it through the mountain underground. But we had the experience. We had been digging in mountains all our lives. When digging gold you go straight down first and then you drive a passage horizontally. If you have been doing this for a whole lifetime, you can sense what is straight and what isn't. Besides, we have a simple method which is always applied in our work. We use three lamps for marking, which is really terribly simple. Then you only have to decide whether the tunnel should go up or down or to one side or the other. Three lamps in line guarantee perfect accuracy. We told the party committee: 'If your technicians can't solve this problem, we can.' The technicians then accepted our method."

Kasem Suchi and Ruzi Khalla were made responsible for the project. Their experience guided the work of the two people's communes in their work.

"You must understand the comrades in the party committee as

well," Mattusun Chirip said. "It was an immense project. The two people's communes had only eight thousand inhabitants. And whatever the method, you also needed concrete and iron."

"The work took five years," said Ruzi Khalla, the man responsible for irrigation within the party committee. "On August 18, 1966, we started to dig, and in August 1971 the canals were opened. The tunnel itself was completed in February 1970. The work was financed in such a way that the production brigades of the two people's communes contributed manpower and tools. Concrete and iron were supplied by the state. The number of working days was about 100,000. The remuneration given by the production brigades was between 0.7 and 0.9 yuan per working day.

"The tunnel is completely cemented, so no water is lost through trickling or leaking. The fall is 120 meters. We have already completed a first water-power station giving 250 kilowatts and are preparing a second stage which will give 1,000 kilowatts. We are planting shelter belts along the canals. We reckon that these will have matured by 1980. We have almost tripled our yields and will increase them even more. We are also getting a guaranteed supply of energy thanks to the water power."

"The masses took this work very seriously," Ruzi Khalla said. "A woman comrade worked here for four months without even going home to take care of her family. I myself worked underground for eighteen consecutive months. The rule was that nobody should work more than three months underground. But I was used to it, I had worked like that all my life.

"There were so many technical problems that had to be solved. It's always like that when you work underground. You have to build proper supports for sand and stones, which slows down the work. The roof may fall in unless it's properly supported. Also, there is too little oxygen and you have difficulty breathing in a long tunnel. Then you have to dig fresh air channels. But all problems can be solved by discussion."

"One comrade sacrificed his life," Mattusun Chirip said. "The roof fell in over him, and he was jammed under a stone. One of the cadres rushed in to help him but got jammed himself and injured. There were several other accidents but they were less serious."

"It was an enormous job done by only two people's communes," Wang Wen-ho said. "But it has really given results. They used to have only corn; now they grow winter wheat on 10,000 mu. In 1970 the cereal production was 4 to 5 million jin. Now it is 11 million jin, and when the whole project is completed and all the canals are working, we expect 44 million jin."

"For two consecutive years we worked underground in three shifts," Kasem Suchi said. "Seven men in each shift. All we had was our usual tools, digging and hoeing our way, six kilometers underground. The tunnel was two meters wide and two meters high."

"Don't forget," Ruzi Khalla said, "that the tunnel serves not only for irrigation. It will also be useful in case the social imperialists attack us."

"The other people's communes here in Niya county are extending the other waterways," Mattusun Chirip said. "The Eighteenth of August project showed that we could build by relying on our own strength."

We walk through the tunnel, wearing oilskins and rubber boots. We wade through the water. People light the way around us with flashlights. The tunnel walls are properly masoned.

"This is learning from Tachai," says the party secretary Li Shu-shan from Khotan, who is walking next to me.

When we get out, it is already midday. The sun is burning and the heat stifling. We are to eat and rest before returning to Niya. They have spread rugs and blankets for us on the earth floor in the canteen of the canal builders, and we are given sour milk, bread, and mutton. The floor is of stamped earth and the walls are of stone. It is cool in here. Abdullah suddenly says:

"This was a huge job for these poor people's communes. But do you realize what 0.7 yuan is? Seventy fen. That is not quite the price of a packet of those cigarettes that foreigners in China prefer. And that is what these comrades were given for a night shift underground! To follow in the steps of Tachai is a necessity to us, if China is to develop. But it is not a stroll for pleasure!"

20
The Politics of Sand

They wake us up before daybreak.

"It's raining in the mountains," they say. "We have to leave in fifteen minutes, or we shan't get past Keriya and onto the proper roads before the water comes."

Just after sunrise we are on our way west, but the air is stuffy and yellow from drifting sand, and we can't see the sun. It is raining in the mountains; it is hot and difficult to breathe. The dunes are smoking and the fine dusty sand blows from them as they move across the road. The yellow sand splatters around the wheels as we cross the road through the new dunes.

"This is the way it is," our driver says. "The new road south of Takla Makan will be a step forward but we won't be able to have reliable communications until we get the railroad."

The riverbeds are still dry. We drive fast. The jeeps have a hard suspension; they bump and bounce. As we go through the bends I can see the other two jeeps behind us. All three of them are Chinese made. I turn around, saying, "I'd like a word with the comrade who designed the air inlet and the side windows." They only open halfway, and one can't even put an arm out. The air is stuffy.

"What was that?" Abdullah says. "I can't hear you."

The noise from the engine is loud, and the sand is spattering.

"I said this jeep seems to have got its body designed for midwinter use," I shout.

"Oh yes," Abdullah replies. "These cars are good in winter. Driving in snow is almost like driving in loose sand; it is the same technique."

We laugh. He produces a thermos flask and pours me a mug of tea. We are hot and the sand is spreading like a veil over the road ahead of us. As we reach the top of a hill, the driver brings the jeep to a halt.

The once dry riverbed down there is already a hissing stream of yellow water, meandering, twisting, cutting into the earth.

"You see why you have to hurry when it rains in the mountains?" Abdullah said.

The water was rising but the stream had not yet had time to swell into a river. The other cars caught up with us, and the drivers went down to the water to decide on the crossing.

"We'll get over," said the driver when he returned to the jeep. "But it won't be possible in another hour or so."

"If we hadn't left so early this morning, we would have been stuck in Niya for a week," Abdullah said.

"We'll go first," said the driver.

He applied the four-wheel drive and the cross-country gear before going into the water at the ford. It was not deep yet, not even 75 centimeters. But the current was strong, and he had to drive at an angle against it to keep his direction. It was difficult to get onto the bank; the sand was loose and the water was eroding it and had formed a step. But the jeep crawled up out of the water, and when we got onto the firm gravel of the other side, we stopped. The second jeep now drove into the water. It came across but couldn't get up; it had got stuck in the loose sand and the wheels dug in.

"People who wonder about desiccation and believe dry gullies in deserts are proof of desiccation because they are dry, and who don't know that the rains can come and gullies dry for decades can become roaring rivers in a matter of hours, can't have traveled much in countries like these," said Gun.

The third jeep had come across and had managed to get onto firm ground. It was now backing down a bit, very cautiously. The tow lines were attached, and they tried to pull up the jeep that got stuck. But it had gone too deep into the sand.

"We'll have to dig," Abdullah said.

"You needn't help," the driver said. "We know how to do it! You just make sure that the wheels grip, and that there are no deep drifts of loose sand in front of the wheels."

It was windy and we were sheltering behind the high sandbank, looking at the water whirling past. The air was yellow and the water seemed to be rising.

"Let's talk about women," Gun said.

"That's an important issue," Atik Kurban said. She was the vice-chairman of the revolutionary committee of the Khotan district and was sitting next to Gun.

"We have to work politically and combat prejudice. We have to change the thinking. It was a religious problem at first. Women were strictly forbidden to take any part in politics. It was unthinkable. At first, when women spoke up in politics, they would be flogged. Then just after liberation the party sent out women cadres to agitate among the women that they should take up the fight against religion and against unreasonable prejudice. Women then joined various political movements. They became active when we put a limit to the tenancy fees. When we crushed the local despots, the party mobilized women to step forward and accuse landowners and religious fanatics. It was very important that the women stand up and tell in a loud voice what they had experienced.

"The land reform meant that women had a right to own land and a right to vote. This was legal equality. That was an important step forward. The new marriage law was the next step, arranged marriages were forbidden, and the marriage age was raised. At the same time the party mobilized the women to take part in production. That gave them incomes of their own and thereby the economic basis for equality.

"In the administration the party gives preference to women cadres. It's the same within the party. We have to educate women cadres and give them responsible positions. We also strive to increase the number of women who go on to higher education and who become workers. All these are practical measures taken to break the old male dominance and create the proper relations between the sexes. There are three forces driving this development. The first is the leading role of the party. The second is the support of the poor peasants and those exploited who were most oppressed. They are a strong driving force. But even more important is that the party has succeeded in mobilizing the broad masses of the women. That changes the situation. So in the end the issue is determined by the policy of the party."

When we have another 114 kilometers to go to Khotan, we drive into Chira. The oasis is situated behind sand dunes thirty meters high. Between them reeds are growing. Chira is in the desert, tens of kilometers from the nearest oasis. Its area is 64 square kilometers, and 4,500 families live there. They now have thirty-three tractors and a truck, and they are battling against the sand. That is a political struggle.

"If the work stops for just a moment, the sand will take over," says Abdur Rahman, party secretary of the sixth production brigade. "Here we wage a constant war against the desert.

"But," he continues, "we do not just fight the desert. It is also a political struggle between the classes. We are now digging away the dunes and binding the sand and extending the arable land. We are bringing more water here from the mountains in a new canal, which we have paved. We are also using the ground water; it's not too deep here. But digging away those dunes is hard work.

"There's no easy way of doing it. One has to work. In itself, it is not too difficult a problem; we dig and we plant. The masses have always known how to plant shelter belts. They know that the desert can be driven back meter by meter according to the water supply. But in the old days, the social structure was such that we could never carry out these jobs.

"It has been and is even today a hard class struggle here in Chira regarding these issues. There used to be cultivation around the sand dunes. The land was privately owned. At the liberation there were about 9,000 people here belonging to 2,700 households. There were about ten local despots. The number of landowners amounted to about a hundred. The rest were poor peasants, rural proletarians, and beggars. The people had two main enemies: the sand and the oppressors.

"We began changing all this in earnest in 1964. Chairman Mao then gave the call to learn from Tachai. For example, look at the sixth production brigade. There are 478 households here, with 600 workers. Since 1964 we have planted 407,700 trees, which is more than 220 trees for each one of our 1,850 inhabitants. We have removed 132 sand dunes and built a whole network of irrigation canals. The yield in this brigade has increased from 280 tons of grain in 1965 to 670 tons. We now sell to the state. It's all thanks to Chairman Mao. But it has been at the price of a hard class fight.

"The 600 working members together devote about 8,000 working days a year fighting the desert. This is what the disputes are about. It is the same all over Chira. A lot of hard labor is required: a couple of working weeks for each person each year in the construction. We are not rich here. We were very poor, and we are still not well off. But we do support ourselves now. What can the commune members earn in one working day? Not much—only 50 to 60 fen. I have been to see the new settlements north of the mountains, where the commune members earn seven times more. We know that. But we can only improve our situation by increasing our production, and we can only increase our production by fighting the desert. And that fight claims about two working weeks a year from each inhabitant here in Chira.

"This is where the class enemy has started to fight us. The class enemy says: Why should man drudge like that? Why should he keep striving so to raise production? We would survive even if we didn't toil so hard. We don't have to try to combat the desert; let's be happy keeping the desert in its place. That would give us more time for ourselves, and we wouldn't have to work so hard. Each person could then look after his own garden better. That is the argument of the class enemy. And we have to apply systematic propaganda against this.

"We are preparing for mechanization. It is necessary, as part of the plan for China's modernization. That is why we level out all fields and remove all sand dunes within our area. We bring irrigation canals forward and plant shelter belts; we transform nature. This is also where the class enemy attacks us and uses God against us. The class enemy claims that it is unlucky to move the dunes. God himself created them, it is not up to man to move them. We should do what God wants us to do and what they have always done before here in Chira: cultivate the land around them. But the class enemy does not believe in God; he just believes that saying this will give him back his power. The old landlords haven't changed their attitudes; they think they will regain power. And although they don't oppose us with weapons, they fight us with ideas. Therefore, we have to fight back with arguments.

"We explain why it is necessary to remove the dunes. We demonstrate how production can increase. We show that we are able to do this with our own power, and we reveal the reason for the class enemy's arguments and show what he really means when he talks about God's will. There is a very real reason why the class enemy tries to stop us from removing the dunes and leveling the fields and making them suitable for tractors. This, you see, would remove their old boundaries. They are used to looking out over the fields, saying this is mine and that and that one. But now that we are removing the dunes, their fields are disappearing, and that means they can never reclaim the land again. They don't want any changes. They think they'll regain power and that everything will be restored to what it used to be.

"They employ all kinds of methods. They try to take advantage of people's superstition, using God. God doesn't want us to increase our arable land, they say. They make use of bad old customs, saying that man was not intended for hard work. They also try to gain influence with certain cadres. You and I are educated people, they say. We know that projects of this size can only be carried out with appropriate management. We need some good engineers from Kashgar or Urumchi or at least Khotan to accomplish all this. We can't let the ignorant masses do it; they will just make a mess of it. It's much better to wait awhile and have it done properly."

"We have a difficult fight here in Chira," Abdur Rahman said. "We know that all their various arguments are only excuses. We also know that what we need at the moment is to utilize the knowledge the old poor peasants have gathered for generations. In that way we can build up China and at the same time learn to master the new techniques. But if we want to succeed in increasing production, the masses must agree to devote almost all of their spare time to the fight against the desert for many years to come. There is no other possibility. This means increased input on the collective level now, when our standard of living is yet low. The class enemy exerts himself to make people think of their private economy instead. But we struggle to convince them that the collective economy is the only possible basis.

"In 1964 when this fight started, the production brigade was in such bad shape that we had had to borrow 17,000 yuan from the bank in order to manage. We have now paid this back, and we have accumulated 100,000 yuan in collective funds. This year we can distribute 60,000 yuan to our members. We have been able to get two tractors and thirteen rubber-tired wagons. We have bought two diesel engines for the water pumps. That's progress. We can show concrete results of our fight against the class enemy, but this means that we must struggle with the desert all the time, and that struggle is mainly political. We take a firm grip on the revolution, and carry through the class struggle in order to raise production."

As we drove into Khotan the posters flapped in the dying storm. Painted slogans proclaimed that party secretary Li Shu-shan was a capitalist roader. He holds the production foremost, they said. The phrases were tumbling about on the posters. There should be some real kind of revolution: one which did not talk of digging against sand so much. The mass struggle for irrigation and tree planting according to the Tachai spirit that now was carried through all around in the various counties of the Khotan district, was not truly revolutionary. Party secretary Li misled the masses onto the capitalist route, it was said.

"How strange," Gun said. "It seems the class enemy in Khotan has become a phrasemonger and an ultra-left revolutionary. In Khotan he does not talk about God but about the revolution. Still, the contents are the same."

21
Turfan

The Gobi Desert is grey and huge under the red mountains far north. We are driving toward Turfan, and the road becomes a thin line on the rim of an immense bowl. From the red edge of the mountains far north, the bowl slopes toward the green center. Far down below the vegetation the mist shows through. Turfan is a depression under the mountains; its lowest point—the central lake in the middle of the depression—is 130 meters below sea level.

The town of Turfan has 20,000 inhabitants. In the whole of the Turfan district there are about 100,000 Uighurs, 21,000 Hans, and 11,000 Huis. It is a rich agricultural area, dry and hot and sunny. The summer heat lasts for 90 days, with an average temperature of $+40°$ C, the highest summer temperature being $+47.1°C$. The temperature of the earth surface goes up to $+75°C$. The annual rainfall is 16.6 millimeters, and the evaporation 3,000 millimeters. Sandstorms ravage through Turfan thirty times a year, sometimes growing into hurricanes. Turfan is known as one of the glowing ovens of China. It is a rich agricultural area with excellent melons, grapes that melt in the mouth, long-staple cotton. Since ancient times it has been one of inner Asia's grain stores. All agriculture is irrigated with water brought from far away.

The road slowly takes us in toward the center of the bowl. Long rows of mole holes seem to run from the mountains in the north to the green center, but that is an illusion. The holes are as large and rough as wells, this being a kareze area. The karezes conduct water from the mountains to the arable land. They are a strange invention, and have many names. In Persian they are called *qanat*. Sometimes they are named "underground canals." But they are not underground canals, although the water is protected from evaporation; they are really horizontal wells.

Tomb painting from the late T'ang dynasty (mid-ninth century) at Astana, Turfan

Seventy-year-old Ismail the builder, Turfan

Amin Hodja's mosque in Turfan, erected in 1777

New buildings constructed by the second production brigade of the Burning Mountains People's Commune

Builders like Ismail maintain a tradition that has existed in Turfan for centuries—new houses are built next to ruins.

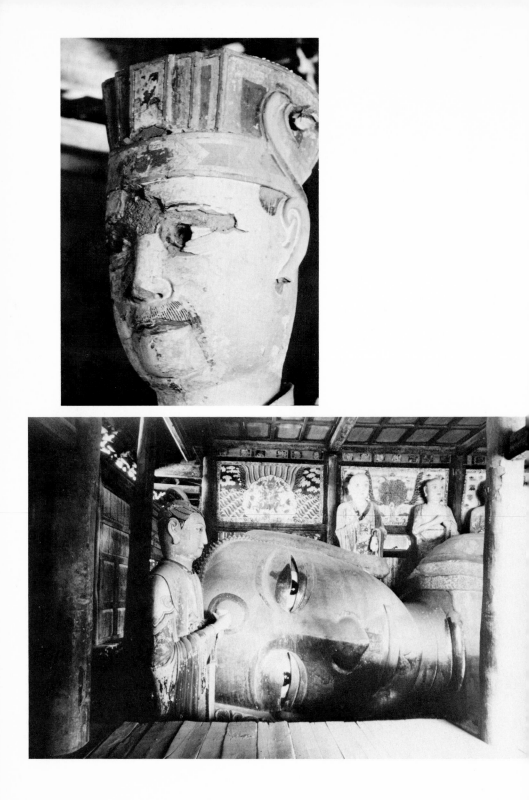

The reclining Buddha in Changyeh, formerly known as Kanchow, is famous. The temple was erected during the Sung dynasty in 1098. The sculptures were given their present shape in 1776. The temple is now a protected monument at the provincial level.

The steel city of Kiayükwan is completely new. It did not obtain its city privileges until 1971.

In 1980, the steel production and rolling mills are due to be completed.

Life in the streets at the oil field of Yümen

The clock tower in Kiuchüan

A drum tower in Wuwei, built during the T'ang dynasty, rebuilt during the Ming dynasty, and restored during the Ch'ing dynasty. It is now a provincial monument.

The water-bearing strata are very deep below the surface. Digging a well as deep as that would be impossible from the technical point of view, and even if it were possible would present such great hauling problems that the project would be too costly. Instead, the well is driven toward the water-bearing strata in the distant mountains.

Far away at the foot of the mountains, the water trickles away into the spongy ground before reaching the impenetrable layers of clay. The vein can be drawn there and led under the desert floor up to the cultivated fields. The water-bearing strata are deep underground at the foot of the mountains, but they are higher than the cultivated fields in the desert.

The solution is to dig shafts with even spaces between them, from the spring to the fields, and connect these with a dug tunnel. The shafts are necessary to give the diggers air and to enable them to haul up the earth they dig out.

The kareze is a great technological achievement. It demands a full knowledge of hydrogeology from the builders. They must be able to find the rich water-bearing strata, and dig their tunnels through varying strata without losing too much water. They must manage to drive a tunnel with an even upward inclination one, two, four, eight, or more kilometers, avoiding loose sand, and give the kareze an inclination such that it cleans itself and does not silt up again immediately.

I was fascinated by the kareze the first time I saw one in 1958 in Iran. I have talked to kareze builders in Iran and Afghanistan. They were popular technological experts. Now their tradition is dying, their craft and lore being pushed aside by engineers trained in the United States and Germany. I was told in Soviet Uzbekistan in 1965 that the kareze was an outdated and useless technique. The karezes were silting up around Bukhara. But here at Turfan were newly built shafts, and here they were still developing the art. Recently 150 new karezes had been added to the 400 older ones. Of course people build reservoirs in the mountains and construct ordinary canals; of course people in Turfan drill deep wells (619 of them since the Cultural Revolution), but they still keep the karezes; maintain the old ones, build new ones.

The road had been asphalted, but the asphalt had been plowed up by the waters during the spring floods. Now, however, the ground was completely dry and the car jerked and bumped as we crawled over the break.

"As you see, we still have water to take care of," said Ruzi Turdi, chairman of the revolutionary committee and deputy member of the CPC central committee.

"There is another use for the karezes," he went on. "They give drinking water. We prefer cold water. I myself drink fresh cold water. The kareze water is clean, and cold even in the hottest of summers."

But the Turfan karezes are a problem. I have read in learned German books that they are ancient, but as far as I know, there is no proof of this. Sir Aurel Stein stated, like Huntington and Pelliot, that the Turfan karezes had been introduced "a century or so ago" and built according to Iranian tradition. He also describes how the building of karezes had been encouraged after the Chinese administration was reinstated, and that this meant that land cultivated only every three years, owing to the lack of water, could then give annual yields.

This is far from unlikely. I haven't heard of any research proving that the Turfan karezes go back to medieval—not to mention even older— traditions. But farther west the karezes are old. If Jørgen Laessøe of the University of Chicago was right in 1951 in his reading of the cuneiform report on Sargon's eight campaigns in 714 B.C., there would then have been an extensive kareze system at Lake Urmia in northwestern Iran.

In the Kharga oasis west of old Thebes far out in the desert in Egypt, there is a kareze system in use, built under Darius I about 500 B.C.

When I was told in Peking that the kareze system had probably been brought to Turfan from the inland in the Han dynasty and been developed after a Shensi pattern, I first found this a good expression of cultural Han chauvinism. But before I had time to protest, they went on saying that other authorities claimed the karezes came from the West.

The situation became slightly more complicated when they stated that Ssu-ma Ch'ien in 100 B.C. described in his *Historical Notes* what must have been a kareze construction in eastern Shensi.

In July 1887, when Captain Younghusband passed here on his way from Peking to Kashgar and India, he made a note that he had been told that the well systems he saw were built by the Chinese army. He himself was more inclined to believe that they were karezes of the type to be found in "Persia and Afghanistan." The discussion about the Turfan karezes is not new.

The first Chinese description of Western karezes was given in the mid-thirteenth century. In 1256 Hulagu had defeated the Ismailites in Persia. (In Europe, these are mainly known as assassins and hashish addicts and devilish intriguers. That, however, is a political legend, created by Baron von Hammer-Purgstall, so admired by Balzac, in 1818 when he wanted to demonstrate the danger of secret societies like Freemasons and Jesuits. This legend is very much alive in books and newspapers and encyclopedias even today. But it is possible to see the Ismailites' as a peasants' revolt, veiled in a mystical ideology.) The

Chinese chronicle writer Chang Te notes that there is a special type of
hunchback ox in the land of the Ismailites; it is called zebu by us and
exists even today from India to western Asia. He also noted that "this
country lacks water, so the people dig wells on the mountain tops and
then take the water tens of li down to the plain to irrigate their fields."

The afternoon is hot, but the shadow under the vine leaves is cool.
I am eating melon and drinking tea and discussing the Turfan karezes
and their origin with two of the responsible kareze builders in Turfan.
Kurban is seventy-eight. He says:

"Our family has built karezes for several generations—for how many
I couldn't tell. But the art was not born here in Turfan; it was brought
here, I think from the inland. You see, most of the oldest karezes here
have Han names. Even the words for the tools we use are Han and not
Uighur. The winch, for example, with which we haul up the containers
of earth has a Han name. If the art had come from the West, it would
have had a Western name. Other arts have words from the West, you
know!"

When we discussed this in Peking, they had said that the question
had not found its final answer. The karezes could have been brought
by soldiers in the Han dynasty but could also have been introduced
from the West. In Kansu, anyway, they are called "Persian wells."

I asked the historians in the local museum in Turfan, and later the
archaeologists of the Urumchi museum, if there were any exact details
known about the history of karezes in Sinkiang. But they, too, replied
that this matter had not yet been sufficiently researched.

Still the karezes in Turfan, as far as I could see, were exactly like the
ones I saw almost twenty years ago outside Teheran. And the winch
that had a Han name here looked just like the one they used in Iran.
At the same time the description from the inland seemed to apply more
to underground canals of the type we had seen in Niya. The real kareze
system as it could now be seen in Turfan, and in other places in Sinkiang
and down through Kansu and farther east in Mongolia, seemed to be
a new technique spreading eastward. It gave—as Stein said—possibilities of larger yields and more regular ones on irrigated land.

The night is stiflingly hot and it is difficult to sleep. The darkness is
dry and solid. We try to quench our thirst with tea and discuss the
karezes:

"All knowledge does not have to emanate from one focus," Gun said.
"When people face similar problems, they achieve similar solutions.
The kareze may have been created in both China and Iran."

That is reasonable and plausible, and she may be right. But the old
systems created well before the Christian era seem different in Iran and

China. The particular system of karezes, though—the horizontally driven well, not just an underground canal—seems to have come specifically from Iran.

"You don't have to be a diffusionist to find it likely that people learn from each other," I said.

"But if there weren't any karezes in Sinkiang until 1780, but there were kareze constructions in Shensi, how could that knowledge spread from Iran to Shensi then? Did the teachers fly over Sinkiang? It is rational to assume that the problem was solved independently."

The question is not answered. The archaeologists haven't examined all the old irrigation systems. All literature has not yet been examined. But if it turns out that, in fact, there weren't any kareze systems in Sinkiang until recent times, and that the construction of karezes only started in the nineteenth century, mainly after Yakub Beg had fallen and the Chinese administration had been reinstated; or if it turns out that once—in the Han dynasty—there were actually kareze systems but they fell into decay and were rebuilt only fifteen hundred years later . . . that is, if what is now usually said of karezes in China is proved true, then there is an explanation that can cover this.

Gun has fallen asleep but I wake her up to say:

"Building karezes demands great skill. It is not enough for a man to see a kareze and then go home and dig. The kareze builders have always been organized in guilds and families and have had their own kareze lore. That means the art will not spread by itself. In other words, our friends may be right and the Turfan karezes may come from the inland and the tools have Chinese names although the technique is from Iran, because what they build in Turfan is not Ssu-ma Ch'ien's underground canals but proper karezes!

"In that case the Chinese administrators must have taken over the Iranian technique deliberately and introduced it to increase the yield. That would certainly agree with their general policy, and it would explain why the old karezes and the tools have names in Han."

"The kareze builders in the old society were despised," Kurban said the following day. "We were at the bottom of the social ladder. We had to work hard and remain poor. My father taught me. I have built karezes in Turfan and Toksun and in many other places. We used to work for the landlords. That was hard. Chairman Mao set us free. We were given no respect in the old days. I and my father and his father before him built karezes and brought water to the fields, but no one respected us.

"It's a demanding job. We dig the karezes here sixty to seventy meters underground up at the head. I'm too old now to work underground. But the cadres and the masses use me as their technical adviser when they build karezes. The cadres show great respect now, and there are many good youngsters and young cadres who come to learn from me. I'm old and arthritic and can't go into the shafts, but I stand at the edge giving advice and inspecting the earth brought up. One has to know the different strata in the ground and what they are like at various depths. People also come to me from several brigades for advice on wells. I tell them how the water flows underground and where it is and what they ought to do. We old peasants and kareze builders are given respect now."

"Karezes need to be well maintained for the water to flow properly," Ushur Nijaz said. He is forty-one and builds karezes like his father before him. "The kareze will silt up. Before 1966 the work teams tried to look after their own karezes, but that didn't work. Since then we have organized the maintenance and construction in a different manner. The party committee discussed the kareze issue at length, and we now have a new system. Unit No. 2 comprises 25 work teams with 50 karezes altogether, maintained by a special kareze team of 150 men. The task is partly to look after the karezes, which is a dangerous job. But it has to be done; if it isn't, it becomes even more of a risk. We try to enlarge the karezes up at the water-bearing strata to increase the water supply. Also, we clear away silt. This we do with great care. We remove the sediments even from the time of the old society. In that way the water supply increases and the agricultural yield too.

"In the old society no real maintenance was done. The water supply thus decreased. Karezes could run dry. I myself work in a kareze group of six with one leader.

"When it comes to building new karezes or doing larger jobs we are 40 to 50 people. This is a job for specialists which demands great skill. Enthusiasm isn't enough.

"We will work ten days at a time underground when necessary. It's a heavy job. Before the liberation my father did not get as much as an hour's rest; the landlord was over him constantly driving him to work on. His body became worn down and he fell ill."

22
The New Monuments

It never rains in Turfan, but it did now! Large heavy raindrops, rolling in the dust, lying like dark wet stains in the street. But it is true that it never rains in Turfan, for although it was pouring high above us, and the sky was black with drifting rain, the heat was so intense that the drops evaporated before they hit the ground. A few did manage to get down, however, and I felt a proud joy as I opened up my black umbrella over us when we walked out of the town during the siesta.

Everybody seemed to be asleep. But the air was stuffy, and the weather weighed heavily. Gun and I had gone out alone to try to find Amin Hodja's mosque. When we got out of the town we could see it in the distance. The minaret, conical like a sugar loaf, stuck out behind some domed tombs far away on the other side of the fields. We had walked for three-quarters of an hour and made our way across the fields, followed irrigation canals and climbed ravines, and now arrived at the large burial place. The domed tombs did not look very old, perhaps a few generations. We zigzagged between the graves to avoid walking over them. Here and there we could look into a grave. Turfan is Moslem and Moslems are anonymous after death, unless they have been saints or great men.

We arrived at Amin Hodja's mosque. It was a remarkable building; its shape was mighty. It was built of brick and sun-dried brick, with decorations all in brick. The masonry was decoration.

"It could have been in Khiva," Gun said. "Without tiles and glazing and with stricter decoration. So it isn't really like Khiva."

We went around the monument. Large placards with Uighur and Han texts proclaimed that this was a protected monument. The autonomous province had declared it protected. Any damage was prohibited.

"But visitors have been here and scratched their names only a month

178

ago," Gun said, pointing at the wall filled with names and dates. "In two thousand years these will be precious graffiti from the time of the revolution, but I do feel that Turfan ought to protect its monument better."

We were to attend a discussion about barefoot doctors in the afternoon and went back into Turfan after a short hour's visit to the mosque. The road from the mosque went through old Turfan, where the houses had beautifully carved porticoes. Outside them women were chatting while their children played. They stared at us as we passed.

"They will have to get used to visitors," Gun said. "Abdullah said that they will soon open Turfan, first to diplomats and journalists and in due course, when the hotel is completed, to tourist groups with archaeological interests."

The following day we returned to Amin Hodja's mosque, now with Ruzi Turdi, chairman of the revolutionary committee, and Mehmed Jusup, party secretary of Turfan county.

"Of course the monument is protected," Mehmed Jusup said. "We do try to teach people not to damage it. And they don't do it intentionally, they just can't see why they shouldn't scratch their names there. It is a bad tradition. The Chinese emperors and the high mandarins used to scratch their names as soon as they saw a monument. You must have seen that in Sian and Loyang and other places. Now everybody does it. It's a nasty habit. We are fighting it, but as you can see, we haven't quite succeeded. We could keep a guard out here, but that wouldn't be very nice. Still, you're quite right. We must be more serious about this, it looks bad."

"They even write their names on the placard saying that damage is prohibited. They can't claim that they thought it was allowed," Gun said.

This is great architecture, but it is also an important historic monument. Suleiman Hodja had it built for his father, Amin Hodja, when he died of old age at eighty-three in the forty-second year of Emperor Ch'ien Lung's reign. That was in A.D. 1777. Amin Hodja had associated himself with the Chinese administration at an early stage. In 1732, in the ninth year of Emperor Yung Cheng's reign, he had been given the title of Count. In 1756, in the twentieth year of Emperor Ch'ien Lung's reign, he was given the title of Duke, and two years later he was promoted to Prince and adviser to the viceroy. Amin Hodja's career in the hierarchy of the Ch'ing dynasty is typical of the way this dynasty used the feudal relations to transform more or less independent rulers with power of their own, based on landowning and religious influence, into vassals, then integrating them into the Chinese administration.

The minaret is forty-four meters high. The panorama is magnificent. But the wall has cracks.

"In 1957 the edifice was declared a monument on the provincial level, and in 1958 the necessary reinforcement work was carried out. You can see the iron bands around the minaret and the iron clamps holding the walls together. We will restore it, as soon as the budget permits. But the danger is not imminent, and we have so many demands to safeguard historical relics here in Turfan, so we can only do what is necessary. The other monuments will have to wait."

We are driving toward Karakhoja, which was the Uighur capital up to the fifteenth century.

"We Uighurs were converted late," Ruzi Turdi said. "That is why the religious prejudice doesn't go too deep."

As we went through the old ruined city, the heat lay over us like a weight of lead. Gun took photographs.

"Keep the camera cases in the shade," she said. But I couldn't find any shade.

"What about your own?" she said.

Ruzi Turdi spoke about the archaeologists:

"They started coming at the turn of the century, and then they kept trying to get in here for several decades. British and Frenchmen and Germans and Russians and Japanese and Hungarians and all sorts of people. But what kind of people were they?"

Ruzi Turdi gave the answer himself:

"Thieves! Thieves and spies!

"What else could you call men like Aurel Stein and Albert von Le Coq and your own Sven Hedin? They traveled and researched and dug, and they were called scientists and they were knighted and given medals and rewards.

"But the right name for a man like Aurel Stein is a military spy and a thief. What was Le Coq if not a thief?

"They traveled here, measuring march routes, drawing military maps. Aurel Stein didn't even draw himself; he brought two Indian servants to do the job for him! So they were explorers! How could anyone explore countries, roads, and towns that had been known and described for two thousand years? The towns they described and visited had traded with Europe long before Berlin or Stockholm or St. Petersburg had even been thought about. We had cities when those were but forests and marshes and wilderness! And they come here to explore! Spies! Look at that wall! Can you see the recesses? Can you see the paintings? There were sculptures there once. You can see where they were. These so-called researchers discovered them, Le Coq and Aurel

Stein. Now they are gone, they took them. What do you call that? We call it theft.

"Not to mention what they destroyed. Our archaeologists cry in rage when they visit places excavated by these gentlemen. Not a trace of scientific method! Just robbing and stealing and destroying. They were worse than graverobbers. They destroyed our priceless assets. And besides, they drew military maps all the time.

"What they stole was only a fraction of what they destroyed, and much of what they took has been lost or bombed to pieces in the Second World War. These so-called scientists devastated more cultural monuments in a few decades than the number destroyed by wars and barbaric invasions in two thousand years! We'll never admit them here again!"

I have met people who believe that Ruzi Turdi's aggressiveness was due to general xenophobia. But suppose instead it had been groups of Chinese traveling around Europe, exploring. Suppose these explorers, by an unfortunate accident, happened to burn down South Råda church while they were taking the paintings from the north wall. Suppose they happened to drop and lose a devil when they chiseled off the sculptures in Trondheim cathedral in Norway, and then had half the load of carved wood from the Urnäs stave church washed off the deck of their junk returning home . . . we would hardly call them cultural heroes.

Is there any reason why people in Sinkiang should regard Aurel Stein and Albert von Le Coq and all the others in a different manner? What would that reason be?

Even long before 1949, patriotic forces in Sinkiang tried to stop the plundering. Eventually it was virtually impossible for foreign treasure hunters to dig in Sinkiang. The last one to try officially was, as far as I know, the German Trinkler. He and his companions were expelled in April 1928 after patriotic Chinese officials had caught them vandalizing, destroying, and stealing priceless sculptures near Khotan. When Sven Hedin made his last journey in Sinkiang, he traveled on behalf of the then central Chinese government, and he had been forced to commit himself not to try to excavate. He still did. Since 1949, as far as I know, only one or two foreign archaeologists have been admitted for a quick tour of Sinkiang.

This does not mean that Sinkiang is closed to researchers. It is, however, closed to plunderers. It is quite likely that foreign researchers in the future will be able to take part in excavations, but this will then be as part of a mutual scientific exchange based on total equality and mutual respect. China is not xenophobic. But the road may still be long, because the "Western" researchers still like to regard Sir Aurel Stein and Albert von Le Coq as scientific researchers and explorers. As long as they maintain that attitude, they have little chance of cooperating with their Chinese colleagues in any field work.

In the burial grounds of Astana we enter tombs with wonderful paintings dating from the latter part of the T'ang dynasty. The tombs are cool in the heat. They are like the underground rooms which people build for themselves in Turfan, as in Iran and India, to get away from the summer heat.

"These tombs were examined in 1972," Ruzi Turdi said. "They were plundered long before that, probably even in the T'ang dynasty. But we still made quite a few finds. Some we keep in the museum here in Turfan, but most of them are in the provincial museum in Urumchi.

"When the social imperialists conducted their propaganda, saying we were not China, and tried to create conflicts, and kept their radio transmitters going day and night a few years ago, we used to have huge mass meetings here in Astana and other places. Tens of thousands of people arrived. We then showed them on site how the connections between Turfan and the inland had developed. We told them about the Silk Road. We took the masses into these tombs to let them see the murals for themselves. The people must take hold of their history!"

When we were leaving Astana, I saw that they were building new low houses with barrel vaults in a village in the production brigade. The houses were large. I walked over to them. There was to be a performance in the evening. But I said we still had time to study the new village. They were using sun-dried brick. They went looking for the master responsible for the work. He was an old man with a sharp gaze, named Ismail.

"I am responsible for the construction work of the second production brigade of the Burning Mountains People's Commune," he said. "The work is planned by the production brigade. The lots are distributed by the work team. My father taught me to build, he was taught by his father. We use the same technique as the one our ancestors used for building the ruined cities over there. It suits the climate and it suits us. We build houses to keep the heat out.

"But the technique is changing. My father, for example, used large bricks for the vault, of about eighty by twenty centimeters. That meant he had to use centering to support the vault as it was bricked. I use smaller bricks. It has the advantage of enabling us to brick the vault without any supporting frame.

"In practice it's done like this: the family who is to have a new house makes sun-dried bricks in its spare time. It is not very difficult to make them if you've learned it as a child. Then a master works with five men on building the house. It's done with mutual help; everybody helps everybody. The master and his apprentices are paid directly by the work team, and the family then has to pay this back to the work team in two or three years. That makes building easy, and anybody can have a new house. The main thing is the planning and the mutual help, which must be used.

"On principle we build a large barrel vault from the front garden to the back. That is ten meters long and four meters wide. The height of the walls is two meters, and the greatest height three meters and sixty centimeters. The external walls are ninety centimeters thick, the inner ones seventy centimeters. The roof is twenty-four centimeters thick.

"From this main room we then build side rooms if needed. Here in this house we have two barrel-vault rooms of six by four meters on one side, and a storage room with the same dimensions, but with a flat roof. On the other side we have one open room of three by four meters and behind it a lavatory of the same size and a storage room of four by twelve meters with a flat roof and a support in the middle. The total area of this house, not counting the garden, will be 180 square meters. The family has seven members and their total expense will be 400 yuan. Not counting all storage rooms and such, they have more than ten square meters in which to live.

"As I said, this type of house is traditional with us. But it's worth remembering that we have changed the technique as such ourselves. Our ancestors and my father used a lot of wood for supporting frames while they worked. By using smaller bricks we have managed to get away from that, so we can work more effectively. Our aim is to provide new houses for all families. We have now built 240 new houses here. Some have seven rooms, like this one, but most of them have five. Unless the family is very large, that is quite sufficient. Counting each space as a room—that is, including the storage spaces—one could say that, as a general rule, a family of five needs five rooms and a family of seven needs seven."

On our way back Ruzi Turdi says:

"We have achieved a few things in Turfan. It's a rich fertile land. The trade turnover of consumer goods here has gone up from 8,870,000 yuan per year in 1962 to 15,700,000 yuan per year in 1975. That means it has doubled. Every family now should have the main four: a sewing machine, a bicycle, a transistor radio, and a watch. When every house has a radio, the isolation is broken. That means a lot.

"This is the way we practice Marxism-Leninism and Mao Tse-tung Thought."

23
Stalin's Cleft Shadow

Stalin stands as a statue under the poplars in the yard outside Secondary School Number 7 in Ining. Gun wants to photograph the teachers, and they form a semicircle under Stalin's eye. The sun shines on the left half of his face, but the right half, turned toward the school building, is in darkness. The windows of the schoolrooms are filled with students staring down at us. Then the windows are opened, the sun's beams are reflected, and they pass over us, glistening, as we watch the teachers arranging themselves to be photographed under Stalin's bust. The students cluster like grapes and lean out of the windows. Now a window on the ground floor just above Stalin is opened, the right half of his face is bathed in a heavenly light. He has a halo of light under the trees with all the teachers stiff around him. He is as beautiful as a painting by John Everett Millais: "Joseph Blessing the Grail Seekers." But behind him, Stalin's shadow is cleft where it extends under the trees. The two different shadows are lost in the darkness. It is a strange sight. It disappears as quickly as it came. The window has been opened wide, and the reflection moves on. Another cluster of schoolchildren presses forward. Stalin's right side is again in darkness against them, and now the sound of laughter and chatter rises toward the leaves, while Gun takes photos of the teachers.

But Stalin's shadow is certainly cleft in Sinkiang. In Sinkiang and in China and all over the world. This school once bore his name; it was the Russian school of Ining. "The secondary school named for Stalin." It was directly responsible to the Soviet consulate and employed exclusively Soviet schoolbooks. The order was Russian. And the exodus of May 29, 1962, was organized from here. With the teachers in front, the children formed ranks on the command of the Soviet consular staff, and then they had to march to the frontier. Those children still haven't returned. Half the school marched off. Now the Soviet influence has disappeared. The school has been integrated in the ordinary school system. It has changed its name, and is now called just "Secondary School Number 7." But Stalin's statue is still there, respected and honored. They give him flowers on memorial days.

In Urumchi, too, there is a statue of Stalin. And on T'ien An Men Square in Peking, Stalin looks out toward the Gate of Heavenly Peace along with Marx, Lenin, and Engels. He is one of the great. His books are read, not without criticism, and the cleft shadow is seen behind his work. His positive part to the negative is as 70 to 30, they say. And 30 means almost a third, which is quite a lot.

Mao Tse-tung gave this judgment, which guided the Chinese Communists from the mid-thirties onward. It means that Stalin's historic assets are considered greater than his mistakes and shortcomings. Many people find this attitude hard to accept. They have been taught that yes is yes and no is no. If Stalin is not the great and glorious leader Khrushchev claimed he was up till 1953 when Stalin died, he must be the mad crook Khrushchev claimed he was when Stalin was safely dead and buried in 1956. They seem to have difficulty seeing Stalin in his historical perspective, as a man of his time.

Mao Tse-tung did. That is why, while Stalin lived, he could praise him for his contributions and consider the general analysis correct, but at the same time he would, in practice, avoid accepting all the unsound advice and erroneous decisions delivered by Stalin and the Stalinist Komintern. The Chinese Communists were faithful to the basic line of the Komintern policy and analysis, with which they agreed, but they did not follow unreasonable decisions based on ignorance; and after 1935 did not allow its representatives to lead the Chinese people to defeat. They reached early that conclusion which was officially accepted—at least verbally—by all member parties, by even the Soviet leaders, when the Komintern was dissolved. The Komintern was an organization that had outlived itself in a situation where the communists had grown into mass parties leading the national liberation struggle.

The total disdain shown by Chou En-lai and other veterans of the Long March and the Yenan Period for such people as the unsuccessful and useless "military adviser" of the Komintern, Otto Braun ("Li Teh") with his Prussian-officer manners, was balanced by their sincere respect for Stalin's general analysis and historic significance. The Chinese Communists would never have managed to establish a broad national front in their fight against the Japanese aggressors, nor would they have managed to triumph in 1949 and start to build the new China, had Mao Tse-tung and Chou En-lai and the other Communist leaders not ended the possibility of Moscow's interference in China's affairs. This was done out of concern for the Chinese revolution at the Tsunyi Conference in January 1935. They considered the general line of the Komintern correct, but found its practical advice disastrous.

This was obvious to everybody as early as 1936. Chiang Kai-shek had been captured in Sian on December 12 by Chang Hsueh-liang, who was the leader of the KMT Northeast Army, and Yang Hu-cheng, who led the KMT 17th Route Army. They demanded that he defend China against Japan. Mao Tse-tung sent Chou En-lai to Sian as a representative of the Chinese Communist Party to negotiate a solution. Chiang Kai-shek was forced to accept a united resistance against Japan, and was released. He returned to Nanking, where he made a weak and ambiguous statement, saying among other things that he had been held up by "reactionaries." In a statement on December 28, Mao Tse-tung pointed out that this was quite impossible. He discussed the issue in detail, showing that the "Sian intermezzo" had been the result of concern for the nation's existence. Three days later, on December 31, the Komintern condemned the action. The "Sian intermezzo" was not only reactionary; it was, Moscow stated, the first outcome in China of the German-Japanese anti-Komintern pact.

This judgment on the situation in China was as absurd as the judgment of the German occupation of West Europe, which made the Komintern at the end of June 1940 advise communist parties to contact the German occupation troops and ask to be declared legal and to be given German permission to publish their newspapers under protection of the occupying power.

Unlike the Chinese Communists, the West European communists obeyed such commands from Moscow.

Thus, they failed to become parties expressing the needs of their own people. In France it was Charles de Gaulle and not Maurice Thorez who took the responsibility of declaring, in the name of the French nation, the national war against the occupiers.

One could say that a judgment like the one made by the Komintern on December 31, 1936, regarding the "Sian intermezzo" was incorrect, and the order cabled by the Komintern in June 1940 to the communist parties of occupied Europe were mistakes.

But when do the mistakes grow to major errors? Let me give an example, which has the advantage of being disputed through and through: the pact between the Soviet Union and Germany in August 1939. In the situation of that time and with the policy maintained by England and France, this pact was a reasonable and rational political act. This view is not undisputed. I do not feel I have to repeat all the arguments in favor of it here. They are well known.

The secret agreement, which implied the division of Poland in case of a new political and territorial arrangement, can be defended; a diplomat must be able to take future events into account and protect himself against every conceivable development. But it was not a correct judgment of the general political situation. One could say it was necessary to stop the German armies from conquering the whole of Poland, and that the Soviet Union thus tried to save as much as possible of Poland from German conquest. But even so, the secret agreement was a mistake, as was the command to the West European communist parties to be legal parties by the grace of the Wehrmacht.

The Soviet invasion of Poland on September 17, 1939, was, however, given a completely different character by the decision made by the Supreme Soviet of the Soviet Union on November 1, 1939, according to which the western Ukraine was included in the Soviet Union; plus the decision of November 2, 1939, according to which western White Russia was included. Those decisions were no longer incorrect judgments or mistakes or deviations; they were errors.

In these decisions—and later in a series of similar ones regarding the Baltic states, the Finnish borderlands, the eastern provinces of Rumania, the eastern part of Czechoslovakia, the Japanese Kuriles, and Tannu Tuva—the Soviet Union, Stalin-led, followed in the footsteps of the Russian czars and did not act as a socialist state with a Leninist policy.

When Mao Tse-tung pointed out that the Soviet Union occupied the Japanese Kuriles unjustly, and when Chou En-lai said he did not know what Kaliningrad was, although he knew of a town called Königsberg, and at the same time maintained that Stalin was a great Marxist and an eminent political leader, then by so doing he pointed out that the errors committed really were serious even though the general policy might be positive. The errors for which Stalin was politically responsible, which include this czarist territorial expansion, were so great that Mao Tse-tung saw them as making up a third of Stalin's complete political work. But the errors must not conceal the great assets Stalin had. And the Chinese leaders who were not servile to him when he was alive do not damn him now that he is dead.

There are many issues concerning Stalin and his policies that are never discussed in China. Some of them are discussed internally. The Stalin issue does not concern China only, but other countries as well. In 1964 the Albanian leaders complained to Peking because Mao Tse-tung had criticized Stalin's policy of territorial expansion. Since then it has been obvious that opinions differed between the Chinese Communist Party and the Albanian Party of Labor as far as the attitude to Stalin was concerned. In other matters also and with other brother parties and other socialist countries there may be different opinions. In such cases, China has not without necessity opened a discussion which might have a disintegrating effect. Therefore, many concrete historic situations where Stalin was involved are quietly passed over in China, or are discussed only internally, within the party. This, however, does not mean that these matters have been forgotten or that their principal significance is neglected.

The documents have been kept, but the concrete discussion will have to be postponed. One could say this is a traditional Chinese attitude. But the principal stand has already been taken: Should towns and mountains be given names after various leaders? How and when is capital punishment to be applied? How should conflicts and differing political lines within the party be treated? How should the economic planning be carried out? Many other issues included in the whole complex "Stalin question" are discussed in principle, but Stalin's name is not mentioned.

Other matters are also difficult to discuss, because many of the people involved are still alive, and there is not yet access to all the documents. This goes for matters concerning Sinkiang in the thirties and forties and into the fifties.

"Don't expect any comprehensive answers about Stalin when you ask questions in Sinkiang," one of my Chinese friends told me in Peking, as we were about to leave for Urumchi.

Another friend lent me *Sinkiang: Pawn or Pivot?* by Allen S. Whiting and General Sheng Shih-ts'ai, just as we were off.

"Read it on the plane," he said. "It can give you some odd information. But use your own sense when you read it. It is written by the CIA, and as far as General Sheng is concerned, it is a defense writ. You won't have many confirmations in Urumchi, and neither will I discuss the details with you. You must use your own common sense."

"You have talked a lot about Stalin during this journey," I was told six months later by a very responsible leading Chinese political cadre in a private conversation just before leaving Peking. "You must realize that the battle in Sinkiang was never about Stalin. We want to keep him out of the conflict. We have great respect for him. We did not remove

Stalin's picture after Khrushchev's black, so-called secret, speech. One could say, generally, that Stalin was a great Marxist. We do criticize him, too; we have published two comprehensive articles about him, 'The Historic Experience of a Proletarian Dictatorship' and 'More About the Historic Experience of a Proletarian Dictatorship.'

"We think an analysis of Stalin's work shows that there were mistakes and errors, even major errors. But most of his work was correct.

"When we discuss these things we don't blame Stalin. I hope you take note of this. No serious conflicts occurred in Stalin's time, not even concerning the issues of dual nationality. As long as we had the same interests, our relations were good. The Khrushchev clique later took advantage of this issue and others."

It's true that the Chinese have not taken up the issue of Stalin where Sinkiang is concerned. One of the reasons is that Stalin did not actually take over Sinkiang. He may have had plans to do so; he had embarked on a number of measures which could have enabled him to do it. But he did not, and however his actions are seen, the fact is that he did not actually question China's sovereignty. That is why he is still standing in the yard of Secondary School Number 7 in Ining and is regarded as a great Marxist-Leninist. But the shadow behind him is cleft, and that must not be ignored in a discussion about Sinkiang. He represents an epoch between the Leninist revolution and those who, according to the Chinese view, have become new Russian czars, following the Russian czarist foreign policy. He inevitably enters the picture of Sinkiang history in that perspective.

No state has been expanding for so long and by such methods as that despotism which first appeared as a Tatarian tax collector and as an authority created by the Tatars in Moscow, then grew with cunning and violence into Russia and a world power. The only possible exception would be the English colonies on the northeast coast of America which were united and expanded into the present United States of America. But that history is shorter and its development more jerky and less stubborn. It is, however, typical of the two superpowers of today that they have a radically different historical background from other states.

Karl Marx, as a nineteenth-century politician and historian, kept warning the world of the danger of this Russian state of a peculiar despotic type. It was not only generally reactionary, a European gendarme prepared to intervene against any liberation movement. It was also aspiring on an international and long-term plan for world rule. Its history, from its origin as a Tatar authority to its position as a czarist world power was an unbroken chain of atrocities and broken pledges, and the explanation of Russian behavior in the nineteenth century could easily be found in Ivan Kalita of the fourteenth century: the same sly, cunning, servile, cruel, despotic, stubbornly forceful exercise of power prevailed.

What I'm writing now does not sound very sympathetic. It opposes the whole liberal nineteenth-century image of Russia. That is intended. Marx meant that this very liberal Russophilia was a deadly threat to Europe. He also pointed out that European liberty was smothered by this hidden cooperation of British liberalism and Russian despotism. If I add that Marx had a view of the great Nordic war and Charles XII that was radically different from that of Swedish liberalism and Bernadotte policy, I do this not to challenge but to show how thoroughly the Marxist tradition has been distorted in a time when large groups of European university students have been official Marxists.

The distortion is not accidental; it has been consciously created by the Soviet Union. Books have been suppressed. References have been concealed in huge masses of text. The Marxist views on history, on Russian history, on Russia's role, have been transformed into "un-Marxism," and at the same time—especially from 1936 on—Soviet historical writing has become increasingly apologetic. Stalin contributed to this development; he may even have considered it favorable in a situation where a major war against Hitler's Germany became more and more inevitable. That war would demand much of the Russian people. But the development continued after he died, and the distortion of Russia's role in history now has become the legitimization even for the current policy of Honecker in the DDR. The "de-Stalinization" did not bring a return to Marx but a final removal of Marxist thought from the Soviet ideology.

Marx held that this Moscovite despotism was striving consciously and continuously, century after century, for an empire that would expand to rule the whole world. He also emphasized that Russia had the strange habit, when preparing countries for inclusion in Russia, first of declaring their independence. Seemingly unselfish Russia fought for the independence of the Crimea, Poland, and others before swallowing them. Engels described Russian diplomacy as a Jesuit order, a closed corporation which, in spite of the internal decay and corruption of the empire, was skillfully extending the despotic Russian power in the direction where the defense wall was temporarily weakened. This is the dark picture of Russia and Russian power, which not only Marx and Engels but also the great Russian Marxist saw. Plechanov and Lenin in different ways (Russia, the prison of the people) saw Russia and its history along these lines. They considered the breaking of Russian power as not only a general liberation but a generally necessary liberation. And this was the background of Lenin's views on the right of the nations. This picture of the old czars should be remembered, now that China refers to the "new czars."

It is also necessary to describe Stalin's dark side, or the cleft shadow he cast over Sinkiang will not possibly be understood.

24

The Russian Game

The road from Ining to Dzungaria and the inland first runs north to Huocheng and Chingshuhezi, where it joins the road from Alma-Ata and the frontier. Traffic is lively at the bus station. This is the route for transport trucks. The road then turns west, cutting through the Takli ravine, turning and twisting up toward the pass over bridges and through tunnels. The road is famous in Sinkiang. I saw it for the first time as a model in the provincial exhibition in Urumchi. Model trucks climbed a model road between model trees in a perspectively intricate module. Now we were driving it in reality, and all the heavy traffic between the inland and the Ili valley drives through this ravine.

The road is new, although the route is ancient. It was the Chinese mail route. It is said to have been founded in 1219 by Genghis Khan's second son, Jagatai. In the autumn of 1221, when the Taoist Ch'ang Ch'un and his disciples traveled down this route on their way to Genghis Khan's court, there were forty-eight bridges across the Takli River.

"They have been built with wood taken from the mountainsides and are wide enough to enable two men to meet," his disciple Li Chi-chang remarks in the account of their journey published in 1228.

Once over the pass, the horizon opens up. In front of us in the white valley is the immensely deep blue Lake Sairam. This is Ch'ang Ch'un's "Heavenly Lake," and the sight is remarkable. In the middle of a landscape of sweeping lines and high white mountains against the dark sky, a large round lake lies clear and marvelously blue, surrounded by light stillness. It is so beautiful that breathing becomes nearly painful. We leave the cars and stand at the edge of the road. We look out over the valley deep under us. The guard at the pass comes up to us. He is wearing a long green padded coat and has the fur collar turned up against the wind. He points at the yurts in the meadow near the white

192

shore far away: "That's the camp, where we're going."

An icy wind is blowing over the pass but the air is clear. The outlines of the landscape could have been cut with a chisel. The colors form distinct contrasting fields, and the scenery has such pure beauty that my chest and my eyes ache from looking at it. There are people down by the yurts, several of them. They have come out and gather into a little group. A fine streak of blue smoke from one yurt can be seen clearly rising straight up before turning off and disappearing in the wind. The yurts down there must be sheltered. People have seen us; one of them is waving. I can't see whether it's a man or a woman. The guard shows me that they are waving to us. They are waiting for us.

For ten years the Cossacks guarded this pass for the czar of Russia. In 1871 the Russian forces had seized the opportunity of conquering the Ili valley. To protect it, they said. In 1861 the first Russian traveling reporter had found his way here. Sixty years later the area was occupied. Then Lake Sairam was mapped out. Russian land surveyors and geologists wandered through this pass on towards Dzungaria.

The occupation of the Ili valley was part of the general Russian advance. There had been Russians in China ever since the Yuan dynasty. They were the vassals of the Mongols. Russian troops were also included in the bodyguard of the emperor in Peking. Even in 1544 the ambassador from the khan of Kazan to Emperor Chia Ch'ing of the Chinese Ming dynasty had a bodyguard of Russians. But in 1552 Kazan was conquered by Ivan the Terrible and the route east was opened. Astrakhan fell in 1556, and the Russian trade company around the Stroganov family expanded east across the Ural. The company general, Yermak Timofeiev, on its behalf conquered the capital of Siberia in 1581. The czar took over what the merchants had conquered, and the Russian advance east continued: Tomsk in 1604, Yeniseysk in 1618, Krasnoyarsk in 1628, and Yakutsk in 1632. The Russians were now far east of the river which had once served as a national frontier, Yenisey, and they pressed on toward the Pacific. However, when the Cossacks approached the rich countries around the Amur, they were coming into lands where people were Chinese tributaries.

The inevitable conflict was sharpened by Russian cruelty. When the Cossacks under Poyarkov made their expedition to the mouth of the Amur, for lack of food they ate the opponents they had killed. This created a spreading horror of the Russians among the Amur people. The Russian atrocities, even measured by the standards of those days, were enormous. They could easily be compared to those of the Spanish in South America and the British in North America. Still, there was one essential difference. The Spaniards managed to defeat the Indian kingdoms which tried to organize resistance. The British did not need to fear that there was a Indian kingdom ready to defend itself behind the Indians they killed. But the Peking court received one report after another about barbarian raids against the people of the northeast and about bloody aggression against peaceful and defenseless farming villages.

After a period of fighting and negotiating, the frontier between Russia and China was then drawn by the Treaty of Nerchinsk in 1689. Russia had to give up all pretensions of conquering the Amur country. That frontier served until Russia, almost two hundred years later, took advantage of the weakness of the Chinese emperor's court and the Franco-British war in China to conquer by cunning the Chinese territory up to the mouth of the Amur and then all of the coastal area toward the Sea of Japan, for which they had striven ever since the first expeditions in the 1640s.

The Nerchinsk treaty drew the frontier between Russia and China where the two empires now met. But west of the river Argun, Russia was still far to the north. There was no common borderline in existence there. But Russia pressed on. According to plan Russia built fortifications south along the Irtysh through Kazakh country. Omsk in 1716, Semipalatinsk in 1718, Ust-Kamenogorsk in 1719. The Russian advance had been triggered by rumors of great finds of gold in Turkestan. On May 22, 1714, Czar Peter had commanded the advance. He had given orders that captured Swedish mine technicians and engineers should be mustered and made to join the troops. Peter was prepared for an alliance with the Oirats, who were in revolt against the Chinese Empire. This preparedness he showed time and time again, while his troops fought the Oirats and founded one fortified camp after another south of what had been the Russian frontier. On December 31, 1721, Czar Peter charged Captain Ivan Unkovsky with the task of securing the Oirat submission by a treaty of friendship and mutual assistance between Russia and the Oirats. If the Oirats recognized Russia's supremacy and gave Russia the right to their gold finds, Russia in turn would protect the Oirats against Peking.

Captain Unkovsky brought gifts to be used in the creation of a friendly attitude among the leading Oirats. Mining experts accompanied the delegation. Czar Peter wanted Unkovsky to stress that the Russian use of Oirat natural assets would be in the Oirats' own interest. The Oirats and the Russians had the same interests, and the Oirat ruler would be given a commission on the Russian profit, and the Oirats themselves would be given lucrative jobs as miners. The mines would have direct connection with Russia by a new series of fortified armed camps.

This suggestion sounds strangely modern. One could say that Czar Peter portended the tactics of a highly developed imperialism. But he failed. In November 1722, when Captain Unkovsky reached the Oirats, the situation was changing. The Oirats were not willing to submit to Russia. China demanded Russian restriction. During negotiations in Peking, China stressed that it could not accept any Russian settlement in the Chinese Uriankhai (Tannu Tuva), that Russian fortifications along the Irtysh would force China to fortify the Irtysh, and that a restricted Russian advance was the condition for trade with China. Russia had just defeated the Swedish kingdom, and there was no possibility of its mustering forces enough for a war on then powerful China. In the Treaty of Nystad on August 30, 1720, Russia had obtained Livonia, Estonia, Ingermanland, Dagö, Oesel, Möen, and parts of the counties of Viborg and Kexholm. It was busy mustering its forces to advance farther west and—as Marx said—make Czar Peter's eccentric capital the center of a new European empire.

In 1727 a new border treaty was signed between Russia and China, fixing the border west from the point where it ended in 1689. This still forms an international border. Along most of its extension, it now runs between the Soviet Union and the Mongolian People's Republic. Only at its extreme west is it no longer an international but an administrative frontier within the Russian Soviet Federated Socialist Republic; because in 1944 the Soviet Union incorporated Tannu Tuva, an area of 171,300 square kilometers and transformed the previously Chinese territory into the Tuvinial Autonomous Region. Stalin thereby completed the policy commenced by Czar Nicholas II when in 1912 he made Tannu Tuva "autonomous" from China and in 1914 granted Tannu Tuva Russian "protection." This is one of the actions which the Chinese consider belong to Stalin's bad third.

The diplomat leading the negotiations from the Russian side was one of the foreign experts described by Engels. Sava Lukich Vladislavich was originally from Bosnia. In due course he worked as a merchant in Constantinople, where he became a secret agent for Russia in what was then the capital of the Turkish Empire, the aim of the Russian plans of conquest. Eventually he was made a Russian diplomat and became the head of the Russian embassy in China. At the termination of the ambassadorship, when he had returned to St. Petersburg, he worked as an adviser to the government, specializing in Far East issues.

In 1731 he left a memorial in two parts regarding the matter of war and peace with China. The basic ideas of this memorial then became the guidelines of Russian foreign policy:

Local wars around Amur would incur great expenses and give limited results. To go to war only for Amur was not worth it. It would then be better to keep to the treaties in force. A real war of conquest on China would, however, be a different matter. Provided Russia had peace for a long period in Europe and could save up a large war chest, the conquest of China would be practically possible. China was Asia's richest country; it had the biggest assets among all states of Asia and Europe. Moreover, the Chinese, though diligent and numerous and in a way well armed, were not warriors. Since the ruling Manchus were no more than 4 million and the ruled Han people were 200 million, Russia ought to strive to get the Hans to revolt against the dynasty. That would mean a civil war in several provinces. Russia could then advance from the north over China. The forces Peking could dispose of would then have to be divided into three: one part to keep the garrisons all over the country; one to fight the rebels; and one to take up the fight against the advancing Russian troops. Under these circumstances it would be possible eventually to defeat China and conquer the whole country.

This memorial is not uninteresting today. In that game played in China by the Soviet Union from the mid-50s onward, the chance of supporting a civil war that might disintegrate China and enable the Russians to invade has always been kept alive. Lin Piao's desperate idea of establishing his own base in southern China, making Canton his seat, and cleaving China as in the Sung dynasty would create that very situation that Vladislavich saw as a condition for a successful Russian attempt to conquer China: civil wars in many provinces and a division of the Chinese military power. But if Vladislavich's memorial is still included in the traditionally expansionist Russian strategy, it is known in Peking as well.

My Chinese friends in Peking point out that the Kremlin leaders now follow the old czarist policy to commence an attempt at incorporating an area by ceremonious declarations demanding its independence and autonomy. They refer to Marx and his description of a course of events that relates to Tannu Tuva as well as the Crimea—not to mention Angola. And they are also extremely well aware of which foreign power could take advantage of the attempts of "the four" to obtain power over part of the military forces and bring the country almost to the point of a civil war. Sava Lukich Vladislavich died in 1738, and the dynasty he served is gone, but Russia is expansionist—is again Russia—and this makes his memorial valid. And Peking takes it seriously, as before.

In the nineteenth century the Russian advance continued down toward Turkestan. The Chinese were forced back to the place where the border is still open; they had to surrender territories and accept changes of the border where the Russians could take advantage of Peking's difficulties and move their positions forward. In 1871, when China seemed to have lost its power over inner Asia, the Russian troops invaded Ili. At first the Russian government, as usual in invasions like this one, let the local commanders take responsibility. But there were definite reasons for the advance: not gold any more, but greater interests. The Ili valley is the most fertile area of the whole of Turkestan, and its capital is a center for trade. In 1891, when Sven Hedin was still pro-Russia, twenty years after the Russian invasion and ten years after the partial retreat, he described the situation like this:

> Kuldja is a Chinese town, where Russia, due to the treaty agreed with China in 1852, has a consulate and a factory. Its geographical situation, as a focal point for Russia's trade with China, Tibet, and the towns of Little Bucharia, as well as the innumerable roads leading there from all directions, give this town very great importance, politically and financially. It is the capital of the Chinese border province of Ili, 5,400 verst from Peking and 5,000 verst from St. Petersburg. The town has 80,000 inhabitants.
>
> In 1876 the Chinese defeated the Dzungans, who for thirteen years had driven them from their land north of Tien Shan. In 1887 the Chinese, favored by Yakub Beg's death, took back Kashgaria or East Turkestan, which ever since has remained in their hands. In this way only the Ili province, or the Kuldja area, stayed under foreign rule, as it was occupied by the Russians in 1871, with the agreement of the Chinese government.
>
> Negotiations over several years brought the result of most of the Kuldja area being returned to China, and on August 19, 1881 the Russian-Chinese border treaty was signed in St. Petersburg. It was a very peculiar and unsuccessful policy that made the Russians waive their rights and submit to the Chinese, who hereby gained a more than suitably high opinion of themselves.*

The interesting thing about Hedin's description is not the incorrect information of the Russians occupying Ili "with the agreement of the Chinese government," but the genuine dismay he expresses because the Russians had to give back most of the area they had invaded and occupied without any right whatsoever.

Sven Hedin here reflects pretty well the attitudes of official Russian

*Sven Hedin, Introduction to *General Prschevalskys forskningsresor i Centralasien* (Stockholm, 1891), p. 28.

circles. They found the constant Russian expansion century after century just as natural as they found each retreat unnatural. Ground trodden by the Cossacks became *ipso facto* Russian, and so Ili from 1881 onward became a Russian irredenta.

The Russian retreat at Ili was, however, connected with a general change of direction of the Russian expansion. Khiva, Bukhara, and Khokand were taken, the advance on Kashgar was temporarily interrupted, and it was now time for Turkmenistan and the road to Merv and Herat. At the same time as the advance was made, England should be made neutral and given a chance to retreat from Afghanistan. When the Russian troops left Ili and retreated from Kuldja (Ining), the conqueror of Khokand, General Skobelev, again advanced east from the Caspian Sea. He had a railroad built, kilometer upon kilometer east. He swore that Russia had no ambitions east of Ashkhabad and sent spies before him to Merv. The Russian foreign minister Gorchakov was old and tired, but his niece's husband—and his own closest aide—the Swedish-German noble Nikolai von Giers, was on good terms with the British liberals, declaring that the Russian troops were by no means advancing toward Merv but simply punishing robbers. The retreat from Ili confirmed the peace-loving Russian policy, and Gladstone, who had withdrawn his troops from Afghanistan, was a peace-loving Russophile.

After Giers had become foreign minister, his policy was careful. He knew the miserable internal weakness of Russia. But he substituted cunning for strength, and in his time Russia continued its expansion in Central Asia and its infiltration into Chinese Turkestan. Russia and Britain were now playing the great game over Asia, but the players were not equal. Britain had the most powerful commercial empire of the time, with seemingly inexhaustible economic resources, and Russia was a corrupt, weak despotism, but Russian diplomacy—as Engels emphasized—was superior to the British in all respects and managed a long-term operation. In the year of the retreat of the Russian troops from Ili, when Gladstone had been in power only a short time, all British goods were by decree excluded from Russian Central Asia. When, later in Gier's time, Captain Younghusband met Russian officers up in the Central Asian mountains, he felt that the two nations understood each other as they played for Asia. But he did not notice—not even when the Russian officers forbade him to stay on Chinese ground and blocked the passes against him—that he was really just an amateur and a traveling gentleman who confronted professionals.

The Russians were convinced that they were there to stay, while the British were just making a guest appearance in Asia.

In the years before the First World War, Russia tried to move its positions forward. Even the military defeat by Japan offered new possibilities to the Russian diplomats, who turned the defeat into a secret Russo-Japanese alliance. Russia seemed to change policy, but its aim was, in fact, the same.

The secret alliance included the plan of dividing Manchuria and fixing the demarcation line between Russia and Japan in northeast China. At the same time, the Russian government intensified the penetration of Mongolia. Scientific and geodetic research teams were sent in to survey the land, the Russian political agents tried to contact the Mongol princes, and the Russian press demanded autonomy for Mongolia.

The fall of the Ch'ing dynasty was used by Russia to declare Outer Mongolia and Tannu Tuva independent. On December 28, 1911, the summoned Mongol princes proclaimed that Outer Mongolia was independent. Russia, by lending the new state two million rubles, was given the mineral rights of Mongolia; the Mongol national bank was founded by Russian financiers who had as security the natural riches of Mongolia; Russian experts were nominated for all executive positions within the new administration; and Russian officers began to prepare the establishment of a Mongol military power.

The Chinese government did not recognize this independence. Only in the autumn of 1945 did it give up its demands on Outer Mongolia. The KMT foreign minister T. V. Soong then negotiated with Stalin in Moscow. China gave up its supremacy over Outer Mongolia on condition that the Soviet Union promise to "respect the political independence and territorial integrity of the Mongolian People's Republic." On October 11 the previous year, the formally independent Tannu Tuva had been annexed by the Soviet Union, Soviet troops were holding northeast China, and Stalin pointed out that China might lose Inner Mongolia too, if it was difficult about Outer Mongolia. At the same time the Soviet Union obtained the naval base on Chinese territory in Port Arthur, from which the Japanese had driven the Russians in 1905. In Yalta the Western Allies had promised this to Stalin; now China had to pay the bill.

The secret alliance between the two greedy powers, Russia and Japan, which was the outcome of the war of 1905, was reinforced by additional agreements in 1912. The border line was now drawn farther through Inner Mongolia. Russia and Japan committed themselves to work not only in their own individual interest on either side of the demarcation line, but also in the interest of the other party on the other side of the line. The alliance was kept secret, but Britain was informed, when Russia declared that it was prepared to let Britain take over Tibet on condition that Russia could expand freely in western Manchuria, Mongolia, and Sinkiang, with the exception of Kashgar, which was to be kept open.

The strategic railroad toward China in 1914 reached from Novosibirsk on the Trans-Siberian Railroad to Semipalatinsk. The Russian officers at this time claimed that China was a constant threat to Europe, and Russia must take it upon itself to close the opening which had let out Genghis Khan's hordes. For the sake of European security, Russia had to occupy Ili, for Europe was threatened as long as Ili remained Chinese.

Russia now placed five divisions in the border area of Sinkiang and awaited an opportunity to act. Then the First World War broke out in Europe, and following the example of Czar Peter two hundred years before, these Russian forces were deployed in the European theater. The Allies had promised that Russia, for its efforts in that new war, would obtain Constantinople and the Bosphorus and the Dardanelles and Erzurum and Trebizond and Turkish Kurdistan. The Western Powers also promised to keep silent about Poland's fate. And so on and so forth, even to French support of Russian fortification of the Åland Islands off the Swedish coast in the Baltic Sea. After all, it was a great war for democracy and liberty and national rights of free action. It was a war to end all wars.

If this, however, was the reason why Russia could not accomplish its invasion of Sinkiang in 1914, it did not mean that the plans had been abandoned. They had merely been postponed. And even if Russia's main interest was now concentrated on the European war, Russia did support—according to the secret alliance—Japan's demands on China of 1915. These "twenty-one demands," given to Yüan Shih-k'ai by Japan's ambassador on the night of January 18, 1915, meant that Japan demanded China's transformation into a satellite state. Even the police districts in the most important Chinese cities were to have "joint Japanese-Chinese administration." But Japan took scrupulous care to fulfill its share of the secret agreement with Russia, and what Japan demanded in Manchuria and Inner Mongolia were only parts of *southern* Manchuria and *eastern* Inner Mongolia. China was to be partitioned.

In the summer of 1916, Russia and Japan signed the document, which transformed their agreement on China's partition to a military alliance against that "third party" which could disrupt Russian and Japanese interests in China and try to gain political influence for itself there.

This secret military alliance was made in the middle of the war that was to end all wars, and it presaged a future war against a "third party." Viscount Motono, who signed this secret military alliance for Japan, said to the Russian minister in Tokyo that they might certainly have difficulties with the United States because of this Russo-Japanese agreement, but that by the time this happened, Japan would be in a stronger position than the United States. Russia and Japan in reality had signed a military pact against the United States for a coming war to divide China and gain supremacy over the Pacific.

Beyond that future war still other wars could now be discerned. The Russian troops had been withdrawn from the Sinkiang frontiers only temporarily. China seemed doomed to be the sacrifice.

Then the October Revolution upset the whole dirty imperialist game. Lenin published the disgraceful documents from the secret archives of the Russian foreign office. His Soviet government stated that revolutionary Russia had forever given up all attempts at a chauvinistic foreign policy; that the workers' and peasants' state condemned the Russian czarist policy against China; and that the people living in areas conquered from China by czarist Russia should decide for themselves to which state they belonged. The Soviet government also announced from Moscow that it considered the Chinese brothers in their fight for freedom. On May 4, 1919, the Peking students had demonstrated with the slogans: "Guard our sovereignty! Punish the traitors!" The anti-imperialist movement united China's people, and in June 1919, the Chinese working class conducted its first political strike and took the lead in the fight against imperialism.

The October Revolution gave the signal. The guard next to me in the Takli pass wore a shining red star in his fur cap. When we were invited to enter the yurt prepared for us down by the lake and were received by our host, the old Kazakh Nebi, I saw Lenin's picture next to that of Mao Tse-tung.

25
People's Defense in Dzungaria

It's true that the border between China and the Soviet Union here in Sinkiang is not a peaceful one. But how did this come about? What has happened here in the sixty years since the October Revolution gave the signal for the century to advance?

In Kweitun Gun and I talk of Stalin almost all night. Among the mail waiting for us there were some newspaper cuttings. Gun suddenly snorted:

"Here is another stupid ass from the fifties who has been to China and reports that the country is poor and the problems great. He has met some wooden cadres who speak like leading articles from the *People's Daily,* so he concludes that those who describe a China in construction are as cheated as the Western intellectuals who visited Stalin's Soviet Union in the thirties and returned full of enthusiasm for the U.S.S.R. in construction."

That was how it all started. We belong to the generation who had to take a stand toward Stalin's thirties during the war against Hitler. That the travelers of the thirties certainly were right to be enthusiastic has to me always been self-evident. People like Julius Fucik or Nordahl Grieg or all the others who described how the five-year plans transformed lousy and filthy Russia into a Soviet Union strong enough to resist Hitler were right. History proved that. Stalin had said that it was necessary in ten years to transform this backward Russia into a modern industrial nation. It was done, and he was the political leader of this period. However you look at him, that is his greatness, as it was the greatness of Winston Churchill that he managed to unite an England driven to defeat by the Munich politicians and lead a national war against Hitler's Germany.

I cannot understand how anyone who has been a contemporary of

202

these men could possibly deny their historic significance. Whoever described the Soviet Union of the five-year plans or the isolated small island fighting on had a right even to be enthusiastic.

"And the executions," I added, "and the deportations and the suspicions. I agree with Mao Tse-tung that they were wrong. Far too many people were killed and imprisoned. There was no difference made between friends and enemies, between real enemies and people who had different opinions. But I know what I thought of this in 1942. That is also a truth to remember. I then agreed with Nordahl Grieg that the Popular Front in Spain was wrong in not lining up the reactionary generals against the wall as soon as they gained power. This humanitarian softness cost the Spanish people immense suffering. I said in 1942, when all Europe and Asia were at war and millions of lives were sacrificed, that if an innocent general or so had been executed in Spain, it would have been a small price to pay for the peace and future of the Spanish people. And if Stalin had ordered that no one was to be given the benefit of the doubt, with the consequence of innocent generals and party functionaries in the Soviet Union being executed, that too was a small price to pay, since the Soviet Union was now resisting Hitler in Stalingrad. I didn't hold these views because I was unusually cruel as a teen-ager. But the Fifth Column had crawled out all around occupied Europe, and many old communists like Doriot and Flyg had become fascist traitors. In the Soviet Union there was only one Vlassov; the others had already been shot. That was how I saw it. That was how we in our generation saw it.

"Many turned to the fascists in those days. Wang Ching-wei and Subhas Chandra Bose were once great leftist heroes; they then changed color and became the servants of Japan. There were plenty of the same sort in Europe. Bucharin had in fact considered it advisable to use individual terror against the political line of Stalin, and the pamphlet Radek wrote in 1934 about Stalin (seemingly servile but in reality hateful) was obviously treasonable at a time when the question whether Russia would be able to build into a Soviet Union strong enough to resist the coming attack was not yet determined. Stalin had the duty to render them harmless before they took the opportunity to play the role of a Doriot, a Bose, or a Wang Ching-wei. Each one of us in our generation in Europe who was an antifascist will remember that this was our view those years when millions upon millions of people were killed in that war Stalin had foreseen and warned against, but had not been able to make the European politicians aware of.

"You can phrase it in a nicer way, but if you prefer clear text to political tactics—what alternatives did Stalin have in 1936? The cowardly and corrupt French general staff did not even succeed in uniting itself to recommend that the government strike back at Hitler's troops as they were marching into the Rhineland. Stalin took on this responsibility. He pointed out in 1939 that the purges had been too large and that there had been serious excesses. But in 1942 we did not hesitate to say that the purges were right. It is easy for the late-born to be anti-Stalinist. They are living a life brought about by his victory. They were given life by the millions who had to sacrifice themselves. I did not praise Stalin when he was alive, but I refuse to deny the experience of my generation."

"You don't need to shout," Gun said.

"I'm testing," I said, "wondering how I can possibly make Stalin visible in his time to readers much later in a different time and a different world. Much in China is understandable only when one sees how Mao Tse-tung consciously tried to avoid repeating the mistakes of Stalin. To describe Sinkiang without discussing Stalin's chauvinism and his erroneous policy against Sinkiang is not possible. But in order to see these errors and understand how they later grew into an overwhelming Russian reality after his death, you need to see them in relation to his true historic greatness."

The Chinese, along with Mao Tse-tung, claim that the positive side of Stalin's work well balances his faults and shortcomings. I agree with them. It is not a question of his personality. Surely he had personal shortcomings and dark sides—but who has not? His real shortcomings were political, and they came to have disastrous effects.

The errors he committed were to a certain extent inevitable. No one can take the leap out of his own time. But some of them could have been avoided. Among those were the manner in which the purges were carried out in 1937 and later, and even in those people's democracies where the Stalinist police methods gained a foothold. But I stressed my feelings so strongly from 1942 in order to show how a generation came to accept even that. In China, Mao Tse-tung has striven to learn also from the negative experiences of Stalin's Soviet Union. When a head is cut off, you can't put it back. Killing should be avoided and imprisonment kept to a minimum. Western and Moscow-oriented mass media have never overcome their surprise that political personages in China can "reappear" and not have all been executed after being criticized and thrown out of power. They seem to base their norms of a communist state structure on the court of Ivan the Terrible, and they seem to think that it is natural and right to a communist that Eisenstein in the Soviet Union thought of making a film to praise Stalin in the form of a dramatic tale of the work of Ivan the Terrible. The revolution is certainly no tea party, and people have certainly been killed during the hard class struggles in China—not only the approximately thirty million who died in the wars or in the famines up to the liberation, but also local despots and war criminals executed after the liberation. There was certainly assault and manslaughter when the Cultural Revolution in various places deteriorated into all-out civil war, as Mao Tse-tung called it, and of course there is still capital punishment in China. But people should not be killed for having the wrong political opinion or for political actions: that is an important principle. Several groups have tried to break it, but Mao Tse-tung and Chou En-lai were immutable on that point. Otherwise the revolution would deteriorate.

That is why the Chinese, in spite of all conflicts, do not talk about the steel broom of revolution sweeping away the enemy, or similar euphemisms for the method of solving political discussions with a bullet in the back of the head of the opponent.

"In Peking," Gun said, "Liu Jen-ching lives as an old-age pensioner. He used to work as an editor for the press. But he was one of the founding members of the party, he was one of its first leaders, he organized the opposition against the party in 1927, and he was excluded as an active enemy of the party. But he lives. It was correct to understand Stalin's purges in the Stalingrad winter of 1942. We meant that it was better to shoot some innocent generals than to let the whole people perish, but in retrospect we should be able to see other possible solutions. Liu Jen-ching was not shot. If asked what happened to him, the cadres will reply that one has to distinguish between political enemies and criminals. Stalin was unable to do that."

Neither in economic development does China follow Stalin. It walks on both legs, developing both the agriculture and light industry. The cadres in China are not to become a technological elite, Red directors. Mao Tse-tung learned from Stalin and from the experience of Stalin's five-year plans. He also learned from critically watching the development of the Soviet Union. He managed to see the enormous progress as well as the mistakes and errors.

Stalin had been right in saying that Russia would perish if it was not modernized within ten years and had not by then become an industrial nation. The construction work was necessary. The five-year plans were correct. Those who reported on them in the thirties had been right. The plans saved the Soviet Union and the peoples of all Europe. But the mistakes made during the construction led to errors with serious consequences. In due course they enabled the Red directors to seize the power of the state and transform the Soviet Union from a friend of the Chinese people into an enemy. The Soviet Union changed from a socialism with great shortcomings to fascism.

In China, Stalin is seen as a great historic figure and at the same time as a political leader with shortcomings. His works are read, but they are read critically. His portrait is next to that of Lenin opposite the Gate of Heavenly Peace in Peking. Such is his historic place; he did carry political responsibility in a difficult period. But his work at the same time is one-third bad, and if his greatness is historic, that third assumes vast proportions.

"That is why the Dzungarian people's militia study Stalin," Gun said. "They have military exercises to defend the people, the revolution, and the future and their homes against the rapacious military machine of that state which after all was built and developed by Stalin. It is not always so easy to keep both aspects in mind."

Especially here in Sinkiang it is both most necessary and most difficult to discuss Stalin's policy and find out what the Chinese see as his positive 70 percent and his negative 30 percent. Here it is not a discussion about his policy in general, not about the Komintern's advice and decisions. Here it is a question of direct interference (as under different circumstances in the northeast of China). Sinkiang during most of the thirties was almost a kind of Mongolia, a part of old China where, however, development seemed to pass via autonomy and independence to a client condition under Moscow and—perhaps—eventually to incorporation into the Soviet Union. Later, at the end of the war, when Tannu Tuva had already been annexed and the Mongolian People's Republic had formally abolished all ties with the Chinese government and had openly become a Soviet satellite state, the question seemed to be whether that "East Turkestan Republic" which had been formed under Soviet protection in the west of Sinkiang would become incorporated into the Soviet Union like Tannu Tuva, or become formally independent like the Mongolian People's Republic.

Sinkiang in the thirties was, however, at the same time a Chinese warlord province and a Chinese province with a strong official anti-imperialist movement. And the democratic movement that brought about the East Turkestan Republic was considered by Mao Tse-tung to be part of the democratic and revolutionary struggle of the Chinese people; the East Turkestan Republic joined the revolution and several of its leaders are still in the political leadership of party and state.

The questions this raises are complicated and have no easy solutions. Many of today's conflicts have their roots in the thirties. We discuss this in Urumchi and the hosts say:

"Sheng Shih-ts'ai came into power in 1933. Chin Shu-jen had usurped the power over the province after the murder of Governor Yang Tsen-tsin and then, owing to the unsettled conditions, had fled. At the request of Sheng Shih-ts'ai the Soviet Union then sent six regiments across the border into Sinkiang to secure Sheng Shih-ts'ai against the warlord Ma Chung-yin. In 1936 Sheng Shih-ts'ai invited another regiment from the Soviet Union. And in 1937 another one, which was stationed in Kashgar.

"One has to say that the Soviet policy against Sinkiang was bad even in Stalin's day. Sheng Shih-ts'ai controlled Sinkiang from 1933 to 1944. For most of this period the Soviet Union tried to achieve and maintain supremacy over Sinkiang through Sheng Shih-ts'ai. The character of that regime was pro-Russian and anti-British rather than actually anti-imperialist. The Soviet Union used Sheng Shih-ts'ai against the KMT and the central government, but did this in its own interest. It utilized its influence to gain economic advantages. The trade was far from equal. In the thirties Sinkiang was dependent on the Soviet Union. The Soviet Union used its position to gain economic advantages. Sheng Shih-ts'ai eventually entered into an agreement giving the Soviet Union extraterritorial rights concerning Sinkiang's mineral riches. It was the type of agreement to which all Chinese patriots objected, the type that Lenin had declared abolished forever by the Russian worker and peasant state, in the relations between Russia and China. But during the thirties the Soviet policy in Sinkiang was becoming a continuation of Russia's century-old intentions. Unequal trade and military infiltration were to force Sinkiang into becoming either directly annexed or transformed into a client state under Moscow.

"One must say that Stalin's policy in Sinkiang was not only to protect the country against Japanese and British imperialism and to keep the Silk Road open in order to give China access to material aid in the war of resistance against Japan, but it also had its own chauvinistic character."

There are three issues from this time which the Chinese did not discuss: the exact text of the agreements giving the Soviet Union supremacy over the mineral riches of Sinkiang; whether Sheng Shih-ts'ai was in truth made a member of the Soviet Communist Party by Stalin personally and subjected to the discipline of this party; the role of the Soviet Union in the extensive "Purge of Trotskyites" in Sinkiang in 1937 and the formation of Sheng Shih-ts'ai's secret police, which was thereafter used to seek out and destroy all communists and progressives in Sinkiang.

The so-called Sin-tin agreement of November 26, 1940, where the

Soviet Union secured for itself the "exclusive right" to mine tin and similar minerals in Sinkiang, had such an extreme character that it surpassed Czar Peter's planned agreement with the Oirats and is a model agreement for imperialist exploitation. The Soviet Union was given all rights, including the right to build power stations and railroads, use all conceivable means of communication, establish radio stations and telephone exchanges, and import freely whatever they needed. Total freedom from taxation and from any levy for the first ten years. The right to re-export equipment and materials without any levy or duty. The right to use Sinkiang workers and technicians and engineers and workers from the Soviet Union, who would have permission to travel and stay anywhere in Sinkiang without restrictions. The right to import and distribute food supplies without any tax or levy or duty. The right to export raw materials or finished products, without any levy or duty, from the production centers that the Soviet Union would construct in Sinkiang. The obligation of the Sinkiang government to evacuate all inhabitants from the areas the Soviet Union was to exploit. And so on.

For this the Soviet Union was to pay the Sinkiang government 5 percent of the average mineral value for tin and such minerals as mined by the Soviet Union in Sinkiang. This would increase to 6 percent after five years, and the sum was payable in goods. Besides, the Soviet Union was to pay 2 percent of the export value to the Sinkiang government, as remuneration for the total freedom from levies and taxation. The Sinkiang government in this agreement renounced any right to inspect, survey, investigate, or revise anything concerning production, finance or trade in relation to the agreement. All property concerned was given extraterritorial status, and the property of Soviet citizens could not be seized. Also, the Soviet Union was allowed to keep armed forces to protect its Sinkiang property, according to this agreement into which the Soviet Union and Sheng Shih-ts'ai entered. The text was published by the KMT in Taiwan in 1950 and by Allen S. Whiting and Sheng Shih-ts'ai in 1958.

"Yes, we too have read books where that agreement was quoted," our hosts said to us.

"The so-called Sin-tin agreement entered into by Sheng Shih-ts'ai goes back to the time before the liberation when the party did not control the country. But generally, we never approved of the dual ownership of companies, mixed companies where the Soviet Union owned one part and China the other. It became one of the reasons for conflict.

"At first we weren't experienced enough. Lenin had used capitalists after the October Revolution. That can be done. But we were quite new in this field. That is why these agreements on mixed companies came about in 1950.

"Immediately at liberation, Chairman Mao Tse-tung, though, had another opinion about mixed companies than the Soviet Union. Mixed companies defied our fundamental principle to rely on our own resources. And we were determined, in accordance with the basic policy emphasized by Chairman Mao Tse-tung, not to give in. We would no longer accept companies co-owned by the Soviet Union and China. They were abolished in 1955.

"But it is important to keep in mind that we did not, at that time, see this as a matter of Soviet exploitation but as a question of political line. It was a question of following Chairman Mao Tse-tung's line on how to build socialism. We demanded equality in our relations with the Soviet Union.

"We wanted to learn from the Soviet experience. Therefore we received experts. The Soviet Union gave us credit. Later, the Soviet Union took advantage of this, when they withdrew all their experts. We have now repaid all loans. And we are against mixed companies."

After the Sian incident when the united front between the KMT and Chinese Communist Party was established in the war of national defense against Japan, more Communists arrived in Sinkiang and worked there to modernize and democratize the administration, and tried to carry out reforms. In this situation, when Sheng Shih-ts'ai got closer to China, he himself claims that he applied for membership in the Chinese Communist Party. During the negotiations he held about Sinkiang in Moscow in 1938, Sheng Shih-ts'ai is said to have been forbidden by Stalin to join the Chinese Communist Party; instead Stalin gave him membership number 1859118 in the Communist Party of the Soviet Union, thus subjecting him to the Soviet party discipline. Sheng Shih-ts'ai has claimed that the Soviet negotiations of 1940, using the party discipline as whip, forced him to sign the Sin-tin agreement.

I have no confirmation of this membership. But it is clear from his words and actions that Sheng Shih-ts'ai in those years was not a progressive Chinese politician friendly to the Soviet Union with an anti-imperialist and patriotic united front policy. He was a Chinese warlord under direct Soviet control. Whether he also was formally under Stalin's personal command in a vassal situation disguised as party membership, I do not know. But that's what he himself claims in the autobiography published by Allen S. Whiting.

Sheng Shih-ts'ai's Sinkiang in the thirties became a strange and distorted reflection of the Soviet Union. Even in Sinkiang great conspira-

cies were discovered and extensive purges were carried out. Trotskyism
—led by the consul-general of the Soviet Union—was to have infiltrated
the whole of the province and won the men in key positions in the
administration with the intention of transforming Sinkiang into a German-Japanese base against the Soviet Union. Soviet representatives—
according to Sheng Shih-ts'ai—were to have arrived in Sinkiang to look
into this conspiracy he had discovered. Many people were imprisoned,
tortured, executed, or annihilated. It is a well-known fact, generally
confirmed, that he organized a cruel secret police force in the warlord
manner. Nobody wanted to talk about the role Stalin or the Soviet
authorities played in this 1930s development.

"Don't forget," Gun said, "why Stalin maintained this policy. He did
not believe that the Chinese people could resist Japan. He did not trust
the masses, either in China or in Europe. So he saw himself forced to
use the Soviet state power to resist the evil and gain with intrigues and
secret diplomatic maneuvers what he considered lost politically. Was
that so strange? The Chinese Revolution had been defeated in 1927. All
the organizations of the German working class had collapsed in front
of Hitler like punctured balloons. The French Popular Front was more
concerned with giving the working class holidays than uniting the
nation in the face of the threat to its very existence. Wherever Stalin
looked, it was the same picture. And the intellectuals who had recently
called for a world revolution now spoke of dreams and poetic revolt and
sexual liberation. He had on the desk in front of him exact data and
extensive intelligence reports showing that Germany and Japan were
striving consciously for war and world rule. If you don't see this picture, then Stalin's actions will be incomprehensible. This is why he was
compelled to use Sheng Shih-ts'ai as a puppet and keep troops and
police in Sinkiang and take out of Sinkiang whatever he could and plan
the incorporation of Sinkiang into the Soviet Union. His error cannot
be understood unless his motives are realized."

Those years, when the warlord Sheng Shih-ts'ai had in reality the
function of a Soviet vassal and the relations with China's inland were
more or less nonexistent, were used by various patriotic and progressive
forces to improve the educational system and spread knowledge. Sheng
Shih-ts'ai's anti-imperialism was false, a mask he had assumed to suit
Moscow. But it could be used by sincere patriots and anti-imperialists.
Sheng Shih-ts'ai's secret police, however (which according to him had
Soviet advisers), tried to make sure no Communists came into Sinkiang.
The progressives had great difficulties in their work, in spite of all the
thundering anti-imperialist speeches made by Sheng Shih-ts'ai.

The united front against Japan then enabled China's Communist

Party to send representatives to Sinkiang. It was also in the interest of the Soviet Union that China's people should unite against Japan and keep the Japanese aggressors at bay. Therefore, the old Silk Road through Sinkiang—now from the Soviet border above Urumchi and down through Kansu—became the supporting link of fighting China. China's Communists had followed Mao Tse-tung's policy, made their own analyses, and did not let themselves be controlled by Moscow. Thus they were more successful than Stalin had ever expected. They had been able to use defeat as a victory, and when they reached Shensi after the Long March, they established a secure base. The masses were awakened to patriotic awareness, and the KMT was forced to national unity in the anti-Japanese defense struggle.

Only a year or so earlier, Stalin had been prepared to hand over the East China Railroad to the so-called Manchukuo authorities and thus give a *de facto* recognition to the "Empire of Manchukuo." He now gave, on the Soviet Union's behalf, more extensive and unselfish support to China to help it fight Japan than any other foreign state did. This must be kept in mind when one talks about Stalin.

In May 1937 the Eighth Route Army could open its liaison office in Urumchi. In due course 150 party workers were sent to work for a patriotic Chinese united front in Sinkiang. Sheng Shih-ts'ai's position was sensitive, and the national united front gave the formal opportunities for the united front work, while the Soviet interest in China's continued resistance against Japan gave the real opportunities.

"It was only a small number of comrades, but they did some very important work for the people in Sinkiang. They were to organize the anti-Japanese united front. They published propaganda material for the united front as well as the classics of Marxism-Leninism and the basic works by Chairman Mao Tse-tung. They distributed works like the ones by Mao Tse-tung called *On Protracted War* and *On New Democracy.* They edited newspapers and magazines.

"As teachers they organized elementary and secondary schools. The secondary ones had 3,000 students. They worked with these schools all over Sinkiang. An important task was to create political consciousness among the students and develop the anti-Japanese united front work in the schools and among the masses. It was also important that patriotic and progressive young people of various nationalities could be sent from these eleven secondary schools run by the party to Yenan for further studies. They then returned and worked with the masses. The party rooted itself deeply thanks to this work.

"The comrades were also responsible for leading trade and banking. They reorganized the administration and the currency, established a special school to train administrators for finance and general administration. They also began to reorganize health services and build hospitals.

"It was a very difficult, very sensitive united front work. The party had certainly sent experienced, trusted comrades to lead it. When Hitler attacked the Soviet Union, the situation deteriorated badly. Chen Tai-chu was then the representative of the central committee in Sinkiang, a member of the party central committee, and a founding member of the party. He knew the situation well. Mao Tse-min, the younger brother of Chairman Mao Tse-tung, was a leading administrator in the province. He too was greatly experienced in revolutionary work in difficult circumstances.

"In the autumn of 1941, the Soviet Union found it increasingly difficult to send materials to Sinkiang. It began to be apparent that Sheng Shih-ts'ai was prepared to change his ruler. He did not believe that the Soviet Union would be able to resist Hitler, and neither could it supply as much as before. From the first days of 1942, the party realized that Sheng Shih-ts'ai could betray it at any moment. But it was impossible to withdraw any comrades in the normal way. The party then gave orders that everyone had to stay where he was, nobody was to flee. They were playing for time; every moment was valuable. The task was to work among the masses and explain the situation to them, so that Sheng Shih-ts'ai would completely unmask himself once he changed sides. The task was to prepare the ground for the next stage of the fight. All the comrades knew that Sheng Shih-ts'ai would attack them. But they stayed till the last minute. They were good examples of steadfastness, as well by their simple life as by their modest behavior. In the spring of 1942 Sheng Shih-ts'ai acted. That was the year when all party comrades in Sinkiang were arrested. Even the children were imprisoned.

"Sheng Shih-ts'ai was just a warlord looking for a new master. He considered Moscow defeated and the Germans sure victors against the Soviet Union. But the KMT did not trust him. He imprisoned the Communists to please the KMT. In the end he had Chen Tai-chu and Mao Tse-min and Lin Chi-lu executed, after terrible torture. Chiang Kai-shek wouldn't believe him when their deaths were reported. Sheng Shih-ts'ai had to send him photos of the execution of Chen Tai-chu, Mao Tse-min, and Lin Chi-lu and of their dead bodies to make Chiang Kai-shek believe it. Now the KMT took over all of Sinkiang, but let Sheng Shih-ts'ai live. Losing Sinkiang made Sheng Shih-ts'ai desperate; he realized that Chiang Kai-shek was more cunning than he was. He eventually escaped to Taiwan with Chiang Kai-shek, from where he later went on to Hong Kong. He is now dead.

"One hundred thirty-one people survived the prison, twenty-two children among them. Apart from the three executed, another twenty died from torture."

To what was told in Urumchi some details from other sources can be added to indicate that Sheng Shih-ts'ai's game may have been even more obscure. It is obvious that, at the time of his action, he expected Hitler to triumph over the Soviet Union. Sheng Shih-ts'ai's torturers had been trained to extract suitable confessions from their victims. He says himself that the first set of confessions obtained by his interrogators claimed that Wang Ching-wei—Japan's puppet politician—had planned the conspiracy against him. Such tortured-out confessions seem parallels of the confessions his interrogators produced in 1937 during the great purge of Trotskyites in Sinkiang and could keep the door to Moscow ajar. But as Moscow refused to accept these trials and protested against the imprisonments, and Hitler at the same time was defeated at Stalingrad, Sheng Shih-ts'ai suddenly had double need to be protected by Chiang Kai-shek. The second set of confessions extricated by the interrogators of Sheng Shih-ts'ai thus claimed that Chou En-lai had planned the conspiracy.

In October 1943 the Soviet military forces had been withdrawn from Sinkiang. Even the Soviet technicians were gone. Sheng Shih-ts'ai had, with photographs, convinced Chiang Kai-shek that he had really had Chen Tai-chu, Mao Tse-min, and Lin Chi-lu executed. The KMT now sent forces into Sinkiang to take over the power, but by the time this was done—Sheng Shih-ts'ai still had the formal power in Sinkiang— it became apparent that the Soviet Union would be victorious over Hitler. Still, the Japanese advanced into China, and the KMT government was weak. Sheng Shih-ts'ai then started to arrest KMT staff. In August 1944 Sheng Shih-ts'ai proclaimed a state of siege. He had discovered another conspiracy. At the same time he is said to have turned to the Soviet consul-general, asking for Soviet forces to march in to maintain law and order in Sinkiang. He thus made an offer to Stalin to incorporate Sinkiang into the Soviet Union. But Stalin no longer listened to the pleas of Sheng Shih-ts'ai, who had to give up Sinkiang and accept being transferred to the Ministry of Forestry and Agriculture in Chungking to save his life.

But then the three districts of Altai, Tarbagatai, and Ili were already in revolt. On November 12, 1944, a central military staff was formed in Ining, and on November 15, 1944, the "East Turkestan Republic" was proclaimed. In the winter of 1944–1945 its forces carried out military operations, establishing its power all along the Soviet border from Tashkurghan to Altai. On January 5, 1945, the East Turkestan Republic government issued a declaration, stating that its task, among other things, was to establish friendly relations with all democratic countries—especially, however, with the Soviet Union.

In August 1945 Molotov, on behalf of the Soviet Union, renounced any involvement in Sinkiang's affairs. But the Soviet government naturally took an interest in what happened at its borders, and "demanded that the Chinese government stop its discriminating measures against Soviet subjects." Considering the fact that the Soviet Union a few months later silently made 120,000 Sinkiang inhabitants Soviet subjects, Molotov's statement becomes slightly ambiguous. In the game that followed, the Soviet negotiators kept this joker up their sleeve. Moscow now took direct part in the discussion regarding Sinkiang's future. At the same time, the KMT government threatened that the United States might intervene in Sinkiang's affairs, since it showed an increasing interest in Sinkiang, and Moscow then sent a message to the KMT government in Chungking, stating that the democratic movement of the East Turkestan Republic was prepared to negotiate. Moscow was considered to have intervened to make sure that a compromise was possible. The East Turkestan Republic became the "Three Districts of Ili, Tarbagatai, Altai," and Sinkiang was to have regional autonomy.

The following years were complicated. The Soviet Union, as well as the United States, tried to advance its position in Sinkiang and establish various contacts. The Soviet Union at the same time gave strong support to the democratic movement in Sinkiang; but it tried to gain influence and control over it that way. The Soviet Union also carried out direct military operations in Sinkiang. In 1947 Soviet forces, together with Soviet-led troops from the Mongolian People's Republic, commenced regular fighting in the "Peitaishan incident" to move the frontier into China's territory.

The negotiations and fights and political changes taking place at this time in Sinkiang were difficult to survey. But even if the Soviet Union inspired and supported—and tried to infiltrate—the democratic movement in Sinkiang (and secretly made 120,000 people Soviet subjects), the main character of this movement remained that of a democratic popular movement in Sinkiang, with no intention of seceding from the rest of China. National independence for the East Turkestan Republic was never proclaimed and never set as a goal, and the Three Districts of Ili, Tarbagatai, Altai formed a liberated democratic base in the Chinese war of liberation. But it was a base where the Soviet Union had gained extensive rights of precedence, even if it had not achieved sovereignty or suzerainty. The mineral riches, however, seemed to be controlled by it.

The development leading up to the peaceful liberation of Sinkiang went along a meandering path. But the negotiations and discussions carried out in 1949 enabled an overwhelming majority among the previously leading military and political personages in Sinkiang to join the new China. The long-term and patiently carried out negotiations made it possible to achieve unity in Sinkiang, and the most reactionary groups were isolated and unable to show more than occasional resistance. This was the policy that wiped out the plans the United States had tried to realize in Sinkiang of uniting the extreme right-wing groups in an armed fight against the new China.

In July 1949 the People's Liberation Army had reached Lanchow in Kansu. It was now possible for it to advance into Sinkiang to defeat the KMT forces. Instead, a series of meetings and discussions followed. Chang Chih-chung, who had been the governor of Sinkiang and had led the KMT negotiations with the Three Districts of Ili, Tarbagatai, Altai, who had led the KMT delegation during the peace negotiations in Peking in the spring of 1949, had now taken a stand in favor of the new China and strove to settle the transitional difficulties in Sinkiang without bloodshed or violence.

When Chairman Mao Tse-tung, on September 21, 1949, opened the Chinese People's Political Consultative Conference, there were representatives of the various Sinkiang groups present; from the Three Districts of Ili, Tarbagatai, Altai as well as from the Urumchi KMT and from the people in different parts of Sinkiang. On September 25, there was an official break in relations between the military command and the provincial government in Sinkiang on one side, and the remains of the KMT regime on the other. They wanted a peaceful liberation of Sinkiang and the union of their forces and the People's Liberation Army. Chairman Mao Tse-tung replied to their telegram. His reply was published in Sinkiang on September 28, 1949. He stated that this decision "corresponded to the will of the whole Chinese people." When Mao Tse-tung, on October 1, 1949, proclaimed the Chinese People's Republic from T'ien An Men Square in Peking, all Sinkiang was already part of China.

On October 30, 1949, units of the People's Liberation Army arrived in Urumchi. The local authorities themselves had by then already smashed attempts to establish an armed counterrevolutionary base in Sinkiang with the assistance of the United States. The real reactionaries had been isolated as a small number without any real power and were fleeing. After continued negotiations, on December 18, 1949, a united provincial government and a united military command for Sinkiang were formed. On January 10, 1950, the units of the "National Democratic Army" from the Three Districts of Ili, Tarbagatai, Altai, were incorporated into the People's Liberation Army.

This peaceful liberation, which terminated long bloody civil wars between different groups in Sinkiang, was a great victory for Mao Tse-tung's policy. It made it possible to begin economic development and also to achieve the Sinkiang Uighur Autonomous Region in September 1955. Behind the skillful diplomacy and the farsighted policy with which the negotiations regarding Sinkiang were conducted, it is not difficult to discern the wisdom of Chou En-lai.

It is, however, not quite clear how the Soviet authorities reacted in Sinkiang in 1949. Some sources claim that the KMT in the spring of that year repeated Sheng Shih-ts'ai's suggestion to Stalin to take over Sinkiang. They are said to have offered Sinkiang to the Soviet Union as a barrier against the Chinese Communists. This is told for instance in a long news story to the *New York Times* of February 1, 1949, by Henry R. Lieberman in Nanking. The intention was to establish "a pro-Soviet border area all the way from Central Asia to the Japanese Sea through Sinkiang, Outer Mongolia, Manchuria, and North Korea." According to a telegram to the *New York Times* on March 30, 1949, from Walter Sullivan in Urumchi, Sinkiang was going over to the Soviet Union, and "it is doubtful whether the Chinese Communists will ever gain more than titular control here."

According to a third source, Allen S. Whiting, the Soviet consul-general in Urumchi should have contacted General Tao Shih-yueh, who then still belonged to the KMT forces. The People's Liberation Army had advanced into Kansu and were approaching Sinkiang. The Soviet consul-general then should have suggested to General Tao Shih-yueh that he declare Sinkiang independent like the Mongolian People's Republic. There should have been groups within the KMT in Canton who wanted General Tao Shih-yueh to follow the directions of the Soviet consul-general. They held the opinion that this was the only way to block the road for the People's Liberation Army.

General Tao Shih-yueh, however, never declared any such Soviet independence for Sinkiang. In September he broke with the KMT and went over to the new China, joining the People's Liberation Army.

The different rumors coincide. They seem to revert to some factual Soviet intrigue in Sinkiang in 1949. But they all stem from United States sources. The real background of these reports is difficult to find. It is apparent that great diplomatic skill was required to enable Sinkiang to declare itself part of the new China on its own initiative, prior to the proclamation of the People's Republic of China; and that without any bloody confrontations between different national groups, without being partitioned, and without extraterritorial rights being given to any foreign nation in Sinkiang.

One should, however, also keep in mind that Stalin during this period was holding back. Whatever plans he had made, he never annexed the East Turkestan Republic as he had annexed Tannu Tuva. Neither did he push through any form of independence for Sinkiang as he had done with the Mongolian People's Republic. The jokers he kept up his sleeve were never laid down on the table. Only when Mao Tse-tung's policy had proved victorious in practice and the People's Liberation Army had reached the inner Asian border of the Soviet Union did Stalin accept the facts and change his policy.

Mao Tse-tung then spent two months, up to mid-February 1950, in Moscow, negotiating seriously with Stalin. The latter admitted to the Chinese representatives that he had done wrong in relation to China. One might say that when Stalin arrived in civilian dress as a guest at the Chinese ambassador's reception at the Hotel Metropole in Moscow, on the occasion of the Soviet-Chinese treaty, and apologized to Mao Tse-tung for the errors and mistakes he had made in his relations with China—and Sinkiang—that seemed to be the final ending of the two-hundred-year-old Russian policy against what was called Chinese Turkestan.

Perhaps it was—for Stalin. The Chinese say that Stalin was an extremely tough negotiator, but that once having given his word, he kept it. In Urumchi they said:

"A total judgment of comrade Stalin shows that he was a great Marxist-Leninist and a great politician and statesman. His good points balance his shortcomings. But since his good points were vast, so too his shortcomings were vast.

"Comrade Stalin generally had the right attitude toward the Chinese Revolution, but he did commit many errors. These errors must be seen in relation to the whole. They were chauvinistic errors, and to a certain extent he followed the czarist policy.

"After his death the smaller part of his policy took over completely. The Soviet Union changed its color. The czarist policy is no longer an exception in the Soviet Union; the over-all policy is now czarist.

"We did not pay enough heed to this change. Liu Shao-ch'i's line made us trust that our solidarity, after all, was decisive. We were therefore unprepared in 1962 when they started their serious campaign. We knew that some of those responsible during the democratic fight against the KMT in the Three Districts of Ili, Tarbagatai, Altai had Soviet passports. They had been Chinese citizens but had lived in the Soviet Union in the early forties. In 1944 they crossed the border and took part in the popular revolt. They were reliable in the democratic struggle. Many of them contributed greatly. They had a base in the Soviet Union, which supported them. At the liberation their forces joined the People's Liberation Army. They were made the Fifth Army Group of the People's Liberation Army.

"From 1949 on, our security work was imperfect. As long as Stalin lived, there were no serious conflicts. And we believed the remaining problems we had inherited from history could now be solved step by step between the Soviet Union and China. We did not take heed sufficiently of what should have been apparent at least from 1955 in Sinkiang. The Soviet consulates worked as centers for organizing an extensive political network. When we realized what was happening, the damage was already done, and the Soviet authorities could carry out the May 29 intermezzo in 1962.

"That was a rude awakening! It turned out that even in our central military administration the Soviet Union had people who not only were Soviet citizens but also served as Soviet representatives. We then let them choose, once and for all, which side to take. Most of them were of course honest. They had joined the democratic revolution for patriotic reasons. But some of them had stronger ties with the Soviet Union than with their own people. These were allowed to travel to the Soviet Union. They could leave, whatever their rank, even if they were generals. Among those who left then and went over to the Soviet Union was the chief of the general staff of the People's Liberation Army in Sinkiang, Sulungtaiev. Another was Leskin, who had commanded the troops at Ili in 1944 and had then been the commander of a group of the People's Liberation Army in Sinkiang. Another was Markov, who held a high position in the People's Liberation Army.

"Quite frankly, this was a shock to many among the comrades here in Sinkiang. But we allowed each one to leave, regardless of his position and the responsibility he had had. When Sulungtaiev applied for a visa to leave China in 1963 and showed his Soviet passport, he was granted an exit visa, in spite of the fact that he was the chief of the general staff and we knew that he was going to the Soviet Union to fight us. He is now in Alma-Ata, leading what he calls a 'liberation movement.' He has strong radio transmitters at his disposal, and they keep transmitting his articles and speeches against Sinkiang.

"The Soviet Union uses transmitters to jam our internal radio communications. They are very skillful at that. But we are overcoming these difficulties. They also transmit broadcasts toward Sinkiang. The main characteristic of their propaganda is that it tries to sow doubts and despondency. This they do by picking up and spreading various kinds of rumors. The other characteristic is that they consciously try to incite the various nationalities of Sinkiang against each other.

"Sinkiang has a history of bloodshed and cruelty. There have been bitter struggles between different groups of people. There still remains a certain amount of distrust and thus the possibility of misunderstandings. The Soviet propaganda tries to blow this up into a national conflict. All reactionaries have tried the same trick to control Sinkiang.

"Our national frontier here is many thousands of kilometers. It runs over high mountains, and is difficult to guard. Our patrols are not always sufficient to maintain control all the way; it is always possible to sneak into the country between the border patrols. But we trust Chairman Mao's instructions for a united defense. The border guards, the people, and the People's Liberation Army work together to defend the mother country. The people of the border area have been mobilized, and we rely upon them to keep the frontier secure.

"We know that they send in quite a few agents to gather military and economic intelligence and also to carry out certain commissions. We also know pretty well how many they send in. We get most of them— most, but not all. They must pass through the border zone, and it is much easier for them to get in than to return afterwards. The people's militia is prepared. We have captured agents who had managed to get all the way to Urumchi. The class enemy supported and helped them. I wouldn't call this a great problem; we have now organized the border security in such a way that only few of their agents are able to return to the Soviet Union.

"We are prepared against war. If they really attack us, we shall annihilate them. China is no longer the China of 1949. We have still a long way to go before we are a modern, highly developed industrial nation, but we have both the will and the ability to defend ourselves. If they attack us, it will be a long war, but the outcome will be the total destruction of the aggressors. They will probably be able to cross the border, but they will never get back home alive."

Nearly all night Gun and I talked of Stalin and what had happened in Sinkiang during the last decades and all that we had heard. It was hot and we were drinking large bowls of tea in the dark. Then Gun said:

"You can't possibly describe this in a way to make European and American liberals realize that yea is not yea and nay is not nay. It is what goes beyond that is the actual reality. They can't see Stalin as a historic figure; they want a *deus ex machina* or a devil from the underground trap door. Like Saint Paul, they think it's a sign of weakness to look upon a political leader of Stalin's stature as both good and evil, as very good and very evil, in his own historical setting. They thus believe that the Chinese are speaking darkly when they do so."

The next morning we went to see the underground tunnels. These tunnels were air-raid shelters and evacuation roads and defense fortifications. We descended deeper and deeper and passed gas locks and steel shutters. Deep down in a canteen we had some tea, and the representative responsible for the defense work said:

"Chairman Mao Tse-tung is right. We shall never attack. But if the social imperialists attack us and invade our land, we shall fight them to victory."

26

The Production and Construction Corps

We are driving east on the main road through Dzungaria. To the north are the Karamai oil fields. The oil pipeline now runs from there down to Urumchi.

"That pipeline saves us a lot of money," Jen Yuang-chang says. He works in Ining but is going to Urumchi for meetings and accompanies us in the jeep. He is thirty-four. His wife is a doctor. They have two children.

"You should stop smoking," Gun says.

"It's difficult," he replies.

"Nothing is difficult if you just decide to do it," Gun says. They laugh, for Jen Yuang-chang is a chain-smoker. He is a cadre working eighteen, twenty hours a day, and his right forefinger is yellow from nicotine.

"I shall go to the cadre school soon," he says. "In two months."

"That will be good for you," Gun says.

The main road to Urumchi has been destroyed by too much traffic. The jeep rocks and bumps.

"The pipeline will enable us to maintain the road," says Jen Yuang-chang. "Before, we had to use a whole stream of trucks to transport the oil. We couldn't keep up the condition of the road then; it was ruined the moment it was repaired. Now that the oil can be carried by a pipeline, the whole transport situation will improve. That will be a relief for all Sinkiang, because we'll be able to use those trucks for other kinds of transportation."

We drive for some time along a railroad embankment without tracks. Concrete bridge vaults stretch across the ravines. But there is no rail; the railroad-building project has been interrupted. The idea was to construct the railroad from Urumchi to the Soviet border, where it

221

would connect with the Soviet railroad network by that built from Aktogai on the Turkestan-Siberia line down to the border at the Dzungaria gate. But China interrupted the construction work when it became apparent that the Soviet Union's policy against Sinkiang was again czarist.

"We must not be careless."

The railroads in Sinkiang are being built, however, even north of Tien Shan. But now there are lines being built which cannot be used by the Soviet Union in case they should make a sudden surprise attack against China. It is the same security-conscious policy that made China move the capital of the Kazakh Autonomous District from Ining near the border to Kweitun farther inland.

Here in Dzungaria north of Tien Shan China has carried out one of its great cultivation projects. And the massive migration from the inland has come here. After the vast extermination of people in Dzungaria in the eighteenth century, the agricultural areas there were deserted. The Kazakh immigration did not suffice to populate them. The disturbances and the wars and the civil wars and the battles between different groups had laid waste large areas of arable land during these centuries. At the time of the liberation the land that could bear was lying fallow and the water was running from the mountains, creating vast areas of marshland at the edge of the desert.

The work was carried out by the Production and Construction Corps of the People's Liberation Army. Out of pure wasteland it has created, by its own work, one of the richest agricultural areas of northwest China. The Corps has also on its own built up an industrial base, which is now taking the step from being a consumer-goods industry to a machine industry, developing an over-all modernization of Dzungaria. The average wages of the commune members are higher here than in most other parts of China. The corps has now been abolished and the ordinary civil administration has taken over, but the construction of Dzungaria is a monument of that style of work, that organizational ability, and that discipline which characterize the People's Liberation Army. Still, most of the people doing this work were originally from the KMT forces; the great task of transforming the marshes and deserts was given to the KMT troops that joined the People's Liberation Army.

In order to understand what the Production and Construction Corps in Sinkiang really is, one has to keep in mind that for more than two thousand years it has been traditional Chinese policy to let the army cultivate land, support themselves, and not cost the country any money. It was also here in Sinkiang that the Emperor Wu Ti in the first century

B.C. founded the first military colonies. His policy was maintained by successive dynasties.

The policy of making the army cultivate the land and thus contribute to production had several aims. One was to secure frontiers by settling military colonies in the border areas. Another was to enable the army to support itself and to maintain a defense capability which would not be too much of a burden on the people. Yet another was precisely to cultivate land that had been deserted. After the devastating wars that destroyed and depopulated whole provinces in China, military cultivation groups were established in different dynasties. Their task was to put agricultural land back into production.

The basic thought, as it took shape during the Han dynasty in the first century B.C. in various memorials, was that it is cultivated land, more than expensive troops, that secures the border. That soil cannot be tilled by deported criminals and all sorts of riffraff gathered up by chance, but only by hard-working and steady people who become settled farmers, and thus at the same time will defend themselves and their country. In this way—the politicians of that time wrote—the empire will not be drained of its troops; one avoids those temporary expeditions which only exhaust the army and cause severe losses without any permanent success. Instead one has, in the right place, a great many people maintaining military discipline and, at the same time, cultivating the land and defending the empire. This enables the empire to keep its resources for unexpected events and also to open up new land.

Mao Tse-tung used this two-thousand-year-old policy. Conditions have changed since the period of the Han dynasty, but Mao Tse-tung was always willing to learn and let the present be served by the past. The good side of this Han dynasty tradition was developed by that revolutionary movement whose armed forces during decades built up the liberated areas of China. Mao Tse-tung shaped this policy there. When the People's Liberation Army was on its way to complete victory, he cabled the instruction of February 8, 1949: "Time is now set for us to make the army a working force." In his instructions of December 5, 1949, the tasks were more detailed. This fulfilling of the traditions from Yenan and the early Chinese Soviet area also meant a return to the best of Chinese tradition.

In Sinkiang especially this policy had great significance. On the whole it had been possible to avoid armed struggles there during liberation. The large KMT forces—unconquered and without any humiliating conditions—together with the "National Army" of the Three Districts of Ili, Tarbagatai, Altai joined the People's Liberation Army. There the three formed one single force.

This force was not demobilized. The KMT soldiers from Honan and other inland provinces were not sent home; nor were the soldiers of the People's Liberation Army. In the unified force, cadres and men from the People's Liberation Army worked side by side with officers and men from the KMT forces. One of the tasks was to transform this whole force into one, influenced by the traditions of the People's Liberation Army and fulfilling its aims.

This new uniform force became the "Production and Construction Corps" and was given the task of cultivating the deserted long-time wasteland north of Tien Shan; of cultivating and transforming the desert at Aksu and in other places. It would rely solely on its own resources. No capital or help was to be given by the government. All it had was its organization, its discipline, and its experience.

The military forces were thus step by step transformed into civil administration. Until the end the staffs operated as economically administrative bodies; now they too have become ordinary civil institutions. The corps is a memory, but in Dzungaria especially its working style has set its mark on the new towns, where they still talk about the different regiments and the farm of this regiment and the industry of that.

Many young people from the inland and the coast came to join this Production and Construction Corps. Many of them found the adjustment difficult and demanding. There were various political forces that tried to stop this stream of young people going to the recently cultivated areas. They called it deportation and implied that the young people were going to perish in the deserts. But Chou En-lai considered it a great task for the young people of Shanghai and the inland to follow the call of Chairman Mao Tse-tung to go to the border lands and take part in the work there. He had to struggle on this issue. Many of the young people who had settled in Dzungaria talked about Chou En-lai's visit to the Production and Construction Corps. The work in Dzungaria was heavy and unusual and difficult for the young people who were used to being students in Shanghai and now had to take responsibility for breaking ground in the marshland next to the desert far away in inner Asia. But that also created a pioneering spirit.

Yang Yung-chen, thirty-four years old, was the work team vice-leader of what had been called the 9th Company of the 145th Regiment, before the transition to civil administration. She said:

"I came here in July 1964, to make my contribution to the mother country. I was then a student at the technical university in Shanghai. I wanted to become a radio engineer.

"But I developed tuberculosis and had to interrupt my studies. I decided to overcome all difficulties and go out to the border and work. This was what Chairman Mao Tse-tung had recommended that the young people do.

"My father tried to stop me. He is an overseas Chinese, living in Hong Kong. He wrote to the Youth League, threatening them. If they let me go out to Sinkiang, he would report them to the control commission of the party's central committee. Father wanted me to go to Hong Kong instead; he promised me I would be able to go on studying there. I could go around the world and study semiconductor technology.

"The Youth League told me that I had to solve my problems with father on my own. 'Your father now has written us three letters,' they said. I then wrote to my father to say that he, an overseas Chinese, had to realize too that it was essential that our mother country progress. I wanted to put my life to proper use. I didn't want to be a high expert in foreign countries and study at the Hong Kong university and go around the world and be famous. I wanted to go to the border. He had no right to stop me.

"The Hong Kong climate, by the way, was as bad for me as Shanghai's, I wrote to him. My lungs would recover in Sinkiang near the Gobi Desert. That made him give up his opposition. Granny was on my side too.

"It is a good life here. I've learned much. But naturally it's not always easy. Not everybody can take up this work. I got married in 1968. My husband is from Honan. We had started to write to each other, and we got married when he was demobilized from the People's Liberation Army. I convinced him to come to me out here. But he had difficulties. He went back inland in 1972, and now he is again in Honan, working in a ball-bearing factory.

"He wants me to go there. He writes that we are married, so it's wrong of me not to follow him. He wants the children as well. He writes that it is certainly right to work. People can go out to work in the Gobi when young, he writes, and then it is glorious. But what will happen when you grow old? You'll regret it then. He has made my brother write too. Do not split the family! my brother wrote.

"I've been working with the cultivation here for twelve years. I have been elected group vice-leader. I'm a party member. It is not easy to be a woman and a leading cadre with responsibility and have small children and no man about the house. In a way I miss him too. I married him because I wanted him. I lie awake at night thinking about it. It has been a difficult struggle for me. My throat goes so dry, I can hardly swallow when I think of him having left. But I shall not give in. That would be like following my father's Hong Kong advice and taking the easy way out. I myself have been building this up. I have broken this ground, and this is where I belong.

Even some comrades here say I ought to follow my husband, since we are married and I'm a woman. But I am a party member. We have discussed the matter carefully, and all the comrades take my view now. We have written to the party organization of the factory where my husband works and asked them to have a proper heart-to-heart talk with him. I have written to him myself too, I have asked him to read Marx and consider what being a Communist really means. You can't sneak away from your mission in life, I wrote. That would be wrong.

"Now he writes to me again, saying he might come out here again. I hope he will. He is not a bad man. He is just a little too weak."

27

The Revolution Marches On in Nylon Stockings!

In 1963, when Mao Tse-tung gave his instructions for the work in Sinkiang, he summarized them in six points:

The second point dealt among other things with the necessity of letting politics lead. The material dealing with revisionism had to be translated into the different languages. The Han cadres who came to Sinkiang to work were obliged to learn the local language. They had to keep strictly to the party policy for relations between the different nationalities of China.

The third point dealt with assistance to people settling in newly cultivated areas.

The fourth point dealt with safeguarding of the border.

The fifth point dealt with increased preparation of the people against subversion and military aggression from the Soviet Union.

The sixth point dealt with unity.

But the *first demand* of Chairman Mao Tse-tung was that the struggle against revisionism necessitates a firm grip on production. The livelihood of the people must improve every year. The improvement should not only be compared with the past; Sinkiang must pass the revisionist Soviet Union and in practice show which road was the correct one.

That is why they fought over women's nylon stockings in Sinkiang in 1975. That is why it may be more important to discuss nylon stockings than oil fields.

Sinkiang has mines and oil fields, heavy industry, highly developed electronics, and fine mechanical industry. Large railroad-building projects are carried out in Sinkiang, and little workshops that until recently repaired bicycles have grown into industries for agricultural equipment, aiming at truck production. Sinkiang manufactures its own tractors.

227

Chairman Mao Tse-tung has said that every province ought to have its own car factory.

In Shihezi we visit the large diesel-engine factory started by the Production and Construction Corps in 1952.

"There were ten of us working here," said chief engineer Wang Shiao-yi. "We had two lathes from the time of our ancestors, museum pieces really. We were supposed to manufacture tools for the cultivation work. We made spades and wool shears and repaired what we could. We have grown by our own power. We have produced and invested, and we haven't cost the government a fen. We now have seven workshops, and we are a thousand workers. Up till 1974 we organized the production step by step, going from small to large, from repairing to producing. We made harvesters and we made our own machine tools, as we developed the factory.

"In 1974 we decided to go over to manufacturing diesel engines. The model is called 195, and has twelve horsepower. It suits us here. The reason why we made this decision is that we had reached a stage of development where we could take a big step forward. We follow Chairman Mao Tse-tung's directives that the road to take for China's agriculture is mechanization.

"More than half the machines we use have been built by us. In 1974 and 1975 we created six production lines. We work in two shifts. After the first period when we tried the machines and built 200 engines to be tested and criticized by the members of the commune in practical operation, we could start production. The masses then agreed that the engines were good and fulfilled the technical demands. At the same time our ordinary production of wagons and harvesters continued.

"It is important that we plan the production of spares while we build the engines. Engines must not become unusable because there are no spares. That is bad planning. We now have an annual production of 1,500 engines. In 1978 we will reach 3,000. We have planned for an annual production of 10,000 engines.

"The technical problems with this transition are vast. There were many difficulties to overcome. We followed the guidelines from the Anshan steel works. The cadres participate in production work, and the workers in administration. Technicians and workers and cadres work together, and in that way we have been able to carry out more than one hundred technical innovations in less than three months. During this major transition, it is vital that the vast experience of the masses be really expressed.

"Chairman Mao Tse-tung advised us to study the guidelines for the Anshan steel works. They break with the bad influence of the Soviet guidelines for the Magnitogorsk steel combine. There the director has all the responsibility and makes all decisions. We have seen where that leads: it leads to technological stagnation. The guidelines for the An-shan steel works mean that the cadres are not isolated and that the working-class power finds its expression in both political and technical work.

"Politics must lead. The discussions we have had here during the present fight between two lines have led to a decision to double the production of spares. The production is a political issue."

But what is the aim of this whole production? That is the content of Chairman Mao Tse-tung's first point in his directives of 1963 for the work in Sinkiang and that is why there was a fight over nylon stockings in 1975 in Kweitun.

In the summer of 1975 the garment factory in Kweitun was completely taken over by the civil administration. It had been set up by the seventh division. Initially it was very small, but by now it had by its own power grown into a garment factory with 673 employees—362 of them women. The raw material was cotton from the large cultivations around Kweitun, on ground broken and drained by the Production and Construction Corps.

But in the summer of 1975, the Production and Construction Corps of the People's Liberation Army had fulfilled its task and been completely demobilized. The workers then initiated mass criticism to change the direction of the production.

It was certainly good to manufacture underwear. The people needed drawers. The people needed long underwear and undershirts and scarves, and the millions of undergarments manufactured by the plant had a good market. One Sinkiang inhabitant in four used drawers from the Kweitun clothes manufacturing plant. But now, the workers said, the revolution and the fight against revisionism demanded nylon stockings!

It was not a question of profitability. Production should not be directed by concerns of profit but by the needs of the people. Liu Shao-ch'i's line was to follow the demand for profit, but that would create a situation like the one in the Soviet Union, where profit ruled. We, said the Kweitun workers, must let politics come first. We have to serve the people.

After extensive discussions the production was changed and the plans reorganized.

"It was not just a question of stockings, it was a question of the bitter fight against Soviet revisionism," said party secretary Shang Li-sheng of the Kweitun garment factory. "The masses raised the question, and the party took it seriously. The revolutionary committee of the district asked us whether we could manage to manufacture nylon stockings as well. We had mass discussions about it. The workers thought we had to do it. So we did."

In September 1975, the Kweitun garment factory started to produce ladies' stockings in cotton and nylon. Since the local industry in Sinkiang was for some time not able to produce the nylon fiber required, nylon was brought from Shanghai and even imported from Japan. In 1975, 4.8 million pairs of ladies' stockings were produced for Sinkiang.

But why nylon stockings? Is that politics? Is that following Mao Tse-tung? Does the revolution march onward in nylon stockings?

Most women in China wear trousers. But not all of them. Uighur and Kazakh women wear skirts. They used to wear long trousers under the skirt, but now they wear short skirts and stockings. The skirt may be short, but they would never go out barelegged.

Cotton stockings, although not plentiful in the shops, did exist. But silk dresses cling to cotton stockings. The women have to pull at their skirts to make them fall properly. Besides, cotton stockings wrinkle. Nylon stockings do not. The Sinkiang women preferred nylon. Some were brought in from Shanghai, but by no means in sufficient quantities.

The Soviet Union then started a propaganda offensive. They sent gift packages of nylon stockings to Sinkiang. They wrote letters of the luxury and welfare of the Soviet Union, where every woman wore the finest nylon stockings and where even workers could afford a private car.

Soon there was a black market of nylon stockings in Sinkiang. The price went up to 15 to 20 yuan a pair, a third of the monthly wages for an ordinary worker or cadre. On principle such trade was prohibited. Still, it was not a police matter but a political question. That was how the workers put it when they started the criticism in July 1975, demanding a change in the production plan.

The Kweitun garment factory now manufactures stockings for the women in Sinkiang. There is no longer a black market for nylon stockings.

"The selling price," said party secretary Shang Li-sheng, "is now 1.40 yuan a pair for cotton stockings, 2.70 for rayon stockings, and 4.70 for nylon stockings. Cotton cloth is rationed, nine meters a year for adults, but cotton stockings are not rationed, and material apart from cotton is free.

"When we decided to begin production of stockings, we had no experience at all. We sent staff to Shanghai to buy equipment and to learn. We also got a few experienced workers from my home province;

I come from Shantung. But if we say that we manufacture enough stockings now, that does not mean that we are satisfied. The quality is not high enough. See for yourself! Compare our nylon stockings with those which can be bought in Shanghai. The masses criticize us, with good reason. But we have our difficulties. Our premises are inadequate, partly outdated, and impractical. We have plenty of machinery that is old and technically inappropriate. We have not mechanized the manufacture as much as we should. We are dealing with these matters. We have built this factory with our own power, and have now an annual production of about 50 million yuan. We are producing over 0.6 percent more than the plan. We have to plan our investments and carry out a mass campaign for technical innovations.

"Other difficulties stem from the fact that the quality of our products is below that maintained by the best inland industries. There is a motivated criticism against our selection being too limited and not well enough considered. Also, we have administrative difficulties. We want to discuss these issues, and it would be a great step forward if a broad discussion could be initiated.

"However," says Shang Li-sheng, holding out a pair of nylon stockings, "the fact that we are now producing nylon stockings in Sinkiang is already a great victory for the revolutionary line."

The nylon stockings manufactured in Kweitun are thick and do not wear out. They look like the nylon stockings that came to Europe at the end of the war; they have the same dull luster.

One could say that the new Sinkiang that is being built also looks like the best of Europe of the 1950s. The Urumchi houses are four stories high, situated in new residential areas in row upon row with trees around them. In the streets there are trolley buses, trucks, and cyclists. Just like the early 1950s.

Demolition is in progress all over Sinkiang. The old slums are being removed, the clusters of houses taken away. The meandering alleys are disappearing. They are digging in Urumchi for the new sewage system. The streets are being broken up, and the traffic is diverted around the city center.

The romanticism is disappearing too. The yellow clay huts with blue carvings are replaced by four-story brick houses. Sinkiang is becoming more like a Swedish or German or French or Norwegian province in the fifties. But the people are getting rid of what was to them misery and overcrowded homes and bad hygiene and nasty smells. That romanticism which cannot survive water conduits and sewage systems and asphalted streets and trolley buses and new housing is certainly not romantic to the people who have to live with it.

Sinkiang is being modernized quickly. This modernization will naturally bring problems. They may be able to avoid traffic problems; the new town planning is carried out consciously for collective traffic. But I know what traffic problems are like in Shanghai and Peking. And all Shantung is jammed up by trucks and cyclists when the traffic swells forth into the main roads in the afternoon. Sinkiang is bound to have its traffic problems and its traffic jams.

And what about the older citizens who have to live on the fourth floor without an elevator? What about the disabled? And what about the children on the stairs?

So far these matters are not discussed in Sinkiang. So far the main ambition is to find a way out of the alleys and clay huts. But there are bound to be plenty of debates in Sinkiang during the next few years.

28
Kansu

The province lies like a huge strangely shaped piece from a jigsaw puzzle inserted in China's map. It is one of the classic Chinese provinces which have formed part of the Chinese state territory since ancient times. It was long administered together with Shensi and up to 1882 included even the present Sinkiang.

The name of Kansu is derived from the old names of two of the most important market towns on the classical route west—the Silk Road as it is now called, the Emperor's Route as it was called then: *Kan*chow, today's Changyeh, and *Su*chow, now Kiuchüan. Here in Kansu the roads met from western Asia and inner China, from the Gobi Desert north and the Tibetan high plateau south. Near the present provincial border to Sinkiang was the Great Wall of the Han dynasty, and here was also its Jade Gateway. The Great Wall of the Ming dynasty now runs across the road at Kiayükwan, and its west gateway is there.

Kansu is an earthquake area. In the big earthquake of 1920, 264,000 people perished, despite the fact that the country was then depopulated and laid waste by the huge peasant wars toward the end of the nine-teenth century.

Since 1949, the administrative borders between China's provinces in the northwest have been adjusted several times. Kansu is now slightly larger than Sweden, about 530,000 square kilometers with about 18 million inhabitants. It has one national boundary in the north where it borders upon the Mongolian People's Republic. In the northwest Kansu adjoins the Sinkiang Uighur Autonomous Region; in the west, Tsinghai province; in the east, Shensi; and in the northeast, Ningsia Hui Autonomous Region.

Kansu is an administrative unit, to a certain extent a historic unit as well. It is not, however, a geographical unit. Eastern Kansu is a part

233

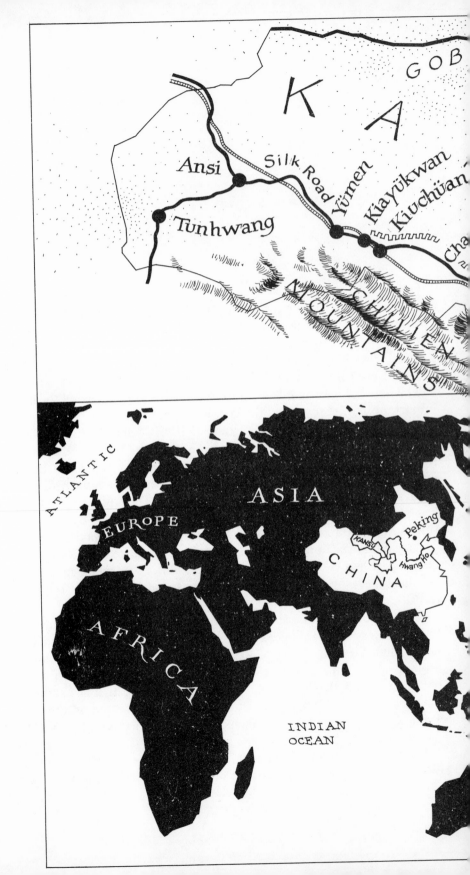

of the loess land of northern Shensi. Southern Kansu around Tienshui is almost as luxurious as South China. From the Lanchow area up toward the mountains beyond Linsia there are good agricultural areas. Hwang Ho—the Yellow River—cuts right through Kansu and "Hohsi"; the land west of the river has a different character. The 3,000-meter-high pass across the Wuchiao Mountains—Wuchiaoling —forms the watershed between eastern and inner Asia. There beyond is the 1,200-kilometer-long Kansu corridor. Oases are strung like pearls along the old trade route between the Chilien Mountains in the south-west and the desert mountains toward the Ala Shan Desert and the great Gobi in the northwest.

The majority of people in Kansu are Han. But there are also large groups of Hui, Mongols, Tibetans, Kazakhs, and others. There are two autonomous districts in Kansu: the Linsia Hui Autonomous District and the South Kansu Tibetan Autonomous District. Eight of the seventy-four counties are autonomous. Generally speaking, this distribution corresponds to the traditional picture. But it also is a result of the cruel genocide carried out after the great peasant revolts in the last century during the "Moslem War."

Kansu has natural riches but is an underpopulated and poor province, now developing into one of China's new industrial base areas. It is situated right next to China's inner defense area, along with Szechuan and Tsinghai provinces. Isolated, long-forgotten places like Linsia have become the centers of the most highly developed modern industry. All of Kansu is developing and the towns are being industrialized and transformed, from Tienshui in the east to Ansi in the west. New towns have also been created in the wasteland, like the steel city near Kiayük-wan—the West Gateway of the Great Wall—which was unknown to the world until recently.

Kansu was famous for its old trade route along the corridor west of the river with its great Buddhist monuments and old cultural towns. Now Kansu is developing its oil and coal, its ore and copper, its various other minerals. The provincial capital, Lanchow, once a focal point for the trade along the great routes, is now being transformed into one of China's important big cities with more than a million inhabitants, an industrial scientific base for China's great leap forward into modernization.

A wooden pagoda in Changyeh, built during the Sui dynasty (583) and rebuilt during the Ch'ing dynasty (1890). It is now a monument at the county level.

The copper works at Paiyin, Kansu

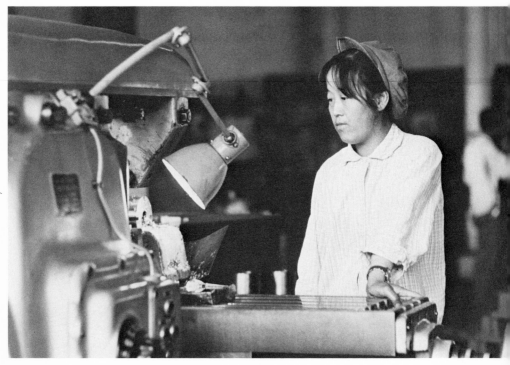

A laborer at the electrotechnical factory in Tienshui, Kansu

A production line at Linsia

A craftsman in Tienshui, Kansu

The old oil field at Yümen

A laboratory at the phototechnical institute of Kansu province, Linsia

A teahouse in the city park in Lanchow. Old-age pensioners are playing backgammon.

The bus station in Lanchow

Dancing-school girls. Only fifty years ago, girls like these were sold as maids and concubines.

The new department store in Lanchow

The old iron bridge over the Yellow River. New esplanades are breaking up the old town of ramshackle houses.

Housewives living at the copper mine of Paiyin clean the service vehicles

In southern Kansu the country is fertile. The Silk Road goes on toward Sian, formerly Changan.

29
Crescent Lake

It was the sixth day in Tunhwang. The previous evening we had completed work at the Caves of the Thousand Buddhas in Tunhwang. Or—more correctly—we had worked there for as long as we had permits. When the sun set, the week was over and with it the permit. Most of the work was still unfinished.

When darkness fell and Gun could no longer take photographs, we left cave number 220. Gun was tired; her knees were shaking as we descended the stairs. These short days, while the possibility lasted, we had worked from sunup to sunset without granting ourselves breaks for rest and meals.

Of course, you can take photographs without daylight. There are lamps and there is flash. But the artists who worked here more than a thousand years ago had neither. The flash turns the perspective of light back to front, and I know of no lamps that can re-create the light-saturated dusk in such caves protected, by corridors and galleries, from the harsh desert light of the valley. Our permit to stay at the Caves of the Thousand Buddhas was limited, so Gun had had to take advantage of every minute of daylight. When we walked toward the guest house, she was so tired that she spewed green gall by the roadside.

In the morning we left the guest house near the Caves of the Thousand Buddhas. It was not late morning and hot already. We were resting at Crescent Lake on the other side of the Tunhwang oasis.

It is a strange little lake. A spring amid the sand dunes in the desert. A clear blue lake shaped like a crescent, framed by high dunes. The fine sand smokes from the dunes in the wind, and they rise high and menacing above the lake, looking as though they were advancing on it, about to throw themselves into it to smother it. But the sand never fills it.

Crescent Lake does not change its outline, even though the sand dunes roll on toward it. It remains. It could be called a fresh-water pool in the midst of the desert.

The lake cannot be seen until one is quite near. One plods through the sand, leaving the last of the oasis far behind. All cars and jeeps were stuck. The sand was like newly fallen snow, the desert sterile, the heat trembling in the air. Then, all of a sudden, Crescent Lake lay clear and still and deep blue down below between the dunes five kilometers south of Tunhwang.

We slid along the high sand dune down to the lake, and the whole desert started to sing beneath us. Mighty strings were struck and the tones rose to the sky. Crescent Lake has been famous since the Han dynasty for this music. The desert here sings and thunders beneath the wanderer approaching that lake which can never be filled by sand. Men created the Caves of the Thousand Buddhas, but the gods created Crescent Lake, they say.

We were sitting in the shade of the trees, having tea on a nicely worn Khotan rug with a bold flowery pattern and a meander edge, in an unusual shade of pink. We looked out over the blue water toward the pearly, shimmering dunes. The water curled in the wind, and near the shore a shoal of fish passed. It was very lovely and very still. This beauty is one of the prides of Tunhuang.

Temples and pavilions should be behind us. The buildings themselves were not very famous, but they were erected on ancient land. In the Han dynasty temples and pavilions had been built here. Tunhwang was then the major cantonment on the edge of the great desert. Troops gathered here to rest before marching on through the waterless desert toward the western provinces and the large oases. Even then Crescent Lake was an excursion goal and a pleasant garden. But the pavilions from that period disappeared long ago.

In the town of Tunhwang there was an oil painting of Crescent Lake on the wall of the reception room of the revolutionary committee. Han Shu, the vice-chairman of the revolutionary committee of Tunhwang county, showed it proudly. The temples and pavilions could be seen in it. The picture had been painted by a young local artist.

"He began to paint after the Cultural Revolution."

But the temples in the picture were not very old; they did not look very remarkable. They dated from the last dynasty.

But when we turned around to look behind us, there were no temples and no pavilions. No buildings at all; only a shepherd's hut and then, beyond the edge of cultivation, a desert with sterile sand. Crescent Lake has been devastated.

"That was not done in the Cultural Revolution," said Chao Yu-yeh from the cultural department in Kansu.

"There were bad elements among the Red Guard. They tried to turn the campaign against bad old customs to a fight against cultural relics. Even Kansu suffered for this; a great deal was demolished in this province. In order to stop that, the party began the large popular movement to care for the monuments and take over archaeology. The Cultural Revolution therefore became the greatest archaeological campaign in our history. Archaeology became a popular movement. But before that, certain bad elements and provocateurs had time to ruin some of the people's monuments. However, these elements did not destroy the buildings at Crescent Lake."

"That happened a couple of years ago," Han Shu said. "The temples and the rest were tended by a man who had previously been a monk. We thought he was changed. At least, we did not realize his true character."

"So what did he do?" Gun asked.

"He burned it all down one night. He also burned down the temple over there on the other side of the dunes near the Sand Mountain Production Brigade."

"Why was that?" we asked.

"There was no special reason. He was in fact a counterrevolutionary at heart and burned all the things for which he was responsible in one night. No one had expected it; we all thought he was long since changed. He had been responsible for these temples for twenty years after the liberation. Then one night he set fire to them.

"But," Han Shu added, "the revolutionary committee of the area will have it all rebuilt. Perhaps not all of it, and in any case not the temple on the other side of the dunes. That was not very interesting. But we are reconstructing most of it as it was; a decision for that has been made, and the plans have already been designed. Everybody in Tunhwang loves Crescent Lake. The next time you come you must come when the grapes are ripe. Then we shall sit in the pavilion and eat grapes, and it will be as lovely as in the painting in the reception room of the revolutionary committee."

Attempts had been made to pump water from Crescent Lake and bring it via a canal to the Sand Mountain Production Brigade. But the canal kept filling with drifting sand. The dunes wandered, and the canal could not be kept open.

"A pipeline all that way would be more difficult and expensive than drilling a well. We would have to pump the water anyway," said Han Shu.

The Sand Mountain Production Brigade is famous. It has removed ninety sand dunes in ten years, and regained 40 hectares. They plan to regain another 70 hectares in the next ten years. The yield per hectare has been multiplied four times since 1966.

From the top of the dune, we could see how the Sand Mountain Production Brigade was advancing in close formation toward Crescent Lake. The vegetation marched in well-disciplined squares. In front was the farthest trench of the irrigation system. Nine wells, 80 meters deep, distributed their water through them.

"This year we shall drill another six wells."

There, at the far irrigation canals, the tree plantations could be seen. They stopped the wind and were a barrier to the desert. Behind them the desert could be divided into squares, binding the flying sand. Bit by bit, the dunes were removed. When the melting water from the mountains reached the outer branches of the irrigation system, and people had plenty of water for a brief period, it was directed to dig its way among the dunes. The dunes already bound were undermined and collapsed, so that the fields became even. Now tractors should be sent out over this chessboard that was rolled out like a carpet across the desert. But so far all Tunhwang has only 118 tractors.

"We're making preparations! By 1980 our whole agriculture will be mechanized."

Not only the Sand Mountain Production Brigade was advancing toward the desert. The whole Tunhwang oasis was on the move. It had passed the extreme borders of ancient settlements several years ago, and was now conquering land from the desert.

"The thing is," said Han Shu, "that more than 35,000 of the 41,000 square kilometers of this county are pure desert. Sterile sand or stone desert, Gobi. The arable land is very little, about 15,000 hectares. We do, however, reckon that it is possible to cultivate 33,000 to 34,000 hectares. We follow the example of Tachai. We shall be a county of the Tachai type."

Learning from Tachai is one of the great political issues in China. The production brigade of Tachai in Shansi province is the example. In a consciously organized way, it has by its own power fought its way out of poverty and backwardness and low production and has overcome severe natural catastrophes. Conscious leadership by the party; using its own resources; all-round development!

In 1964 Chairman Mao Tse-tung gave the call: "Learn from Tachai in agriculture!" Since then Tachai has been not only an example but also a focal point of great political confrontations. The question whether this way was the right one and whether it was at all possible to develop the country in this way with its own resources, was central in the political fight of the Cultural Revolution. Liu Shao-ch'i and his followers denied it.

China is a huge country. China is an old cultural nation. China has great scientists and a developed industry. But China's poverty and backwardness were enormous. They are still great. What misled Liu Shao-ch'i and his partisans was the overwhelming sense of hopelessness before the problem of China's heavy poverty. They, unlike Mao Tse-tung, did not see the possibility of all these hundreds of millions coming together in a united development, using their own potential power. Mao Tse-tung saw the fable about the foolish old man shoveling the mountain away not only as a fable; to him it was true. It showed the only way China's people could possibly go. But to lead China on this road a strong faith in the creative ability of the masses and in the greatness of man was needed.

Mao Tse-tung did have this faith, even in the worst of circumstances. But Liu Shao-ch'i did not. He could not rely on the masses. He was without faith.

During the years following the Cultural Revolution the issue of Tachai as an example became the central conflict in China. In the autumn of 1975 it had reached the stage of a large national conference on learning from Tachai. And during this conference, Hua Kuo-feng appeared in the general view as a national leader. He gave the final report on the month-long conference and set out the result. By learning from Tachai it would be possible to carry out that agricultural mechanization by 1980, which the Fourth National People's Congress had decided.

It would be possible to mechanize agriculture and so guarantee a development of a modern industry, defense, science, and technology. By the turn of the century China would achieve its aim of being one of the most highly developed nations in the world.

But the issue was disputed. Learning from Tachai implied dealing with matters of production in practical work. The aims laid down by Chou En-lai at the Fourth National People's Congress, and made more specific by Hua Kuo-feng at this large national conference in the autumn of that year—October–November 1975—were attacked more and more blatantly and desperately during the political struggle in China in the spring and summer of 1976, when Tachai began to disappear from the mass-media picture. Hua Kuo-feng's speech was more and more pushed out of view. At the same time attacks were becoming open against that very modernization which Chou En-lai and Hua Kuo-feng had stated as goals in their reports—written on the advice of and

approved by Mao Tse-tung. Names were not mentioned, apart from
Teng Hsiao-p'ing, but their policy was beginning to be described as a
"capitalist-road," nonrevolutionary—or even counterrevolutionary—
policy.

However, anyone who—like Gun and me—traveled through China
in the summer of 1975 and the spring, summer, and autumn of 1976
and talked to party secretaries, brigade leaders, and people in practical
work, noticed very little of this mass-media opinion from the universities of Peking and Shanghai. The structure of power that later became
evident showed that those then called the "gang of four" had had power
only over mass media and such channels. Their words filled the air for
a while, but they were just husks and odd grain, blowing in the wind.

The responsible cadres on various levels whom we spoke to in Sinkiang and Kansu during this period behaved as though this whole
debate, which filled the air and showed itself on posters and in newspapers, did not concern them. They referred in Sinkiang to the first point
of Mao Tse-tung's instructions of 1963 to grip economic work so firmly
that the standard of living of the people would surpass that of Soviet
Central Asia. The revolutionary road must show its superiority in
practice. In Kansu they spoke about the Fourth National People's
Congress and the goal of modernization, at the very same time as the
mass media condemned that modernization as revisionism.

There were leading cadres influenced by the "Gang of Four"; there
were areas, towns, and even provinces where the "Gang of Four" had
considerable influence. After their fall I visited some of these places.
But in the summer when they reached for the greatest power, I traveled
through provinces where their words seemed like air. This should be
mentioned, because many readers will believe that China went through
a fundamental transformation in the autumn of 1976. In places, perhaps, but not generally. People went on working along the guidelines
of Premier Chou En-lai fixed by the Fourth National People's Congress, regardless of the attempts to declare these aims revisionist or
capitalist.

Han Shu in Tunhuang, like other local politicians and authorities to
whom we spoke in brigades, communes, counties, and districts in Sinkiang as well as in Kansu, considered the main, overwhelming task to
be to carry out the decisions concerning the modernization of China.
Politics are—in China as anywhere else—an issue of real human problems.

"In the old days," Han Shu said, "we only used 30 percent of the
water of the Tang River. Now we use 57 percent. We have built three
reservoirs with a capacity of 16 million cubic meters. Besides, there is

a margin by which we can increase the use of water in the Tang River. In principle our county has been electrified. We yield 3,200 kilowatts from six local power stations. The network now reaches 55 of the 77 production brigades in our eleven people's communes. It is fifteen years since our area achieved self-sufficiency in agricultural products, and we have started to build industries. In 1965 the value of our industrial production within the area had reached 1.8 million yuan. Now ten years later, the value has passed 11 million yuan annually. More than half of the arable land has already been prepared for tractor use.

"Still, the degree of mechanization is low. Manual work is by far the greater. And we have not yet any real protection against sand storms. Even if we are proud of the average income now having reached 226 yuan per person—105 of this in cash—and we have good grain reserves apart from that needed for consumption in storage, it is not very much. Compared with how we used to live, it is naturally much better, and we have a right to call it great progress. But looking to the actual requirements of the people, we have not much to boast about.

"That is why the campaign of learning from Tachai is so important to us. We must build up this area by our own power. The help from the government is great. It is of a general nature. The price of the industrial products we buy has been stable for twenty years while the supply has increased. The tax on agricultural production has in reality been decreased constantly, at the same time as the official buying price of our agricultural products has increased every year. This is a great help and stimulus, it enables us to develop this county—like other counties in this country—with our own resources.

"Regarding production, we have well-defined planned figures for our county up to 1980. We plan to build 439 kilometers of irrigation canals, construct three water reservoirs for a total of 40 million cubic meters; drill one thousand new wells; erect three new water-power stations which will increase the electricity supply by 3,000 kilowatts and secure the energy for our new industries; we shall reclaim 2,000 hectares of saline land; prepare another 7,000 hectares for use with tractors; on the whole, gain protection against sand storms by planting 50 kilometers of shelter belts and 20 million trees. We shall increase the average cereal yield from the present 6.3 tons per hectare to 7.5 tons per hectare and raise the average cash incomes by 50 percent per person. That is our present guideline. If we manage to achieve it by 1980, we shall have created the very first beginning of what could be called a socialist countryside. But we shall certainly have to take a firm grip on the revolution, if we want to increase production in this way."

It was steaming hot when we returned to Tunhwang from Crescent

Lake. Tunhwang is a desert town with a typical continental climate. January has temperatures as low as −28°C, while the temperature reaches over +43°C in July. The annual evaporation is 2,484 mms but the rainfall is only 29.5 millimeters. Still, as we now were arriving in Tunhwang town from the desert, it was as though all the sluices of heaven had opened, and rain poured down.

The water gushed forth hissing in the irrigation canals. We ran into the guest house to get under a roof. But the Tunhwang houses had not been built with rain in mind. After a few minutes, the ceiling was leaking heavy drops, and the walls were wet. We spread our raincoats over the camera equipment, the typewriter, and the notebooks, and as we looked out into the rain from the window, we could see men on all the flat mud roofs, stamping them down to keep the water out.

It was still raining in the morning. The courtyard was a thick yellow-clay paste. Before we got the car onto the road we were clotted with mud up to our knees. The clay stuck to our soles, and the car skidded, spinning its wheels, before it could be steered into the road. But Han Shu, soaking wet in the middle of the heaviest rain, laughed toward the sky:

"It hasn't rained like this for years," he said. "I couldn't sleep all night. I just kept running out to feel the rain. This rain means more than one million jin of grain this year. Five hundred tons of grain rained down from the sky over Tunhwang last night. It's in truth a lucky day."

The road up through the desert was slimy in the rain now pouring steadily down over a stony desert. We were going to Ansi. There were large grey watchtowers standing in the rain.

"They date back to the Han dynasty," Han Shu said. The mountains were to our right and the desert was open toward Sinkiang on our left. We turned right at Ansi and had begun to drive the Kansu corridor eastward along the Silk Road down to the land of the Yellow River.

30
It Rains in
the Corridor

"Women," said Chang Yu-lan, a woman of thirty-five, "women must learn to stand up and address a meeting." She was the party secretary of the Chauyang production brigade of the Santakuo People's Commune right on the border between the counties of Ansi and Yümen in the Kansu corridor. We were in her house eating *mien,* noodles with a strong spicy sauce. She had made the noodles that night while awaiting our arrival. She had discussed production and results with us and the plans up to 1980, and now she said:

"It is important that the women learn to understand they are capable of doing whatever a man can do. Both my husband and I have been active all along. And it was during our political work that we grew together and got married. We took part in the great debates. We criticized certain cadres, since we considered their style of work wrong; they were hiding behind their desks and had taken refuge in their offices and never saw daylight. I stood up and addressed the meetings. After that they said that I ought to be elected a cadre. That's how it happened. Nobody actually said anything against having a woman cadre, but I suppose many thought that way.

"There are 1,301 people in this brigade. Of these, 67 are educated young people who have settled in the countryside and want to stay here. There are 50 of us in responsible positions of various kinds, cadres. None of us are on salary from the state, and we all work in the fields. We are short of workers, and now no cadre stays behind his desk in the office any more.

"My husband was elected to the management of the production brigade. They said he did a good job, and so he was selected for the county revolutionary committee over in Ansi. We see each other when we have a chance. I live here with our son, who is now five. When my

243

husband went over to the county revolutionary committee, I was elected secretary of the party organization of the production brigade."

The road up to the Yümen pass was totally straight over a stony, bushy steppe. Only when one turned around did one see how long and steep the incline was. Far down below were the farms of the oil field.

"The family members work there," said Fu Wai-chen, the chairman of the revolutionary committee in Yumen. "We follow Taching. The Yümen oil fields are not just self-sufficient in agricultural products, they are also important suppliers to the state. We have just broken new ground in an oasis fifty kilometers from here. We produce each year enough cereal, edible oil, and meat to supply our whole population for twenty months. We follow Taching. Yümen does not consume the country's resources.

"How are we to build China? We have our own resources, that's all. So we have to rely on that. We must exploit every drop of oil, and not have eyes bigger than our bellies."

The constant upward slope led to the oil fields. The engine hummed in second gear, after the driver had to give up the attempt to keep it going by pressing the accelerator. The flat steppe was all grey, but the mountains now appeared gradually redder through the dusty air.

Yümen is not an example, it is a pioneer. Taching is the example. Taching is an example to industry, in the same way as Tachai is to agriculture. Over on the steppes in northeast China, the workers opened China's first really great oil field during three years of hard work in the early sixties. In those years the Kremlin leaders tried to drive China to surrender by economic warfare. The Peking buses puffed around with large balloons filled with methane gas on their roofs. The factories stood still in the country. All Soviet technicians had been withdrawn. They had taken blueprints and spares as they left.

In various embassies the young cultural attachés were talking to us. They were excited.

"China is in crisis," they said.

In the autumn of 1962 we went to a drunken party with the Russian correspondents in Peking. They wanted to pump us for news from northern Shensi, where we had lived in the Liu Lin production brigade. But they were also telling us that they had it from reliable sources that people were starving to death in southern China.

That was the time the "iron man" Wang Chin-shi and his comrades overcame all difficulties and made China self-sufficient in oil by managing to open the oil field at Taching in northeastern China. That was where the Kremlin leaders were conquered. That was also a victory over Soviet ideas of how an industry should be run. No director's autocracy! Cadres to take part in the manual work and the manual workers in the administration: workers, cadres, technicians in unified groups to develop techniques and liberate the masses' initiative.

In the bitter struggle China had to go through after those years when plans miscarried and natural catastrophes had been hitting the country —difficulties used by the Soviet Union to still more fully disrupt the whole economy by sabotage and thus try to bring about a political landslide giving the pro-Soviet group political power and the Soviet Union military bases in China and hegemony over China—in that bitter struggle so full of disappointments and when so many former friends turned their backs on a China in need of solidarity, the victory of the oil workers of Taching gave enthusiasm to China. And during the years of the sixties and seventies, when the political struggle went on undiminished in China, Taching remained an example of the new great development.

Taching may be the example; but Yümen is the father of the example.

"This is where Wang Chi-ching gained his experience as an oil worker," said Fu Wai-chen. "In the KMT period he worked here from the beginning, but up to the time of the liberation he could not even buy himself a pair of trousers. The life of the working class was hard. But China's oil workers were brought up here at Yümen. We sent workers from here to the new oil fields and cadres to responsible positions in party and state.

"We got started in 1939, in the KMT period, and during the anti-Japanese war. Those years were bitterly tough. At the liberation there were four thousand of us here, but we could not yield more than 60,000 to 70,000 tons a year. After the liberation the working class took over and developed Yumen. We reached a peak in 1958, when 46,000 people worked here. We had built up this town, schools and hospitals and everything.

"In 1960 the party demanded that we send cadres to the fight for China's self-sufficiency in oil. We were to send workers up to the steppes in the northeast, where oil had been discovered. The imperialists said that China had no oil, but our scientists proved them wrong. China had great oil reserves; we had only to open the fields. That was not an easy task.

"The party said that life would be hard where the workers were being sent. There were no houses and no roads. Food would be scarce, the climate rough. They had to be prepared for hardships in their fight for oil. China's resources were more strained than ever then, and many high cadres lost all faith and followed Liu Shao-ch'i.

"But the working class of Yümen could be trusted. The veterans, having been through the difficulties in the old days, were the first to volunteer. So we could send at once 18,000 oil workers headed by the veterans to the steppes in the northeast. Wang Chin-shi went. He became known as the "iron man" in Taching. He died in 1970 from cancer of the stomach. But we shall never forget him.

"We have sent many comrades from Yümen to various parts of the country. Kan Shi-en, for example, China's oil minister. He worked so hard that he died quite young in 1976; Sung Chen-min and two other vice-ministers for the oil industry; Chan Chi-min, who is responsible for oil and coal and chemical technology in Kansu; Chen Li-nin, vice-chairman at Taching; Pei Hu-chung, vice-chairman of the Takang field at Tientsin; and Tsiao Wei-han, vice-chairman of the Shengli ("Victory") oil field in Shantung. Veteran workers from Yümen have been leading the victorious battle to transform China into a country that is not only self-sufficient in oil but even an oil exporter! Since 1960 we have sent 64,000 oil workers from Yümen to work at other oil fields in China. Yümen has been a center of education for China's working class.

"In Yümen 19,000 people now work in the oil and the service industry; 3,700 of them are women. Besides, there are 22,000 family members who are able to work. They are building up our agriculture and have enabled us to be self-sufficient in that too. That is Taching's line: all-round development.

"About ten years ago, some leading comrades thought that Yümen was finished as an oil field, emptied, and had to be abandoned. They were wrong. During the Cultural Revolution we re-examined the Yümen finds, and now we have a regular annual production of 600,000 tons. Whether we can increase production or not is a political issue. We have learned to drill deeper. We have reached new oil-bearing strata.

"The main thing is to get the masses mobilized. This policy has saved us 50 percent on equipment since 1960. One must keep asking if whatever is done cannot be done in a cheaper way. It is just a matter of getting into the habit of asking while one handles a machine: What can I do to make this machine work better and last longer? Initiative, inventiveness, care, thriftiness. When politics lead and everybody knows that the work is done in the interest of the whole country and socialism and not just for private welfare and the owner of the factory, the creative potential of the masses can be realized. That's the way we have carried out an annual plan in six months. Our new refinery is now in production.

"This is also the basis of the school we have founded here in Yümen. We have our own workers' university and the oil ministry has its technical college here in Yümen. Workers are educated there to become highly qualified technicians, specialists in oil drilling and extraction. In three years we have sent 5,500 educated technicians from here to other oil fields."

There is a heavy grey sky over Yümen in the morning. Rain hangs in the air over the steppe, and we have gone east to the new oil fields.

"Work here is fully automatic," Chu Yu-chen said. He is an oil technician and responsible for the work. "The oil runs in pipelines at a frost-free depth to the refinery eighteen kilometers from here. All this work was carried out between 1969 and 1974.

"We had to solve a whole series of technical problems. The frost-free depth was not the least, but got solved by the three-in-one combination. I was responsible for the work. We don't have autocracy here as in the Soviet, the type of autocracy the Soviet experts tried to force on us. That applies not only to the general management of the work but also to the technical issues. An almighty chief engineer can have the best education in the world and still know less and make more mistakes than a collective comprising technicians with both theoretical and practical knowledge, oil workers with plenty of experience, and politically responsible cadres, who have both experience of work and knowledge of the administrative and financial long-term planning. The three-in-one combination is more effective than the KMT's despotic chief engineers and the autocratic Soviet directors."

"It is a political issue," said Chu Yu-chen. "The people are the driving force of history, even in technology. The people's potential for technological innovation must be liberated. In our construction, we have to exploit and develop the knowledge and experience of the whole of the working people."

Chu Yu-chen had led the work of constructing the automatic control plant that directed the work of this whole field. His twenty-five-year-old assistant was called Chou Wen-chi. He showed us the plant.

"I come from Shanghai. After school I worked in the country to learn to understand reality better. Later, the brigade I worked in noticed my technical aptitude, discussed the matter, and sent me here to work and learn from older technicians.

"Then I was given the chance of working with Chu Yu-chen when he led the construction of this control plant. Now that it is completed the field is totally automated. Eight of us do the work that took forty-seven before. There's less manual work. We survey and control the operation of 83 oil wells here, but we have the capacity to extend them to 130 and no more staff will be needed.

"I shall stay at the oil fields. I don't want to go back to Shanghai. I live in Kansu now and I shall get married here."

The road from Yümen goes southeast across the high plain. We are driving at an altitude of 1,800 meters and the weather is strange. A brisk wind is blowing against us and dark clouds amass in the sky. Swift little clouds chase each other, dragging their shadows across the landscape. Beyond the wide asphalt road the ground is barren and stony. It is gobi. But here and there this sterile grey landscape is becoming black in patches, and water puddles gleam in the hollows. They shouldn't—it never rains here.

The low mountains on the left nearer the great desert in the north are black. The farthest parts of the Great Wall pass by there. On top one can see old watchtowers silhouetted against the sky. The wall runs alongside us, for the route is ancient even if the road is new. The trucks we meet greet us with howling horns, and the drivers wave as they pass us on their way west to Yümen and the oil fields or the new industrial towns beyond or Ansi and Tunhwang or perhaps farther on to Sinkiang.

This is the emperor's route. Not only caravans and merchants and ambassadors traveled here, troop upon troop of the emperor's soldiers marched west to their distant barracks. When they trod past here they were not even halfway from Peking and still had more than 2,000 kilometers to go, as the crow flies. Eighty-five generations have lived since the route became a guarded road. This is the long road through the Kansu corridor, the corridor through Hohsi, the Country West of the River.

The river in question is the Yellow River on the other side of the water divide. Here on the high plateau we are approaching the edge of inner Asia, but 600 kilometers still remain to the watershed. To our right are the Chilien Mountains. On European maps they are called the Richthofen range. But the mountains were named long before German aristocrats traveled in China.

There is rain in the air; that is in truth remarkable. No rain-carrying clouds can ever reach here from the Atlantic Ocean. They get as far as Dzungaria, but they do not manage to cross Tien Shan.

No rain comes from the Indian Ocean. Hundreds of miles of the highest mountains of the world bar the way. And the summer monsoon blowing from the South China Sea is not supposed to carry the rain across the mountain ranges and the high plateaus. The clouds are supposed to discharge themselves before arriving here, and the wind is supposed to blow hot and dry. It doesn't. Last week at Tunhwang all the heavenly sluices were opened above us and the rain poured down. Rain and cold in inner Asia when it should be dry and warm.

"The weather is strange," Wang said. "It may have something to do with the earthquake."

China is having a bad year. There have been earthquakes and floods. Later toward autumn and winter, there will be a bad drought over many agricultural areas.

Forty years ago this would have caused famine and plague and chaos. Now it is just a year of natural disasters. Many people were killed in the 1976 earthquakes. How many? I don't know. Somebody said 800,-000, and that may be right. But there was no plague and no famine and the social fabric did not tear apart. The preparedness proved reliable. Mao Tse-tung's instructions concerning preparation for war and natural catastrophes had been followed. But of course, the catastrophes were felt. The industrial areas in the northeast were as if they had been attacked with nuclear weapons. But the catastrophe could be mastered with preparedness and foresight.

On the road through the corridor west of the river, at this strange time, when there was rain in the air and China was shattered by natural catastrophes, we talked about bad years of famine, and Chen said:

"China is a vast country. And our whole history is full of vast natural disasters. They have cost innumerable millions of lives. But if the people realize that these natural disasters have occurred and will occur again, that great natural disasters are inevitable, and if the people don't let themselves be frightened or paralyzed by this knowledge but really decide to fight them—then man will triumph over disaster. We must be prepared for war and natural catastrophes. It is quite possible to fight these threats rationally and keep the number of victims as low as possible and limit the damage. We Chinese realize the importance of being prepared for war and natural catastrophes, but that certainly does not mean that we want either!"

In such a year of catastrophes, which tries China so greatly, we drive across the high plateau in a rising storm.

31
At the Western Gate

The railway roadbed is coming closer. Suddenly the road turns to the right. It should cross the railroad. But the gates close in front of us and the bell rings. The train takes its time coming. Far away on the plain, black smoke. It grows. It becomes a mighty plume. The train is coming. The telephone starts to ring in the hut beside the crossing. Now the train is quite close. It thunders and hisses and the ground shakes as the locomotive rushes toward us. It is a mighty Santa Fe–type locomotive, black and gleaming. A 2-10-2. In Sweden we would say a 1-E-1. The heavy train rattles past and the cars look as though they are going the Union Pacific westward. Even when the locomotive is far away and growing small on the plains toward Sinkiang, the cars continue to clatter past us. A real heavy freight train. At the end comes a caboose looking like a real caboose should look.

The Chinese railroads look American. That is not surprising. Many of the characteristic features of American railroading, considered so typically American, were designed by Chinese engineers in China.

If this train came from Peking, it has probably come via Tatung, Tsining, Huhehot, Yinchuan, and Wuwei. If the train left Peking on what once was called the Kalgan line, after about an hour it would have passed the Chinglungchiao station. There a bronze statue of a man wearing a suit looks out over the railroad just before it dips in under the Great Wall north. It is a statue to commemorate Doctor Jeme Tien-yao.

He was one of the world's greatest railroad engineers; he developed the railroad technology. He led the construction of this railroad just after the turn of the century. At the beginning of this century—before the fall of the empire—the Chinese engineers had already reached and surpassed the world level. They solved tasks that were more difficult

250

than those tackled by the foreign railroad constructors, and they solved them beautifully. But these engineers were hampered by foreign imperialism and by Chinese warlords and corrupt officials. Even this large railroad high up past Lanchow and through the Kansu corridor into Sinkiang was planned and discussed by Chinese technicians before the First World War. However, only when the Chinese people after a long, cruel and bloody struggle had been able to smash their fetters, unite the country, and thoroughly clean it up did the Chinese railroad engineers have the freedom to carry out their rational plans. The railroad is designed for heavy traffic. It has opened up the great northwest of China.

As the train passes and disappears westward, the gates open and the broad asphalt road lies ahead to the east. The corridor becomes narrower here. The hills approach each other, and a wall stretches right across the valley. There is a huge fort there. This is the present West Gateway of the Great Wall: Kiayükwan. The asphalt road sweeps past the old castle in a wide bend, but the caravan route goes straight up to the wall and in toward the heavy doors closing the gate of the Great Wall.

There is not one but many Great Walls. The actual length is therefore always a matter for discussion. Its extent has varied in different periods. In the Han dynasty it ran west of Tunhwang. Now its western keep is down here in this long pass where the old caravan route led over the barren tableland between the mountains. From this fort of Kiayükwan over to the east keep of the Great Wall at Shanhaikwan on the border between the provinces of Hopeh and Liaoning, where the wall reaches the sea at Po Hai Bay, the American geographer Fredrick G. Clapp at the time of the First World War estimated its length at 6,323 kilometers. The Chinese claim the wall is 10,000 li long, that is, 5,000 kilometers. But *wan*, ten thousand in Chinese, like "myriad" is not a number, it is numberless. The Great Wall is certainly long—it is one of the greatest building works of man. In fact, the greatest.

The Great Wall was built by various rulers and in various dynasties. It is not—as is sometimes claimed—a work commanded by Shih Huang Ti, who united China, but in 220 B.C., when the kingdom was united, General Meng T'ien, with 300,000 men, was commanded to reinforce and extend the Great Wall.

The Great Wall has been called a boundary. It was not. Its function was different. It was a fortification and a system of checkpoints. It had several functions, one being to offer protection against raids and wars by the nomad horsemen. The Great Wall of the Han dynasty can thus be said to form a part of that defense of civilization against the barbarians which was continued in the so-called Wall of Alexander against the Turkmen steppe to the Caspian Sea, and then in the Roman fortifications through Europe all the way to Hadrian's Wall across England. But the Great Wall does not belong only to ancient times.

It can also be compared to the system of inner borders established by the British at the outposts of their Indian Empire. The British had both an inner and an outer fortified border, and so had the emperor's China an inner guarded border at the Great Wall.

Marco Polo traveled here, but he does not describe this fortification at Kiayükwan. He couldn't; it was not built until 1372, two generations after his death. China was then again united. It was in the Ming dynasty. Two generations later, on August 27, 1420, an ambassador from Shah Rukh, the ruler of Herat, the son of Timur, came this way to the gate in front of us. The ambassador had been traveling since December 4, 1419. The ambassador's report reads:

> On the following day they continued through the desert. When they arrived at a mighty fortification called Karaul (advanced post, guard) situated in a mountain pass and through which the road passed, all the travelers were counted and their names taken down before they were allowed to continue their journey.

Here at this checkpoint all travelers were registered. If they were traveling without valid documents from the emperor and if the commandant had not had previous notice of their arrival, they were detained while the Peking authorities dealt with the case and decided on it. Messages from this fortification in the far west were sent to Peking by fire and smoke signals. The guard towers were within sight of each other all the way and were constantly in communication.

It could, however, take time before Peking reached a decision. The Jesuit Father Benedict Goes, who arrived here in the New Year of 1606, had no valid passport. He was given a preliminary permit to continue to the next big town, then called Suchow and now Kiuchüan, where he would be informed about the decision. But he died in 1607 before the matter had been decided in Peking.

The present buildings were built when the fortification was strengthened in 1539. They were then rebuilt in 1566 and were given their present look. The walls are 11.6 meters high, built of burnt brick around a core of sun-dried brick. The building was used as a fortification until the fall of the empire in 1911. The tariff valid then was 120 tsien (small copper coins with a square hole in the middle; at that time there were about 20 tsien to a United States cent) per traveler and 400 tsien per animal. There was a special customs tariff for merchandise. This customs duty within the country was misused to enrich the officials.

Kiayükwan was declared a national monument after 1949. During 1957 and 1958 extensive restoration was carried out, and another huge restoration was begun in 1974, which will take years to complete.

Now there are telephone poles of concrete and power lines of iron in the middle of the fortification.

The lines haphazardly run to and fro across the courtyard. "That was built in 1967 when the central coordinating authorities did not function too well," Wang said. "A certain anarchy was prevalent. Various authorities erected their own power and telephone lines with no regard for the fact that this was a national monument, and disregarding the central planning, which would have saved them a lot of money. Now politics are in command again and the anarchy is over. All this is to be razed. It is neither practical nor pleasing."

There is yet another story about this confused network of lines and cables. If they were erected under a certain degree of anarchy, it was still not done without any plan. They are reminders of a period that was heroic, too. We are standing upon the gate leading to the east. Here below us Sven Hedin and his expedition left Kiayükwan in their "Ford automobiles" on December 27, 1934, on their way inland. Sven Hedin had then been commissioned by the Chinese central government to investigate the chances of extending the Silk Road—the Imperial Way —and he was driving back east from Sinkiang. The route was to become a modern motor road.

> One hardly leaves Kiayükwan behind, before the sterile desert begins again. But the country is not totally devoid of life. A herd of antelopes pass here, as swift as the wind, and in a side road a camel caravan marches forth.*

But now that we are standing on the wall looking east from this gate, we can see a town. A big town, with about 80,000 inhabitants. It is one of China's new steel cities and work on it was begun in 1965.

The town is so new that Theodore Shabad in 1971 was not quite sure how much of it existed. He wrote the standard work *China's Changing Map*. He mentioned that a news dispatch of 1971 might indicate that the project of erecting an iron and steel combine in Kiayükwan had not been totally canceled. When he wrote this, production there had been going on for more than a year.

The seemingly confusing network of cables and lines that various authorities have drawn through this old gate at the extreme west of the Great Wall are a memory of the period when China, during a sharp

*Sven Hedin, *Sidenvägen* [The Silk Road] (Stockholm, 1936), p. 336.

inner struggle between different lines, was gathering its strength in order to build the country. Kiayükwan was made a steel town during the Cultural Revolution.

China is huge. There are cities that cannot be seen in any atlas. There are huge industries not mentioned in any standard work. There are whole railroads not shown on any map. There are large bridges—technical engineering of world importance—which have never been mentioned in news dispatches or seen in pictures or discussed in the Hong Kong reports. As we looked out over the steel town of Kiayük-wan, it had never been mentioned in any report—ever.

"But as you see," Wang said, "this steel town does exist. We're showing it now, we don't mind if it's known. Take a photo, Gun; take as many as you like. It's not a secret any more."

There are reasons for being secretive, understandable reasons. Once in this six-months long journey we arrived at a huge railroad bridge where there should have been neither railroad nor bridge, at least not according to our maps. "We would not like you to take a photo of the bridge," Wang said to Gun. "And we'd like you to say nothing definite about its situation and position," he added to me.

"What does it matter?" Gun asked. "Both Russians and Americans must have taken photos of it already from their satellites."

"Well," Wang said, "I suppose you're right. But satellite pictures aren't all that explicit. For example, they don't show how you are to approach the bridge if you want to bomb it. Neither do they show the exact construction. If satellite pictures were sufficient, the Russians wouldn't need to send in spies to inspect the locations. But they do. We capture them. They haven't come here yet, though."

Ever since the liberation, China in its industrial construction has tried to adjust the lack of balance which is a legacy of the past. Imperialism and the foreign powers had left behind a lopsided location of industries. Shanghai and other coastal cities became huge swelling metropolises exploiting the rest of the country.

It has been a well-known fact that China has tried to change this picture. But exactly how well they have succeeded in their redistribution has not been published as yet. The provinces of Kansu and Tsinghai are being developed into a strong industrial base in inner China. But no full details have been given and satellite photos cannot reveal precisely the production and capacity of the new industries. In various international studies it has therefore been stated that China has perhaps failed.

I find it sensible of the Chinese to be secretive. As I was standing on top of the old fortification walls looking toward the new steel town, I knew of course that one of China's large rocket bases was only some hundred kilometers away. But I didn't ask them to take me there, and if I had happened to see it, I wouldn't have described it. For the same reason I have not described or marked the camouflaged Swedish military airfields or Iranian fortifications I happened to drive past. Both Sweden and the countries of the Third World have a right to protect themselves. There is no journalistic interest in serving the superpowers in their intelligence service.

So I do find it reasonable of China to keep quiet about some of its progress. But at the same time, I think it's wise for the world to remember that the actual progress in China often is greater than is shown by Chinese propaganda. China does not conceal its mistakes and its conflicts very much—one can read about them on the posters in Shanghai and Peking, and the news then passes through various channels in Hong Kong to all the papers of the world. However, it happens frequently that China hides its success.

32
The Kansu Iron Combine

"This," said Chia Chang-yun, vice-chairman of the revolutionary committee, "is the 'Kansu steel plant.' But that name does not cover what it really is; we are not yet a steel plant. We are an iron combine with a mine and a transport system and power stations, and so on. We are an iron plant and we are already producing iron. A steel plant we shall be within the next five years. The steel plant and the rolling mill will then be in production. We are called a steel plant but we are an iron plant and a steel plant-to-be. Write that!"

Kiayükwan, the steel town, was designated a town by the state council in 1971. Its area was then established at 1,798 square kilometers. This means that its area comprises the town center and also large areas around it. The aim is that Kiayükwan should strive to be self-sufficient in agricultural products. This is in accordance with the general line in Chinese planning. In 1976 the town achieved full self-sufficiency in vegetables. Before 1980, it is to be fully self-sufficient in meat and vegetables. Concerning cereal production the matter is more complicated. Here at the edge of the desert, agriculture needs irrigation. More than five years' work will be required to enable the town to produce enough grain for its own needs. The town now consumes about 16,500 tons of cereal annually, and the production reaches only 10,000 tons annually. The mechanization of agriculture is to be completed before 1980, but by then the number of inhabitants will have grown. Even more work, in other words, will be necessary before self-sufficiency can be achieved.

"Fisheries are another difficulty," Chia Chang-yun said. "Fish is an important part of our diet. We stock dams and canals with fish, this year about 600,000 fry. But that's insufficient, and the masses complain."

It was in 1958 that the decision was made to build a base for the steel industry in Kansu. That was done in accordance with Chairman Mao Tse-tung's policy on planning the location of industries. This iron base in the northwest was necessary to reach a balanced national development.

In the Chilien Mountains southwest of Kiayükwan, there were great reserves of iron ore, though of moderate quality. The ore held 37 percent. The preliminary geological examination carried out showed that there were at least 420 million tons of ore.

Construction was begun that year. A railroad had to be built to the mine fields, and the iron plant had to be erected. Fifty thousand building workers arrived.

"But the work was interrupted in 1960," said Chia Chang-yun. "Liu Shao-ch'i forced that decision through. He claimed that the project was unprofitable and useless. China's difficulties were too great. There was no food for the people. There was nothing else to do but to stop construction and disassemble the equipment. Liu Shao-ch'i and his followers had panicked, and they stopped many construction projects.

"From 1960 to 1964, there were only a thousand men here keeping guard. In 1962 Mao Tse-tung heard that the iron-plant project in Kansu had been stopped and the plans abandoned. He said he became sleepless with concern. He could not sleep all night after being told that the whole project of a base for the steel industry in Kansu had been written off. There were violent debates in the central leadership. The conflicts between Liu Shao-ch'i's line and that of Mao Tse-tung showed very clearly.

"However, Mao Tse-tung's line triumphed in 1964, and the decision was taken to resume the work. But a cold wind was blowing from a certain direction in 1964 and 1965, claiming that the northwest did not need a metallurgical base. That had to be overcome before construction could be resumed.

"At the same time we began to build the town around the iron plant. There was only wasteland here before, so it all had to be done from the beginning. We also founded small industries at the same time, plus all the service institutions necessary to a town. Now we have thirty-two small industries of various kinds.

"All this work was carried out without the help of any foreign specialists. Only Chinese technicians have been active here, working out plans and studies, from the very first project.

"The production of cast iron started in April 1970. The production value of 1975 was 57 million yuan, and that of 1976, 70 million yuan. Only in 1980 will steel production begin. We shall then be 19,000 people working here. The low production volume is a problem. The technical knowledge is insufficient. We have great deficiencies.

"Most of our workers are young—about 70 percent of them. They come from the People's Liberation Army, demobilized after completing their service. Others move in from the countryside. We have only few experienced workers. They volunteered to come here from Anshan and Peking to participate in the construction work and guide the young workers. This lack of trained workers of course makes for low productivity. Still, the young people learn as they go along, and difficulties are there to be overcome."

Li Yu-chan is a woman teaching at the Sian Metallurgical Institute and working at the plant with her students.

"These pupils study metallurgy at the institute. We have discussed the aim of education a lot these decades. We consider it necessary for these students not to be separated from the practical work. They now spend three months here, studying metallurgy and simultaneously grappling with the problems in practice.

"They are second-year students. When they work here we create special groups comprising the teacher and the students, together with workers and technicians. Such a combined group can make use of experience in a better way."

As we were leaving, Chia Chang-yun suddenly said:

"I read your third report from the Liu Lin Production Brigade in northern Shensi. It was very interesting, I feel I know the comrades there. Some of us decided to go for a visit there after having read what you've written about it. We have discussed the possibilities, and it is not at all unlikely that we shall go. I want to go myself if I can."

The road beyond Kiayükwan had been flooded. It had rained hard in the mountains and all the irrigation canals were overflowing. The fields were under water. And this was where it is never supposed to rain.

33

The Reclining Buddha

"Look out!" Wang shouted. "The planks may be rotten up there!"

Gun was taking photos of the reclining Buddha in Changyeh and had climbed the loft to get closer to the large face. The planks were old and they creaked and gave way. The reclining Buddha stared past her with huge eyes in the large dark hall.

The reclining Buddha in Kanchow, which was the old name of Changyeh, is famous. The figure is 34.5 meters long and 7.5 meters high. The temple was erected in the Sung dynasty in A.D. 1098 and was restored in the Ming and Ch'ing dynasties. The later reconstruction was done in the twelfth year of Emperor Ch'ien Lung (A.D. 1776), when the temple was given its present exterior. In 1963 it was declared a protected monument on the provincial level. Restoration work was then carried out in 1965, 1971, and 1975. Our hosts are very proud of the monument.

It is not so remote, even if it is distant, this temple in an old town on the large trade route. It has been visited by foreign travelers, ambassadors, merchants, and other passers-by. The reclining Buddha in Kanchow was never unknown. In reality, it forms part of our own background.

Gun is working in the loft; I can hear her in the darkness above. I draw closer to the large figure; its eyes look through me. One day around 1550 a party from Venice went over to Murano to dine and talk. They were four people, hosted by the learned writer and statesman Gian Battista Ramusio. He had long since become a widower and had retired to complete his great geographical work: *Navigationi e Viaggi*. And it is in the foreword of its second volume of 1556 that he describes this particular afternoon.

Among his guests were his close friend and publisher, the printer

259

Giunti, and the famous architect and fortification specialist Michele Sanmichele, plus the Persian merchant Hadji Mohammed, who was in Venice to sell a large amount of genuine rhubarb root from the mountains around Suchow, now Kiuchüan.

After the meal had been cleared away and the gentlemen were sitting over their glasses, the Persian told them about China, saying among other things that the temples in Kanchow were built rather like the churches in Europe,

> with columns from one side to another. . . . Also, there are two remarkable statues in that town, one of a man and one of a woman. They both measure forty feet and have been sculptured lying on the ground.

Rhubarb root from Kansu had been among the remedies supplied by Master Lukas, court apothecary to King Gustavus I of Sweden. And when the court pharmacy was moved from the palace into town to become the old royal pharmacy, he went on selling rhubarb root from Kansu. Whoever is constipated and buys a laxative in that pharmacy—now called "The Lion"—in Stockholm, can buy the same remedy as that brought to Europe by Hadji Mohammed on the voyage when he told Ramusio about the reclining Buddha in Changyeh. The pharmacy of today in the center of Stockholm is, in fact, that same pharmacy that served King Gustavus I in what was in China the Ming dynasty.

That night I took a late walk around the town. On my way home, I saw a strange spindly construction against the starlit sky, like a palace built of toothpicks. I wondered what it was.

"A pagoda," Wang Li said. "A wooden pagoda from the Sui dynasty. It is in the yard of Secondary School Number 1."

We went to see it the following morning. It was a remarkable building, said to have been built in 583. But old Chinese buildings are rather like Granddad's old stick. Granddad bought it fifty years ago. The handle was replaced forty years ago, and the ferrule thirty years ago. The stick itself was replaced twenty years ago, but it is still Granddad's old stick. I couldn't tell how many times the wooden pagoda had been rebuilt between the Sui and the late Ch'ing dynasty. But in 1890, in the Ch'ing dynasty, it was restored and reinforced with brick walls. In 1925 it was repaired once more, and in 1953 the county decided to declare it a protected monument.

"This monument must be protected and tended with great care," the county authorities have written on a large placard next to the pagoda. "The pagoda is a county monument, a monument of local history. It is not a national monument like the west gate of the Great Wall, and not a provincial one like the reclining Buddha. It is only a county monument."

"We've got so many similar things," said Wang Li. "The town is full of temples and old monuments. We try to use them for schools and meeting rooms and such. But don't worry about the pagoda; a county monument is just as protected as a national one. It is in the care of the people."

But if Tunhwang and the gate of the Great Wall and the reclining Buddha and the wooden pagoda were protected, there were things that were not. Shantan a little farther east in the Kansu corridor had been devastated. Red Guards had arrived there, and not just any Red Guards, but those who called themselves "real leftists," determined to destroy all old customs and all the old imperialist influence.

Shantan had had the only large Asoka stupa in China, an enormous dome of sundried brick, whitewashed and huge. It was said to hold a strand of hair of King Asoka of India. These Red Guards, who claimed to be the real leftists, destroyed the whole stupa in their attempts to wipe out the imperialist influence.

In Shantan there was also a wooden house from the Sung dynasty. It had been owned by the same family since the eleventh century. The house was surrounded by legend; it was said to be cursed, and no one lived in it or had lived in it for almost a thousand years. It had been left as a monument, one of the oldest preserved buildings in China. Only few wooden buildings exist from this period. This house in Shantan was of importance to the Chinese people; it gave them a chance to investigate the technique developed by the craftsmen of olden times, the foundation of today's construction techniques.

But these students, who claimed to represent the real and true left, in convincing themselves that they did not have to believe in ghosts, demolished the house and burned the wood.

There was a simple burial memorial over George Hogg in Shantan. He had been with Chu Teh in southeastern Shensi during the anti-Japanese war. He had served the Chinese people, sacrificed himself for the Chinese people, and shared their conditions without thinking much about it.

In 1943 he wrote a book in Paoki in Shensi about the struggle of the Chinese people. This book was to decide my own and many other people's attitude to the power of the people and to the inner weakness of fascism: *I See a New China.* My copy was given to me by a British soldier in Oslo in 1945. The soldier came from London and was a communist. We had met at the large demonstrations after the liberation. We talked about the new world after the triumph over the fascists, and he spoke a lot about China. He gave me Hogg's book to read, before he was transferred to Germany. I never had time to give back the book; I've still got it. Now in Shantan, I wanted to visit Hogg's grave.

That was not possible. This George Hogg, an internationalist who had given his life in support of the Chinese people in the war against fascism and died on July 22, 1945, before the victory had been won in the anti-Japanese war, kept his burial memorial for only twenty-two years. His memory was respected by the new China. He was one of those many who had come from foreign countries—India, Canada, England, Germany, and many others—out of solidarity. Mao Tse-tung had taken them as examples of the international solidarity of working people and of "serving the people."

Combatting imperialism in a revolutionary way—as they said—these Red Guards, who called themselves leftists, attacked George Hogg's grave. "Weeds away!" they shouted, as they threw over the tombstone, smashed it, and scattered the fragments until they could never be found again. The grave was wiped out.

"You understand why people hate these self-styled rebels?" said Wang.

34
Toward the Divide

We are driving toward Wuwei and have driven from Ansi a thousand kilometers in Kansu. We followed the old imperial road down through the Kansu corridor. But we did not keep to it. We turned off here and there onto smaller roads, before returning to the main road going east.

The road runs between mountains and desert. To the south are the snow-covered Chilien Mountains. Beyond them, Tsaidam, with its marshes and salty lakes on the desert plateau that is now being transformed into the industrial base of innermost China. To the north low mountain ranges started to appear after Kiayükwan. Beyond them, the great deserts. The road we drove kept to the edge of arable land below the mountains. The melting water from the Chilien Mountains allows agriculture. Around the rivers coming down from the mountains are the oases. The farther east we drove, the larger were the oases and the closer together they came. But between the oases were stretches of gobi and bushy steppe. As we drove on, the arable land, however, took over. The Great Wall, which had accompanied us since Tunhwang with guard towers and stretches of wall, had now become a long wall running along the road mile upon mile after we left Shantan. Only in the desolate mountain passes did the wall turn off north and become watchtowers on the heights.

The land now was mainly arable. The desert and the wasteland had been pushed back to patches of gobi along the road through the countryside. We could see the fields advancing. The dunes were being removed, and the tree plantations marched forward over the plains. Dams and canals gathered water for the attack on the desert, and commune members were working with spades and hoes in the trenches by the edge of the desert. The odd tractor made its way forth between the wheelbarrows.

The rain had passed before Changyeh and the wind was as dry and hot as it was supposed to be. The stars burned at night like holes in the black sky. But at night, when we reached Wuwei, the air had changed both taste and color. It was smooth in our throats and had a soft sweet scent of inhabited land. The moon was mild and gentle over the landscape, like a north European moon, no longer white and sharp-cut like the moon farther up in the corridor, over the inner Asian mountains and deserts. We arrived at Wuwei, and even here, before reaching the water divide, we had left inner Asia.

The towns on the way down through the corridor had been old cultural towns. Now they were quickly being transformed, industrialized. But it is not enough to say that this development must be shown against its appropriate background. We traveled through a Kansu that had not only been poor and hit by natural catastrophes, but, from being a poor part of imperial China during the last century, had undergone a fate worse than that of the German lands during the Thirty Years' War. The peasants here had risen in a just war of liberation against imperial power, against the tax collectors, and against hunger. They did so under religious slogans, as did the European peasants in the sixteenth century. Here in Kansu and Shensi the peasants' war was fought from 1862 to 1878 with Moslem watchwords, just as the huge peasants' wars for freedom fought by the Taiping armies against the empire from 1847 to 1864 had Christian watchwords.

In the sixteen years while the empire was fighting against the rebel peasants in Kansu, its war was financed by loans from foreign trade companies, such as Jardine, Matheson & Co. To them it was only business. They traded in Chinese peasant extermination; the annual interest from this operation was 10.5 percent. They got the customs and taxes as security, at the same time as the troops they financed and made profit on made China safe for foreign capital by suppressing rebels and nationalists and all kinds of revolutionaries. In 1878, when the imperial general Tso Tsung-t'ang finally defeated the Moslem peasant armies in Kansu, the population in Kansu had gone down in sixteen years from 15 million to 1 million. If Tso Tsung-t'ang played a partly progressive role against Yakub Beg in Sinkiang, his contribution in Kansu was purely negative.

The struggles had not been—as is sometimes thought—national struggles. They were social struggles, peasant risings, class struggles. The empire used its Manchu "kinsmen" to stay in power by dividing and ruling. The Manchus were not a ruling class. General Tso Tsung-t'ang was a Han. He was one of the rulers. The life of the Manchu families after the fall of the empire, when they were no longer even in

service, was reported by the Swedish treasure hunter and Chinese civil
servant Johan Gunnar Andersson in 1926:

> Liangchow (Wuwei) has the strange and, one could say, the doubtful
> fame of being a center for the trade in young girls. The reason why so
> many young girls are offered in this place is said to be the preponderant
> Manchu population since the late Manchu dynasty. These Manchus now
> live in extreme poverty. The girls offered for sale are of all ages, from
> small children to 15–16, and the little girls are usually cheaper, since they
> will have to be fed and tended for many years before they can be used
> as servants or second wives. I was told at the time of our visit that about
> 2,000 girls were then being offered for sale. The price was between 50
> and 200 dollars or in exceptional cases considerably more, if the girl was
> unusually attractive.*

Fifty-year-olds in China talk of these bitter memories to the young
people. But the bitterness with which they talk about the past turns into
ice-cold wrath when they remember what these strangers and their own
ruling classes had to say about the unbearable oppression:

> One might find this trade in little girls a repulsive traffic, but a person
> aware of conditions in China will have a different view. These wretched
> Manchu families, who supply most of the girls, are so extremely poor
> that even the little objects of speculation themselves, if they are old
> enough to reflect on their situation, will see it as a better fate to be taken
> away from their home and its hopeless destitution.†

Andersson was probably not a bad man—no worse than his class then
were in China. He is very much like the businessmen one comes across
in Bombay and Calcutta who tell stories about life in India, and then
tell you how you see things "when you get used to India."

European and American liberals touring China usually complain
that all the middle-aged and older Chinese they talk to "tell the same
tale" about the old society and its misery. They would prefer a greater
variety of material. They do not realize that the Chinese would certainly have liked it too, but their past was just as monotonously bitter
as is related.

Wuwei was a center for the trade in small girls. Kansu was a center
for opium-growing. Local warlords and despots ruled northwest China.
China was looted by foreign armies and was sucked dry by their merchants and experts and plunderers. Her own government was corrupt
and tyrannical.

*Johan Gunnar Andersson, *Draken och de främmande djävlarna* [The Dragon and the Foreign
Devils] (Stockholm, 1926).
†Ibid.

The great oppression spawned revolt. The hopeless poverty made it necessary for the people to rise against misery, united and relying only on themselves. But Mao Tse-tung and the People's Liberation Army were supported not only by the poor peasants and the proletariat; liberation was supported by the vast majority. Only a handful followed the KMT and Chiang Kai-shek when they fled, and very few remained real counterrevolutionaries or utterly hostile to the new China after 1949.

That is easy to understand. Only classes and groups and individuals who are totally base and morally depraved can accept corruption, oppression, drug pushing, prostitution, and national humiliation. That was why the support for liberation was so vast: old teachers praising Confucius, officials who did not want to be corrupt, officers who had after all gone into the army because they wanted to defend China against the Japanese aggressors. But also merchants, capitalists, and even landowners greeted the liberation. They did so because their experiences were so extremely bitter that they felt Mao Tse-tung had saved China.

"I was thinking about how they finished off the opium dealers here," Gun said.

We were having a late walk through Wuwei. We had visited the agricultural machinery factory that day and were going to the textile factory the following day. Now we were talking in the warm night. The town was silent, the shops closed. The windows were lit up in the hotel, but the streets were almost empty. A cyclist appeared under a lonely streetlight far away. Chinese towns go to bed early.

"When the People's Liberation Army came here on its march up Kansu to Sinkiang, people gathered all the opium dealers. They were tried and convicted and shot, and that was right. All the opium was collected and burned.

"When the opium was burned, all freedom to kill oneself by taking drugs ended in Kansu. The freedom to prostitute oneself as well. The humiliation ceased. It is not even thirty years ago. I don't think any of our friends here in China could listen to that passage written by Andersson about the trade in small girls in Wuwei without reacting sharply; they would hardly be able to control their anger.

"They haven't shot such great numbers in China. But drug dealers, dealers in girls, and local despots were shot at the liberation. It served them right."

We walked home to the guest house through sleeping Wuwei. It was getting close to eleven o'clock. Gun continued:

"Many members of the so-called academic left in Europe and the

United States have projected their liberal and anarchist dreams on China. That has damaged China. How many times have we not read how the Chinese rehabilitated prostitutes and opium addicts gently, without violence, to a better life where they could regain their human dignity in collective work. All that is true, but little has been said about the procedure before this adjustment could begin."

The People's Liberation Army behaved just like the big revolutionary people's army it was, just like the Taiping, just like the peasants' movement in Hunan described by Mao Tse-tung, just like all peasant armies in similar situations. The gambling houses, the opium dens, the brothels were closed once and for all. The victims were removed. The criminals were taken to the main square, to be brought to trial by the masses, convicted, and executed in front of their victims. All opium was burned immediately and all use of opium stopped immediately. Many of the heavily addicted suffered, they say. I asked the comrades about it. They replied that the withdrawal shock certainly was severe. Many addicts did not survive it. They had sunk too deeply in their opium addiction. They died or committed suicide when the opium stopped. But that was the price necessary to get rid of opium forever in China. There was no other way. The people demanded instant abolition of all drugs.

Revolutions are not tea parties, but neither are they some kind of psychotherapy. Chu Teh and many people along with him had risen from addiction themselves, and they knew there is no middle course to take between the total extermination of drug use and the humiliation of addiction.

35

The Yellow River

At an altitude of 3,000 meters the road passes the Wuchiaoling, and then all rivers flow to the sea. We had passed the great divide, Chuanlang Ho ran next to us down toward the plain, growing into a river. The landscape was green and undulating where Chuanlang Ho joined Hwang Ho, the Yellow River. Huge water wheels here turned up the water of the river slowly in their buckets, bringing it through the irrigation canals out into the fields high above the surface of the river.

"Look," Gun said. "Here the irrigation technique is changing tradition!"

But we turned off the Lanchow road, driving up along the Yellow River. The hills grew like mountains around us and the wide river was gushing forth down below. In Liuchia we were standing in the mountain room of the power station. The Yellow River here produces 1,-225,000 kilowatts in five large generators. The mountain around us was thundering and trembling. Over the distant mountains the pylons rose.

"High-voltage lines of 330,000 volts down to Shensi and of 220,000 volts up to Tsinghai, away to Ningsia Hui and into Kansu," said Wang Tu-kiang, vice-chairman of the revolutionary committee of the Liuchia power station.

The Yellow River here grinds forth energy for the new industries of inner China. This power station is one of China's large constructions and part of the huge project to control the whole of the Yellow River.

"This was one of the one hundred projects with which the Soviet Union was to assist us," said Wang Tu-kiang, "and we began planning it in 1956. We started work in 1958. The Russians left in 1960. They use assistance and loans as means of political blackmail. Whoever does not obey is punished. They said we'd never accomplish this by ourselves.

268

"They might have been right. Those experts stole drawings and geological examination material when they left and we stood here with ten thousand men without any actual blueprints and with the enormous task of building a power station on the Yellow River which would alone generate more energy than all China produced before the liberation.

"But I also want to point out that many of the Soviet experts were sincere friends of the Chinese people. They were in tears when their government forced them to go home and sabotage our economy.

"Those years were difficult. Moreover, the country was hit by great natural disasters, and Liu Shao-ch'i in August 1962 decided to have this project stopped. That was bitter for us; many of us refused to accept that the reasons given for the decision were valid. Liu Shao-ch'i claimed that the natural disasters had been so serious, and the damage caused by the Soviet leaders so extensive after they broke their contracts with us and paralyzed vital parts of our industry, that it was pointless even to try to continue building this power station. Especially since we had severe technical problems, and the Soviet experts had plundered the archives and the laboratories of drawings and maps and geological survey material. It was a painful, inconceivable decision to us who worked here.

"Several large projects in Kansu were stopped in those years. It was a difficult time. The work had to stop, but we continued with surveys and planning.

"The workers who had been employed here were transferred to some other and smaller power stations not far away: the power station at Yankow, thirty kilometers from here, which now supplies 300,000 kilowatts, and the one at Papan, forty-three kilometers from here. But this power station at Liuchia was to be the largest one, and it was essential for the supply of energy for the new industrial construction. We kept discussing it. We did not accept that it had been excluded from the plans.

"The lengthy discussions, the struggle between the two lines and the Movement for Socialist Education eventually helped us fight back at Liu Shao-ch'i. In July 1964 the guidelines were decided for the industrial construction in northwestern China. We were then given permission to resume work here. We were at that time 20,000 workers. We had changed the plans. We went down another twenty meters in the rock.

"The whole plant has been designed and completed in China. The large 300,000-kilowatt generator was made in Harbin. We completed the dam and the power station in ten years, and it started to work at full capacity in 1974.

"Our task is not only to produce energy but also to contribute to the control of the Yellow River. We are one of the plants forming part of this huge project. The dam has been built to resist and control even enormous floods; we can control it so that not even catastrophic situations will lead to devastating floods in Lanchow. In normal cases, and even with abnormal floods, we can stop completely the floods that used to be common in Lanchow.

"Our problem—and the over-all problem with the Yellow River— is the silting. Here in the upper course of the river, the difficulties are not quite so bad as farther down. Still, they are bad enough. There are various solutions. To protect the dam itself we use the short-term solution of rinsing and flushing away sediments. We do this when the floods come. But about 4,000 cubic meters remain every year in the dam, and we must get rid of that. We must stop the erosion in the upper course of the river long-term. That would be the only permanent solution. It would mean planting trees, building dams to prevent erosion, terracing. This all forms part of the large Yellow River plan. It is to be done both above and below us. Every production brigade in the drainage area of the river has its place in that plan. We are going to transform China on a permanent basis."

Almost a week later we continue above Liuchia in a river boat. Higher up, the Yellow River was closed to boat traffic. It would open only in October, after the floods. But we could get as far as where it joins the Tacha River. We would disembark there and take the road to Linsia.

We were standing by the railing, looking out over the water toward the red mountains to the southwest. Over by the Tsinghai border was Pinglingssu. Before the arrival of the floods it is difficult to get there. The road from Linsia is rough. It had been especially hard to take the road down through the ravines. But the result had been well worth the effort. Pinglingssu has perhaps the best-preserved sculptures from the Northern Wei dynasty of the sixth century A.D.

The caves were so remote that no archaeologist had been able to go there before the liberation. Therefore they were never plundered. As far as I know, no other foreigner had been to Pinglingssu.

"I'm glad I've been allowed to see Pinglingssu. I just hope the pictures will turn out well."

It was a still afternoon. The water was like a mirror and we were sitting on deck wrapped in blankets, drinking tea and reading our mail. We had received a whole sack of mail from Lanchow. The atmosphere was strangely Norwegian. It was like having taken the boat from Revsnes on the Sogne Fjord and then gone down the Aurland Fjord and the Näröy Fjord to Gudvangen. The precipices were reflected in the water, and the sky high above us was incredibly blue. We went through letters and book packages and newspapers, sorted them, and read them.

Wherever we had been these months people had been involved in extensive political discussions. Here and there, as in Khotan, these discussions had filled all walls with posters. In other places, the discussion had seemed to us to be a silent neglect of the themes prescribed by the Peking newspapers. These discussions in China were not formal or theoretical; they concerned fundamental issues.

But in the letters and newspapers we received in our mail from Europe, China was something else. While we traveled up the river, and the rocks rose steeply from the still water, we discussed this.

"It's strange," Gun said, "they seem to be describing a world totally different from the one in which we travel. The world where we travel is so much more usual. Chinese politics are not strange. But they move in another China, and seem to be listening to another discussion."

We talked about *why*. Because it is quite obviously so. It is enough to read what we have published over the years to see that we talk about the same countries as they, the same places, perhaps even the same people—but not the same world. That goes for China and for India or Pakistan or Afghanistan or any other country we have traveled in much and often. Sweden, for example. Or France. But now, sitting on the deck of a river boat on the upper reaches of the Yellow River, it was China we were talking about.

We traveled in China during a summer and an autumn when the most intense discussions ever were being held in the country. They were more tense than in 1962 and in 1969. These discussions appeared to us to be real ones about important issues, involving deeply all those who took part. But when we read about them in the Swedish press, they sounded like top-level intrigues in Peking. As if millions upon millions of Chinese rattled off their lines in different political roles.

But here in Liuchia, Wang Tu-kiang had told us how bitterly disappointed many people were in August 1962, when their project was stopped. He had described their protests and their struggle to make as many workers as possible continue, and how this debate went deeper during the Movement for Socialist Education in 1964, and how they eventually obtained a decision in July 1964 so that they could resume the work.

"They tell us similar stories everywhere," Gun said. "It was the same thing at Niya and at the iron plant. They describe real struggles and real issues."

There are student circles and journalistic circles in China where the problems are presented as abstractedly as in London or Paris. This is a serious problem for China. People moving in those circles or reading those articles must see China as a strange country. To them it therefore seems reasonable to see China as a mess of topside palace intrigues where private interests are disguised as ideologies. In the same way it seemed reasonable to people moving in certain French journalistic circles in the thirties to see France as controlled by Freemasons' intrigues. However, these images of China in the sixties and seventies and of France in the twenties or thirties are absurd, even though there *are* intrigues in China and there *were* Freemason politics in France between the wars.

We have tried to avoid these problems by staying away from such circles, in China as well as in those other countries we visit, live in, or describe, including Sweden.

In the case of China we have another advantage, apart from that of staying away from students and journalists. We have traveled and been together with people we know. In 1962 as well as now, we have been traveling with friends and colleagues from way back. People we have known and with whom we have talked and worked and had discussions in different times and different countries.

If you have known each other and have talked about big things and small, world politics and everyday questions and private matters for ten, twenty, twenty-five years, and have had time to have different opinions on some questions as well as to change opinions about different questions and quarrel about others—then it is easier to understand. The struggle between two lines was no secret.

Not that they reveal state or party secrets. But if you know each other for a long time, and your friends begin to sit up at long meetings every night, you can't avoid knowing what it is all about and what is being discussed and how the party people are reacting.

Twilight is falling over the river and Gun says:

"Well, it is then really the politics of Premier Chou and the decisions of the Fourth National People's Congress that are at stake. Here in Kansu there's no doubt where the local cadres in general stand. We haven't seen anything indicating organized rebel activities, apart from, possibly, that notice board in Changyeh."

Gun packed up the mail. The books we had ordered in Urumchi were coming already.

"The world works," she said. "The mail reaches you."

She had been reading Sir Aurel Stein's *Ruins of Desert Cathay.* She now packed the heavy volumes in the book bag. It was large and brown and strapped with black leather bands to stay shut.

"But it's an old-fashioned way to travel," she said. "I think we must be among the last people to travel with a proper library. And our journeys do take time. We have spent more months traveling abroad than at home since 1956; I checked."

The boat had docked. It was low tide and the landing stage had high banks. I balanced along the swinging plank, my brown book bag in one hand and the typewriter in the other and Gun's camera cases slung over my shoulder.

"Look, what a beautiful sunset," Gun said.

The clouds were now burning high up in the western sky, the shadows around us were heavy, and in front, in the dusk, were the jeeps, waiting for us, their headlights on. We loaded our luggage and drove to Linsia.

36
Where the Roads Separate

Linsia is an autonomous district. The town was once the seat for the Ma brothers, warlords and feudal rulers who kept this as their land. Since 1956, it is the Linsia Hui Autonomous District, a rich agricultural district. They give us millet cakes and discuss agricultural and economic planning. Of the 1,254,000 inhabitants in the district 1,140,000 are active in agriculture. But we had really gone there for the industry.

Here by the border of Tsinghai, in what used to be the most remote part of China, is now one of China's most modern industries: the phototechnical industry of Kansu province.

The plant has many large modern buildings right next to the mountainside. In case of war the factory can go into bombproof mountain rooms and continue production. Part of the plant is already inside the mountain. That the phototechnical industry of Kansu province was founded and was located here has both economic and defense-political reasons. The production fulfills civil as well as military needs.

"We moved up here from the coast in 1966," says party vice-secretary Kao Yong-chin. "Chairman Mao Tse-tung had encouraged us in a planned geographical relocation of the optical industry to increase preparedness. Four factories and institutes were moved up here. We came from Harbin, Nanking, Sian, and Shanghai. In the winter of 1966–67 four hundred of us came up here. There were neither houses nor workshops here then; we had to build it all with our own hands. The winter was cold and hard. Since then we have constructed this industry bit by bit. We are now 3,700 employees. We contribute to the industrialization of hinterland China.

"Before liberation China did not manufacture its own photographic lenses and other photographic equipment. The Shanghai shops were then a world exhibition of expensive import goods. After liberation we

274

began to build up our own industry for photographic equipment. We have had some success. This is one of our new industries; there are others in the same field, elsewhere in the country.

"The part of the production we now show you is partly film projectors for 35mm, 16mm, and 8.5mm; partly cine-cameras for newscasting by television. Light hand cameras. We also manufacture tape-recording equipment and various types of tapes and such for computers. Finally, we manufacture optics for photographic and other important uses. That is an area where we have been able to develop a new technique and achieve a technical breakthrough on our own.

"The first big political problem was the energy supply. We had by no means enough for our needs. It was a political problem, because we could have requested that the state bring a high-voltage line from the Liuchia power station to us, but we discussed the matter in a principled way and decided to carry out the work with our own resources. We had two technicians with good experience, who led the work. The line was brought here in 1966 in a hundred days. We crossed forty mountains and five reservoirs and had to cross the Yellow River twice. But we did it.

"There are many technical problems connected with our production. Utmost precision is required. We have to substitute our own homemade equipment for expensive imported equipment. But finding a substitute for the foreign equipment is not enough—we must surpass the precision and the performance of foreign equipment. We must reach and surpass the most advanced world level. It can be done, provided we rely on the working class and carry out the task properly. Scientists, cadres, and experienced workers in the three-in-one combination can overcome even the worst problems.

"One issue seriously discussed is whom our production serves. It is fine that we manufacture 35mm projectors; we make good projectors, appreciated by the masses. They are durable and easy to handle. But the workers asked, Whom do we serve? The big cities only? We have to take a stand in the class struggle. We must serve the poor peasants, the film must serve the people. But our projectors are too heavy and require too much tending to be used all over the countryside.

"The problem was solved in 1973 when we designed a projector that can be used by the production brigades. It is portable and weighs only twenty kilograms. We now have an annual production of 30,000 such machines.

"We are now discussing the Super 8. The 8.5mm is excellent, it gives high quality. We now must conquer this format and achieve the highest quality possible. It's a format the masses themselves can use. The question of the direction production is to take is political. So we frame the question, and thus we have now begun to tackle the Super 8.

"In 1975 we produced goods worth 26 million yuan. In 1976, 30 million yuan. And in 1980 we shall, according to plan, produce goods worth 90 million yuan.

"The copper industry in Payin or the petrochemical industry in Lanchow are well-known, but the optical industry in Linsia is one of the typical new projects in China that rarely get into the news."

"China is a poor country in the Third World," said Gun when we drove down to Lanchow. "Whoever comes here to find a country that has overcome its environmental problems, where the women are all equal, where the social conflicts are solved by relaxed friendly discussions, and where no one tries to take advantage of someone else—that person will be bitterly disappointed and can go back to Europe and write about his disappointment. China can't fulfill such hopes.

"But whoever travels in China, eyes open, seeing the change, will understand what the Chinese mean when they say that they will modernize China and make it a flourishing, highly developed socialist country with science and technology at the highest world level by the turn of the century. And don't forget that they say a socialist country, not just a highly developed one."

In Lanchow we met the Yellow River again. Here it runs through the city 250 meters wide. The town is old, and has long been a focal point for trade. Since the first five-year plan in the early fifties, it has developed not only as an administrative center and a focal point for trade but also as an industrial and scientific base in northwestern China.

Most of the old maze of tumbledown houses has been demolished to give air and light. Broad, luxurious esplanades have been driven through the old slums. But a heavy yellow blanket of industrial exhaust covers this new town. There is smog over Lanchow, and we start to cough.

But industrial pollution still smells of progress in Lanchow, and even if people say something has to be done about it, the cough tickles them like development and future in the bronchial tubes.

The old route, the Silk Road, the imperial road, passes here through Lanchow. We had come all the way here down from the Soviet border in the extreme west. It was early in the morning, the air was misty and thick. The street had not yet filled with workers going to the factories. But they would be coming soon.

Here in Lanchow most families now have the four big items: a bicycle, a sewing machine, a watch, and a transistor radio. They already have bad traffic problems when the streets fill with bicycles in the rush hour. The traffic propaganda is intense: Pedal in single file! Keep both hands on the handlebars! Only one person per bicycle! Give signals!

The production brigades enter the town with their tractors and block the streets. The revolutionary committee has forbidden tractors and heavy trucks in the town center. They have to stay on the outskirts, where they have their halting places and their motels.

"It is impossible to have the traffic bound for the corridor and Sinkiang right through the city," said Ho Ying, chairman of the revolutionary committee of Lanchow. "We must build the main road past the city, construct a new road with new bridges over the Yellow River, and exclude the through traffic.

"It is difficult for other reasons, too. The young drivers who got their licenses in their military service drive carelessly and dangerously.

"We must raise the standard for licenses," said Ho Ying. "There are those, too, who drive without a license."

But on this early morning, the imperial road through Lanchow is still empty and still. Then two men come with night-soil barrows. They have been to collect night-soil in the town and are going back to their production brigade in the suburb! They pull their barrows, and we look at them. The smoke of progress might make us cough, but these two men in the early morning prove that Lanchow is sure to overcome its smog and its traffic problems and its growing pains.

The sewage is not flushed into the Yellow River. Chinese agriculture is based on the use of all human waste. It is carefully kept, treasured, and composted to fertilize the fields. Sewage is not despised "filth" in China but riches to be used. Mao Tse-tung stressed that the idea that excrement was dirty and that people working with shit had shitty jobs was a miserable upper-class notion. Whoever can't see that shit is valuable and serves agriculture and thus serves the people in their work can never be a Communist but will always remain a rebellious upper-class intellectual.

We looked at the men pulling their night-soil barrows down the imperial road, and Gun said:

"Who cares about the smog? There goes China's future!"

Glossary

1 yuàn	About 50 cents
1 li	500 meters
1 chi	33.33 centimeters (the metric system is being introduced)
1 jin	500 grams
1 liang	31.25 grams
1 mu	.0666 hectar
cadre	Originally, a "professional revolutionary" (hence the expression "to join the revolution" for taking employment in the civil service). Now, a functionary or an official in government, industry, party administration, or mass organizations.
KMT	The Kuomintang was founded in 1912 by Sun Yat-sen as a bourgeois, democratic national party. Later it joined the Komintern. The Communist Party of China formed part of the Kuomintang. Sun Yat-sen died in March 1925. Eventually, when the Kuomintang seemed to triumph all over the country, Chiang Kai-shek carried out his long-planned blow against the Communists and left-wing radicals in the great "April Massacres" in 1927. The final outcome of this action was Chiang Kai-shek's escape to Taiwan in 1949 together with what remained of the Kuomintang.

Index

Abbas I (shah of Persia), 67
Abd-er-Rahman, 89
Abdur Rahman, 114–15, 119–20, 168–71
Abdurchut Kur, 77–79
Afghans and Afghanistan, xi, 7, 8–9, 10, 23, 26, 34, 42, 86, 99, 101, 103, 104, 105, 140, 173, 174, 198, 271; origin of state, 88–9; Russian border, 29–30. *See also* Pamir
Afro-Asian states, 43
agriculture, 23, 25–26, 110, 132, 133–4, 205; bad years, 249; and border security, 223; Chinese Empire, 46, 148–9, 158–9, 174–5, 222–3; Cultural Revolution in, 173, 238, 239–40; desert, 157–65, 168–77, 237–42; irrigation projects, 145, 151, 152, 155–6, 160–5, 167, 168–71, 174–6; land-reform movement, 74–82; Mao's policies, 74–82, 169, 228, 238–42; modernization of, 144–5, 169–71, 228, 238–42; politics of, 238–42; pre-1949, 158–9; Production and Construction Corps, 223–6; for silk production, 113, 116, 120; traditional, 172–7
Ahlbert, Gustaf, 67
Ahmad Khan, 88–89
Ahmed Shah, 89–90, 93
Aigun, Treaty of, 94
airports, 42
Akbar, 67, 69
Aksu, 97, 224
Ala Shan Desert, 234
Albania, 188
Alexander the Great, 11
Alexander II (czar), 99
Algeria, 97
Alley, Rewi, xv
Altai, 41, 213–15, 218, 223

American Eugenics Society, 154
Amu Darya, 99
Amur River, 193–4, 196
Andersson, Johan Gunnar, 265, 266
Andijanis, 102
Angola, 196
animal husbandry, 6, 23, 25, 26, 131
Anshan, 258; steel works, 228–9
Ansi, 242, 243, 248
antiquities: Amin Hodja's mosque, 180–2; Asoka stupa, 261; Astana burial grounds, 154, 182; Caves of the Thousand Buddhas, 235–7; Cultural Revolution and, 236–7, 271–2; Hazrat-i-Afak mausoleum, 50; Hodja mausoleum, 66–68, 72–73, 86; jade, 138; karezes, 174–6; modernization and, 144, 149–51; preservation of, 150, 151, 178–82, 270; reclining Buddha, 259–60, 261; Silk Road, 111, 115, 116, 118, 119, 182; Tashkurghan, 11, 22–23; Western researchers, 84–85, 180–2. *See also* Great Walls
Apak Hodja, *see* Hodja, Hidajetulla
Arabia, 127
archaeology and archaeological finds, *see* antiquities
architecture, 179; Moslem, 67; traditional, 182–3
Arctic Ocean, 41
Aristotle, 126
Armenia, 30, 53
arts and artists, 18, 60, 84–85, 132, 236; architecture, 67, 179, 182–3; Khotan rugs, 139–41; music and dance, 159–60. *See also* antiquities
Ashkhabad, 198
Asia: American presence in, xi–xii; Brit-

ish imperialism in, 29–30, 34–35, 98–99, 101–9, 198–200; changing attitudes to, 59; China's position in, 196; Christianity and, 49–57; Russian expansion in, 97–100, 101–7; Western view of, 84–86. *See also* China; Japan; Pamir

Association of American Geographers, 154

Astana, 154, 182

Astrakhan, 193

Atik Kurban, 131–2, 167–8

Aurelian (emperor of Rome), 127

Azad Tiliwaldi, 79

Aztecs, 138

Babur, Zahir ud-Din Mohammed, 68, 83

Badakhshan, 7, 22, 72, 89, 101, 111

Baghrash Kul, 110

Balkhash, Lake, 95

Baltic states, 187

barefoot doctors, *see* health and health care

Beg Kuli Beg, 86, 87

Bengal, 112

Bhutan, 43

Bismarck, Otto Eduard Leopold von, 104

Bosphorus, 30

Brahmaputra River, 26

Braun, Otto (Li Teh), 185

British Empire, *see* Great Britain

Buchanan, Andrew, 99

Buddhism and Buddhists, 52, 53, 54, 69, 116, 117, 118

Bukhara, 95, 99, 100, 173, 198

Bulun Kul People's Commune, 25

Burma, 43

Canton, 139, 196

capital punishment, 188

Caspian Sea, xi, 198, 252

Castiglione, Giuseppe (Lang Shih-ning), 73

Catherine the Great (czarina), 39

Catholic Church, 55–57; Jesuits, 55–56, 69–70, 72. *See also* Christianity

cattle breeding, *see* animal husbandry

Central Asia, *see* Asia; Pamir; Sinkiang Uighur Autonomous Region

Chan Chi-min, 246

Chang Ch'ien, 45, 46, 115

Chang Chih-chung, 215

Ch'ang Ch'un, 192

Chang Hsueh-liang, 186

Chang Shih-ling, 31

Chang Te, 175

Changan, 115, 116, 117, 118

Changyeh, 233, 259–61, 264

Chao Hui, 71, 72

Charles XII (king of Sweden), 190

Chavannes, Édouard, 111

Chen Jung-ju, 137

Chen Li-nin, 246

Chen Tai-chu, 212, 213

Chia Chang-yun, 256, 257

Chia Ch'ing (emperor of China), 91, 193

Chiang Ching, 6

Chiang Kai-shek, 27, 63–74, 212–13, 266; "Sian intermezzo," 186. *See also* Kuomintang

Ch'ien Lung (emperor of China), 71–73, 91, 179, 259

children, 26, 62, 137, 212; mortality rates, 26, 134. *See also* education

Chilien Mountains, 234, 248, 257, 263

Chimkent, 97

Ch'in Shih Huang Ti (emperor of China), 45, 46, 251

Chin Shu-jen, 207

China: and Japan, 186, 199–201, 207, 209, 210–12, 245, 261; Kuomintang era, 15, 16–17, 23, 24–25, 64, 120, 186, 199, 207, 208, 209, 211, 212–13, 214, 215, 216, 218, 222, 223–4, 245, 247, 266; new, xi, xii–xiii; poverty, 239; religions of, 52–56; Western attitudes on, 59, 84–86, 266–7. *See also* Chinese Empire; Chinese People's Republic; Chinese–Russian relationships

China's Changing Map (Shabad), 253

Chinese character, 89–90

Chinese Communist Party, 24, 185–6, 188; in Sinkiang, 207, 209, 210–12. *See also* Chinese People's Republic; Chou En-lai; Mao Tse-Tung; People's Liberation Army

Chinese culture, 63, 84–85, 124–5. *See also* antiquities; arts and artists; Chinese Empire

Chinese Empire, 12, 27, 45–47, 68–73; agriculture, 46, 148–9, 158–9, 174–5, 222–3; Ch'ing dynasty, 22, 55, 63, 71–73, 90–96, 120, 179, 199, 259, 260; Christianity and, 49–57; coinage, 91; decay of, 90–97, 99–102, 151–2; Five Kingdoms, 119; Franco–British war, 94, 194; Han dynasty, 11, 45–47, 63, 115, 116, 119, 128, 144, 153, 174, 175, 176, 223, 233, 236, 242, 251–2; Manchu dynasty, 11, 70, 71, 90, 196; military colonies, 222–3; Ming dynasty, 63, 68,

70, 91, 96, 193, 233, 252, 259, 260; Northern Chou dynasty, 15; Oirat wars, 70–72; Opium Wars, 56, 91–92; peasant wars, 264; religion and, 52–56, 67, 69–72; Russia and, 29–30, 37–40, 94–107, 193–9; Sung dynasty, 63, 196, 259, 261; Taiping Revolution, 56, 91–92, 95–96, 264, 267; T'ang dynasty, 52, 63, 84, 116, 119, 151, 182; trade and trade routes, 42, 46–47, 56, 69–70, 91–92, 93, 110, 129, 139, 248; unification of, 45–47; Wei dynasty, 63, 115, 116, 119, 270; Yuan dynasty, 63, 68, 193. See also China; Chinese People's Republic; Chinese–Russian relationships

Chinese People's Association for Friendship with Foreign Countries, xv

Chinese People's Political Consultative Conference, 215

Chinese People's Republic: alleged Siberian demands, 27, 43–44, 107; arts and culture, 18, 60, 84–85, 132, 139–41, 159–60, 236; cities vs. hinterland, xiii; economic development, 205; education, 13, 18–19, 23–24, 26, 61–62, 64–65, 75, 77, 79, 132, 134, 137, 159, 168, 184–5, 210, 211, 246; family planning, 17, 134; foreigners and, 84–85, 254–5, 262; Gang of Four, xii–xiii, xiv, 3–4, 240; health care, 12–13, 14, 16, 26, 57–59, 75, 132, 134, 147–50; housing, 146, 148, 182–3; intellectuals, xiii, 114–21; international trade, 121, 139–41, 142; marriage in, 109–10, 168; National People's Congresses, 77, 239–40, 272; nationality policies, 17, 61, 65; natural disasters, 144–5, 146, 155–6, 167, 249, 269; in 1976, xi–xii, 3–4; nuclear experiments, 42; political issues, 135–7, 160, 167–71, 238–42, 243–4, 246–7, 271–2, 275; proclaimed, 215; railroads and roads, 42, 110–11, 122–3, 133, 146, 158, 160, 161, 166, 192, 198, 221–2, 233, 250–1, 257; Vietnam border war, xi; women in, 17–20, 61–62, 77, 109–10, 137, 147, 150, 159–60, 163–4, 167–8, 224–6, 243–4, 246. See also agriculture; China; Chinese–Russian relationships; industry and industrialization; Kansu; Mao Tsetung; Sinkiang

Chinese Revolution, 16–17, 23–25, 185–6, 210, 217. See also Kuomintang; People's Liberation Army

Chinese–Russian relationships, 18, 20–21, 29, 93; borders and border disputes, 24, 25, 27, 28–36, 43–44, 94–96, 199, 202, 214; in China–Vietnam border war, xi; industrial, 268–9; Protocol of Novy Margelan, 28–29, 44; Sin-tin agreement, 207–8, 209; trade, 94, 98, 99, 139, 140, 141, 197, 207–8; treaties, 194–5, 197. See also Chinese Empire; Russian imperialism; Soviet Union; Stalin, Joseph Vissarionovich

Chinese Turkestan, see Sinkiang

Ch'ing dynasty, 22, 55, 56, 63, 71–73, 90–96, 120, 179, 259, 260; fall of, 199; national revolts against, 91–92, 95–96. See also Chinese Empire

Chira, 168–71

Chou dynasty, 15

Chou En-lai, 25, 43, 77, 185, 186, 187, 205, 213, 216, 224, 239–40

Chou Wen-chi, 247

Christianity, 49–59, 69, 91, 96; missionaries, 49–51, 55–57, 67, 129; politics of, 53–57; view of silk, 126–7. See also Catholic Church; religion

Chu Teh, 261, 267

Chu Yu-chen, 247

Chuanlang Ho, 268

Chuguchak, 99, 100

Chungking, 4, 125, 214

Clapp, Fredrick G., 251

class struggle, 169–71

climatological historical theory, 153–6

colonialism, 59, 97–98, 106, 111. See also Great Britain; imperialism

Communist China, see Chinese People's Republic

Confucius and Confucianism, 38, 54, 55, 56–57, 125, 159

copper industry, 276

Crescent Lake, 235–6

Crimea, 190, 196

Crimean War, 94

Cultural Revolution, 16, 19, 130, 133, 162, 163, 246; in agriculture, 173, 238, 239–40; archaeology and antiquities, 236–7, 261–2; education and, 19, 64–65, 75, 79, 132; health care and, 26; industry and, 139, 253, 254; Red Guard, 163, 261–2; violence of, 205

Czechoslovakia, 187

Dandan-Oilik, 118

Danube River, 128

Darius I (king of Persia), 174

de Gaulle, Charles, 186

desert: agriculture, 157–65, 168–77; cli-

mate, 172, 178, 242; reclaiming, 160–5, 168–71, 224–6, 237–8; roads, 158, 160, 161, 166; water supply, 166–7. *See also* Chira; Keriya; Niya; Tunhwang; Turfan
desiccation theory, 153–5, 167
Diderot, Denis, 59
drug use, *see* opium trade
du Jarric, Peter, 69
Dzhambul, 97
Dzungaria, 3, 41, 42, 71–72, 158, 192–201, 248; modernization, 222–6. *See also* Sinkiang

earthquakes, 4, 233, 249
East Turkestan Republic, xi, 206, 213–17. *See also* Sinkiang
education, 23–24, 26, 62, 64–65, 75, 77, 79, 210, 211; Cultural Revolution and, 19, 64–65, 75, 79, 132; "Seventh of May universities," 134; Stalinist era, 184–5; of women, 19–20, 61–62, 168; workers', 137, 246
Egypt, 111, 157, 173
Eisenstein, Sergei M., 204–5
Emperor's Route, *see* Silk Road
Engels, Friedrich, 13, 24, 106, 107, 185; on Russian diplomacy, 38–39, 190, 195, 198
Europe, 59, 92, 153, 196, 200, 210, 252; communists, 186, 190, 203, 210, 266–7; compared to China, 62, 63; history of silk in, 112, 116, 119, 126–7; Napoleonic wars, 105; peasant wars, 95–96; trade with China, 128–9, 140, 141. *See also* imperialism; West and Westerners; World War I; World War II; *and* names of countries

Fa-Hsien, 9, 117
family planning, 17, 134
Fan Li-chen, 84
Fan Shi-hung, 11, 12–14, 15, 16, 22
fascism, 206
Fergana, 45
feudalism, 67, 69, 90, 158–9. *See also* Chinese Empire
floods and flood control, 144–5, 146, 155–6, 167, 249, 270
France, 97, 125, 140, 271, 272; Popular Front, 210; war in China, 94, 194; in World War II, 186, 187
Franco–Prussian War, 104
Fu Wai-chen, 245
Fucik, Julius, 202

Gabain, Annemarie von, 155
"Gang of Four," xii–xiii, xiv, 3–4, 240
Gates to Asia (Myrdal), 7–8
Gazi brigade, 35–36
Genghis Khan, 70, 192, 200
geography and geographers, 27, 111, 251
Germany, 85, 96, 103, 140, 173, 174, 190, 210, 248; anti-Komintern pact with Japan, 186; DDR, 190; pact with Russia, 187. *See also* Hitler; World War I; World War II
Ghez Darya, 27
Giers, Nikolai von, 198
Gladstone, William Ewart, 39, 198
Gobi Desert, 85, 172, 233, 234, 238
Goes, Benedict, 69–70, 252
Gorchakov, Prince, 97–99, 198
Grand dictionnaire universel du XIX siècle (Larousse), 59
Great Britain, xi, 27, 44, 49, 51, 56, 97, 104, 139, 207; in Asia, 29–30, 34, 98–99, 101–7, 198–200; colonies, 151, 152, 189, 193; in India, 252; Kabul war of independence, 89; opium trade, 56, 91–92, 129; and Russia, 29–30, 34, 98–99, 101, 190, 198, 199–200; Sinkiang policies, 87, 90, 100, 101, 102; in World War II, 187
Great Walls, 233, 248, 251–3, 260–1
Greece, 119
Grieg, Nordahl, 202, 203
Gros, Baron, 94
Gustavus I (king of Sweden), 260

Hammer–Purgstall, Baron von, 174
Han dynasty, 11, 45–47, 63, 116, 128, 144, 153, 174, 175, 176, 223, 236, 242, 251–2; Eastern, 115, 119; Great Wall, 233; Western, 115, 116
Han language, 13, 64, 71, 175
Han people, 17, 42, 61, 62–64, 75, 93, 96, 124, 159, 172, 196, 234, 264
Han Shu, 236, 237, 238, 240
Hazrat-i-Afak mausoleum, 50
health and health care, 12–13, 14, 16, 75, 132, 134, 147–50; barefoot doctors, 26, 58, 147, 149; patriotic movement, 147–9; traditional vs. modern, 12–13, 57–59
Hedin, Sven, 26, 34, 38, 40, 83–86, 154, 180, 181, 197–8, 253
Herat, 67, 68, 198, 252
Hitler, Adolf, 190, 202, 210, 212, 213. *See also* Germany; World War II
Ho Ying, 277

Hodja, Amin: mosque, 178–80
Hodja, Hidajetulla (Apak), 66, 67, 70, 88, 89
Hodja, Makhdumi Azam, 69
Hodja, Mamrisim (Fragrant Concubine), 72–73
Hodja, Suleiman, 179
Hodja, Tursun, 77
Hodja family, 66–68, 69–70, 72–73, 80, 100; mausoleum, 66–68, 72–73, 86
Högberg, Lars Erik, 51
Hogg, George, 261–2
Hohsi, 248
Holdich, Thomas Hungerford, 27, 34–35
Holland, 97
Hong Kong, xiii, 225, 254, 255
Hopeh, 251
hospitals, see health and health care
housing, 146, 148; traditional construction, 182–3
Hsüan Tsang, 6, 9, 116–18, 158
Hua Kuo-feng, 78, 239–40
Huhehot, 250
Hui people, 41, 61, 63, 64, 91, 95, 96, 97, 100, 172, 234
Huns, 45, 46, 47
Huntington, Ellsworth, 154–5, 174
Hwang Ho, see Yellow River

I See a New China (Hogg), 261
Ibn Ustad, Muhammad Riza, 67
Ignatiev, Count, 94
Ili, xi, 3, 23, 45, 71, 92, 95, 97, 99, 100, 105, 130, 213–15, 218, 223; Russian occupation of, 193, 197–8, 200
imperialism, 111, 118, 245, 254, 262; historical justifications, 154–5; religion and, 52, 55–56. See also Great Britain; Japan; Russian imperialism
India, 23, 27, 59, 63, 89, 97, 102, 152, 153, 211, 261, 265; border disputes, 42, 43; British in, 252; Mughals, 67, 68, 69; trade routes to, 42, 47, 69, 115, 127
Indian Ocean, 248
Indians, American, 194
Indus River, 23, 26, 116
industry and industrialization, 42, 48, 77, 110, 131, 205, 227–32, 234, 268; in Chinese Empire, 91; clothing, 229–32; copper, 276; Cultural Revolution and, 139, 253, 254; diesel-engine factory, 228–9; following Taching, 244–5; jade, 138–9; letting politics lead, 227, 229, 246–7, 275; Mao's view, 227, 228–30, 257, 274; oil, 41, 42, 221, 244–7; photomechani-

cal, 274–6; pre-liberation, 245, 247, 274; rug manufacture, 139–41; silk, 119–21; Soviet vs. Chinese policies, 244–5, 247; steel, 228–9, 253–4, 256–8. See also modernization; science and technology; workers
Ining, 41, 71, 184–5, 189, 192, 222
Institute of Uighur Medicine (Khotan), 50, 57–59
Iran, xi; karezes, 173, 174–6; trade routes to, 47, 115. See also Persia
irrigation and irrigation projects, 145, 151, 152, 155–6, 167, 256; Chira, 168–71; Kansu, 238; Niya, 160–5; traditional, 172–7, 268; workers, 163–5. See also agriculture; water supply
Irtysh River, 41, 194, 195
Isfahan, 67
Islam, 22–23, 50, 51, 52, 53, 54, 55, 63, 67, 69, 70, 178; architecture, 67; "Moslem war," 234
Ismailites, 174–5
Ivan the Terrible (czar), 193, 204, 205

Jacobites, 53–55
jade, 137–9
Jade Gateway, 233
Jagatais, 68, 69, 83
Jahangir, 67
Japan, 33, 56–57, 101, 107, 203, 230; anti-Komintern pact with Germany, 186; pact with Russia on China, 199–201; war with Chinese, 186, 207, 209, 210–12, 245, 261; war with Russia, 33, 199; in World War II, 33, 56, 200–1
Japan, Sea of, 194
Japanese Kuriles, 187
Jardine, Matheson & Company, 264
Jarring, Gunnar, xv
Jeme Tien-yao, 250–1
Jen Yuang-chang, 221
Jesuits, 55–56, 69–70, 72
Jin Ching, 114, 115–19
Jo Li-chun, 114, 115, 120–1
Journey to the Source of the River Oxus, A (Wood), 89, 90
Justin I (emperor of Rome), 54
Justinian (emperor of Rome), 126

Kabul, xi, 50, 69, 88–89, 95, 103, 104, 105; war of independence, 89
Kafiristan, 22
Kalmucks, 71
Kan Shi-en, 246
Kanchow, see Changyeh

K'ang Hsi (emperor of China), 70–71
Kansu, 42, 69, 84, 92, 96, 100, 175, 211, 215, 216, 233–73; agriculture, 237–42, 246, 256; archaeology and antiquities, 235, 236–7, 251–3, 259–62, 270; autonomous districts, 234; Cultural Revolution, 236–7, 240; earthquakes, 249; education, 246–7; energy projects, 268–70; Great Walls, 233, 248, 251–3, 260–1, 263; imperial, 259–60, 264; liberation of, 266–7; name, 233; natural assets, 234; oil fields, 244–7; opium growing, 266–7; peasants' war, 264; people, 234; photomechanical industry, 274–6; politics, 271–2; pre-liberation, 264–6; roads and railroads, 233, 250–1, 257; Sand Mountain Production Brigade, 237–8; Santakuo People's Commune, 243–4; steel industry, 253–4, 256–8; trade routes, 234; water supply, 237, 240–1; weather and climate, 248–9. See also Kansu Corridor
Kansu Corridor, xii, 3, 52, 234, 242, 243–9, 250–1, 263. See also Kansu
Kao Yong-chin, 274–6
Karakhan, Leo, 31
Karakoram Mountains, 43
Karamai, 41, 221
Karashahr, 83
karezes, 172–7. See also irrigation and irrigation projects
Kasem Suchi, 163, 165
Kashgar, 9, 12, 22, 24, 27, 35, 41, 42, 48–52, 57–68, 86, 97, 140, 142; agriculture, 60, 74–82, 110, 155; Apak Hodja mausoleum, 66–68, 72–73; Christianity in, 49–52, 53, 54, 57, 67, 69–70; foreign struggles for, 103–7; imperial, 47, 66–73, 90, 93, 94, 102–3, 110, 111, 151, 197; modernization, 48, 60–62, 64–65, 108–11; Russians in, 37–40, 49, 87–88, 94–95, 103–7, 198, 207; Silk Road, 116. See also Sinkiang; Tashkurghan; Uighurs
Kashgaria, see Kashgar
Kashmir, 42
Kazakh Autonomous District, 41, 222
Kazakhs, 61, 64, 109, 222, 230, 234
Kazan, 193
Keriya, 110, 122, 123, 144–56; agriculture, 144–5, 146, 151; bazaar, 145, 146–7; health care, 147–9; housing, 146, 148; modernizing, 146–51; water supply, 155
Kessle, Gun, xi, 3, 4, 6, 37, 38, 40, 48, 49, 50, 52, 57, 59, 60–61, 83–87, 88, 104, 106, 107, 122, 123–5, 126, 129, 146, 147, 149–50, 151, 153, 155, 167, 175–6, 178–9, 202, 205, 206, 210, 254, 259, 272, 276
Khiva, 67, 68, 178, 198
Khojend, 99
Khokand, 93–94, 95, 97, 99, 100, 101, 102, 198
Khotan, 3, 4, 42, 43, 50, 97, 109, 110, 111, 114–26, 129–43, 149, 150, 153, 160, 167, 181, 271; agriculture, 133–4; Cultural Revolution, 132, 133; education, 134; history, 114–21, 124, 127; jade industry, 137–9; modernization, 119–26, 130–7, 138–43; politics, 129, 130, 132–3, 171; problems, 132–4; rugs, 137, 139–42; silk production, 114–21, 124, 127, 135–7, 142–3; transport, 133; water supply, 155, 156. See also Sinkiang
Khrushchev, Nikita, 185, 189
Kiayükwan, 233, 251–4, 256–8
Kirghiz people, 24–27, 34–36, 41, 69
Kirghizistan, 45
Kiuchüan, 69, 233, 252. See also Changyeh
Kizil Jik, 28–29, 30, 44
Kizil Su Kirghiz Autonomous District, 24–27
Kokrash Kol, 30
Komintern, 185–6, 206. See also Soviet Union
Korea, 216
Korla, 83, 85, 110
Krasnoyarsk, 193
Kuldja, 41, 197. See also Ining
Kunduz, 23
Kunlun Mountains, 41, 138, 155
Kuomintang, 186, 199, 266; Han chauvinism of, 17, 64; industry, 245, 247; in Production and Construction Corps, 222, 223–4; revolution against, 15, 16–17, 23, 24, 217–18; Russia and, 199, 207; silk production, 120; Sinkiang policies, 207, 209, 211, 212–13, 214, 215, 216, 218; in war against Japan, 207, 209, 211
Kwangsi, 91
Kweitun, 202, 222, 229–32

Laessøe, Jørgen, 174
Lahore, 103
Lanchow, xii, 234, 251, 270, 276
land-reform movement, 74–82; Taiping

Revolution, 91–92; women and, 168. *See also* agriculture

Larousse, Pierre, 59

Lattimore, Owen, 156

Laufer, Berthold, 111

Le Coq, Albert von, 180–2

Leihon, Per-Olow, xv

Lenin, Krupskaya, 30

Lenin, Vladimir Ilich (Ulianov), xi, 13, 24, 33, 36, 185, 206, 207, 208–9; "Declaration of Workers' Deputies," 30–31; "The Fall of Port Arthur," 33; on Russian power, 190–1; on Russo–Chinese borders, 30–31, 32, 201. *See also* Marxism–Leninism

Lennartsson, Anders, xv

Lhasa, 37 n, 50, 70, 71. *See also* Tibet and Tibetans

Li Chi-chang, 192

Li Kuang-li, 47

Li Sheng-tian, 119

Li Shu-shan, 160–1, 165, 171

Li Yu-chan, 258

Liaoning, 251

Lieberman, Henry R., 216

Lin Chi-lu, 212, 213

Lin Piao, xii, 196

Linsia Hui Autonomous District, 234, 270, 274–6

literacy, 18–19, 132, 159. *See also* education

Liu Hou-shan, 132–4

Liu Jen-ching, 205

Liu Kai-shan, 61

Liu Shao-ch'i, 19, 162, 217, 229, 239–40, 245, 257, 269

Liuchia, 268, 269, 271–3

Long March, 185, 211

Lop Nor, 42, 156

Ma Chi-min, 162, 163

Ma Chung-yin, 83, 84, 85, 86–87, 88, 89, 152, 207

Ma Hua-lung, 96

Ma Ming-hsin, 96

Mahmud Tailaki, 141

Mai Chi Shan, 4

Manchu dynasty, 11, 70, 71, 90, 196; Taiping Revolution, 56, 91–92, 95–96, 264, 267. *See also* Manchus

Manchuria, xi, 199, 200, 216

Manchus, 63, 91, 93, 96, 100; after fall of Empire, 264–5. *See also* Ch'ing dynasty; Manchu dynasty

Manicheism, 52, 54

Mao Tse-min, 212, 213

Mao Tse-tung, xi, 6, 13, 16, 24, 33, 84, 163, 176, 201, 205, 211, 215, 225, 266, 267; agricultural policies, 74–82, 169, 228, 238–42; on antiquities, 150, 151; death, 4; health-care policies, 58, 148–9; industrial policies, 227, 228–30, 257, 274; instructions on Sinkiang, 17, 227, 240; *On New Democracy,* 211; on preparedness, 219, 220, 249; *On Protracted War,* 211; proclaims republic, 215; Production and Construction Corps, 223, 224; on silk production, 120; on Stalin and Stalinism, 185, 186, 187, 204, 205, 209, 217

Mao Tse-tung Thought, 77, 183

Map of Mainland Asia by Treaty (Prescott), 30

Maram Khirip, 64–65

marriage, 109–10, 168

Marx, Karl, 13, 24, 92, 106, 107, 185, 196; on Russian growth, 189–90, 195

Marxism–Leninism, 24, 183, 211, 217; Soviet revisionism, 24, 25, 229–32, 240

Masjid-i-Shaykh Lutfullah, 67

Mattusun Chirip, 158–9, 160, 162, 164, 165

Mayas, 138

Mazar-i-Sharif, 22

medicine and medical care, *see* health and health care

Mediterranean countries, 23, 111; religion and politics in, 53–54; Silk Road, 116, 126, 127; trade routes to, 42, 47

Mehmed Abdullah, 74, 75, 79, 80

Meng T'ien, 251

Merv, 103, 198

Minfeng, *see* Niya

Ming dynasty, 63, 68, 91, 96, 193, 233, 252, 259, 260; fall of, 70, 91

Ming-hsu, 99

missionaries, 49–51, 55–57, 67, 129. *See also* Christianity

modernization: agricultural, 144–5, 169–71, 228, 238–42; great leap forward, 234; learning from Tachai, 145, 161–5, 169, 171, 238–42; Liu Shao-ch'i line, 239–40, 245, 257, 269, 271; and preservation of antiquities, 144, 149–51; Soviet, 205–6; trade, 145–6. *See also* industry and industrialization

Mohammed, Hadji, 260

Molotov, Vyacheslav M., 214

Mongol Empire, 68

Mongolia, 30, 175, 199, 200, 216

Mongolian People's Republic, 42, 195, 206, 214, 216, 217, 233
Mongols, 41, 55, 63, 96, 193, 234; Oirats, 70–72, 194–5
Monkey (The Pilgrimage to the West), 6
Moslems, *see* Islam
Movement for Socialist Education, 271
Mughals, 67, 68, 69
Muhammed Beg, 147–9
Münzer, Thomas, 96
Mur Imat, 58
Mussolini, Benito, 56
Myrdal, Jan, 83, 84–88, 103, 104, 176, 202–4, 240, 254, 258, 260, 261–2; *Gates to Asia,* 7–8

Nadir Shah (king of Persia), 88
Nanking, 216, 274
Navigationi e Viaggi (Ramusio), 259–60
Needham, Joseph, 111, 118
Nerchinsk, Treaty of, 194
New York Times, 216
Nicholas II (czar), 195
Ningsia, 84, 233, 268
Niya, 158–65, 175, 271; archaeological finds, 110, 115, 116, 119; irrigation project, 161–5; modernization, 159–65
Norberg, J. P., 51
Nur Ashim, 76–77
Nuristan, 9
Nystad, Treaty of, 195

oases, 153, 156, 157–8, 234. *See also* Chira; desert; Keriya; Niya; Tun-hwang; Turfan
October Revolution, 33, 201, 202, 210
oil industry, 41, 42, 221, 244–7
Oirats, *see* Mongols
On New Democracy (Mao), 211
On Protracted War (Mao), 211
opium trade, 129, 266–7
Opium Wars, 56, 91–92
Oriental despotism, 152
Örn, Torsten, xv
Oscar II (king of Sweden), 34
Oxus River, *see* Amu Darya

Pakhtaklik People's Commune, 50, 74–82
Pakistan, 8, 12, 23, 109, 271; Indian border dispute, 42; modern silk trade with, 121, 142
Palestine, 154
Palmgren, Gottfrid, 51
Pamir, xiii, 7–8, 72, 95, 105; border disputes, 25, 27, 28–36, 43–44; British–

Russian treaty, 29–30, 34; Russian occupation, 40. *See also* Sinkiang
Paoshan, 150
Payin, 276
peasant wars, 56; European, 95–96; Kansu, 234, 264
Peking, xiii, 3, 4, 42, 55, 67, 125, 156, 185, 206, 258; French–British occupation, 94; National Institute, 136
Peking treaty of 1860, 94–95
Pelliot, Paul, 174
People's Liberation Army, 18, 23, 81, 82, 123, 130, 162, 215, 216, 217, 218, 219, 258, 266, 267; Production and Construction Corps, 222–6, 229
People's Republic of China, *see* Chinese People's Republic
Persia, 23, 30, 32, 67, 88, 98, 99, 101, 103; Ismailite war, 174–5; Sassanid Empire, 53–54; Silk Road, 115, 116; trade routes to China, 42. *See also* Iran
Persian rugs, 140
Persian wells, *see* karezes
Peshawar, xi, 103
Peter the Great (czar), xi, xii, 194, 208
Petrovsky, Nikolai Feodorovich, 37–38, 39, 40, 49, 105, 107
photomechanical industry, 274–6
Pinglingssu, 270
Pliny the Elder, 127, 129
Po Hai Bay, 251
Poland, 107, 187, 190
politics: agricultural, 238–42; of desert reclamation, 168–71, 271–2; industrial, 135–7, 246–7, 275; women in, 137, 160, 167–8, 243–4. *See also* Chinese People's Republic
Polo, Marco, 6, 7, 8, 9, 69, 125, 158, 252
Portugal, 128
Prescott, J. R. V., 30
Protocol of Novy Margelan, 28–29, 44
Ptolemy, 10, 11
Punic Wars, 45
Punjab, 103

racism, 111, 154–5
Radek, Karl Bernardovich, 203
railroads and roads: American, 250; desert, 158, 160, 161, 166; East China, 211; Kansu, 233, 250–1, 257; Sinkiang, 42, 110–11, 122–3, 133, 146, 160, 166, 192, 198, 221–2, 251; Trans-Siberian, 200. *See also* trade and trade routes
Ramusio, Gian Battista, 259–60

religion, 49–59, 93, 170, 178; and peasant war, 95–96, 264; women and, 168. *See also* Buddhism and Buddhists; Catholic Church; Christianity; Confucianism; Islam; Taoism; Zoroastrianism
religious feudalism, 69–70
Richtofen, Ferdinand von, 111
roads, *see* railroads and roads; trade routes
Roman Empire, 252; Eastern, 53–54; Punic Wars, 45; and Silk Road, 126–8
Rome and China: A Study of Correlations in Historical Events (Teggart), 127–8
Rotsemi Salan, 139–41
Ruins of Desert Cathay (Stein), 271
Rukh, Shah, 252
Rumania, 107, 187
Russian imperialism, xi, 26, 37–40, 51, 94–95, 97–107, 193–8; Asia policies, 34–35, 97–100, 101–7; atrocities, 193–4; and Chinese Empire, 29–30, 37–40, 94–107, 193–9; czarist, 43, 83–84, 85, 90, 93–95, 97–107, 189–91, 193–8; diplomacy of, 37–40; Engels on, 190, 198–9; Great Britain and, 34, 98–99, 101, 190, 198, 199–200; Japanese alliance, 199–201; Marx on, 189–90; and Mongols, 70, 71; Peking treaty of 1860, 94–95; Treaty of Aigun, 94; World War II, 187. *See also* Chinese–Russian relationships; Soviet Union; Stalin, Joseph Vissarionovich
Russian Revolution, xi, 33, 201, 202, 210
Ruzi Khalla, 163, 164, 165
Ruzi Turdi, 173–4, 179, 180–1, 182–3
Ryukyu Islands, 101

Sadik Beg, 100
Sadit Tude, 24
Sairam, Lake, 192, 193
Samarkand, 99
Sanmichele, Michele, 260
Sargon, 174
Sassanid Empire, 53–54
Science and Civilization in China (Needham), 111
science and technology, 13, 77; Han, 174, 175, 176; of silk production, 113. *See also* industry and industrialization
Semipalatinsk, 194, 200
Semiryeche, 100
Shabad, Theodore, 253
Shang Li-sheng, 229–31
Shanghai, 42, 125, 136, 224, 230, 246, 254, 274

Shanhaikwan, 251
Shansi, 238
Shantan, 261–2, 263
Shantung, 3, 4, 246
Sheng Shih-ts'ai, 83, 120, 188, 207, 208, 209–10, 211, 212–13, 216
Sheng Tupan, 85
Shengli, 246
Shensi, 3, 92, 95, 174, 176, 211, 233, 234, 261, 264, 268; Liu Lin Production Brigade, 244, 258
Sian, 210, 258, 274
Siberia, 31, 94, 99; alleged Chinese claim to, 27, 43–44, 107; Russian conquest, 193
Sibos, 41
silk production, 47, 114–21; aesthetic traditions, 142; agriculture for, 113, 116, 120; history of, 112, 114–19, 124, 127; Mao's view, 120; modern, 119–21, 142–3; moral view, 126–7; politics of, 126–9; workers, 136–7. *See also* Silk Road
Silk Road, 11, 110–11, 114–19, 233, 242, 253, 276; archaeological finds, 111, 115, 116, 118, 119, 182; and European history, 112, 116, 119, 126–9; history, 114–21; location of, xii; Myrdal-Kessle route, 3; name, 111; in 1930s, 207, 211. *See also* Kansu; silk production; Sinkiang; trade and trade routes
Sind, 103
Sin-tin agreement, 207–8, 209
Sinkiang, *see* Sinkiang Uighur Autonomous Region
Sinkiang: Pawn or Pivot (Whiting), 188
Sinkiang Uighur Autonomous Region, 41–44, 139, 233, 240; adherence to China, 86–90, 152, 214; agriculture, 23, 25–26, 42, 48, 110, 131–2, 133–4, 144–5, 146, 152–3, 155–6, 157–65, 168–77, 205, 228; archaeology and antiquities, 11, 22–23, 50, 66–68, 72–73, 86, 111, 115, 116, 118, 119, 151, 154, 178–82; area, 41–42; autonomous administrations, 41; borders, 42–47, 218–20, 223; British in, 87, 90, 100, 101, 102; climate, 42, 163–4; Communist Party, 207, 209, 210–12; as East Turkestan Republic, xi, 206, 207, 213–17; imperial period, 18, 47, 92–97, 151–2; industry, 41, 42, 48, 77, 110, 119–21, 131, 139–41, 208, 221, 227–32; Mao's instructions on, 17, 227–32, 240; natural assets, 42, 131; peaceful liberation of,

215–17; as pivot of Asia, xi; population, 42, 153; Production and Construction Corps, 222–6; purges, 207, 210, 213; roads and railroads, 42, 110–11, 122–3, 133, 146, 160, 166, 192, 198, 221–2, 251; role in world history, 127–8; Russian policies and presence in, xi, xii, 83–84, 85–88, 90, 93–95, 99–103, 184–5, 188–9, 193–4, 197–8, 200–1, 204, 206–20; Soviet withdrawal from, 213–14; U.S. and, 214, 215, 216; warlords, 83–90, 100–2, 103, 106, 120, 151, 152, 176, 188, 197, 207–13, 216, 264. *See also* Dzungaria; Ili; Kashgar; Keriya; Khotan; Niya; Pamir; Tadzhiks; Takla Makan Desert; Tarim basin; Tashkurghan; Turfan; Uighurs; Urumchi
Sino–Iranica (Laufer), 111
Sino–Soviet relationships, *see* Chinese–Russian relationships; Russian imperialism; Soviet Union
Soong, T. V., 199
South Dansu Tibetan Autonomous District, 234
Soviet revisionism, 24, 25, 229–32, 240
Soviet Union, xiii, 30–31, 45, 94–95; current China policies, xi, xii, 20–21, 24, 25, 29, 32–33, 43–44, 93, 107, 230, 245, 254; expansionism (new czarism), 32–33, 187, 189, 196, 199; Komintern, 185–6, 206; modernization, 202, 205–6; in Sinkiang, 83–84, 85, 93, 200–1, 206–20; Stalinism, 202–6; in World War I, 200; in World War II, 186–7, 190, 202–4, 212, 213. *See also* Chinese–Russian relationships; Russian imperialism; Stalin, Joseph Vissarionovich
Spain, 128, 193–4; Popular Front, 203
Ssu-ma Ch'ien, 174, 176
Stalin, Joseph Vissarionovich, 13, 24, 184–91, 199, 202–20; accomplishments, 202–4, 206; Chinese view of, 185–6, 187–9, 195, 204, 206, 217; on czarist foreign policy, 32; economic policies, 202, 205; foreign policy, xi, 32–33, 84, 188, 195; purges, 203–5; Sinkiang policy, 184–5, 188–9, 200–1, 204, 206–20
steel industry, 228–9, 253–4, 256–8
Stein, Aurel, 87, 118, 151, 153–4, 155, 156, 174, 175, 180–2, 272
Stolpe, Jan, xv
Strindberg, August, 92
Suchow, *see* Kiüchuan
Sufism, 96

Sui dynasty, 11, 260
Sullivan, Walter, 216
Sumer, 111
Sun Yat-sen, 63, 64. *See also* Kuomintang
Sung Chen-min, 246
Sung dynasty, 63, 196, 259, 261
Sweden and Swedes, 13, 34, 71, 106–7, 123–4, 125, 155, 190, 194, 195, 233, 250, 255, 265, 271, 272; Ethnographic Museum, 84–85; missionaries, 49–52, 67. *See also* Hedin, Sven
Swedish Broadcasting Corporation, xv
Syr Darya, 97
Syria, 53
Szechuan province, 3–4, 115, 234

Taching oilfields, 244–5, 246
Tadzhiks, 3, 5–6, 8, 15, 16, 17, 18, 23, 41, 61, 64. *See also* Tashkurghan
Tadzhikistan, 45
Taiping Revolution, 56, 91–92, 95–96, 264, 267
Taiwan, 213
Takla Makan Desert, 3, 4, 42, 110, 142, 144, 166. *See also* desert
Takli River, 192
T'ang dynasty, 52, 63, 84, 116, 119, 151, 182
Tang River, 240–1
Tannu Tuva, 195, 196, 199, 206, 217
Tao Shih-yueh, 216
Taoism, 54, 192
Tarbagatai, 95, 213–15, 218, 223
Tarim basin, 41, 42, 47, 68, 93, 110, 153–4. *See also* Sinkiang
Tarim river, 138
Tashkent, 10, 11, 68, 98
Tashkurghan (Afghanistan), 10
Tashkurghan (Pamir), xii, 5–24; archaeology and history, 10–12, 16–17, 22–23; authors' route to, 5–10; climate, 13–14; Cultural Revolution, 16, 19; effects of liberation on, 13, 16, 17–20, 23–24; Tagarmi People's Commune, 5, 6, 23–24. *See also* Pamir; Tadzhiks
Teggart, Frederick J., 127–8
Teheran, 103, 104, 105. *See also* Iran; Persia
telephones, 253
Teng Hsiao-p'ing, 240
Tertullian, 126–7
Third World, 59, 129, 255, 276
Thorez, Maurice, 186
Tiberius (emperor of Rome), 127
Tibet and Tibetans, 17, 27, 37 n, 43, 63,

70, 71, 119, 197, 200, 233, 234
Tien Shan, 41, 128, 224, 248
Timofeiev, Yermak, 193
Timur, 252
Torguts, 71
trade and trade routes, 90, 264; British, 56, 91–92, 128–9, 139, 234; Chinese Empire, 42, 46–47, 56, 69–70, 91–92, 93, 110, 129, 139, 248; desert, 93, 101, 158, 234; modern, 12, 121, 139–41, 142; opium, 56, 91–92, 129, 266–7; with Russia, 94, 98, 99, 139–41, 197, 207–8. *See also* railroads and roads; Silk Road
travel and travelers, 9–10
Travels of Marco Polo, The, 6, 7. *See also* Polo, Marco
Treaty of Nerchinsk, 194
Treaty of Nystad, 195
Trotskyism, 207, 210, 213
Tsaidam, 263
Tsiao Wei-han, 246
Tsinghai province, 42, 84, 96, 233, 234, 268, 270, 274
Tsingtao, 3, 4
Tsining, 250
Tso Tsung-t'ang, 90, 92, 100, 102, 264
Tsungli Yamen, 99
Tsunyi Conference, 186
Tu Li-shen, 71
Tungans, *see* Hui people
Tunhwang, 4, 115, 119, 160, 235–7, 240–2, 248, 251, 261
Turfan, 42, 71, 140, 153, 154, 172–83; agriculture, 172; Amin Hodja mosque, 180–2; housing, 182–3; karezes, 172–7; rainfall, 178; Turkestan, 97, 99, 197
Turkey, 13, 32, 87, 100, 195
Turkmenistan, 106, 157, 198

Uighurs, 17, 41, 42, 48–52, 60–65, 75, 80–82, 87, 101, 123, 124, 131, 135–6, 145, 172, 180, 230, 251; in Ch'ing dynasty, 92–93; and Christian missionaries, 51, 52, 57, 59; language, 13, 64, 132; medicine, 57–59; music and dance, 159–60. *See also* Kashgar
Ukraine, 187
United States, 97, 173, 189; Asian role of, xi–xii, 101, 201; China policies, 214, 215, 254; CIA, 188; as colony, 189, 193; imperialism, 104; leftists, 267. *See also* West and Westerners
University of California (Berkeley), 127
University of Chicago, 174
Unkovsky, Ivan, 194, 195

Urmia, Lake, 174
Urumchi, 11, 22, 41, 42, 67, 84, 97, 110, 119, 147, 149, 156, 185, 188, 192, 211, 217, 219
Ushur Nijaz, 177
Ussuri River, 94
Ust-Kamenogorsk, 194
Uz Bel pass, *see* Kizil Jik
Uzbekistan, 45, 173

Vietnam-China border war, xi
Vladislavich, Sava Lukich, 195–6
Volga River, 71

Wahab, R. H., 34
Wang Chi-ching, 245
Wang Chin-shi, 244, 246
Wang Ching-wei, 203, 213
Wang Di-tse, 84–85
Wang Shiao-yi, 228
Wang Tu-kiang, 271
Wang Wen-ho, 161–2
warlords, 120, 152, 251; *See also* Ma Chung-yin; Sheng Shih-ts'ai; Yakub Beg
water supply, 133, 155–6, 161–5, 172–7; hygiene and, 148–9; Kansu, 237, 240–1. *See also* floods and flood control; irrigation and irrigation projects
Wei dynasty, 63, 119; Northern, 115, 116, 270
West and Westerners, 174, 175; archaeologists, 180–2; attitude on China, 59, 84–86, 266–7; intellectuals, 202; journalists, 124–5; missionaries, 49–51, 55–57, 67, 129; silk trade, 115–16; view of communist state structure, 204. *See also* Europe; Hedin, Sven; Stein, Aurel; trade and trade routes; United States; names of countries
Whiting, Allen S., 188, 208, 209, 216
women: 17–20, 25, 26, 60–61; Chinese Empire, 92; clothing, 124–5, 230–2; education, 19–20, 61–62, 168; in industry, 135–7, 139–41, 258; and land reform, 168; liberation of, 17–20, 109–10, 147, 150, 159–60; in politics, 137, 160, 167–8, 243–4; pre-liberation, 265; Production and Construction Corps, 224–6; revisionists' use of, 25; Tertullian on, 126–7; workers, 77, 163–4, 246
Wood, Alexander, 89, 90
Wood, John, 89–90
workers: benefits and wages, 136–7, 165; education, 137, 246; housing construc-

tion, 182–3; irrigation project, 163–5, 169–70, 171; kareze builders, 175, 176–7; oil, 245–7; pre-liberation, 141–2, 176, 177; railroad, 250–1, 257; rugmakers, 140, 141–2; silk industry, 136–7; steel, 258; women, 77, 163–4, 246. *See also* industry and industrialization
World War I, 93, 199, 200, 251
World War II, 186, 187, 190, 202–4, 212, 213
Wu Ch'eng-en, 6
Wu Ti (emperor of China), 45, 46, 47, 222–3
Wu Tsung (emperor of China), 52
Wuchiao Mountains, 234
Wuchiaoling pass, 234, 268
Wuhan, 3
Wuwei, 250, 263, 264, 265, 266

Yakub Beg, 86, 87–90, 100–2, 103, 106, 151, 152, 176, 197, 264
Yakutsk, 193
Yale University, 154

Yang Hu-cheng, 186
Yang Yung-chen, 224–6
Yangtze River, 3, 52, 115
Yarkand, 67, 69, 97, 100, 101, 115, 122, 123
Yellow River, 47, 96, 110, 111, 115, 234, 242, 248, 268–74, 276, 277; energy projects, 268–70
Yenan, 185, 223
Yeshil Kul, 72
Yinchuan, 250
Yipek Yoli, *see* Silk Road
Younghusband, Francis, 37, 40, 174, 198
Yuan dynasty, 63, 68, 193
Yüan Shih-k'ai, 200
Yümen, 243, 244, 245–8
Yung Cheng (emperor), 179
Yunnan, 4, 150
Yusup Hadji, 57–58, 59
Yutien, *see* Keriya

Zorkul Lake (Lake Victoria), 29
Zoroastrianism, 53

About the Authors

Jan Myrdal has written five previous books on China and Asia, three of them in collaboration with his wife, Gun Kessle. His autobiography, *Confessions of a Disloyal European,* received considerable attention. In addition, he has published novels, books of essays, and a collection of radio plays in Sweden, where his weekly column is a continual source of controversy. He is currently editing the novels of Balzac in Sweden and has made several television documentaries.

Gun Kessle is well known in Sweden as an artist and photographer, and has also published several books of her own. Her most recent book, *Daily Life in China,* describes, in words and photographs, a street in the city of Chengtu.